VEIN OF
IRON

"*Effort, and expectation, and desire,
And something evermore about to be.*"

ELLEN GLASGOW

VEIN OF

IRON

&s Afterword by Anne Firor Scott

University Press of Virginia
Charlottesville and London

THE UNIVERSITY PRESS OF VIRGINIA
Copyright © 1935, 1938, by Ellen Glasgow
Copyright renewed 1980 by The Richmond Society
for the Prevention of Cruelty to Animals

Afterword copyright © 1995 by the Rector and Visitors
of the University of Virginia
Expanded Paperback Edition

First University Press of Virginia printing 1995

Published by arrangement with Harcourt Brace & Company

Library of Congress Cataloging-in-Publication Data
Glasgow, Ellen Anderson Gholson, 1873-1945.
    Vein of iron / Ellen Glasgow ; afterword by Anne Firor Scott.
        p.   cm.
    Includes bibliographical references.
    ISBN 0-8139-1636-4 (pbk. : alk paper)
    1. Depressions—Virginia—History—20th century—Fiction.
2. Married women—Virginia—Fiction.   3. Family—Virginia—Fiction.
I. Title.
PS3513.L34V4   1995
813'.52—dc20   95-14153
                                                                    CIP

Printed in the United States of America

TUCKED AWAY in some hidden recess of my memory, where it had lain unnoticed for many years, there was a novel with a setting in the Valley of Virginia. Thus far, I had written only of the Tidewater and Richmond. I was born in that section, and all my life had been spent there, except for the few years I had divided between New York and Europe. My mother's people had settled in the Tidewater in 1619 and 1634, and she was also one of a tribal multitude who looked back to that too virile progenitor, Colonel William Randolph, of Turkey Island.

But my father's forbears were among the stalwart pioneers in the upper valley of the James River and the fertile wilderness between the Blue Ridge and the Alleghanies. Glasgow, Graham, Anderson, they had first fled from Scotland to shelter in the north of Ireland, and then, when religious persecution still tracked them down, they had sailed from Ulster in search of a safer refuge among the savages of America. The original Glasgow homestead, built on a large tract of land, mostly wilderness, in Rockbridge County, is still standing, though it has been twice burned in part, and has suffered the even greater indignity of modern improvements. The place was named "Green Forest" because Glasgow means "greenwood" in Gaelic.

As a child and a young girl just growing up, I had spent many summers beyond the Blue Ridge, and it is probable that the seeds of this book were even then germinating in the soil of my mind. The Scottish ballads were as familiar to me as my alphabet, and far more beloved. My Aunt Rebecca, a wonderful old lady and Scottish to the core, would sing these ballads, in her thin sweet voice, by the fireside of an evening, or, more thrilling to us, elders and youngsters alike, she would relate in serial form, since she was a born story-teller, all the adventurous plots of the Waverley novels, acting the separate part of each character and slipping, whenever the rôle required it, from her precise English into the exciting accent of Gaelic. Spurred on, at the age of seven, by an interrupted climax in "Old Mortality," I hunted for the worn volume inherited from my grandfather's library, and taught myself, with infinite patience, to spell out the words on the printed page. But I have never forgotten how the glorious adventures seemed to grow stale and flatten out when I read them in cold and faded print, deprived of the magical tones of my Aunt Rebecca's voice.

Years passed, and Aunt Rebecca, with her imposing generation, was almost forgotten. I had written both tragedies and comedies of the Tidewater and Richmond, when I apprehended, with the suddenness of all literary apprehensions, that a social history of the Commonwealth must, of necessity, include the descendants of the Scotch-Irish settlers between the Blue Ridge and the Alleghanies. The Great Valley of Virginia embraces the five smaller valleys of the Shenandoah River, the James River, the Roanoke River, the Kanawha or New River, and the Holston or Tennessee River. But the scene of *Vein of Iron* is restricted to the upper valley of the James, though I have been careful not to use the actual name of any place or person in that region. As I explain at length in my prefaces to *The Battle-ground* and *The Voice of the People*, it was my original intention to depict such aspects of the Southern scene as I had actually known, and to avoid, at any cost of popular approval, the sentimental fallacy, so prevalent in fiction at the turn of the century, that the South was inhabited exclusively by aristocrats and picturesque Negroes, who afforded what used to be called "comic relief" in the novel.

When at last I returned to this theme, I plunged immediately into a state of total immersion. Few of my novels have interested or absorbed me so completely in the beginning, and I even enjoyed my researches, which fortunately left nothing more concrete than the essence of a moment in history. I read innumerable records of the frontier and frontier warfare. Sometimes I would

search through several volumes in order to verify the state of
the weather or the month of the year, and having verified it, I
would dismiss it in a parenthetical clause. For the three full years
while I was writing this book, I projected my consciousness
without effort into that resolute breed from which my father
had sprung. Having held fast through the generations, would
this breed yield nowadays to the disintegrating forces in the
modern world? Would that instinct for survival we used to
call "the soul of man" be content to wear for the future the
tarnished label of "psychology"? Would those intrepid Scottish
metaphysicians, who had placed freedom to believe above freedom to doubt, and had valued immaterial safety more than material comfort, would they sink in the end under the dead weight
of an age that believed only in the machine? Not in vain had my
Aunt Rebecca instructed me, on the Sabbath, in the Shorter
Catechism and the Westminster Confession of Faith. Not in
vain, on the other days of the week, had she sung the Border
ballads and related the Scottish legends. I had learned my lesson
well and long, though I thought I had forgotten it. Nothing remained for me to do but to set the scene and attempt to analyze
the primary elements that composed the Presbyterian spirit and
the Presbyterian theology. And the chief of these elements, or so
it appeared in my examination, was the substance of fortitude.

In Ironside, I combined two mountain villages, and so clearly
was the setting visualized in my mind that I was able to draw a
map of imaginary Shut-in Valley. I knew where every road
climbed, every house stood, every field spread, where every
hill swelled in the plain and every mountain peak soared into
the clouds. From the beginning, I had known that I was engaged
upon a family chronicle, and especially that I was trying to
isolate, not a single character or group of characters alone, but
the vital principle of survival, which has enabled races and indi-
viduals to withstand the destructive forces of nature and civilization. The ramifications of my subject would lead me far back
into the past, and in order that I might saturate my mind with
the atmosphere of the place and the time, I asked innumerable

questions of old and young and devoured every record I could
find of the earliest settlers in the Valley of Virginia. When the
book came to be written, I found that these researches, which
had occupied a year or more of my time, had contributed (if we
except the general sense of security, the feeling that I could move
about freely and safely in the scene and the atmosphere of the
novel) exactly two pages of print. For, according to my dubious
method of writing, it was as necessary to unlearn facts as it was
to acquire them. What I needed, and what I had worked to
attain, was a distillation of the past, not the dry bones and the
decaying framework of history.

Not a few of these characters were suggested by an incident
or an outline or even a gesture. In most of them a single living
cell, or germ, was supplied by the anecdote or appearance of a
"real" person. The merest fragment, it might be, was all I needed
for my beginning; and in the case of Grandmother Fincastle, I
pieced several of these separate fragments together, and so built
up a figure of flesh and blood and spiritual fibre. I had known one
or two Scotch-Irish grandmothers who might have sat for her
portrait; and I am still receiving letters from her descendants who
imagine they have recognized her features and have hastened,
in one instance at least, to repudiate the likeness. The first John
Fincastle may be traced back in outline to one of the earliest
pioneers, a stout-hearted Presbyterian minister, and his picture
also has been recognized, though not so far rejected. In Great-
grandmother Tod, I have united two different persons, one a
connection by marriage of my own great-grandfather. As a
child of ten, she was carried off to captivity by the Shawnees;
but it was another child who grew up in an Indian village to love
and marry an Indian chief. The murder of the young chief by
her two brothers, after the treaty that ended Pontiac's War, is
one of the incidents recorded in the journals of the first settlers.
In the protagonist of my novel, the later John Fincastle, I was
trying to portray the fate of the philosopher in an era of science,
of the scholar in a world of mechanical inventions. His return
to an earlier spiritual age and the philosophy of Plotinus is intel-

lectually and historically accurate. Many of the pioneer ministers were men of intrepid spirit and intellectual vigour, and the
transplanted Scottish mind was still nourished by metaphysics.
In my childhood in Lexington, I had heard points of doctrine
elucidated, though never argued, with all the subtlety of dialec-
tic. Aunt Meggie, I had known intimately and remotely, in
varied forms and fashions, from the Alleghanies to the Tidewater; and I had known too, though only once, the imperfect
prototype of Mary Evelyn.

So the family was grouped round a centre, and the chronicle
was beginning, before I had put pen to paper. My characters,
including the animals, even the pet ram, had gathered as obediently as the creatures in Noah's ark. I had steeped my mind
in the setting of a mood and divided my scene into foreground,
middle distance, and historical perspective. All was waiting
to begin when I suddenly perceived that I had left my children out in the cold; I had provided everything but the right
kind of roof. And, oddly enough, it was the roof alone that was
making the trouble. I had seen the old manse in my imagination;
I had seen the colour of the brick and the architectural design. I
had seen every Fincastle, from Grandmother to little Ada and
Horace, the hound, go up the rounded stone steps to the square
porch and pass through the front door into the hall, and then
through the hall and the dining-room and the kitchen, out on
the back porch and down into the yard. I had seen the pioneer
oak and the rockery and the garden fence of white palings and
the willow beside the little path that led down to the spring-
house. But the house I saw so plainly was not the typical mountain house. It had its own peculiar plan and its own sloping roof
that drooped over the windows in the upper story. Nevertheless, it was the old manse, and the Fincastles had built it. They
had always lived under that roof, within those walls of weath-
ered brick; and they refused obstinately to change their home, or
even to go about their daily tasks, as long as they were threatened
with eviction. Just as John Fincastle collapsed on my hands
whenever I tried to change his name, so the whole family

dropped dead at my feet as soon as I started to pull down the manse. So at last, in desperation, I told myself that an earlier grandfather, probably John Fincastle the third, had altered the original roof when he enlarged the house for his bride.

For the purposes of my theme, I should need, I knew, not only the force of tradition, as exemplified in Grandmother Fincastle and Aunt Meggie, but the break with tradition which comes to Ada through Ralph and his frustrated ego. What I wished to do was to test the resistance of this vein of iron to outward pressure, and to measure the exact degree of its strength. Several critics have questioned the probability of Ralph's surrender to a moral code in which he no longer believed; but none of these critics, I am convinced, had ever lived in a strict Presbyterian community through the pre-war years, or felt the inexorable force of that Calvinist morality which Santayana has called "an expression of the agonized conscience." In his impressionable years, Ralph had been subjected to this agonized conscience (which at its best breeds inhibitions) in forms bordering closely on religious mania. Nor would this surrender of the broken will have been improbable in any long-established society, such as existed all over Virginia and indeed over the entire South, where, until the post-war demoralization, religious precepts were still a power for good or evil. In former years, I had witnessed one such instance in Richmond, and I had heard indirectly of several others. There may be a weakness at this point in my chronicle; but I think the flaw is owing less to the absence of probability than to insufficient analysis. Like other novelists, I suppose, I have my own favourite parts and passages, and those I felt, and still feel, most deeply in this book are the interlude on Thunder Mountain and John Fincastle's return to the manse at the end. Although Ada was nearest to me in many ways, I think the main strength of the book lies in the figures of the old Presbyterian grandmother and the old pagan philosopher. But all these people, including the Bergens and Mr. Midkiff, are so real to me that I can scarcely recall whether nature or I created them in the flesh. Otto Bergen, with his varied pets, was partly founded on a skilled cabinet-maker who used to repair my furniture in Richmond; and he also had his sanguine smile and his dachshund, his canaries and his cages of white mice. Mulberry Street, with its good houses of other days and its balconies of wrought-iron lace-work, exists in fact, and so does the terraced hillside overlooking the canal and the river. Indeed, I have taken few liberties with the actual plan of the city I have called Queenborough. Here and there, it is true, some architectural sacrifice to progress or politics may have been restored; I may have rebuilt a house or repaired a balcony or replanted a tree; but, for the rest, I think my chief, if not my only, offense has been in the renaming of streets. One casual critic (the same critic, I suspect, who imagined that *Barren Ground* was about the cultivation of land) has inaccurately described *Vein of Iron* as "a novel of the depression." But the truth is that the great depression, which occupies only a few chapters, was, like the Great War, an inevitable feature in any record of the time and the place. Both the War and the depression were there without my connivance; and it was impossible, in writing Ada's life, either to ignore them or explain them away. But these things were scarcely more than an incident in the larger drama of mortal conflict with fate.

Technique has interested me since my early years when, with only intuition and a natural ear for words as a guide, I had groped my way toward a method. Consciously or unconsciously, I was forming a style; but I felt that the style I needed must have something more than mere facility. It must be alike elastic and adaptable and equal, on occasion, to the more or less serious emergencies of fiction. No good style can be uniform or expected to fit every subject, or indeed to fit every work by one author. I had seen too much excellent material spoiled either by a velvet style that would not give or by a fustian style that was fraying out. It is the fashion in criticism nowadays to praise the "invisible style." Yet this term is, I think, both far-fetched and indefinite. Style should be no more invisible than a transparent complexion which changes colour in response to the animation within. It should be recognized as a natural part of the organism, not as extraneous decoration which may be forcibly peeled off without impairing the whole structure. It was true, moreover, that, in the matter of style, as well as in the nature of substance, I was disposed by constitution to move always against the literary current. But if this knowledge ever entered my mind, I accepted it as unavoidably as one accepts sultry weather, and it failed to influence or even to retard the general tendencies of my work. If I was aware that I could never become one of the fashionable apocalyptic prophets of literature, I was aware also that I had little desire to be a prophet and still less to be apocalyptic. Even nowadays, when the kindly hearted are no longer unanimous in advising me to write in the manner of Thomas Nelson Page or James Lane Allen, and even my hopeful publisher has stopped urging me to "do an optimistic novel of the far West"—even nowadays, I am still obstinately facing the wrong way. For I have wished to do honest work, and I have found that to do honest work I must begin by not taking advice. At the turn of the century, the Southern skies were brilliant with literary sky-rockets. One after another, I saw them shoot up and sink and sputter out in the darkness. "There were so many promising writers of your generation," a man of letters said to me recently in New York. "I wonder what has become of them." And I could only glance round at the altered scene and murmur, "I wonder."

Although I have had my loyal friends and critics, few persistent novelists, I suppose, have ever received in one lifetime so generous a measure of benevolent neglect. For all such double-edged blessings, I am able to say, since I have attained understanding, that I am not deficient in gratitude. To be choked with cream is, perhaps, the saddest fate that can overtake any promising writer. Not only was I spared this ultimate honour, but the lack of it has provided me with adequate space in which to take root and grow, without artificial grafting into a more popular stock. If I have missed many of the external rewards of success, I have never lost the outward peace and the inward compensation that come from doing the work one wishes to do in the solitary way in which one wishes to do it. It is true that I have seldom received prizes, but it is true also that I have seldom been obliged to return thanks. I wanted "a room of my own," and it was granted me. I wanted a pursuit that I might follow with interest between the cradle and the grave, and that, too, was allowed. As a beginning author, the odds may have been against me, but as an ending author, who has been saved from a sense of diminishing vitality, I think the odds are now even. For the old purpose, or illusion, is unimpaired. Still, I tell myself, after almost forty years of endeavour toward a single aim, that it is possible to reach below the semblance of fiction and grasp the verities of experience.

But to return to this novel. In handling an austere subject projected against a background of hills and sky, I felt that I required a closer adaptation of style. Sophisticated wit and sparkling irony must be drained away from this bare and steady chronicle of simple lives. And so the speech of the heart, not the language of the mind, must serve as the revealing medium for my narrative. After an excursion into civilized comedy, I was reviving the substance and the manner of *Barren Ground* and of those previous novels, which were written in ardent revolt from a literary convention that was formalized and inflexible. Years earlier I had said that Southern literature needed blood and irony; and in writing of a social tradition that had become lifeless from immobility, I found that through an infusion of satire alone could the dry bones be made to appear animate. But these outworn husks of thought had never spread beyond the Blue Ridge into the Valley of Virginia. A living germ still survived in the long tradition of fortitude. Satire would have splintered back from the sober bulk of the Presbyterian mind and conscience. A natural vehicle, the grave speech of a spiritually proud and materially humble race, who disdained the artificial tongue of the sophisticated as heartily as they would have despised the gangster idiom so much admired in the pages of Mr. Hemingway and his imitators,—this natural vehicle, perhaps the most difficult of all speech to translate into English prose, was, I soon discovered, the one inevitable expression for my purpose.

For a generation style, as distinguished from manner, had been among my chief interests and my major preoccupations. I had worked toward a personal form which, however imperfect in the abstract, might become in time an appropriate instrument for my transcripts of life. In all my novels, except the earliest, I have spent hours or days in pursuit of that exact right word which is so seldom recognized when it is found. But the search for the exact right word, it is needless to explain to any writer, is a perennial aspiration. I am, therefore, merely affirming a forlorn hope, not proclaiming an achievement. No one can comprehend more clearly than I do the stony road of failure that lies permanently between the dream and the actuality. Nevertheless, to the writer, the idea will remain always more real than the representation.

As long as a book has the life of reverie alone, it is possessed by the author; and through the stages of prenatal development, it is attached by some vital cord to the writer's unconscious being. It is from this living matter that the structure, shape, nature, and external lineaments must be formed, either intuitively, as in my case, or by a deliberate act of the will. I knew, without knowing *how* I knew, not only the general construction but every small detail of my scene and my characters. I knew whence they had come and whither they were going, and that the imaginary world about them contained ample room in which they might move and turn and walk forward or backward. And I knew, also, what these people required of me if I expected them to stay alive in my hands. The point of view must be clear, straight, and restricted, as in so many of my novels, to two angles of vision. From the beginning to the end, the events must be registered either in the mind of Ada or in the mind of John Fincastle. The eyes of youth must look on life through the courage of emotion, while the eyes of age regarded it through that fortitude which wisdom bestows. Only once do I depart from this guiding principle, and this is when, in the early chapters, I encounter a technical problem. In these chapters, I treat subjectively five different points of view in the family group gathered before the fire in the manse on a December evening. As I used it, this seemed to me to be an innovation, and I employed the device not only because, in my creation of the Fincastle family, I needed these reflective views, but, in a measure at least, because the device was experimental and daring. It is the kind of experiment, as a friendly novelist said to me of my section "The Deep Past" in *The Sheltered Life*, that is either a triumph or a defeat because it cannot simply fall short of its end. The truth is that it took me months to enter completely into the mental processes of these five different human beings, from the old grandmother down to the child of ten, and to immerse myself in their separate moods and visions. After I had written these chapters, I felt that there was little left for me to learn about the inner lives of my characters. For each point of view, it was necessary to discover or invent an appropriate rhythm. Grandmother's retrospect moves with a slow, rocking vibration, as when one is reluctantly falling asleep, and grows fainter and farther away as drowsiness conquers. "Suddenly, without warning, descended upon her a sleep that was not sleep as yet. Her eyes saw; her ears heard; and in her stiff fingers the needles did not slacken. But she was immersed in profound stillness; she rested upon an immovable rock." And in the concluding sentence the five almost wholly metrical lines are followed by the sudden break of the partial line at the end, which "drops off," just as does Grandmother Fincastle:

> "Wéaving ín and oút of her bódy and sóul, and
> knítting her ínto the pást as she knítted lífe íntŏ
> stóckings, móved the famíliar rhýthms and páuses—
> nów—of the hóuse; and móved as a cásual wáve, as
> bárely a mínute's ébbing and flów, in the tímeless
> súrge of predéstinátion. . . ."

And so the stream of reverie flows on and downward, through the metaphysical consciousness of John Fincastle, the practical mind of Aunt Meggie, and the flashes of insight that illumine Mary Evelyn's reflections, until it finally ripples out in the staccato cadences of little Ada's fanciful musings. In this daydreaming, as throughout General Archbald's meditation in *The Sheltered Life*, I have treated the past and the present as coexistent in time, and time itself as a subjective medium.

If these backward flights required density of atmosphere, the whole theme demanded prose of a transparent texture. And it was imperative, as I have said elsewhere, that this style should spring naturally from the characters and the situation, and should be divorced, so far as this is possible in any work of the imagination, from the personality of the author. The substance, as well as the contour, must show clearly through an envelope that was inconspicuous in itself and yet able to transmit equally light and darkness. I was striving in this book, however unsuccessfully, for a way of writing that was strong, terse, without extraneous adornment, and impeccably true to reality. Only in the interlude on Thunder Mountain and the last journey of John Fincastle back to his old home, where burial was cheaper, does beauty break through, not as an objective aim but of its own inward movement, and submerge the naked semblance of life.

From the first paragraph, this theme had been woven, for me, of sounds—of blended sounds, of ringing, of murmuring, of harmonious and dissonant sounds. In the same way, but less emphatically, I had felt that *The Sheltered Life* was shot through with scents and colours, that *The Romantic Comedians* was composed of rippling lights, and *They Stooped to Folly* of laughing animation. In the very beginning of *Vein of Iron*, the rhythm tightens and moves swiftly, to the patter of running feet. Yet, so far as I am aware, Mr. Carl Van Vechten is the only reader who has observed the symbolic movement of my first paragraph, or observing it, has taken the trouble to record his observation in writing. Still, this is scarcely fair, since many readers and not a few professional critics have commented upon the variation of sound accompanying my chronicle.

All this, since it deals with the problems of writing and the architectonic design, does not begin until the substance in hand has assumed magnitude and proportion. With the origin of an idea, there is always the feeling that one is working in an imponderable medium, in some fourth or fifth dimension; but the minute we begin deliberately to break up, divide, and construct a pattern, we have dropped back among the physical unities.

And though the physical unities may not lie at the heart of the matter, it is essential that a novelist should have command not only of his material but of its proper manipulation. Brushwork may not be the highest end of art, but it remains the solitary means by which an artist may arrive at the highest end. It is unfashionable nowadays, it is even considered a little absurd, in an epoch of neo-barbarism, to regard a work of fiction as a form of art. Nevertheless, the most favourable comment to be made upon any literary fashion is that it is only a fashion, which means that it will go out again as suddenly as it has come in. And from my unimportant point of view, only a form of art appears to be worthy of the dedicated service of forty years.

Ellen Glasgow.

Richmond, Virginia,
December, 1937

CONTENTS

PART

ONE

TOWARD LIFE

CHAPTER 1

CHILDREN were chasing an idiot boy up the village street to the churchyard.

"Run, run, oh, what fun!" sang little Ada Fincastle, as she raced with the pursuers. Flushed and breathless, panting with delight, she felt that the whole round world and the short December day were running too. The steep street and the shingled roofs of Ironside rocked upward. The wind whistled as it sped on. Dust whirled and scattered and whirled again. The sunshine was spinning. A bird and its shadow flashed over the winter fields. Clouds flew in the sky. The road beyond the church reared and plunged into the shaggy hills. The hills shook themselves like ponies and rushed headlong among the mountains. The Blue Ridge and the Alleghanies toppled over and tumbled far down into the Valley of Virginia. "Run, run, oh, what fun to be flying!" Then suddenly the world balanced itself, revolved slowly, and settled to rest. She had stopped.

Past the old stone church, on the edge of a field, the idiot turned and spat at his tormentors. His mouth was only a crooked hole in his face; his small dull eyes squinted between inflamed eyelids. Without dropping his pail of refuse, he squawked with rage and dodged from side to side as the boys pelted his shoulders. "Go home, Toby, go home to your mammy!" the little girls mocked, dancing about him. "Go home to your piggie—pig—pigs!"

Across the field, beyond the last sunken mound in the churchyard, the fallow land broke and fell into Murderer's Grave, a bare ravine, once a watercourse, where the body of a hanged man had been buried nearly a hundred years before. Since that time, Ada knew, there had been no hanging at Ironside; but some

3

people said that the lost spirit of the murderer, with a red stripe round its neck, still prowled on stormy nights outside the churchyard. In a hovel perched on the rim of the ravine Toby Waters, the idiot, lived with his mother.

"He's afraid to go home," Willie Andrews cried. "His mother got drunk yesterday and beat him with her hickory stick. She sold her last petticoat for moonshine to the people on Lightnin' Ridge."

Darting into the field, he seized the idiot's cap and stuffed it with cow droppings. Willie, the children shrieked, could always think of something to do. A great sport, he was, with the funniest face and the quickest tongue in the village.

"He wants his cap," Janet Rowan trilled in her childish falsetto. She had an innocent rosebud face, and was fond of sticking out a small rosy tongue which the Sunday-school teacher had once brushed with quinine because it told fibs. "He's crying for his dirty old cap."

"Oh, he won't mind," Willie retorted. "He eats slops. I've seen him."

"But it hurts him," Ada Fincastle answered slowly. "It hurts him to cry."

Excitement had ebbed, and her voice sounded far off and troubled. She glanced uneasily from the idiot's face to the spoiled cap (such a ragged cap!) and back again to the idiot's face, which was sagging with grief. Sudden light broke within. It was just as if her heart, too, had turned over. "I don't like to hurt things," she said, and there was surprise in her tone.

In a flash of vision it seemed to her that she and Toby had changed places, that they were chasing her over the fields into that filthy hovel. But it wasn't the first time she had felt like this. Last summer she had seen a rabbit torn to pieces by hounds (their own young Horace, for all his noble bearing, was among them) and she had heard it cry out like a baby. She had watched its eyes throbbing with fear and pain, like small, terrified hearts. Since then she had never been able to eat rabbit unless she pretended it was chicken. Aunt Abigail Geddy said chickens were not nearly so much like babies. She said chickens didn't really mind having their necks wrung if you did it the right way.

"It does hurt him, Ralph. I know it hurts him." Her voice was firmer now, and she looked round at Ralph McBride, who was the only boy she trusted. She could not remember when her confidence in him had begun. From the time she could crawl she had tried to follow his auburn head everywhere.

"He likes it," Ralph replied impatiently. "If he didn't like it, he could run home."

"But he's lost his cap. Maybe he knows his mother will whip him if he comes home without it." Moved by a reckless impulse, she jerked off her own cap of knitted red wool and held it out to the idiot. "You may have mine, Toby. I don't need it."

"What bedevilment are you up to now?" a voice shouted from the churchyard, and at the first word the children scattered and fled squealing down the village street. "I'm sometimes tempted to think," the voice continued, "that children are more savage than savages."

"He won't hurt me. I shan't run," Ada thought. It could be nobody but Mr. Black, the minister, she knew, and she knew also, though he was a man of humane instincts, that he preferred children in Sunday school.

"Can't you leave off tormenting that unfortunate?" he called again, as he opened the gate and came out into the road where she waited alone. "Did he snatch your cap?" he asked, glancing severely at Toby.

"No, sir, he didn't snatch it. I gave it to him."

Standing her ground, she stared up at the ungainly figure in the long black greatcoat and the scarred face under the slouch hat of black felt. His eyes were dark and piercing; his long bony nose curved in a beak; and his smooth-shaven chin was veined in splotches like spilled blackberry wine. A livid birthmark was branded on the left side of his face between nose and temple, and this, with the drooping eyes above, as defiant as the eye of a caged hawk, gave him the look of a man who had fought his way through a forest fire. Only the fire seemed to be burning not without but within. He was a saint, Ada's grandmother, who ought to have known, had insisted, and because he was a saint he had been able, in spite of his disfigurement, to attach to himself, with brief intervals of widowhood, three excellent wives.

"What will your mother say to that?" The minister's tone was stern.

"I have another, sir. Grandmother knitted two red caps for me. One for every day, and one for Sunday."

He smiled, and she told herself that he no longer frightened her. "And you have a red lining to your squirrel-skin coat."

She looked down. Yes, 'twas true, but she hadn't thought the minister would notice what she had on. Her short coat of squirrel skins stitched together in squares had been lined by Aunt Meggie with the red flannel from one of Grandmother's old petticoats. Beneath the coat she wore a frock of brown and yellow sprigged calico, chosen dark to save washing. She hoped the minister couldn't see the top of her red flannel underbody, which would poke up at the neck, though it was sewed to her petticoat of the same scratchy material. Was there anything wrong, she wondered, while her anxious gaze travelled to her brown woollen stockings with yellow stripes at the top, and farther down, but not so very far, after all, to her stout leather shoes made by old Mr. Borrows, the cobbler, who still sewed so neatly that his shoes lasted for ever. They looked clumsy, she thought; but he had assured her they would wear until her feet grew too big for them.

Though she flushed when the minister glanced down at her, she was not ashamed of her appearance. She had been told, and saw no reason to doubt, that she had a perfectly good face. "A large mouth, but perfectly good," Aunt Meggie had said, and Ada's mother, overhearing this, had laughed and added, "A blunt nose, but perfectly good too." Only, it seemed, her eyes were uncertain, or, so her mother insisted, "improbable." She had discovered this a year before, when she was nine, and Aunt Meggie was writing a letter about the family to a relative they had never seen, a blind and crippled old lady in Scotland. "Shall

I say that Ada's eyes are dark grey or smoky blue?" Aunt Meggie had asked, turning, pen in hand, to the child's father. "Tell her," he had replied quickly, "that she has eyes like the Hebrides." When Ada had demanded eagerly, "What are the Hebrides, Father?" he had answered mysteriously, "The Western Isles."

She would remember this always because it had happened the day she won her gold medal for reciting the Shorter Catechism. The medal was very thin and scarcely bigger than her thumbnail, but it was solid gold, the minister had said when he presented it. Her name was engraved on one side in letters so fine she couldn't read them, and on the other side there was the single word "Catechism," with the year 1900 beneath. She wore the medal threaded on a shoe-string round her neck, except on special occasions when Mother would search in her bureau drawers until she found a bit of old ribbon.

Suddenly, when she thought he had finished, she became aware that Mr. Black was asking another question.

"Why did you give away your cap?"

"The boys spoiled Toby's. And he was crying. He was afraid his mother might whip him."

Mr. Black frowned. He always frowned, as Ada learned afterwards, whenever he was brought face to face with the misery of the world. It was not easy, she could see, too, for him to avoid it. His sacred calling and the whole scheme of salvation depended upon misery, Mother had once complained when she was having a toothache.

"Well, I shouldn't trust her if she can lay hands on him," he said.

While he spoke he wagged his head under the slouched brim, and because she thought it more polite to assent, she wagged back at him like a solid shadow.

"How old are you, my child?" Mr. Black inquired, after a pause.

"Ten, sir. I've been going on eleven ever since last summer."

He nodded abruptly, and then appeared, even more abruptly,

to forget her. His countenance shone in the sunlight, and her own small image seemed to wink at her from its glassy surface. She saw the drift of red in her cheeks, the freckles that never faded from her nose even in winter, and her flying hair, between brown and black, cut short to her shoulders, and curving up till it was like a drake's tail, Aunt Abigail said. She couldn't see the colour of her eyes, but that might be because they had that far-away look.

A stuttering noise at her back made her wheel round, and she saw that Toby was trying to stretch her cap over his deformed head. When she looked at him, he threw the cap in the road and held out his hands, babbling, "Sugar, sugar!"

"Can you understand what this unfortunate is saying?" Mr. Black asked.

"He's begging for something sweet. His mother taught him to say 'Sugar, sugar' like that whenever he meets anybody. No, I haven't anything sweet to give you, Toby," she said severely.

"Go home!" Mr. Black commanded, with a queer distortion of his mouth, and Toby picked up the half-emptied pail of refuse and trotted obediently along the twisted path that led across the field to the hovel.

"You ought not to throw away the caps your grandmother knits for you." The minister's voice had saddened. "Her fingers are not so nimble as they used to be, and her bones are more brittle. But in her prime, before that attack of lumbago last winter, you couldn't have found her match anywhere. Many of our people back in the mountains owe their lives to her and to the medicine in her saddle-bag. Often on stormy nights when word came down from Thunder Mountain that somebody was near death, and the doctor was away on another case, she would pack her saddle-bag with medicine and bandages, not forgetting cloth for a winding-sheet, and start with me on horseback up Lightning or Burned Timber Ridge."

It's all true, Ada told herself proudly, tossing back the hair from her shoulders. Every one spoke that way of Grandmother, especially her daughter-in-law, who had come from the Tidewater and had been a belle in the gay, fast set there, Aunt Meggie said, until she met Father when he had his first charge in Queenborough. A fine church it was, too, the largest Presbyterian congregation in that part of the country. Why had they left there, she wondered, and come back to live with Grandmother in the old manse? Would that always, even when she grew up, be a mystery? From a word Aunt Meggie had let fall, she suspected that the change had had something to do with losing their church. And then, when they were all safely at Ironside and Father had begun to preach in the old stone church, which his great-great-grandfather, John Fincastle, pioneer, and his flock had built with their own hands, he had lost this charge also as soon as the second volume of his book had come from the press. It was dreadful, she couldn't help thinking, though Grandmother had rebuked her for the opinion, the way pastors were dismissed just as soon as they were comfortably settled. Father had been obliged to turn into a schoolmaster and fill the parlour with rows of ugly green benches. She had heard somebody say that he was allowed to teach only profane learning, and even that was on Grandmother's account, because she had done so much good in her life.

"Did your father go to Doncaster this morning?" Mr. Black's question trailed off into the sigh she had learned to expect when any one spoke of her father.

"Yes, sir. He went with Mr. Rowan in his two-horse gig. They started before day, and he said they would be back, if nothing happened, about sundown. It's a long way."

"Not as the crow flies. But all ways are long over bad roads."

"He had to go about the mortgage." A mortgage was nothing to be ashamed of if you were self-respecting. Nor, for that matter, was being poor and doing without things, so long as you saved your pride and didn't stoop to receive charity.

What troubled her was not the mortgage, but the endless sigh that fluttered about Father's name. He had been a more eloquent preacher than Mr. Black, Mother declared, and after the second volume of his book was published (the book that had cost him two pulpits) famous men from all over the world had written to ask his opinion of the philosophers in the olden time. For he himself was one of the greatest. Had he lived long ago, Mother had said, carefully pronouncing the syllables, he might have walked with Socrates, he might have been the companion of Plato.

There was a brief silence while the man and the child gazed up the steep road from the church to a grove of giant oaks and a red brick house flanked by a stony hill which was used as a pasture for three infirm sheep. The dwelling stood slightly withdrawn from the village, on land that had belonged to the Fincastles ever since Ironside had been a part of the frontier and John Fincastle had led his human flock up from the Indian savannahs, running in wild grass and pea-vine, to the bowed shoulder of the mountain. Near the timbered ridges he had felled trees and built the original manse, a cabin of round logs with a stone chimney. He had always believed, Grandmother said, that the Lord had directed him to their grove of oaks in Shut-in Valley. Far into the night he had prayed, asking a sign, and in the morning when he had risen to fetch water he had seen a finger of light pointing straight from the sky to the topmost bough of an oak. After more than a century and a half, in which the log cabin had given way first to a small stone house and then to the square brick house, the Fincastle place was still known as "the old manse," while the minister's home in the village was called "the new parsonage." The child, who had heard all this and much more, imagined that the fine town of Fincastle, and the lost county as well, had been named after the pioneer for whom God made a sign. But the minister might have told her, had he felt the wish to shatter a harmless myth, that these historic scenes commemorated not an act of God, but the family seat of Lord Botetourt in England.

"Is there anybody at the gate?" Mr. Black inquired presently, shielding his eyes from the sun. "It may be only a sheep. It's queer, isn't it," he continued solemnly, "how little difference there is between a human being and a sheep to near-sighted eyes?"

The child laughed shyly because she knew, though it did not

seem funny, that he expected her to be amused. " 'Tis Grandmother," she replied. "She's picking up sticks. Every evening, just before sundown, she goes out and picks up all the sticks that have dropped since the day before."

The queer frown that bore so strong a resemblance to misery, and yet was not misery, distorted the minister's face. "But that is bad for her rheumatism."

"She doesn't stoop all the time. Father made her a pair of wooden tongs to pick up with."

"Do you never help her?"

"We all pick up every evening. Sometimes Father and I go down into the woods and gather the handcart full of lightwood. 'Tis a great saving," she explained in an elderly tone, "on the backlogs Father cut last summer."

"I dare say. Well, you'd better run home now and help your grandmother."

"I'm not going home." Her voice was faltering but brave. "I'm going over to the flat rock by the big pine to watch for Father." Had the minister forgotten that Christmas was coming soon, and the Ladies' Missionary Society was holding a festival on Tuesday to raise money for the heathen in China?

"Is he going to bring you something?" Again he smiled, and again she thought in surprise, I am not afraid of him.

"He's going to bring me a doll with real hair." Her eyes shone and the red drifted back into her cheeks.

"But won't a doll with real hair cost a good deal?"

"I saved up my berry money. Mrs. Rowan paid me two dollars and a half for picking berries for her last summer."

"Will a doll cost all of two dollars and a half?"

"I hope not." She appeared anxious, as indeed she was. "I had to spend a dollar. I simply had to spend a dollar."

"Well, run on. He may come sooner than you expect. Isn't the nearest way through the village?"

"No, sir, I know a sheep track over the fields. The track goes by the flat rock all the way down to Smiling Creek."

But he had not, she realized after a moment, listened to a word she had said. His gaze was sweeping the Appalachian uplands and the unbroken chain of mountains to the farthest and highest blue summit. While she waited for him to dismiss her, she saw his mouth quiver and move stiffly in silent prayer. Then, as she was about to slip away, the words fluttered and came to roost on his lips. "Whenever I look at God's Mountain, I know what is meant by *the peace of God, which passeth all understanding.*"

Vaguely bewildered, but still eager to be all that he required of a child who knew the Catechism by heart, she hesitated and raised her eyes to a face that had become luminous with worship. Then, turning away softly, she tied her knitted scarf over her head and ran into the near field to pick out the old sheep track, which was scarcely wider than a seam in the ground.

HE child lay on the flat rock and watched the road that climbed through the small valleys within the Great Valley.

God's Mountain, Father said, was the over-soul of Appalachian Virginia. Whenever she gazed at it alone for a long time, the heavenly blue seemed to flood into her heart and rise there in a peak. That must have been the first thing God created, and blue, she supposed, was the oldest colour in the world. When she was studying the Alps in her geography class, Father had said that the Blue Ridge and the Alleghanies were older. And the streams were old too. That was why there were no lakes or ponds in the hollows of Indian Rock County, not even in Campbell's Valley or Aunt Mary's Valley or Can't Whistle Creek Valley or, of course, in their very own Shut-in Valley. But there were many rivers and creeks and runs and trickling ice-green freshets from the melted snows in the mountains. Scattered among them, she could see the comfortable farmhouses, with roofs of red painted tin or grey weather-beaten shingles. For Shut-in Valley was not really shut in except at the farther end.

A doll with real hair—the thought ran in a bright skein through her mind. She had never in all her life had a doll with real hair. And she was buying it with her own money that she had earned, so she might look at it as soon as it came, without waiting for Christmas. Mother had given her a scrap of pink baby ribbon to tie round its head; she knew Aunt Meggie was making a dress as a surprise; and Grandmother, she was almost sure, had crocheted a pink coat, and perhaps tiny shoes, of worsted for it to wear when she took it into the village. She would call it Flora because that name sounded pink and smooth and smiling, with yellow hair.

Leaning down from the rock, she looked far over Little River, which reflected the sky through shadows of scudding clouds. Immense, clear, glittering, the even summit of God's Mountain broke on the western horizon. She could smell the crystal scent of winter in the air, like the taste of wild strawberries. Nearer, yet still far away, she could make out the twin crests of Rain and Cloud Mountains, and when she turned and glanced over her shoulder, there was Thunder Mountain, the nearest of all. On the very top of Thunder Mountain, Father said, there was a heap of brown stones. Nobody could tell how it had come there, or why the Indians had raised it. Some people believed it was the burial mound of an Indian chief. But Father thought that when the Shawnees went by on the warpath, each brave had dropped a stone as an offering to the Great Spirit, just as she dropped a penny in the plate Deacon McClung passed in church.

When she was old enough she meant to climb the mountain and see for herself. That was one of the things Mother had always longed to do and had never done. "Some day when we have nothing important to do," Mother said, "and I don't have to lie on a sofa to spare my back, we'll take a whole day out of life and climb to the very top of Thunder Mountain. We'll go up as high as the Indian mound. From there we can see nearly to the end of the world." And ever since she was little, the child had asked, "Is the end of the world blue, Mother?"

Lower down on Thunder Mountain you could still see signs of the Shawnee warpath. Indian trail, they called it; and Ralph McBride had followed it with some deer-hunters last fall. Over that trail the Shawnees had come for the massacre of Smiling Creek. Ralph had found arrowheads and part of a tomahawk down under the rocks in the deepest bottom of the creek. When the Indians went back they had taken Great-great-grandmother Tod away into captivity. A little girl she had been, ten years old, no bigger than Ada. She had lived for seven long years a captive in a Shawnee village. When she was sixteen, they had married her to a young chief, and she had gone into his wigwam. Then peace with the red men had come soon afterwards, and when she was seventeen she was returned under the treaty, Father said, that ended Pontiac's War. After all she had endured, she lived to be over a hundred.

In the middle of the road by the flat rock, two of the mountain people, a man and a boy, were swinging by with a slow, even gait. As they passed, they looked up and nodded gravely, and she nodded back without speaking. "Somebody must be sick up there," she thought; for the mountaineers seldom came down in winter, except to buy Jamaica ginger, or to summon Doctor Updike to visit the dying. Father had told her that they were a stalwart breed, the true American Highlanders. In pioneer days their forefathers had fled from the strict settlements, some because they could breathe only in freedom, and others to escape punishment for crimes against the laws of the Tidewater. But old black Aunt Abigail Geddy, who had Indian blood, muttered that there were fearful sights in the hills if you knew where to look for them. She had once gone to Panther's Gap to help Grandmother take care of a family of half-wits. Three generations of half-wits, from a chattering crone of a granny to a new-born baby barely a day old! And the baby was the worst. If it had been a kitten, she said, they would have tossed it straight into Panther's Run. Aunt Abigail would have mumbled on over her pipe until the child was quaking with horror. But just as she approached the hair-raising part, Mother came into the kitchen and spoke so severely that the old woman could never be persuaded to return to the subject. She would only shake her head and mutter that folks in Panther's Gap were all as poor as Job's turkey.

Ever since she was too little to lace her own shoes, Ada had wondered what it meant to be poor. She remembered, too, the very moment her wondering began. It was when she was five years old, and Grandmother had taken her frock of yellow sprigged calico to give to the poor McAllisters, who lived up the road. She had loved her yellow sprigged frock, and she had hated to give it away. When she had cried, Grandmother, who was rummaging in her closets to find clothes to put into a basket, had reproved her and said she ought to be glad to divide with God's poor. "Are we poor, Grandmother?" she had asked. "Not so poor," Grandmother had replied, "as the poor McAllisters." "What does it mean," the child had persisted, "to be poor"? "It means," Grandmother had answered, "not to have enough to eat. It means not to have enough clothes to cover you." "Oh, then, we aren't poor, Grandmother," Ada had cried joyfully. "We have two bags of cornmeal in the storeroom, and two sides of bacon in the smokehouse, and a patch full of sweet potatoes in the garden. And all of us," she had added in triumph, "have our new red flannel petticoats for next winter." Then Mother had dropped on her knees, crying, while she folded her in her arms. "You're right, darling," she had said, "we aren't really poor, and we have much to be thankful for."

The shadow of the big pine had fallen aslant the rock, and rolling over in the crisp air, which was not too cold, Ada looked across the fields to the village and the stone chimneys of the church above the bare boughs in the churchyard. She knew the story of that church by heart, and she could listen for ever, she thought, to the adventures of the first settlers, as Grandmother told them.

"Ours is a little church, but we have loved it," Grandmother would begin. "Even if we've never been so well off as the congregations at New Providence and Timber Ridge and Falling Springs, still we were appointed to our humble work in the Lord's vineyard. The Fincastles, too, were always simple folk, though they had learning, and were as good as the best."

"And are we as good as the best now, Grandmother?" Ada would ask.

"In everything but circumstances, my child. The Craigies were even less well-to-do than the Fincastles; but they were rooted like oaks."

"Scotch-Irish, people called the pioneers, though after they were driven out of Strathclyde they had stayed to themselves in Ulster, and had seldom or never crossed blood with the Irish.

John Fincastle had brought his flock with him from County Donegal, all the elders and deacons of his church and a few humbler members of his congregation. They had sailed from Ulster in the ship *Martha and Mary*, and it had taken them one hundred and eighteen days to cross the Atlantic Ocean to Philadelphia. At first they had settled and practised their religion in Pennsylvania; but after a few restless years, the bolder spirits among the Ulstermen had pushed southward, with their families, over the old Indian Road, into Virginia. The Scholar Pioneer, the immigrants named John Fincastle, because he had brought not only his Bible, but as much of his library as he could stow away into a pack. Grandmother would chuckle over the legend that he had reduced his wife's pots and kettles to a single vessel in order to make room for volumes of profane learning. "That's how your father came by his reason, if not by his use of it. Though I'm far from denying," she would sigh, "that, in spite of his backsliding, he is still a man of good parts."

But the worst was not over. A thrilling quaver would creep into Grandmother's voice. When the Indian Road led them into Virginia, they found the settlement too contentious for a worshiper who wanted peace with his Maker. After a few months John Fincastle thrust out toward the frontier. The mood of the wilderness flowed into him and ebbed back again. He was pursuing the dream of a free country, the dream of a country so vast that each man would have room to bury his dead on his own land.

The pioneers who had gone ahead had left not a single track, not even the print of a hoof, in the Indian meadows. There was nothing to guide them except the sun and the stars, and occasionally the faint signs of Indian hunters. No wagons could travel the wilderness, and all they needed, even profane learning, had to be carried on pack horses. No wonder, after climbing hills, fording rivers, defying forests, that a spear of light should seem to them to be the finger of Providence. Their first act was to drop on their knees; their first thought was to build a house for Divine worship. But years passed before they could assemble material for the Ironside church, with the floor of walnut puncheons, the high-backed pews, the stone stairways to the gallery.

When the ground was broken, all the families in the clearings left their brush-harrows and plows and hastened with saws, axes, and hammers to the spot where they had knelt in the sunrise. Men and women worked together building the walls, and every grain of sand to make mortar was brought by the women on horseback. Mrs. Ettrick, a woman of great strength, was surprised by a redskin when she was fording a creek, but she felled him with the single blow of a hatchet and galloped back to warn the men who bore muskets. Grandmother's words would drop thick and fast, like the pelting of hail, while Ada's flesh crawled with fear that was somehow delicious.

John Fincastle was a merciful man. Though he was a trespasser on the hunting-grounds of the Indians, he became their friend and protector. Only his renowned piety had saved him from death when he tried to defend innocent tribes. He never forgave the settlers, especially his own militia, for the murder of Cornstalk. In his last years, when he was upwards of eighty, and his eldest son, John II, had succeeded him in his ministry, he abandoned what was then called civilization (here Grandmother would pause to shake her head), and went alone into the wilderness as a missionary to the Shawnees. All his worldly needs, he had declared, could be strapped on his back. He carried with him two Bibles and one other book, a copy in his own handwriting of the Meditations of a heathen Emperor who had not even been converted and saved. That made some people think his years were beginning to tell on him. It seemed, whatever way you looked at it, a strange thing to do.

"Remember, my child, that you have strong blood," Grandmother would end proudly, for her forefathers, the Craigies, had been members of John Fincastle's flock. "Never let it be weakened. Thin blood runs to wickedness."

The sun was going down in a blaze, but as it sank behind the hills it shot up again in a fountain of light and scattered a sparkling spray into the clouds. Cramped from waiting so long, Ada felt that a chill had begun to creep up from the rock, where the sunshine had vanished, through the thickness of her woollen stockings and squirrel-skin coat. Springing to her feet, she jumped up and down until warmth ran in pinpricks over her arms and legs. When she moved to the edge of the rock, she could look through the last faded leaves on the oaks, which glimmered with a bluish tone in the flushed light, and see the dormer-windows and the sloping shingled roof of the manse. The darkness of ivy was flung over the square front porch, with ends that groped toward the western wall and laced back the green shutters.

In the side yard, over the fallen leaves, a dusky shape moved near the ground, and she knew that it was Horace on his way from Aunt Abigail Geddy's cabin, which he visited between meals in the hope of a sop of corn pone and gravy. The Geddys were the only coloured family in Ironside; they were all upright and independent, and they were proud of their Indian blood and straight features. Aunt Abigail had lived at the manse for forty-odd years. After Father lost his church and had no money to pay her wages, she had stayed on because she said it was respectable to work for a minister, whether he preached or not, and her cabin between the garden and the sheep pasture, behind the row of sunflowers Aunt Meggie raised every summer for chicken feed, was all the home that she wanted. It was a good cabin. There were two rooms with a big stone fireplace and a floor of double boards to defend the old woman's bones from the dampness. Her son, Marcellus Geddy, had plastered the walls and whitewashed them within and without.

Between the green shutters the red eye of a window blinked from under the ivy, and while the child watched the flickering gleam she seemed to be in two places at once. The dusky shape of Horace barked at the door. It opened and shut again behind him when he had padded into the hall. Grandmother had filled her basket with sticks long ago, and had gone in to take up the ball of brown yarn and her steel knitting needles. She would sit erect in her deep chair with wings on her own side of the fireplace, near the lamp on the round table and the front window where the shutters were held back by ivy. The big front room was Mother's chamber. A log fire burned there all the time, and after supper the family gathered in front of the great fireplace to pray with Grandmother, and to listen to Father when he read aloud a chapter from *Old Mortality*. In one corner there was a high tester bed, and Ada's own trundle-bed, in which she had slept ever since she was a baby, was rolled out at night from under the hanging fringe of the counterpane. All the furniture, except a rosewood bookcase and sofa from the parsonage in Queenborough, was made of walnut or pine and had furnished the manse in her great-great-grandfather's day.

Grandmother was the kind of person you saw better when you were not looking straight at her. Even when she was young, Mother said, she could never have been handsome; but she had the sort of ugliness that is more impressive than beauty. Her figure was tall, strong, rugged; her face reminded the child of the rock profile at Indian Head; and her eyes, small, bright, ageless, were like the eyes of an eaglet that had peered out from a crevice under the rock. At seventy, her eyebrows were still black and bushy, and in the left one there was a large brown mole from which three stiff black hairs bristled as sharply as needles in a pincushion. Summer and winter, except on the Sabbath, she wore the same dresses of black and grey calico with very full skirts, and a little crocheted shawl of grey or lavender wool was flung over her shoulders whenever she felt the edge of a chill. Ada had never seen her without a cap on her thick hair, which was not white but grizzled. Even when her lumbago was so painful that she could not get out of bed, and a fire had to be kept up all night in her room, she would ask for her muslin day cap with its bunch of narrow black ribbon before she would swallow a morsel of breakfast.

Mother, who could never sit still, would be moving about, helping Aunt Meggie in the kitchen (for three days Aunt Abigail Geddy had been crippled with rheumatism), or running out on the porch to look for Father or for Ada herself. Then in a flash, hurrying and laughing as she hurried, she would dart in through another door, crying, "I forgot something! I know I forgot something, but I can't think what it was I forgot!" She was always like that, gay, amused, beautiful, even when she was faded and weather-beaten, making fun where there was no fun.

For a few years after she lost her two little sons from diphtheria, Aunt Meggie said, the heart had seemed to go out of her. But when Father was obliged to resign from his church in Queenborough, and everything became suddenly so bad it looked as if it could not be worse, Mother grew brighter than she had ever been. She talked all the time, and no matter how poor they were, she could always find something to laugh at, if it were nothing more amusing than poverty. Yet it was true, as she would repeat over and over in her bright, tremulous voice, they had much to be thankful for. Never, as far back as Ada could remember, had they been hungry. Even if they needed clothes, and Grandmother redipped and turned and pressed the ribbon on her caps until it was worn to a fringe, they had never been without corn bread and brown gravy and all the dried beans and peas and canned tomatoes that Aunt Meggie gathered in their garden and put up with the help of Aunt Abigail Geddy.

T HE dying flare of the sun cast a rust-coloured light down into the valley, and across this light a long black shape wavered suddenly from the blue crook in the hills.

That must be the two-horse gig, with Father and Mr. Rowan side by side on the small seat. But was it? She couldn't be sure. Yes . . . no. Oh, it was, it was. . . . Lightly as a squirrel, she balanced herself on the edge of the rock, bounded with a single flying leap into the road, and raced down toward the bottom of the hill, where the gig was splashing through a puddle before talking the climb. Like an enormous crow, the shadow hesitated, flapped, and then flittered onward before the vehicle, as if shadow and substance were two separate bodies. At last he was coming. He was bringing her doll with real hair that she could brush and comb and perhaps roll up in curl-papers. As she ran on, her breath came in gasps and words floated in wisps of fog out of her mouth. Never had she been so happy before. Her heart felt as if it would bubble over with joy.

"Did you bring it, Father?" she called, and he answered in his distant voice, so unlike her mother's near and thrilling tones, "Yes, I brought it, my child. I did the best I could."

When the gig reached her, she was lifted into it and settled snugly between Father's hard lean figure and Mr. Rowan's soft bulging one.

"I reckon he's got something for you stuffed away in that basket with the coffee and sugar," Mr. Rowan remarked pleasantly. She had always liked him, even if he was Janet's father and Janet would tag after her when she went climbing with Ralph. It wasn't any fun to climb with a baby that fell down and scratched her knee and then sat in the briers and cried if you didn't come back for her. But Mr. Rowan had a pleasant face (a red face was more cheerful, especially in wintertime, than a pale one) and he had a good habit of carrying pink and white sugar animals in his pocket. This was because of Janet. Aunt Abigail said they had spoiled Janet till she was rotten, and some day, when the Lord had time to attend to it, they would be punished.

"It's a doll with real hair. I bought it with my berry money."

"Well, well, I wish Janet would turn her hand to making money. She's never bought anything for herself."

"But she's always had a wax doll this high." She measured the height in the air. "It's so beautiful she won't let any of us play with it."

"Is that so? Well, I tell you what we'll do. You bring your doll to Janet's Christmas tree and we'll all play together."

Daylight and shadow had both vanished now, and there was only the thin dusk on the road. Past the flat rock into the village, where she saw Mr. Borrows shutting his shop, and Judge Melrose walking along the cinder-strewn sidewalk with his brown spaniel Ruddy, and a white horse before the door of old Mr. Wertenbaker, who had come from the Shenandoah Valley, and Janet Rowan waving her hand to her father, and Ralph McBride opening the gate before the small house where his mother, a widow but proud, worked so hard to keep a roof over their heads. Then on beyond the church into the steep short road which led through the big gate that sagged on its hinges, and over the crackling dead leaves in the yard of the manse.

"Well, I'll be turning home," Mr. Rowan said, smiling and friendly, as he picked her up and swung her to the ground. "It's been a long day, and we'll both be glad of a good supper with bed at the end of it. A cold wave is coming. We may have snow again by to-morrow."

The gig rolled through the gate; the crackling died away in the leaves; there was the sound of wheels growing fainter; and then suddenly Mother's voice called eagerly from the porch, "Have you come, John?"

"May I have it now, Father?" the child asked.

They were standing under the oaks, and she waited while he glanced down uncertainly at the basket. His figure, tall, spare, with the straight spine of an Indian, seemed to sink into and become a part of the twilight.

"May I have my doll now, Father?" she asked again.

Stooping over the basket, he lifted the lid and drew out an oblong parcel wrapped in brown paper and neatly tied with a store string. "I did the best I could, my child," he repeated, as he put it into her hands. "After the mortgage was settled, it took all I had left to buy coffee and sugar for your grandmother. She is old, and it's a deprivation for her to go without coffee."

But she held the parcel tight, without untying the string or taking in a word that he said. Suddenly the whole world was swimming in bliss, the blue twilight, the dark afterglow, the far-off benevolent shape of God's Mountain. "I'll undo it inside," she whispered, catching her breath. "I'll wait for Mother and Grandmother."

Wheeling round, she ran across the yard, over the dead leaves which sighed as cheerfully as if they were not really dead. She would always remember that happy rustling underfoot, and the clinging smoky scents that sprang up out of the twilight— scents of earth and winter and frosty darkness, all shot through and mingled with a sensation of joy, a quiver of expectancy.

The door opened and shut. She ran into the room, straight to the fireplace, where Grandmother was knitting and Mother had hurried in, after calling Father, to throw lightwood knots on the flames.

"He's come, Mother. He's brought my doll."

"I'm glad, dear. I'm glad you have what you've wanted so much." Mother's eyes, as she turned from the fire, were like lamps under a dark shade, and her thin cheeks, where all the dimples were sucked into hollows, were flaming with colour.

Grandmother peered over her spectacles, though her knitting needles continued to click busily, and Aunt Meggie, who was tying on an apron on her way to the kitchen, stopped and glanced back, with her round cheerful face and funny slanting eyes beneath wisps of sandy hair that strayed over her forehead.

"The only dolls little girls had in my day were rag dolls," Grandmother said, with a smile. "Rag or corncob or hickory nut. I remember somebody, 'twas a member of your great-grandfather's congregation, gave me a wooden doll with arms and legs on hinges, and I nearly went out of my wits for happiness." The sense of fun played over her as dawn skims over a mountain crag.

Mother laughed. "But your day was different. The world has grown, and children have more nowadays." She sighed under her breath, the kind of sigh, Ada knew, that meant she was thinking of all they used to have before Father became a philosopher instead of a minister.

"Hadn't you better keep it for Christmas?" Aunt Meggie asked. "There won't be much for Christmas this year."

"Oh, no, let her open it," Mother said. "She bought it with her own money."

Ada's fingers were trembling so that she could scarcely pick out the knot in the store string that must be saved. "I'm going to name her Flora," she cried. "I think Flora is the prettiest name in the world." Her voice broke off, rose again in a sharp cry, and quavered into a sobbing moan. "Oh, Mother, Mother, she isn't real! She isn't anything in the world but china like Nellie. Her hair is just china!"

It was true. Mother and Grandmother and Aunt Meggie stared down at the black glazed head as it emerged from the sawdust. Then, stooping quickly, Mother snatched the doll from the box, and said in a bright, anxious voice, "She has a nice face, darling. Perhaps there weren't any better." Grandmother's needles stopped for a minute, and Horace, on the rug near the fire, raised his head and thumped his tail slowly.

"But I don't want a china doll, Mother. Nellie is china." Darkness overwhelmed her. All the shining bliss was blotted out as suddenly as it had flashed into light. Her heart sank down, far, far down into emptiness, and instead of the happy sighing of the leaves she heard only a mournful whisper from the flames that crawled over the lightwood knots on their way into smoke. Never, never as long as she lived would she have a doll with real hair that she could comb and brush. Something would always stand in the way. First she had lost all the money she had saved; it had slipped through the lining of her squirrel-skin coat before Mother mended the rent in her pocket. Then one season had been too poor for berries and the next season they had been too plentiful. And she was already outgrowing the age for dolls. Grandmother reminded her of this every day. Little girls of ten years had had their useful tasks in Grandmother's childhood. They had carded wool or hemmed cloth or stitched a sampler like the one Grandmother herself had worked when she was only seven, with the picture of a church and a white steeple and a few birds flying. At the age of ten, Grandmother insisted, little girls should be taught their responsibilities.

"I don't want it, Mother. I don't want china hair."

"We'll hear what Father has to say, darling. Perhaps it isn't so bad as it seems. She has a nice face, and I'll make her a dress and a bonnet out of that pink gingham I'd put away."

"As soon as my hens begin laying again, I'll buy you a doll, Ada," said Aunt Meggie, who possessed the treasure of a practical mind. "Try not to give way to disappointment. Think how sad the world would be if we all gave way to disappointment."

But the child had ceased to care what became of the world. She had waited and saved; she had denied herself sticks of painted peppermint candy when the other children were sucking; and all the time she was growing farther from the age of play and nearer to the dreadful age of tasks. There was the bedstead, too, that Ralph McBride, who could carve almost anything, had made for her last Christmas. It was waiting now in the cupboard where she kept her playthings. The posts were smooth and round and fitted together, and there was a carved acorn in the middle of the headboard. Nellie hadn't looked just right in that bed, especially after Aunt Meggie had given her a tick of feathers to put on the slats and Mother had made sheets and pillows and even a blanket. A doll with real hair that opened her eyes in the morning and shut them at night was what the bed needed. And now Nellie would have a companion like herself, with a body that was sawdust as far as the neck and coal-black hair that was as hard as her face.

"Aunt Meggie is right, Ada," Mother was repeating in her voice of strained sweetness which sounded as if it were on the verge of breaking, yet never broke. "Try not to take things so hard."

"But Janet Rowan takes things hard, Mother, and she has all the dolls she wants."

"I know, Ada, but the Rowans are rich, and we are poor. Don't envy them, dear. We are happier than they are."

Above the murmur of the flames she heard Grandmother heave one of her great sighs which shook her from head to foot, immense as she was, and remark sternly, yet not without sympathy, to Mother, "The child has a single heart, Mary Evelyn, and that will always bear watching. Jealousy is the flaw in the single heart."

"Ada has never been jealous," Mother answered quickly, while the red in her cheeks stained her throat. "You can't expect a child not to feel disappointment."

"I didn't say that to hurt you," Grandmother rejoined gently. "Ada is a good child."

"Don't cry, dear," Mother said, folding the child in her arms. "Your father is coming in. Try not to let him see how much this has meant to you."

First the hall door and then the chamber door opened and shut. Horace sprang to his feet with a bark. The smell of winter was blown into the room on waves of freshness; and her father entered with a step that dragged from weariness after his long drive and his hard day. Crossing the floor, he kissed his wife and held out his hand to his mother, who did not favour casual endearments.

"I did the best I could, Mary Evelyn," he said, flinching from mental or physical pain. "I know the child is disappointed, but I did the best I could. There wasn't a wax doll with real hair for less than three dollars. The cheaper ones had been sold for a festival."

"I know you did the best you could, John," Mother replied quickly, with a gesture as if she were patting and smoothing. "Ada is disappointed, of course, but Meggie is going to buy a doll for her as soon as the hens begin laying well. This one has a pretty face even if she has china hair, and she will look lovely after I've dressed her. You must be half starved. Sit down and get warm while I make the coffee. Meggie has everything ready, and think what a treat it will be to have coffee and sugar again."

With her sprightly walk, she hurried out into the hall, and Ada heard the rustling of paper as the parcels were carried through the dining-room into the kitchen. The other side of the house was dark now and cold. The front room was Father's library, where he worked far into the night, though he never had a fire except when his hands became so frostbitten that he could not close his fingers over his pen. Grandmother had knitted a jersey for him of thick yarn, but in the coldest weather he wrote in his greatcoat and sometimes even with his hat on, or one of Grandmother's little shawls tied over his head. Mother begged him to have a fire, and sometimes she would light one without his seeing her do it. Yet even in winter it was a cheerful room, and in summer it was the nicest place in the house because of the shining backs of books on the walls and the view from the front windows of God's Mountain, which seemed closer there than anywhere else. Some of the books had always been there. They belonged in Great-great-great-grandfather's theological library, and this had been increased year by year in each generation. Then there were all the works on philosophy Father had bought when he was a student in London. He would sometimes talk to them of the two years he had spent there, and Ada would listen breathlessly to his account of the house and the landlady in Bloomsbury, where he had lodged. Every day, as soon as the doors were opened, he would go into the Reading Room of the British Museum, and he would stay there until it closed, except for half an hour when he went out for a cup of tea and some slices of bread and butter. It must have been a dull life, Mother thought, but he had loved it. He had been as happy, he said, as the day was long. Yet Ada had overheard Grandmother telling Aunt Meggie in the middle of the night that his years in London and in the British Museum had been "the ruination of John."

The aroma of coffee was wafted in, and Grandmother tossed her head with a spirited gesture, in the way an old mare will do when she feels the spring in her bones. Presently Mother would call them back into the kitchen and they would pass the closed door of the parlour, where all the ugly green benches and the stove for wood were waiting for Monday morning and the rows of pupils who came to be taught, among other branches of learning, profane history and geography, but not sacred.

The kitchen door must have opened again, for a new smell, the warm, kindling, delicious smell of frying bacon, curled up brown and crisp at the ends, mingled with the aroma of coffee. On any other night, the child would have been the first in the kitchen, helping and watching, but she still suffered from the memory of Flora, and all her appetite seemed to have fled. She thought distantly of the table Mother adorned with flowers or winter berries in the blue bowl she loved, and would let no one else wash, because it was exactly the colour of God's Mountain. The blue bowl had been one of her wedding presents, but the four silver candlesticks, which she set out even when she had no candles to put in them, had belonged to Great-grandmother Fincastle, the one who had been a Graham. Good food, Grandmother said, needed no trimming. But Mother had a way of living that made everything pretty. She was glad that the candlesticks were not solid silver, that copper gleamed through in places where they were worn. The copper, she would say with a laugh, was more precious than silver, for it was the only thing that had kept them from being turned into money. It was Mother, of course, who kept a row of red geraniums on the kitchen window-sill and had arranged what she called her "winter bouquets" in the old earthenware crocks on the hall table.

"You need something to eat, John," Grandmother said suddenly, as she let her knitting fall in her lap. Her nostrils quivered with pleasure when the smell floated in, for she had a hearty relish for food. Not, as she complained, for the dishes provided by her daughter-in-law's pernickety taste, but for coarse, strong, nourishing fare with a body of its own that stayed by her.

"Rowan gave me a bite, but I wasn't hungry." Father spoke dreamily, as if only the fringes of his thoughts were engaged in his answer. "Yes, I shall be glad of a cup of coffee."

Going over to the cupboard in the corner, Ada took out the doll's bedstead and stood it on the floor beside her own trundle-bed. When she had put a nightgown on the new doll, she laid her beside Nellie between the sheets. Even if she couldn't love her, she might still name her Flora.

Hurrying in, with her sweet and anxious expression, Mother said gaily, "Supper is ready, and nobody is going to be disappointed."

Her forehead and temples were pinched with neuralgia; the tendons jerked like cords in her throat; and the colour in her haggard cheeks looked as if it had been burned there by a flame. But the lovely contour, the perfect oval, of her face had resisted time and disease. A strange happiness, more a quality than an emotion, as ethereal and as penetrating as light, rippled in her voice and shone steadily in her eyes and smile.

'T WAS the three cups of coffee that put the heart into me and will make me sleep sound, Grandmother Fincastle thought; for she had scant patience with the feeble folk who are at the mercy of nerves and let anything in the nature of food or drink keep them awake.

Bending over with difficulty, she eased her foot, which had begun to swell, from the square cloth shoe with elastic sides and stretched it out on the warm bricks, where the kettle steamed, the firelight shifted, and a skeleton spider, pale as a ghost, was spinning a single strand of cobweb over the pile of backlogs near the chimney. For an instant, while she raised her head, she felt that the room receded and swam in a ruddy haze before it emerged again in its true pattern. The material form had dissolved into a fluid, into a memory. Then once more the actuality triumphed; the immediate assumed its old power and significance.

She saw the big warm chamber glimmering with firelight. Mary Evelyn now slept here, but she herself had slept here long ago, as a bride, a wife, and a mother. Aye, she had much to be thankful for, shelter and warmth and all the creature comforts she had missed in her youth. . . . There was that mouse again scampering in the far corner. She hoped Meggie had not forgotten to put down the mousetrap.

She liked the soft, bright colours in the rag carpet, woven by her own hands out of scraps the congregation had saved for her. She liked the homemade furniture of walnut or pine better than the carved rosewood Mary Evelyn had brought from Queenborough. She liked the great bed, so substantial that it took two men to push it, and the patchwork quilt which was brought out at night when the fringed counterpane was removed. Nobody nowadays had the patience or the eyesight to make that Star of Bethlehem pattern. Work like that belonged to another time. But it looked comfortable on the foot of the bed, with the child's trundle-bed rolled out and prepared for the night.

All Grandmother's children had slept in that trundle-bed, the seven she had lost, the two who were living, and she had grown fond of it. It was the only piece of furniture she had brought from Giles County, where her father had lived when she was a child. "I'm going to make a sofa out of that old trundle-bed, Mr. Fincastle," she had murmured, blushing when Adam, her husband (though it would not have been respectful to think of him by his Christian name), had smiled at the sight of it. But she had known when she spoke that the trundle-bed would never be turned into a sofa.

Her youth had suffered from hardships; she had spent her childhod in a log cabin, yet she had not been ashamed. When she was five years old her father was called to a mission on Wildcat Mountain, and from that time she had not seen a railway train until she was grown. Mr. Fincastle had met her when he came to preach at the mission, and he had felt from the first minute, he told her afterwards, that this also was appointed. That was the Sabbath she was admitted to sealing ordinances. But even before she had reached the years of discretion, her faith had been strong. When she was no bigger than a slip of a girl she had felt that she was ready to do or die, or even to be damned, if it would redound to the greater glory of God.

Though she knew that bricks are no more than straws in the sight of the Lord, she would always remember how wonderful the manse had appeared to her, as a bride, when she had first seen it on a spring morning. Everything had seemed to her to be provided; the grove of oaks to cast shade; the vegetable garden at the back of the house; the well so close to the kitchen porch; the springhouse at the bottom of the yard under the big willow; and the house inside, with the solid furniture, the rows of books that had always been there, and the shining pewter plates, so bright you could see your face in them, on the sideboard. She could imagine nothing more luxurious than eating in a dining-room, with a cloth on the table, and having hot water to wash in. As a bride she used to say that she praised the Lord whenever she took up that big kettle from the trivet in front of the fire. And she thanked Mr. Fincastle's father, too, for the kitchen, nearly if not quite so large as the front chamber. He had built that for his wife, Margaret, who had brought a family of servants.

Margaret Graham was an extraordinary character, and she was still beautiful as Grandmother remembered her. She had known wealth, for she was the daughter of Squire Graham of Glenburnie, who had inherited a fortune in land and died dis-possessed. When she was married to the third John, she infused a romantic legend, as well as an aristocratic strain, into the Fin-castle stock. There was a cherished tradition that the Graham ancestor who had fled from Scotland to Ireland in 1650 was a near kinsman of the great Montrose. "No, we were not always with the Covenanters," Grandmother thought, shaking her head while she tucked the ball of yarn between her thigh and the cushion. Old John, the pioneer, had said that he fought not against men, but against evil passions both within and without the Kirk. The present John had inherited his grandmother's straight features and her eyes—bright blue, with a crystal gaze that seemed to pierce the heart in its search for truth. When she first came as a bride, the ruling elders had requested her to wear a veil in church, so that her beauty might not distract men's thoughts from the eloquence of her husband. After that, she had worn a green barège veil over her bonnet. But it was not Mr. Fincastle's father, John III, who had built the brick house. They had John II to thank for that. When he was well on in life, a relative in Scotland had left him a legacy. Not a fortune as people thought nowadays, but enough to build a brick manse and to enlarge the church over the old house of worship. With what was left, he had placed a sandstone slab at the head of every Fincastle grave in the churchyard. His father, John I, was buried there. A week before his death, when he was out of his head, the Shawnees had brought him back, mourning as they would have mourned for a great chief.

How in the world, Grandmother still asked herself, had those early settlers been able to enjoy living without such simple comforts as feather beds and kettles of hot water? In fear, too, whenever they had taken time to stop and think, of the savages. Yet they also had loved life. They had loved it the more, John would tell her, because it was fugitive; they had loved it for the sake of the surprise, the danger, the brittleness of the moment. Her husband, she knew, had felt this, though what he had said sounded so different. Life will yield up its hidden sweetness, she had heard him preach from the pulpit, only when it is being sacrificed to something more precious than life.

They had believed this in the old days. Time and again, they had risen from the ruins of happiness. Yet they had gone on; they had rebuilt the ruins; they had scattered life more abundantly over the ashes. There was a near neighbour of her grandfather who had held his cabin twice when others fled to the stockade. For the sake of his crop, he had held his ground. All within the space of ten years, he had seen two wives and two families of children scalped and killed by the savages. He himself had once been left to die, and a second time he had escaped from an Indian village and made his way home through the wilderness. For the rest of his life he had worn a handkerchief tied over his head, and one Sunday morning, while the congregation sang the Doxology, he had fallen down in a fit. In his later years he had married a third wife and had brought up a new family, after the manner of Job, to inherit the land. Though he had seen men burned at the stake, he had never lost his trust in Divine goodness.

And nearer still, there was her own grandmother, Martha Tod. She had liked the young chief too well, people had whispered. He was a noble figure; he had many virtues; she had wept when they came to redeem her. One story ran that her Indian husband had come to the settlement in search of her, and that her two brothers had killed him in the woods, from ambush, and

had hidden his body. This may have been true, and again it may
not have been. The age was a wild one. Many of the men who
had come to the wilderness to practise religion appeared to have
forgotten its true nature. Whatever happened, Martha Tod's
lips were sealed tight. Not one, not even her mother, had ever
won her confidence again, or heard her speak of her life with
the Shawnees. But as long as she lived, after her marriage to an
elder in the church, she had suffered from spells of listening, a
sort of wildness, which would steal upon her in the fall of the
year, especially in the blue haze of weather they called Indian
summer. Then she would leap up at the hoot of an owl or the
bark of a fox and disappear into the forest. When she returned
from these flights, her husband would notice a strange stillness
in her eyes, as if she were listening to silence. But gradually, as
her children grew up, ten of them in all, fine, sturdy, professing
Christians, her affliction became lighter. To the end of her days,
even after her reason had tottered, she could still card, spin,
weave, dye, or knit as well as the best of them. Grandmother
had heard that when she was dying her youth, with the old
listening look, had flashed back into her face, and she had tried
to turn toward the forest. But that was too much to credit. It
couldn't have happened. Not when her mind was addled, not
when she was well over a hundred. Grandmother remembered
her well, an old, old woman with a face like a skull, mumbling
over her pipe in the chimney corner.

Was it true, Grandmother wondered, looping the yarn round
the thought, was it true that wildness could be handed down in
the blood? Could Martha Tod's spells have skipped her own
children and broken out again in John's heresy? Yet Martha
Tod had been as innocent as a lamb. Never, even in captivity,
had she doubted that only through the blood of Christ could she
be redeemed.

Jerking up her head, which had nodded a moment, the old
woman glanced at her son on the other side of the lamp, and
thought in surprise, "But he has a fine face!" Whenever she
looked at him, no matter how many times in the day, she was

startled afresh, as if she had never seen him before. How could a man who denied the Virgin Birth wear a countenance that seemed, when he was plunged within, to be cut out of light? He had looked like that, she recalled with a pang, when he had stood his trial for heresy and schism (nothing, not even the loss of her husband and her seven children, had caused her such anguish); but in later years, since his hair had whitened (though he was only forty-four), the thinness and clearness of his features had become more striking. She had ascribed it all, his loss of zeal, his backsliding, the resignation from his church in Queenborough, the final trial before the Presbytery that deposed him—all these misfortunes she had ascribed to the influence of the British Museum, and to the sinister volumes (never would she have glanced into one of them) that he had bought at such sacrifices (he had gone without a greatcoat; he had even gone without food) when he was a student.

Mary Evelyn, too, had encouraged him when she should have admonished. A cruel doctrine, she had called predestination, and once, while the trial lasted, she had cried out that she believed anything John believed, that she would rather be damned with John than saved without him. Yet Grandmother had loved her better than she loved Meggie, who was one of the elect, assured of salvation. But Mary Evelyn had needed her more. She had made the heartbreaking appeal of the dying or the poverty-stricken. Though she was happy, her happiness, like her beauty, was too ardent to seem natural. And she had never had a family of her own. Her parents had died before she was old enough to remember them, and she had been left—an orphan, and what was far worse in the Tidewater, a poor orphan. The relatives who had brought her up had been elderly and unkind. It is true that she had been, for a few years, a belle and a beauty, but worldliness, as nobody knew better than Grandmother, was without staying power.

After Mary Evelyn's marriage to John her worldly friends had forsaken her. Then the last of her relatives had passed away, and she had turned to Grandmother, when her children died of diphtheria, as she might have turned to the Rock of Ages had her mind been less given to flightiness. A cross she had been, 'twas true, but a cross that pressed into the heart. If only her love for John had been a strength instead of a weakness. And worse than a weakness. In some obscure way, almost an infirmity of the flesh. For how could a man like John, with that queer absent-minded attitude of a thinker who is more dreamer than thinker, satisfy any woman?

His father had been different. Blessed with a robust constitution, he had loved, as he had lived, robustly. They had had perfect sympathy and great satisfaction in marriage. When Grandmother looked back on it now, it seemed to her that she had enjoyed everything, even childbirth. There had been pangs, of course (though never the long spasms of agony that had tortured Mary Evelyn's frail body), but the pains were so soon forgotten in the joy of bringing a child into the world. Could her children be born again, she would bear with gladness every pang, great or small, that she had suffered. But nothing could take her family away from her, not even death. They were still united, the dead and the living. And Mary Evelyn was one of them, as dear as her own. Yet she was wasting away. Year by year, she was wasting away under John's eyes, who had never so much as noticed the change in her. He thought her perfect, he said, when what she needed was plenty of milk and custards and delicate food. That was the worst of being poor, you couldn't give the right things in sickness.

But it was a mercy, with the mortgage falling due, that John had been able to pay the premium on his insurance. Small as it was, they had had a struggle to meet the payments and to find something they could turn into money. There were only a few silver spoons left, and these were so old and thin and brittle that they would break when you washed them. Three thousand dollars wouldn't go far nowadays. But if anything should happen to John, even that little might tide Mary Evelyn over the first year or so. Neither Mary Evelyn nor Meggie would let her speak of the insurance. For her part, she had a practical mind;

she had always looked ahead; she had never expected life to be easy. Not after John's trial, not after he had told the Presbytery he rejected the God of Abraham but accepted the God of Spinoza.

That was the beginning—or was it the end?—of his ruin. The most brilliant mind in the church, they had called him, and then he was ruined, he was finished, he was forgotten. For what place was there for eloquence outside the pulpit? What future was there in a Christian country for a man who had denied his Redeemer? In the eighties people were more strict than they were in this new century, which was already slipping from its foundations. A scholar outside the church then was as blind as a bat in the daylight. To be sure, he had tried his hand at other work, but that, too, had ended in failure. He could not push his own way; he could not even stand on his feet and sell drygoods. All he could do was to think, and nobody (here Grandmother picked up a dropped stitch) could earn a livelihood in America by thinking the wrong thoughts. Then, when they had come to their last crust (for a year there had not been a scrap of meat in the house except bacon for gravy), they had called in Doctor Updike to see Ada, who coughed as if she had croup, and he had stumbled, by chance or benign curiosity, into the bare storeroom. They had the doctor (a better friend never lived) to thank for the school in the parlour. At first the people in Ironside had protested, but at last they had remembered her; they had reminded themselves of all they owed to their Fincastle ministers, from John, the pioneer, down to Adam, her husband. A closed memory unfolded as a fan in her thoughts. She saw the pale red loop of the road round the manse on a spring morning, the narrow valley, deep as a river, and the Endless Mountains thronging under the April blue of the sky. More than fifty years ago, but it seemed only yesterday! From the changeless past and the slow accretion of time, the day and the scene emerged into the firelight . . . from the falling leaves . . . and the sifting dust . . . and the cobwebs . . . and the mildew. . . .

Suddenly, without warning, descended upon her a sleep that was not sleep as yet. Her eyes saw; her ears heard; and in her stiff fingers the needles did not slacken. But she was immersed in profound stillness; she rested upon an immovable rock. And about her she could feel the pulse of the manse beating with that secret life which was as near to her as the life in her womb. All the generations which had been a part, and yet not a part, of that secret life. The solid roof overhead, the solid floor underfoot, and the fears of the night without, the flames and the shadows of flames within, the murmurs that had no voices, the creepings that had no shape, were all mingled now. Weaving in and out of her body and soul, and knitting her into the past as she knitted life into stockings, moved the familiar rhythms and pauses—now—of the house; and moved as a casual wave, as barely a minute's ebbing and flow, in the timeless surge of predestination. . . .

"Grandmother's nodding. She's dropped off. She's beginning to snore," Ada whispered triumphantly. "Maybe—oh, maybe she will forget about prayers. Father"—she turned to pluck at his sleeve—"Father, doesn't God ever get tired of just listening?"

O MAN who has to provide for a family, John Fincastle thought, has a right to search after truth. Perhaps not anywhere in the world. Certainly not in America. But were the Renaissance and the nineteenth century in Europe the only ages when men believed that they could discover truth as they discovered a gold mine? When men believed that the search alone was worthy of sacrifice? Missionaries, Mary Evelyn declared, sacrificed their families all the time, but his mother insisted there was a difference when people were sacrificed to a truth that had been revealed.

Well, there might be. He didn't know. He couldn't pretend to care. That, he supposed, was what religious education had done for him—only his mother thought it was the British Museum. It had condemned him to poverty and isolation while it denied him the faith that makes poverty and isolation supportable. Not that he had been unhappy. Working over his book was sufficient happiness for one lifetime, if only he could have taken care of those who depended upon him.

Deep within his consciousness, so deep that the wish had never floated to the surface of thought, there was a buried regret for the solitary ways of the heart. In London, as a student, when he had lived in Bloomsbury on next to nothing, he had felt this freedom, he had been contented to drift. He was on fire then for knowledge. He had believed that, if only he knew enough, he might defend the doctrine of his church, he might even justify God. This, he saw now, bending over with his gaze on the fire, was the first mistake of his youth. Knowledge does not justify God. All the learning in the British Museum does not prove that man can apprehend God; it proves only that men

have invented gods. A multitude of gods, and all to be reconciled, one with another, before they could be vindicated. He
had turned then to translating Plotinus, and while he pondered
the *Enneads* he had been happy. Happy, yet a failure. For he
had been born with an otherworldliness of the mind. He had
never felt at peace except when he had strained toward something beyond life.

A year later, when he had returned from his studies abroad
(he had held a scholarship for six months in Germany; he had
spent two years in London), any place the church had to offer
would have been open to him. But he had wanted a charge
among the dispossessed of the earth; he had preferred the independence of spirit that comes from not owning things. His
world, he knew, was not, and could never become, the world
of facts; he was, and would always remain, out of touch with
what men call realities.

During a brief visit to Queenborough he had received a call
from the largest Presbyterian church in that city. There had
been no question in his mind of acceptance. Then the next day,
a day in June, while the letter was still unanswered ("Having
good hopes that your ministrations in the Gospel will be profit-
able . . ."), he had met Mary Evelyn; and in an instant, or so
it seemed to him, his past and future had been divided by the
clean thrust of a blade. Even now, after fourteen years, this was
a secret spot in his memory. Was it strength? Was it weakness?
Mary Evelyn had never suspected that the meeting with her had
swept away his vocation. Ada believed that he was the pastor of
his church in Queenborough when he had fallen in love with
her mother. But that first glimpse of Mary Evelyn had brought
ecstasy, and the touch of ecstasy had released the desire for a
home and children and close human ties. For a moment Mary
Evelyn returned to him. Not the woman who sat within reach
of his hand, frail and worn and used up by living, but a girl who
was tender and radiant, with eyes like smothered flames under
black lashes.

Well, he had loved her. No woman, only his seeking mind,

had ever divided them. He would have given all he was for her, but he could not give what he was not; he could not make himself over; he could not prevent that involuntary recoil now and then, as if his whole existence were overgrown and smothered by the natures of women. Even the wincing of his nerves while her voice ran on, strained, bright, monotonous, inexpressibly sweet, was beyond his control.

It was true that the external world and all the part of his life that people called "real life"—his affections, his daily activities, teaching the young, hoeing the garden, cutting logs, picking up sticks (he must remember to tell Ada that the poet Wordsworth picked up sticks for firewood)—all the outward aspects of living seemed to him fragmentary, unreal, and fugitive. He had not willed this; he had struggled against the sense of exile that divided him from the thought of his time, from his dearest, his nearest. Nevertheless, it was there. His inner life alone, the secret life of the soul, was vital and intimate and secure.

He could remember the year, the month, the day, the hour, the very minute even, when the outline of his system had come to him. In the church in Queenborough he had been a success; Mary Evelyn was happy and more beautiful than she had ever been; they had two little sons, the elder only three. For a few weeks he had come back to visit his mother, and he was planning to write his work on *God as Idea*, a history of religious thought through the ages. It was a morning in April. There was a changeable sky and new life on the earth. He had been reading philosophy (was it Schopenhauer? was it Spinoza?), and when he closed the book he had turned and looked over the valley to the companionable mountains. In the very act of turning in his chair he had seen that sudden light on reality, that reconciliation between the will and the intellect.

For years the idea had lain buried. Yet in those years all he was, and thought, and felt had gathered to the bare outline and clustered over it as barnacles cling to the sides of a sunken ship. But when he began the Introduction to his history, the idea came again to the surface and he found that it was not dead but alive.

In the end he had been driven into obscurity, into poverty, into the strange kind of happiness that comes to the martyr and the drunkard. Why? Why? Who could answer? He might have been false to himself, and who would have suffered? But he had craved truth (yet who knows what is truth?) as another man might crave a drink or a drug. Was this endless seeking an inheritance from the past? Was it a survival of the westward thrust of the pioneer?

He had a sudden vision of his grandmother, the one who had been Margaret Graham, with her young blue eyes and nimbus of snow-white hair. Even in her old age she had not lost a certain legendary glamour. Women were not supposed to be students in those days, yet he had never seen her kneading dough without an open book on the table beside her. With much difficulty, no doubt, she had gained a fair knowledge of history and languages. After her marriage she had still kept up her studies, and when her husband had died at the age of thirty-eight and left her with three sons, she had prepared them for college. They had made their mark, too, not one but had done honour to her and her training. How, he wondered, had she been able to overcome all those obstacles? Strong, of course, she had been in mind and body, but what he remembered most vividly was the impression she gave of invincible poise. He had heard his father say that she would have felt at home in any epoch, in any circle.

He had never forgotten, though he couldn't have been more than ten, that several of the elders in the church had surprised her one September morning before breakfast when she was walking barefooted in the wet grass on the lawn (somebody had told her that the Indians considered dew a cure for swollen feet), and she had received them without a word of excuse, and invited them, with her grand air, into the house. Yet she had cherished the queerest jumble of superstitions. Though she was scholarly for her sex, she was not above calling in old Aunt Jerusalem (Aunt Abigail's mother, and a step nearer the savage) when she wished a mole or a wart conjured away. Until they put her to bed for the last time, she had warded off rheumatism by carrying an Irish potato in her pocket. But these beliefs were more absurd nowadays than they had appeared in that credulous era. Would the time ever come when all superstitions, even those about God, would seem as ignorant as his grandmother's faith in an Irish potato?

The muscles in his leg twitched, and he glanced at Mary Evelyn, who smiled and said something in a whisper when she saw he was looking at her. His mother thought he had not noticed the change in Mary Evelyn, but she was mistaken. There were moments when he would have believed anything, acted any part, if only he could have saved her.

I've forgotten something," Mary Evelyn said under her breath, "but I can't think what it is." If she didn't remind herself Saturday night, she would be sure to neglect it on Monday. There was the rent in John's greatcoat; there was the turpentine liniment for Aunt Abigail; there was Ada's best dress to be washed and prettiest hair ribbon to be pressed for the festival— Oh, the new doll's dress! That was what she was trying to think of! Sunday always made a breach in her work; but perhaps she might steal into the closet when they came back from church and look for the pink gingham she had put away, though, to save her life, she couldn't remember where she had put it. It was dreadful the way she forgot things. Her memory was growing worse all the time. Her bringing up was to blame, said Mother Fincastle, who was upwards of seventy and never forgot anything. . . . If that mouse scratched under the wainscoting, she was sure she should scream, and then Mother Fincastle would make Meggie or John set a trap. She didn't mind stepping on spiders, but she couldn't bear to kill things that squeaked.

Flightiness was her infirmity, Mary Evelyn mused, folding her worn hands in her lap, and trying to restrain the impulse to jump up and sweep the hearth clear of the wood embers that had just broken and scattered. Little things filled her thoughts. They rattled about in her mind, like dried seeds in a pod. Important facts would slip away, but her whole inner world was cluttered up with the sweepings of yesterday—mere straws in the wind. It wasn't that she hadn't struggled to be sober and steady. Nobody knew how ashamed she felt just now when Mother Fincastle spoke reverently of her husband, John's father,

45

who had been dead thirteen years. Mary Evelyn had the sincerest respect for his memory. He was a man of God, an earnest Christian, a great preacher, a true father to the poor and the afflicted. All his life he had laboured in the field at Ironside, and he had built up his church here and founded the mission on Thunder Mountain. He was all this, Mary Evelyn knew. Yet, whenever she heard his name, the first thing she thought about him was that he chewed tobacco. His godliness ought to have obliterated that recollection. But her mind wouldn't record in the right way. No matter how long she lived she would remember that Father Fincastle chewed tobacco. And she would think, "How dreadful to be the wife of a man who chewed tobacco!"

It was like this, too, in the present. She was burdened by the litter of trifles. Her appetite was so fastidious that the sight of a bleeding rabbit or a mouse in a trap would take it away. Mother Fincastle said all that was mere silliness. She had the robust relish of the pioneer, and she couldn't understand how one could be sickened and made to turn away from food when one was hungry—or at least empty, for Mary Evelyn could never feel hungry for corn bread and bacon. Well, love was a great power when it could make everything else seem so trivial to her that she could wear rough clothes and eat coarse fare without a regret.

But there were other trials, too, so small that she was ashamed of them. Those black bristles in the mole in Mother Fincastle's eyebrow! For twelve years, ever since John had brought her to live in the manse, she had worried over those bristles. If only somebody would do something about them! Again and again, she had opened her mouth to speak of them and had shut it quickly, deterred by the austere dignity in the old woman's demeanour. It was safe, she knew, to venture just so far, but no farther, with Mother Fincastle, who commanded respect and disapproved of familiarities. Not even little Ada would have dared to speak or think of her as "Granny." Still, the bristles were preying on Mary Evelyn's mind, which had become, she felt, more and more flighty. It's such a trivial thing, she told herself now, but I shall never bring myself to the point of speaking about it. For Mother Fincastle had been more than a mother to her; she had been a fortress of strength.

The evening was very long. John was too tired to read. She had never seen him more exhausted by a day's trip. That mortgage was wearing him out. If only they had a little money. Not much, just enough to keep out of debt. When she thought of the power of money to ruin lives a dull resentment against life, against society, against religion, awoke in her heart. For there was no sorrow greater than living day and night, in sickness and in health, in the shadow of poverty, watching that shadow spread darker and deeper over everything that one loved. There was no sorrow greater, yet there was something, she told herself, greater than sorrow.

Turning her head on the back of the chair, she looked out into the night, where the shutter flapped at the side window and the wind had risen in gusts. Outside, in the troubled darkness, she heard the creaking of boughs, the rustle of dead leaves on the ground, the small tongues of wind lapping the walls under the ivy. Inside (she touched Horace with the tip of her shoe, for he had growled in his sleep) there was the glowing centre of life. She had much to be thankful for. Nobody was ill; nobody was hungry; nobody she loved was out in the cold. Aunt Abigail had a good fire, and Horace (she glanced down at his black-and-tan head) was warm on the hearth.

But I must keep Ada happy, she thought the next minute. I must keep her as happy as I have been. For it was true. Looked at from any angle, she had been happy. Life had been eager, piercing in flashes of ecstasy, tragic at times beyond belief, but never drab, never tedious; never, not even at its worst, when John was standing his trial, had it been ugly.

I T's blowing up colder, Meggie thought, as she picked up her hooked needle and returned to the counterpane she was crocheting. I'm glad John mended that leak in the roof. Half of her mind was still in the next room, where she had turned down her own and her mother's bed, started a fire to undress by, and hung two outing nightgowns and two red flannel wrappers on a small clothes-horse in front of the flames. The woodhouse had been well filled in the summer, and with the help of chips and sticks the back-logs ought to last until the winter was over. While John was away she had had the place tidied up and the paths swept with a brush broom by old Beadnell Geddy, who would work for a cast-off flannel shirt or a worn-out pair of shoes. She must remember to tell John, who would never notice the loss, that she had given the old man a pair of woollen stockings because he suffered from chilblains.

Though she had little patience with John's religious doubts (hadn't he gone out of his way to borrow trouble when he put unsound views into his book?) she could not deny that he was unselfish in little things and ready to help her with any work that she wanted done. And she could never forget (nobody who saw it could ever forget) the way he had nursed his wife when she had pneumonia six years ago. He had never left her bedside, even to change his clothes, until the crisis was over, and then he had fallen asleep from exhaustion with his hand on her pillow. Mother had covered him with a blanket and had left him there, with his knee on the floor, until he awoke.

While she watched him Meggie had felt her heart soften. She still loved him; he was her brother and a Fincastle, and she prided herself upon the strength of the family ties. But she could not forgive the headstrong will that had affronted his father's memory (who should know more of truth than their father, who had been a servant of God?) and broken his mother's heart. "Would you have him live a lie?" Mary Evelyn had asked passionately. But why should he set up his own belief for the truth? Who was John that he should know more of truth than his forefathers had known or the Bible had revealed to them?

Bending over the counterpane, she reached down into the big splint basket near the hearth and tossed a knot of resinous pine on the fire. She loved to watch the coloured flames shoot up quickly, branch out from the stalk, and unfold into flowers. Another pale spider (how she hated spiders!) was lowering itself on a cobweb from the top log on the woodpile. That was the pile they kept there in case of a snowstorm. She must make Uncle Beadnell move the logs on Monday and look for the spiders. A mouse, too, had been worrying Mother in the night, and she must remember before she went to bed to bait a trap with middling rind in case Ada had eaten the last crumbs of cheese.

Mary Evelyn was as thin as a rail. Her face was all eyes, and in spite of her high colour, the skin looked waxen. She was not strong like the Fincastles. When that pain in her back stabbed suddenly, her hand would fly to her heart, and a look of terror would flash into her eyes. Yet she would work on until it killed her. Nothing could stop her. Energy had fastened upon her like a disease. John ought to speak to Dr. Updike about her. Perhaps he would suggest a tonic of bitters or some cod-liver oil. Mr. Greenlee, the apothecary, would always let them have medicine and pay for it when they were able.

Years ago when Meggie was a young girl (she was only thirty-three now, but she felt older), Dr. Updike had treated her for spring fever. His figure was less burly then and there were no pouches under his eyes. He couldn't be over forty now, but he had travelled the roads at all hours in all seasons, and he looked elderly for his years. Whenever she thought of him, though it was so long ago, a pale flush seemed to spread more within than without. Not that she had had any sentiment (for her life was too full of useful activities and her heart was too full of her family), but for a little while she had wondered if —well, if he had cared more than he showed on the surface. She had never forgotten the time he kept his hand on the inside curve of her arm (she was noted for her pretty arms), stroking it softly while he sat by her bed and asked questions about her health. That was all. Yet she had felt startled and shy, with this pale glow breaking out in her mind. It was queer she should remember that after all these years, after he had married Hannah Kelso and had a family of children.

For herself, she had never thought of love-making or marriage. It wasn't that she had been plain or unattractive. She was better-looking than most, especially when she had been plump and fresh, with a neat figure. But she couldn't run after men the way some girls did even in Ironsides. In the old days there had not been women enough to go round, and all had been sought after. There were belles among simple people like themselves, as well as in the more distinguished circles of the upper Valley. Mother said it had been different ever since the war, with most of the young men going away to make a livelihood and marrying in strange places. Well, she hadn't worried about that. If the Lord had appointed her to marriage, He would have arranged it all in His own good time. As it was, she had put her hope in little things, and she had been happy. She was the only member of the family who was never low-spirited, not even in the long winters, when sometimes they were snowed in for a week.

T H E taste of sugar is like pinks, Ada thought. It's like verbena and sweet alyssum. If only a taste wouldn't melt and fade as soon as it had gone down! And when you hadn't had sweetness for a long time (Father had waited because he could get coffee and sugar cheaper from a wholesale house over in Doncaster) it tasted different and sharper. She wished pleasant things lasted longer, and other things, like evening prayers when you were sleepy, wouldn't drag on for ever. Father wasn't going to read to-night. She wanted dreadfully to hear what happened next in *Old Mortality*, but Mother had whispered in the kitchen that she mustn't ask him to read. If she couldn't listen to that, she wished they would let her shut her eyes tight till morning.

Mother had promised to get up early on Monday (Sunday always came when you'd rather it wouldn't) and cut out the dress and bonnet for the new doll before breakfast. Nellie had never had a pink dress. She had never even had a sunbonnet. Maybe, after a long time, she might get used to Flora and begin to love her.

Nights were always short, except Christmas Eve, which was longer than anything. She hoped it would be snowy this Christmas. Aunt Meggie said it was blowing up cold. If there was a deep snow, Ralph McBride was going to make a big snow man, the biggest they had ever had, in their yard. But if there wasn't any snow, he had promised to take her for a climb to the top of Lost Turkey Hill. She had never been more than halfway up when she was picking huckleberries, but this time they would start early, with some bread and meat in their pockets, and climb

to the very top. Then they could look down into the gap between Thunder Mountain and Old Man Mountain.

Oh, she wished Christmas would hurry up! Mrs. Tiller, who
kept a cake and candy store down in the village, had sent Grandmother some raisins and currants and citron for a fruit cake.
Aunt Meggie was trying to save enough sugar and butter, pinch
by pinch. Nobody was going to have any sugar until Christmas,
except Ada, because Mother said children couldn't be expected
to do without sweets. Children and old people, she had said,
handing the sugar bowl to Grandmother. But Grandmother had
replied that she wasn't old enough yet to be childish. "Wait
until I'm a hundred, my dear. Don't hurry me into my dotage."

Last Christmas (it seemed miles away!) had been splendid.
Ralph had given her the doll's bedstead, and she had had a good
package of fire-crackers for him. They had gone out together,
and he had set off the fire-crackers, only not all at a time. He
had shown her how to light one and let it go off a little and then
stamp it out, so it would last longer. She had another package
for him this year. His mother had to give him only useful presents, like shirts and stockings, and things to keep him warm
when he hadn't a greatcoat. Grandmother had knitted a thick
jersey for him, like the one she gave Father. He wore it over a
flannel shirt, under his thin coat, and he said the cold never
really got to him.

Ralph was the brightest boy in school, though Grandmother
insisted he was too headstrong. Already he was saving money
to go to college, and he worked part of the day in Mr. Rowan's
machine shop. In summer he and his mother lived on the vegetables they raised in their back yard. Ralph was a fine gardener,
too, but no matter how hard he worked he could never put by
enough, Father said, to take him to college. A gifted boy,
though, might find some other way, and Father was teaching
him everything that he could. Ralph was going to be a lawyer
when he grew up. Though he was only twelve, he knew already
what he wanted to be, and he read everything he could find
about law and lawyers. He would make up all kinds of games

with a trial in them, and a judge and a jury. Ada would be the prisoner on trial for her life. She didn't know why, but that was the part she could act best. Janet would want to be the judge, but he wouldn't let her. He didn't like Janet. She fibbed, he said, and was a telltale. Blue eyes and yellow curls didn't make her any better to play with. She trotted after them wherever they went, and she was always begging him to make her a doll's bedstead.

There was that white spider again. Did spiders have ghosts? Did they have skeletons? Did they have hearts? She must remember to ask Father when he woke up. But Ralph might know better than Father about things like spiders. There was a mouse, too, that crept out when it thought they were all asleep. She wondered if Aunt Meggie had caught it in her trap. Mother hated to hear them squeak when they were caught. But Grandmother didn't mind any more than Aunt Meggie. She said the Lord had made mice to be caught in traps. "Why?" Ada had asked, but nobody had answered. Only when she had asked a second time, Mother had replied sharply, "Your father must tell you." Then she had asked over again, "Why, Father?" and he had answered slowly, "God alone knows why, my child." Father and Mother worried over such questions. Why God does this? Why God does that? What is the reason for everything? But Grandmother and Aunt Meggie knew straight off, without any thinking. Grandmother said she answered questions "out of conviction."

The wind was blowing loud and rough. She could hear it crashing through the trees, as if it were bringing snow. Lots of sticks would be shaken down. They would have to lie there till Monday, because nobody ever did any work, except cooking and making fires, on Sunday. Picking up sticks didn't look like work, but even if 'twas only useful play, that also was profaning the Sabbath. Wind made Mother feel jumpy, she said, and she didn't like the tap-tap-tapping of the ivy on the windowpane. "I hope Aunt Abigail has plenty of cover," she would say. Or, "Have the sheep sense enough to go into that shelter?" Or,

"Are you sure none of the chickens were shut out, Meggie?" It did seem dreadful that their sheep had so little sense. They were old sheep, and Job, the pet ram, was almost as rheumatic as Grandmother. When Ada was little they had had more. One of the first things she could remember was going into the kitchen one morning in the midst of a spring blizzard and seeing a new lamb, wrapped in Grandmother's red flannel underbody, lying on an old feather bed in front of the stove, while Aunt Meggie fed it from a rag dipped in a mixture of milk and water and a little sugar. That was the sort of recollection, she felt, that stayed with you till you grew up.

She was glad she didn't have to live out in winter, like a bird or a sheep or a wild animal. She wondered if the small furry creatures in the woods could snuggle down under the dead leaves at night and keep the cold wind from nipping them. The wind was the worst. It sounded then as if it had blown off a bough. She hoped the wind would spare their oldest oak, "the pioneer," even if it damaged the younger trees. So many bird and squirrel families would be made homeless if the storm stripped the pioneer. When you looked up in the branches you could see nests sprinkled like houses in a village, and in spring and summer the tree hummed all the time, Mother said, as if 'twere a harp in a breeze. Last year, when Aunt Meggie raised three turkeys (though one of them was mistaken for a wild turkey and shot by a hunter, who took it away with him) they would never roost anywhere but on that low-hanging bough near the gate. . . . Toby Waters must be frightened, out by Murderer's Grave. You'd think the hovel and pigsty would be swept down into the gully, with all the pigs squealing. Grandmother said the church helped Mrs. Waters because, though she was a bad woman, Toby was not to blame for being an idiot.

Well, she was glad, too, that she wasn't an idiot. But why did God make idiots? It seemed worse than making mice to be caught in traps. When she had tried to find an answer to that, Grandmother had replied tartly, "If you ask any more foolish questions, Ada, I shall be tempted to box your ears." And Father had said over again, "God alone knows why, my child." But, whatever God's reason might be, it was a mercy that they lived almost in the village and not, like the Waterses, in a pigsty on the rim of a gully. They couldn't be too thankful, Mother kept saying, though she must know that she had said it before, for a warm room and a good fire and plenty to eat. The words had a singing sound that Ada enjoyed, and they reminded her that the taste of sweetness was still somewhere far down inside her. 'Twas nice, too, to feel Horace's head, as soft as velvet, resting on her foot and keeping it cozy. If the evening didn't stop soon, she was going to slip down on the rug and let Horace be her pillow and sink away, away, while the flames crooned and the kettle sang and the shadows danced and the spider swung to and fro on his cobweb.

Suddenly Father was saying, "It's almost time for bed. Shall I read a page, Ada?"

"Oh, if you would, Father!" She raised her head from the softness of Horace and sprang to her feet. "I want dreadfully to know if they caught Morton."

The leaves fluttered as John Fincastle opened the book. Well, every day had an end. He glanced at his mother's face, furrowed into an expression of grim goodness, at Meggie's cheerful features, which were still comely, at the drooping head of his wife, transfigured by the firelight into its old loveliness. A sigh passed his lips, but his voice when he began reading was strong and thrilling.

" '*Hist,*' *he said, 'I hear a distant noise.*'

'*It is the rushing of the brook over pebbles,*' *said one.*

'*It is the sough of the wind among the bracken,*' *said another.*

'*It is the galloping of horse,*' *said Morton to himself, his sense of hearing rendered acute by the dreadful situation in which he stood. 'God grant they may come as my deliverers!*' "

The pages rustled as they turned, and the book was closed. "He's safe, my dear, until Monday. I'll let Horace out for a minute, and then we'll lock up and have prayers." Every night

Horace ran as far as the gate before he went to sleep in the front hall on the sofa with the sagging bottom. The chamber door was left open, and sometimes Ada would be awakened by the nose of the hound on her cheek. "He's had a bad dream," she would think. "I reckon dogs have bad dreams just like other people."

To-night, after she had said her prayers and slipped into her trundle-bed and drawn the blanket up to her chin, she dropped to sleep saying, "It is the sough of the wind among the bracken." Those were glorious words to have in your head; they seemed to go round by themselves. At midnight, when she awoke suddenly, they were still turning. Outside, the wind was blowing harder than ever. Could the last leaves hold on until morning? Underneath the crashing and the whistling she could hear the murmur of the dying flames in the fireplace, and then the sudden squeak of the mouse in Aunt Meggie's trap. She hoped Aunt Abigail knew when she said mice didn't mind being caught. Perhaps her Indian blood made her wise in such matters. Well, anyway, Flora wouldn't have heard about that. Rising slowly, she picked up the new doll from beside Nellie, who was used to sleeping alone, and brought it to bed with her. Grandmother thought it was only silliness to pretend that things like trees and dolls had real feelings. But they may have, she thought; you never can tell.

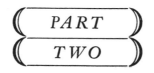

PART
TWO

THE SINGLE HEART

YES, it was true, Ada thought, she couldn't remember the time when they had not cared for each other. Ralph had always been there, no matter how far back she went, with his bright auburn head, his gay nut-brown eyes, his sudden smile that had a power over her heart. There was an Irish strain in his blood. Mother said this gave him his charm and his amused, friendly manner.

Midway between the garden and the front porch, she stopped in the June sunshine and looked toward the rocky road, which plunged down from the manse to the church and then swerved abruptly, as if it shied away from the houses. While she stood there she felt that the little girl of ten years before was pausing close beside her in the tall bright grass. She thought of this other Ada, who had never grown up, not as herself, but as a shadowy companion. She would be happy now, even though she was invisible, because the girl of twenty, who was herself and yet not herself, would be married to Ralph as soon as he had finished his law course. One year at college had used up whatever he had been able to put by, and even then he had worked as a clerk in a hotel at night and had sent home every penny he made to provide for his mother. After that, he had thought he would be obliged to give up the study of law and accept a position Mr. Rowan had offered him in his machine shop. But Father, who could do everything except earn a living, had made the way easy. Dr. Ogilvy, one of the professors at Washington and Lee University, had engaged Ralph as his secretary for several hours every afternoon; and Father had arranged with the Dean of the Faculty that all the classes of the law course might be taken in one year. "With Ralph's wide reading and fine memory, he will be able to do the work," Father had said. "The boy has a brilliant mind, he has a natural bent for the law, and he has read and remembered now more than most lawyers ever know and forget. It is not often," he had concluded, "that life is so straight and so simple as this."

In front of her swallows circled over the steep roof from which shingles were peeling. When she moved nearer the porch, she could see the outline of Mother's head at the window, while a shadow darted as swiftly as a grey wing into her mind. All the past year Mother had suffered from an obscure malady, an injury to the spine, Dr. Updike suspected, though he wasn't sure. Every day she sat from morning till night in a wheel-chair sent to her by one of Grandmother's friends in the Ladies' Aid Society. The strangest part to Ada was that she still wore her cheerful look and talked breathlessly, without stopping or waiting for a reply. She looked as pale now as a wax flower under the greenish light cast by the ivy, with her lovely head, which was still brown and glossy, turning as quickly as a bird's when anyone came into the room. Presently the bulk of Grandmother's figure moved toward the window. The girl could see her massive features, carved into granite fortitude, bending down over Mother. At eighty, Grandmother was still the strongest member of the family, except for her rheumatism. And the happiest, too, until Ralph came home from his year at college, and surprised that shy, startled ecstasy in Ada's face when she looked at him.

"Love, love, love," she said over to herself, as if she were trying a strange word on her lips. Sudden stillness dropped into her mind, and through this stillness there floated presently the absurd recollection of the doll with china hair Father had brought her from Doncaster. Why should she think of that now? Some minds are no better than ragbags, Grandmother had remarked disapprovingly. But there was Flora beside Nellie in the bedstead Ralph had carved, just as she had them tucked away in that old tin trunk in the attic. For she had never had the doll with real hair, and Flora still wore, even in bed, her pink sunbonnet. Aunt Meggie had promised her a doll. Then something had happened. She couldn't think what it was. Had the hens refused to lay? Had they needed the money for medicine? Well, it did not matter now. It seemed silly that she should ever have wanted a doll so much. Grandmother thought it was because she was jealous of Janet. But it wasn't. No, she had never been jealous of Janet, not even when Janet tried to make Ralph fall in love with her.

Was that because she felt safe? Was it because she knew that Janet had always wanted Ralph, but Ralph in his heart had always disliked Janet? The other boys in Ironside admired her. It may have been because Ralph had never liked her that she ran after him. For it was no secret; everybody but her parents had talked of her ways with men. "That was the trouble of a village," Father had said. "All likes and dislikes are inbred until they become like the half-wit families over in Panther's Gap." Grandmother had added severely, "Too much tittle-tattle, that is the worst of it." Then Mother had asked, "But what can you do? If you're different, you have to be sacrificed, just as they used to sacrifice living things on an altar. Heaven knows you were sacrificed, John."

Father had looked at her with his vague but hopeful smile. "Don't make a martyr of me, my dear. You might tempt me to make one of myself. And a self-made martyr is a poor thing."

"I can never understand," Grandmother had insisted, "what has got into the young folks nowadays. It looks to me as if they were clean daft, every one of them. Well, well, I reckon I've outlived my time. Things were not like this when I was young."

"Nor when I was young, and that wasn't so long ago," Aunt Meggie had agreed. "If you'd told us in the eighties that boys and girls would be so wild in 1911, we'd have laughed in your face. Mrs. Tiller was saying yesterday that some of the boys, sons of decent parents, too, think it manly to go up to Lightning Ridge to buy moonshine. Mrs. Melrose had to break up her daughter's birthday party, she said, because several boys were unsteady on their feet. She thinks 'tis all this round dancing that has ruined their morals."

"But the waltz is the only dance worth dancing," Mother had laughed. "I adore it still, and I was so sorry for John when I found he had never learned even to heel and toe in his childhood."

"Mark my words," Grandmother had retorted, "when customs like that come in, moral responsibility is the first thing to go. I may not live to see it, but remember what I have said when you are compelled to live in a world that has lost the sense of responsibility. I doubt if you'll find it any more to your taste than the one you were brought up in."

"There's a point in your argument, Mother," Father had replied, after a pause. "I am inclined to believe that a man may be free to do anything he pleases if only he will accept responsibility for whatever he does."

Grandmother and Ada had exchanged a mystified look. It wasn't always easy to decide how strong or weak was the tincture of irony in Father's remarks.

"I don't know what you mean, John," the old woman had rejoined tartly, "but I know very well what your grandfather meant when he used to say, 'If you flosh the water, you will have scum without fish.' "

No, she wasn't jealous of Janet—well, not what you would call really jealous. But there had been a queer twisting pain far down beneath a tight lid in her heart when Ralph had seemed to like Janet for a few weeks last summer. Janet might have all the pretty clothes she wanted, even pink nightgowns, which Grandmother and Aunt Meggie agreed were unrefined, and silk stockings for the day as well as the evening. She might even have a dogcart with red wheels and a high-stepping bay. All these things did not matter. But when it came to Ralph, Ada knew that she wouldn't give up without a struggle, that she would fight for her own. That was what Grandmother meant by the flaw in the single heart, she supposed. The single heart holds on to its own. "I won't let her have him," she had resolved, "no matter what happens." Then Janet and Ralph had stopped speaking to each other after a quarrel (they were always fussing about trifles), and immediately Janet appeared to become infatuated with Hunt Patton, the son of a well-to-do farmer in the Shenandoah Valley. All winter they had been together from morning till midnight. But early in March, Hunt gave up his work in Judge Melrose's office and returned to the farm. When he went away so hurriedly everybody was astonished that nothing was said of Janet's engagement, that the very next week she should begin flirting with Charlie Draper. In April, Ralph went into Mr. Rowan's big store and machine shop, which dealt in everything you could need on a farm, from a garden rake to a reaping machine or one of the new automobiles, and after that Janet was obliged to be friendly with him, on the surface at least. Fortunately, Ralph wouldn't be there long, only until he went to Washington and Lee in the autumn.

She had been looking toward the house, and when she turned her head she saw that Ralph had entered the gate and was coming across the lawn, where the sheepmint in the grass gave out an aromatic scent when it was crushed. Whenever he came back, after even a brief absence, a sensation of freshness and surprise rushed over her, as if she had never seen him before—as if she had never seen anyone else. He was tall and thin and strong; he was warm and sunburned and eager.

"You're early," she said, smiling. When she was happy words seemed to stop coming.

"I'm on my way to work. I had to see you a minute."

They had turned away under the oaks, and she was in his arms while the whole June landscape and the unearthly blue of the mountains spun round them.

"I simply had to see you," he repeated.

"I know." She loved the leanness and hardness of his body, as if his warm young flesh had turned to bone and muscle. Suddenly, she felt that she wanted to stoop and kiss the dark freckles and the reddish down on the back of his hand. But all she could bring herself to say was, "I know. But you mustn't be late."

He laughed. "Do you want me to go?"

She shook her head while a quivering sweetness ran over her.

"I know you don't," he said presently. "I can tell by your eyes even when you don't speak. They are dark grey in the shade, but in the sunshine they are exactly the colour of huckleberries. That's why I like you in that blue dress."

Her glance dropped quickly. It wasn't that she was shy, she told herself, only she couldn't let him break down some deep reserve he had struggled against ever since he had known she loved him. "It's worn out," she said, stroking his hand. "I have two blue cotton dresses, but both are worn out. I wish," she added, "I had something better than my pink gingham to wear to the dance on Wednesday."

"You'll look all right. You'll look right in anything."

"Janet has a white organdie. Her mother ordered it from a catalogue."

"It doesn't matter. You'll look better than Janet."

"But Janet's lovely. She has real blue eyes." Why had she said that? Was it to hurt herself? Was it to make him praise her?

"I don't care about Janet's eyes, I like yours better." Taking her face in his hands, which were eager and strong, he began kissing it very slowly all over, from the backward wave of dark hair to the full white throat. "There's something about you. I don't know what it is, and I don't care. It's different, that's all. It's you, and if you've got faults, then I like faults. I like a blunt nose better than a sharp one. I like a large mouth better than a small one. I like sunburn better than a peach-bloom skin. Sometimes I think I fell in love with you because of those silly freckles on the top of your nose." His arm slipped to her bosom, crushing her to him. "Well, I ought to go. I'll come as early as I can to-night."

He took a step away and turned back to kiss her again. "It won't be much more than a year," he said. "I'll be through by next summer, and then I'll go into somebody's office, perhaps down in Queenborough. Would you like to live in Queenborough?"

Her eyes dwelt on him. "Anywhere with you. I don't care, except for Mother, and of course Father."

"Well, a year isn't long."

She loved the husky quiver that ruffled his voice.

"No, a year isn't long."

"But it's hell waiting."

She laughed tenderly. "If Grandmother heard that, she wouldn't want me to marry you. She thinks all the young people to-day are headed to ruin." Then she caught his arm. "Did you ask Judge Melrose to lend us his buggy for the dance? How are we going out to the Padgetts'?"

"I forgot to tell you, Janet wants us to go with her in her father's spring-wagon."

"I thought we were going alone."

"I wish we were, but I didn't see how I could refuse. While I'm working for Mr. Rowan I have to be nice to Janet. Do you know, he is going to buy an automobile," he added in an interested tone.

"Is he?" she answered indifferently. "I'd like to see Janet in the sort of motor veils and goggles they put in the papers. Who else is going with us to the dance?"

"Charlie Draper. And she has asked Willie Andrews to take a girl who is spending the night with her."

"That's Bessie McMurtry."

"It's all right, isn't it? But why do you always get miffed when I mention Janet? The only quarrels we've ever had were about her."

"I don't." Her face felt scorched—but it was true, though she denied it. Once she had left him at a picnic for a whole afternoon because Janet had dared him to take a drink of moonshine whiskey with Willie Andrews and he hadn't had the courage to refuse. No man, he had said to her then, would "refuse to take a dare from a girl."

"You don't?" he laughed teasingly. "Well, you don't, darling. It's all right, isn't it?"

He had started away, and when he looked round, she saw the shadow of the leaves flickering over his eyes, which changed from nut-brown to yellow as the sun touched them. Then, while she hesitated, the sudden smile broke on his lips, and she felt that her heart was a wheel turning.

"Oh, yes, it's all right," she answered in a voice that vibrated with tenderness. At the house she saw him stop for a minute to speak to Horace, who awoke from a nap on the sunken mill-stone at the foot of the steps and greeted him with the air of an elder statesman.

I ought to go in, she told herself, but they would see that I am all in a flutter. There was plenty of work to do helping Aunt Abigail. Or, perhaps, Grandmother would be waiting on the kitchen porch beside the big splint basket. Grandmother liked to lean on the garden fence, or walk along the paths, if the dew was not on the weeds, and watch her gather the early vegetables, while they talked of the way the corn and tomatoes and black-eyed peas were ripening.

In the effort to steady her mind she walked over to the sagging gate which failed even to keep out the hens. Inside the broken palings, once straight and white, Aunt Meggie's sunflowers were shooting up in tall rows which would bloom in July and August. Beyond Aunt Abigail Geddy's cabin the narrow hayfield ran on until it sank and was lost in the stony hill, where three sheep and two lambs were nibbling the high weeds. Job was gone, but a sprightly young ram had inherited his place. From where she stood she could barely distinguish the huddled grey stones from the browsing sheep.

Though they had had the little flock only three seasons, the wool had come in well for Grandmother's knitting and to make warm, light interlinings for several of the old quilts. Grandmother and Aunt Abigail Geddy were still as good as ever at washing wool, carding, and spinning. Aunt Abigail and Marcellus sheared the sheep, but Grandmother always watched because she said she couldn't trust either African or Indian blood not to enjoy nipping. Grandmother looked after everything, and Father said she could feed a whole family on what Aunt Abigail threw away. When she was a child they never saw a store, she would say proudly. Their coffee was made of sweet potatoes, just as in wartime, and once or twice her father had been obliged to write his sermons in pokeberry juice. Yet she had been as happy as she was after she learned to crave real coffee.

I hope she has taught me how to live, Ada mused, as if she were smoothing out some tumult within, some exultation and overflow of the heart. I hope she has taught me how to make the right kind of wife. There was no fear of poverty in her mind. She was prepared to meet the future on its own terms, and to take what it gave. If only she had Ralph, she could find happiness, and no one could be easier to make happy than Ralph.

Grandmother called urgently, and Ada turned away from the garden. Over the springhouse at the bottom of the yard she could see the nearer valley laced with the crystal blue of streams, and beyond the valley the throbbing azure light on the mountains. God's Mountain ranged far and free toward the west, beyond the heavenly twins, as Father called Rain and Cloud Mountains. But directly in front of her the dark brow of Thunder Mountain frowned through its summer foliage, with the coloured hills flowing away from it fold on fold.

I never knew before that happiness hurt, she thought. Happiness like this hurts.

Suddenly, from an old lilac tree by the side of the house, a bird's song sprinkled the air with joy. It was a catbird. The pair (was it the same pair?) came back every spring.

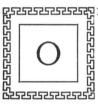N THE porch her grandmother was waiting. "You must run down to the store, Ada, for a box of mustard. 'Twas all used up last night."

"Is Mother worse?"

"That stitch in her back is troubling her again. She's had mighty little sleep for the last two nights."

"I'll go straight down. It won't take me any time." At the sound of her voice Horace peered inquiringly from the side of the house, shook himself twice, and ambled after her when she hurried through the gate into the road.

As she went on, picking her way among stones, Thunder Mountain seemed to push back the brushy hills and move nearer. She had seen the mountain in all aspects and in all seasons, dark-browed, frowning, remote, or ringed with flame while terrified deer and the humble furred and feathered creatures of the forest fled, with the eagles, the buzzards, and the hawks, from the furnace that had once sheltered them. But today she felt only the June softness of the fields, sown with small powdery daisies which looked as if they had been plucked from the stem and strewn over the long grass. Wild lupine was still running in a bluish fire down by Smiling Creek, and clusters of chicory had just flowered along the roadside. All this light and softness and colour streamed within and became a part of her mood. But Mother was in pain. Resolutely, prompted by some inherited instinct, she accepted the fact of pain as the deeper reality.

When she reached the church she threw a glance over the field to the hovel and the evil-smelling pigsty, where Mrs. Waters and Toby scratched the hard soil on the edge of the ravine. She had never spoken to Mrs. Waters, and she tried not to look at her if they met in the road. Though she pitied the old woman (it seemed so hopeless to be old and bad together), she was embarrassed when they passed each other, as if a bodily disfigurement had been thrust under her eyes. Years ago, she had wondered how Mrs. Waters, who was then robust and not ugly, with plump legs in tight black stockings that bulged over her shoes, was able to live and even gain flesh on a pigsty alone. That earlier banishment, for Mrs. Waters had been expelled from church in her youth, differed in some curious particular from the present self-inflicted retreat. In the past she had at least kept her curves in those places where curves were desirable, and she had never failed in summer to flaunt a few gaudy blossoms, usually prince's-feather or cockscomb, before the door of her hovel. One spring, it is true, she had come down with pneumonia at planting-time. Then the church had paid Uncle Beadnell Geddy to hoe her garden and to look after the hogs which Toby would neglect whenever he was given an opportunity.

For a week or more the woman had lingered near death. It was only natural, Ada realized now, that Ironside should have been divided between relief over the removal of sin and reluctance to accept the burden of Toby, who would remain an idiot boy if he lived to be eighty. Doctor Updike had attended Mrs. Waters as faithfully as if she were one of the redeemed; Grandmother had made mustard plasters and sage tea, and had carried a soft pillow and a wool-lined quilt to the cabin; the Ladies' Aid Society had taken up a collection and had engaged Uncle Beadnell's wife, Aunt Pomona, to sit up at night. But the minister and the elders, supported by the entire congregation, including Grandmother and Doctor Updike, had decided that she could not be buried among professing Christians in the churchyard, but must sleep beside the hanged, and no doubt damned, sinner in Murderers' Grave. Even Mother had thought that the decision was "merely human," and Father had remarked, "If they turned her out of the church, it is scarcely logical to expect them to welcome her in the churchyard. Dead Presbyterians are still Presbyterians, only more so."

"Why is it, Father," little Ada had asked, after pondering the fact, "that Mrs. Waters never has any visitors in the daytime? Willie Andrews says she sees company late at night after her lamp is turned down. They are tall dark people, and Willie is sure they're witches. Are there any men witches, Father?"

"There are no witches, my child. Perhaps they are charitable persons who come to bring her food or swill for her hogs. Let us hope," he had concluded, "that Mrs. Waters may live long enough to make peace with God and the congregation."

He had had his wish fulfilled, though only in part. If Mrs. Waters had made peace, it was with God alone, and there was a flaw, or so it appeared, in that tardy reconciliation. After her illness she had fallen into a decline; her bouncing curves had flattened out; the dark company had ceased its nocturnal visits. Presently she had begun to beg for broken bread or hogwash at the back doors of the village. There had been talk of putting her in the almshouse. But the county almshouse was too proud to receive women of a certain character, and at last the village fathers had banished her, on a bare pittance, to her hovel out in the fields. Stringy, bedraggled, raddled with the paint of pokeberry juice, and smelling of moonshine whiskey, she haunted the alleys or poked in the dump heaps between sunset and dusk.

Like the shadow of a crow, the image of Mrs. Waters flapped over Ada's mind and was gone. Only a mild wonder remained. Was religion like that? How could she tell? How could anyone tell? she asked herself, looking at Horace (Mother said dogs were dumb poets), who raised his nose from the cow manure in the road and gazed up at her.

She passed the church and the churchyard. Light shadows were playing over the tombstones. Birds were singing high up in the trees. Uncle Beadnell was trimming the grass on the graves with a sickle. Close by the church, they were painting the shutters and small square porch of the parsonage. Mrs. Black's hollyhocks were gay and bright, and the climbing red rose on the porch was in full bloom. They had it tied back while old Mr. Potter and his son were painting the posts. Mrs. Black, who was watching them, nodded to Ada and asked after her mother. She was a small, active, managing woman, so thin that people said you could see every bone in her body, with a shiny look that ran over one like a swarm of ants when she was excited. But her heart was too big for her, Grandmother insisted; she would go out of her way to do a kindness to anybody.

"She's not so well to-day," Ada answered. "I'm going for mustard."

She passed the doctor's house, and saw him coming out in an alpaca coat with a crape band on the sleeve. He was in mourning for Mrs. Updike, who had died in the winter. But his stout figure and ruddy face, with the beaming smile that warmed the hearts of his patients, appeared as sanguine as ever. Though he had never complained of his marriage, Ada had heard that his wife had been a trial to the flesh, and that in her last years she had formed the habit of drink—or it may have been drugs.

"I'm going to drop in to see your mother on my rounds," he said. "Tell your grandmother to keep mustard plasters on her back until I come."

She passed the big white frame house of the Rowans and saw Janet in a dress of green linen watching her from an upper window. She passed Mrs. McBride's small cottage, lost in rows of potatoes, tomatoes, beets, and turnip-tops that were running to yellow. She passed the post office, where several horses were tethered to the hitching-bar in the street. At the end of the square, which was bordered by wire-grass and dandelions, she went into the general store, and waited for Mr. Robinson to finish wrapping up a parcel before he gave her the box of mustard.

"Hope nobody is sick up at your place," Mr. Robinson said. "Is your mother feeling bad again?"

"She has that pain in her back. It comes and goes all the time."

"I'm sorry to hear that. I'd hoped the fine weather would cure her."

Taking the box of mustard, she went out into the street and stopped to draw breath. I didn't know how fast I was walking, she thought. Missing Horace, she looked about her and found him lying in the speckled shade of a young locust tree. The tree was in blossom, and she paused a moment to breathe in the fragrance. Ironside, so bleak and hostile in winter, was charming in summer, with its leafy shade trees and the hollyhocks and roses in the front gardens.

"I know you're feeling the heat, Horace," she said, "but we must start back right away."

As she reached the Rowans' house, Janet came running down the walk to the gate.

"Oh, Ada, come in and see my new dress. I've just unpacked it, and it's too lovely for words."

"I can't, Janet, not now. Grandmother is waiting for this mustard."

"It wouldn't take you a minute. I've laid it out on the bed."

On the other side of the gate Janet's flaxen head nodded above the sheath of pale-green linen; her pleading face, as vacant as an empty eggshell, was faintly pink and transparent; her eyes of periwinkle blue were round, soft, and innocent of expression. The only flaws in her loveliness were two front teeth that projected from her short upper lip and a dimpled chin that receded abruptly. Yet even these faults had worked, oddly enough, Ada thought, to her advantage. "She's the living image of Queen Victoria as a girl," Mrs. Rowan declared. "That engraving in our parlour of Princess Victoria in a tall comb, picking up a rose from a table, might have been taken from Janet."

"Oh, do come in," Janet begged.

"No, I can't stop now." Ada walked on, and Janet opened the gate and fell into step at her side.

"What are you going to wear to the dance, Ada? Amy Padgett says their new barn is like a ballroom. It's just finished, and they are going to put up Chinese lanterns and chairs and tables around the walls."

Ada sighed. "I haven't anything to wear but my pink gingham." Ralph had said she would look prettier than Janet in all her finery. Still, she wished she had something better. The recollection of the pink gingham pinned on the clothesline at home floated into her thoughts, swayed upward in the breeze, was puffed out in rosy billows, and covered, in a single immense wave, the whole field of vision. It didn't seem fair, she reflected, being human, that Janet, who was so lovely, should have finer clothes than any other girl in the village. No, it wasn't fair. Yet Janet might think it wasn't fair that Ada had Ralph, whom Janet wanted more than she had ever wanted white organdie. But, even then, Ralph wasn't the only man Janet wanted and had run after. Mrs. Tiller believed she had cared most for Hunt Patton, who went away so suddenly—too suddenly, the malicious old woman had whispered, for Janet's good. Only women, Ada had noticed, were severe with Janet.

"I can't come any farther," Janet said when they had passed the churchyard, "but I want you to see my dress. This is Monday. There isn't much time."

"I'll come to-morrow if Mother isn't worse. I'll run down in the morning."

"You're going with us, aren't you? Ralph said you would."

"He told me you'd asked us to go in the spring-wagon."

"I thought we could all crowd in. When did Ralph ask you?"

"Days ago. I can't remember when."

"He would have taken me," Janet said, with abrupt vehemence, "only we'd had a falling-out."

Looking at her in surprise, Ada remembered the Sunday morning when Janet had had her tongue brushed with quinine because she told fibs. She was older now, and the fibs had matured into lies.

"I don't believe he ever thought of asking you," Ada retorted, while her face, flushed already from the sun, burned to a flame.

"Oh, he would have, only we had a falling-out," Janet repeated. "He felt dreadfully when I told him this morning that I was going with Charlie Draper." She bit her lip and her voice trembled with irritation. "Oh, I wish I could go away! I'm so tired of Ironside. Do you ever feel that you want to go away and never come back?"

"I'm going away next year. Ralph and I are going to be married as soon as he has settled in Queenborough." Her tone was defiant, as if she were flinging back Janet's falsehood. Yet she had not meant to tell anyone, not even the minister, until next autumn. It was unwise, she knew, but that twisting pain (was it anger? was it jealousy?) had been more than she could bear. The instant after she had betrayed her secret she began to regret it. "I ought to have known better," she thought in self-reproach, "but I suppose I'll never know better than to let Janet hurt me. Even when I know she is lying, she still hurts me. Well, no matter. . . . If only she will leave us alone."

For a minute Janet's breath came and went with a rustling sound, as if something alive in her bosom struggled to break out.

"Even when we were children I was the only girl Ralph would play with," Ada added. "You and he always quarrelled."

Janet laughed, without effort apparently. "Well, you're welcome to him," she said. "I hope you'll be happy. Yes, it's true we were always falling out. He was never, even when we were children, my sort." Dismissing the subject, she asked lightly, "You will come to see my new dress, won't you?"

"Yes, I'll come. I'll come in the morning." Ada's anger had faded, though she still blamed herself for betraying her secret. "You won't repeat what I've told you?" she asked.

"Oh, no, I shan't repeat it. After all, you're my best friend, aren't you? It was natural that you should tell me first."

That was a nice way to take it. Janet had her pleasant side when she wasn't crossed, and it seemed that Ada's confidence had not ruffled her temper. She did look rather like Princess Victoria in the old engraving, with her small stubborn mouth, red as a cardinal flower, above her childish receding chin.

"I'll keep the dress in the spare room for you to see," she added sweetly. "Be sure to come early."

HEN she passed from the sunshine into the cool greenish light of the hall, Ada felt she had entered an invisible network of affection and security and that something more which is the essence of fortitude. The pine planks of the floor splintered under her feet; the plaster was sifting in a yellow dust from a crack in the ceiling; the walls were streaked and splotched under the peeling paint—but the unity of the house, the way of life, had survived the processes of destruction.

Father ought to mend things, she thought, even if he has so little time between the garden and his book. But I suppose it would take every minute he has to keep the place from falling to pieces.

Horace stopped to drink from the earthenware bowl in one corner, and, after quenching his thirst, looked up at her with moist velvety eyes and his attractive dog's smile. His black-and-tan head was domed like a philosopher's, though he still kept a puppy's heart beneath his shining black coat. When she did not go upstairs to her room under the dormered roof, he followed her, with a wagging tail, into her mother's chamber.

Grandmother was standing in the middle of the floor, erect from the waist up, but bent slightly in her rheumatic hip. She stood much of the time, because her joints were more painful after she rested, and she believed that it was a mistake to give in to infirmities.

"Sit with your mother while I make the plasters," she said. "She hasn't touched a morsel to-day, and she's trying to sip a glass of milk."

"It's delicious milk," Mary Evelyn said in her excited voice from the wheel-chair. Ever since her illness began Dr. Updike had sent her a pitcher of milk from his Jersey cows every day, and she insisted that it had kept her alive. She sipped very slowly, holding up the glass first in one wasted hand and then in the other, and raising her head as a bird does when it drinks. "Yes, the pain is better. It comes and goes," she answered. "Did you see anyone in the village?"

"Nobody but Janet. Oh, Mother, I told Janet! I didn't mean to, but she made me angry, and I told her."

"Did you, dear? Well, I suppose it won't make any difference." In her wrapper of lavender lawn, with a faded purple shawl over her shoulders, Mary Evelyn looked as transparent as a shadow against the greenish light at the window. Only her voice was strong, animated, and intensely alive. "Your grandmother doesn't like Janet, but I doubt whether there's any harm in her."

"She promised me she wouldn't tell anyone."

"Even if she does, it won't matter. Everyone knows that you and Ralph were made for each other. It makes me happy when I think of it, just as if I were living my own youth over again."

"All the same I wish I'd kept my secret. . . . You've forgotten to sip your milk."

"Yes, I know." Mary Evelyn raised the glass to her lips. "You and Ralph have known each other so long and you are so much alike that you ought to understand without having to explain. It's a pity you are both quick-tempered. But you will have to be patient. Women always have to be patient."

"His mother isn't. Does it matter very much that I can't make myself like his mother? She made Ralph unhappy when he was little. He used to say that he felt closer to you than he did to her."

"She's a good woman according to her lights, but your father says"—Mary Evelyn laughed at the recollection—"that her religion has curdled. Calvinism does curdle in some natures. I know how angry I used to feel when she kept Ralph in all Saturday evening because he hadn't had time to learn his answers in the Catechism."

"Well, there's one thing certain," Ada said. "If I ever have children, I shan't make them learn the Catechism. And it isn't only about that. I believe Mrs. McBride enjoys making Ralph miserable. He hasn't told her about us because he knows she will be sure to say the wrong thing. Do you think I shall have to call her 'Mother McBride'? Nothing will ever make me call anyone but you Mother."

"I'm afraid she'll expect it, darling. But that isn't really important. You mustn't say she likes to make Ralph unhappy. You mustn't even let yourself think it."

"It's true. And Ralph doesn't really love her. You can't make yourself love people."

"But he's working to make money for her. He told me he would give her every penny he made in Mr. Rowan's store. It ought to take care of her while he is at Washington and Lee."

"That's because of the obligation. He wants to give her what she thinks she deserves for being his mother. But it isn't because he loves her. You can do a great deal for a person without love. She tried to stand in his way even about the law. There's some bent in her, he says, that makes her recoil to the contrary whenever he wants to do a thing. It isn't exactly spite, but it works the same way."

Grandmother Fincastle brought the plasters and applied them to Mary Evelyn's back under the lawn wrapper and the muslin chemise. "Let them burn well," she said.

"Do you want me for anything, Grandmother?" Ada asked.

"Not just yet. Stay with your mother until the plasters burn too hot. Meggie will give you the peas to shell while you're waiting. Does that feel right, Mary Evelyn?"

"Perfectly right," Mary Evelyn answered sweetly, though she shifted the plasters as soon as her mother-in-law had taken the empty glass and gone back to the kitchen.

In a few minutes Meggie came in with the peas in a yellow bowl. "Would you like me to iron your pink gingham, Ada?"

"Oh, Aunt Meggie, if you have time! You iron so beautifully." As her aunt turned away, she said a little wistfully, "You never wore gingham to a party when you were a girl, Mother."

"No, dear, we wore a great deal of mousseline-de-soie. That was all the fashion when I was a girl. But your pink gingham looks very well on you."

"Aunt Meggie says you were perfectly beautiful when you were young."

"That was long ago."

"Father thinks you haven't changed."

Mary Evelyn smiled. "He sees me as I used to be. He never really looks at the outside of anything. But he has to give his whole mind to his book. That is his life's work. Each volume has taken many years, and he has still two more to write."

"I wish people would read them, Mother. Three years ago, when his third volume came out, nobody, at least nobody in America, seemed to take any notice."

"More than you think noticed it, Ada. There were letters, you remember, from philosophers in Europe."

"They are so far away they don't sound as if they were real. Is the plaster too strong?"

"No, it's my skin. Everything hurts it."

"Your nerves are like that too. It must have been hard on you when you first came to live at Ironside."

"I had to learn. Everyone has to learn. Then I'd just lost your two little brothers. It didn't matter whether I had things or went without."

"Aunt Meggie says you were always in high spirits."

"I had to choose between high spirits and low spirits, and I chose what I thought would be easier on others. Those first years were a trial, but gradually things seemed to get better. Or, perhaps, I got used to their being bad. You were only a baby, and you can't remember the time when there wasn't enough to eat in the house. It was then I fell into the habit of laughing too much. A light spirit, Aunt Abigail called me." Her mouth twitched convulsively, while Ada stopped shelling the peas and bent over her.

"Is the pain worse, Mother?"

"No, it isn't the pain. I was thinking." She made a sudden gesture as if she were brushing away a recollection. Then animation quivered through her nerves in a spasm, and she sprang upright in her chair. "You could never guess," she said in a changed voice, "what was the hardest thing to get used to. After the death of my babies, the hardest thing was having to do without running water in the house. Even going hungry was less of a trial. There were times when I'd have given years of my life to hear the sound of hot water running into a bathtub. Your grandmother and Meggie have the kind of skin that nothing irritates. They could wash with homemade soap in cold water (though your grandmother was fond of her warm bath), but I used to chap and have chilblains that first winter. Your grandmother bound up my heels in mutton tallow, and when she couldn't get Castile soap for me, she tried her hand at boiling down the tallow and scenting it with rose-leaves. Aunt Abigail began then bringing in the big tub every morning to fill with pails of warm water. After they saw how I suffered, they never forgot to keep my kettle steaming on the trivet in winter and the stove in summer."

"I like to splash in cold water. It's the first thing I do when I get out of bed."

"You have the Fincastle skin. It's a blessing because it makes life so much simpler, like the Fincastle constitution. That gives you your fine colour."

"I'd rather be like you, Mother."

"You wouldn't say that, darling, if you knew everything. Many and many a time I've been no better than a thorn in the flesh. Nothing is more trying than nerves to people who have none."

"They love you."

"That has helped. Love has been stronger than religion. But they would smile if they knew how much of my courage depends on little things. These little things mean more than themselves. They mean an attitude of soul, a ceremony of living. Your grandmother could never understand that my blue bowl has helped me more than morning prayers. For me, bare Presbyterian doctrine was not enough. I needed a ritual. That is why I have never, not even when we were poorest, let myself think poor. That is why I have never failed to put the crocheted mats on the table, and the candlesticks, with or without candles, and the flowers or berries in the blue bowl."

"I hope I'm like you, Mother. Oh, I hope I'm like you."

"Well, I've been happy, dear. In spite of everything, I've been happy. But it was a hard struggle at times. I like to look ahead for you and think that your life will be easier."

T H E Rowans' hall was fragrant with the smell of hot gingerbread when Mrs. Rowan, wearing an apron over her fresh print dress, met Ada at the door and told her to run upstairs. She was a stout, unshapely woman, with flaxen hair just going grey, smooth pink cheeks, and eyes like periwinkles that had been rained on. Janet was her only child, and since she should never have been without a baby at her rich bosom, she had spent an immoderate maternal sentiment upon a single daughter. Like all the wives of the upper Valley, she was a conscientious housekeeper; her drip coffee and salt-rising bread and her "light hand" for sponge cake were celebrated even in that region of plain thinking and good living.

"Go straight up to Janet's room," she said as cheerfully as if she had not spoiled her husband's digestion and her daughter's disposition. "I'll bring you a glass of lemonade and a piece of gingerbread as soon as it's done. Janet hasn't been herself for the last day or two. She won't touch a morsel at the table, so I'm trying to make her take a bite between meals. I can't imagine why in the world she should be in the sulks now, and her father and I are driven almost out of our wits trying to think of something that will please her. I've just been up to see about her. Running up and down stairs at my age," she added, pushing her hair back with her wrist, "is no joke."

"She asked me to come and see her dress," Ada answered, while her gaze wandered over the spotless hall and staircase and through the open door of the parlour, where the dim light rippled on the engraving of Princess Victoria picking up a rose from a table.

"Yes, I've laid it out on Janet's bed. She was wild with pleasure when it first came, but she's so moody that nothing ever pleases her for very long."

"She has asked us to go to the dance with her."

"I know. She was going to take a party in the spring-wagon. But this morning she said she wasn't sure she wanted to go. I shouldn't worry about that, though. She always goes contrary at the last minute."

"I know she'll be the prettiest girl there," Ada said, because she knew nothing else would cheer poor Mrs. Rowan so much. "But Aunt Meggie says you were prettier than Janet when you were young."

To her astonishment, Mrs. Rowan appeared vaguely offended. "Oh, no, I couldn't touch Janet," she rejoined stiffly. "There's never been a girl in Ironside who could hold a candle to her. That's why I wouldn't call her 'Jeanie' after me even when she was little. It seemed too common a name for her. It's a pity she wouldn't study; but you can't have everything. After our sending her away to boarding-school for two years, she doesn't seem to know as much as you learned at home."

Ada frowned. "Father taught me."

"Yes, I know. I'm not denying that your father is a scholar. Mr. Rowan says you can know a great deal without being sound in doctrine. Everybody thinks he's done as well as a college by Ralph McBride. That's a fine boy," she continued. "Judge Melrose would have taken him into his office this summer, but Ralph's mother insisted on his working for Mr. Rowan because the salary is higher. There's Janet calling now. Yes, honey, I'm sending her right up. It's a blessing the child hasn't inherited my prattling tongue."

Yes, Janet had never prattled, Ada agreed, as she ascended the stairs. There was no denying, however, that the silence of her pouting red lips could be eloquent.

"Oh, it's you!" she exclaimed as Ada entered, looking round from the window, where she was drying her hair in the sunshine. "Wait a minute, I'll show you my dress as soon as my hair stops dripping."

"What a pity you have to put it up."

"I'm going to let one large curl hang on my shoulder. That fashion has come in again."

"Well, it's nice for girls who have curls like yours." Ada turned to the organdie flounces on the bed and took up the blue and pink ribbons. "Oh, how lovely!" she exclaimed.

Janet laughed with pleasure while she tossed back her hair (it was like a spray of silver gilt, Ada thought) over the checked apron she had slipped round her shoulders. "There are roses at the waist, and I'm going to wear a rose, an artificial one, in my hair. Mother wants me to wear a natural rose as she used to do. She has a perfect half-blown bud she's saving on her rose-bush. But nobody wears natural flowers any longer." Her sullen mood had vanished; she was fresh and animated for the moment at least. "It's a pity you haven't anything but that every-day dress. If you were smaller, I might lend you something of mine."

"Oh, I couldn't." Ada flushed and shook her head. "My pink gingham is good enough. I can't help it if it is an everyday dress."

An everyday dress and an everyday figure, she thought, glancing into the handsome mirror over the dressing-table. Above Janet's face, like a young moon in an empty sky, Ada's own features spun suddenly into vision. A perfectly good face, she said to herself, with a laugh, but more pleasant than pretty when you compared it with Janet's, and almost too vigorous in contour, like the picture of a head on the prow of a ship.

"There's Mother," Janet said in an angry whisper. "I wanted to talk to you alone, but she never leaves me a minute in peace. This morning she tried to make me swallow sulphur and molasses."

Panting from her exertion, Mrs. Rowan pushed open the door with her foot, and brought in the lemonade and ginger-bread on a painted tray. "I stopped to rinse out your best stockings," she said, as she put the tray on the table where Janet could reach it. "Alberta's hands are so rough, I was afraid she might tear them."

Silk stockings too! Ada thought, with a stab of envy. How lovely it must be to wear silk stockings to a dance! Her own best pair (a gift from Aunt Meggie at Christmas) was woven of a fine mixture of lisle thread and cotton. "I wonder how it feels to wear silk stockings," she sighed, and continued happily, with her mind on the future, "Some day I shall know."

Mrs. Rowan was pouring lemonade into tall amber glasses. "Well, I've never had any myself. We were too poor when I grew up to bother about what kind of stockings we wore as long as we weren't barefooted. But Janet has so many she won't even take the trouble to darn them."

"She'll have to marry a rich man," Ada said, thinking of Ralph, who was so poor that he had his shoes half-soled until they were dropping to pieces.

"Oh, Father will take care of that," Janet retorted.

The doting bliss in her mother's look faded to anxiety. "He will as long as he is able, honey," she replied. "But your father isn't so well off as he once was. I know he worries to think what would become of you, with your expensive tastes, if anything should happen to him."

"But what could possibly happen to him?" Janet inquired. "He's as strong as an ox. No, I don't want any gingerbread. Just give me a sip of lemonade."

Mrs. Rowan seemed disappointed. "I made it the way you like it, Janet, with plenty of butter."

"Well, I don't want it now," the girl returned, so pettishly that Ada could see she was longing to be rid of her mother's attentions. "I wish you wouldn't keep poking things at me."

"I declare, I don't know what is the matter with her," Mrs. Rowan remarked helplessly. "She isn't often like this. You'll take a piece, won't you, Ada?" she asked almost timidly.

"Of course I will. But I'd rather take it home with me. Grandmother has such a sweet tooth."

"No, you eat this now with your lemonade. I'll wrap up some in a napkin for your grandmother and put it on the hall table." Her tone was sprightly again. "Well, I'd better be going down if there isn't anything I can do. Poor Alberta is crying with toothache, but I can't persuade her to have her tooth pulled. If you want anything before dinner, just call me."

As soon as she had left the room and her heavy tread was heard descending the stairs, Janet flew to the door and turned the key in the lock. "I thought she'd never go," she breathed impatiently. "I never can talk before Mother."

"She's so devoted to you, Janet. It makes me feel sorry for her."

"I know. I love her, too, but she fusses over me until I feel as if I should scream."

"What is it you have to tell me?"

"Nothing much. Only some of the boys went up to Lightning Ridge yesterday, after they stopped work, to buy moonshine. They're going to hide it in the loft to-morrow night. Of course, it's just for fun. They don't mean anything but a joke. Willie Andrews started it, and you know how he is."

"But they oughtn't to. Nobody has anything but lemonade at a barn dance. The Padgetts wouldn't like it."

"Tommy Padgett is one of them. He is going to fix a table up in the loft because his mother won't let him put anything in the punch."

"How do you always hear things?"

"Oh, the boys tell me. They know I won't give them away. You mustn't say a word about it, you know."

"Who are the others?"

"Charlie Draper wouldn't go. But there was Fred Robinson, and there was Ralph McBride."

Ada started and put down the glass of lemonade she was holding. "What made Ralph go?" she asked. "He can't touch that whiskey without its going straight to his head. Charlie Draper can't either. That's why they don't drink anything."

Janet laughed. "Oh, the boys were teasing Ralph. You know Ralph can't bear to be teased. I suppose Willie Andrews dared him to go. But he's all right to-day. I saw him when I went to speak to Father in the office."

"Well, it may be just fun. I don't know. But why didn't you stop them? That moonshine is too strong."

Janet shook her head. "I'd rather be anything than a killjoy."

That was meant for her, Ada told herself, with a flash of anger. Janet thought she was a killjoy. Well, no matter . . . Beyond the window a cloud of bees had settled on a blossoming locust tree, and she thought, I never saw bees so golden.

"Wouldn't you like to have some pink roses to-morrow?" Janet asked sweetly. "Mother will give you as many as you want. They will match your dress."

"If I can come for them, but there's so much to do at home. Mother has been sick, and neither Grandmother nor Aunt Abigail can stoop to pick up things."

"I should think you'd need a more active servant."

"Aunt Abigail stays for her cabin and meals. She doesn't do much, and we have to bring in all the wood. But it's a help having her in the kitchen. Anyway, she's like one of the family. She'll never leave us as long as she lives."

"That's the trouble," Janet remarked, "with family servants. They always hang on after they've ceased to be useful. I'm glad we haven't any old ones left. Then, if I don't see you before to-morrow evening, Mother will send the wagon at half-past eight."

There wasn't any reason in the world, Ada thought, descending the stairs, why the visit to Janet should have dampened her spirits. Of course, it was foolish of those boys to go up to Lightning Ridge, but then, weren't young people, especially boys, always doing things that appeared foolish? Ralph was only twenty-two. His mother had been too strict with him as a child. When he became a man, Father said, he would feel less need to assert his personality. And, strangely enough, this headstrong will was one of the qualities in Ralph that moved her most deeply. There was something childlike and helpless in his defiance. She felt the wish to protect him in the very moment when she surrendered. Well, she wouldn't change him if she could. She loved him for what he was.

On the hall table she saw the neatly folded red-and-white napkin, and as she picked it up Mrs. Rowan came out of the dining-room.

"I put in some sponge cake for your mother. It isn't so rich as gingerbread, and I hoped she might fancy it."

"I know she will. Yours is always as light as a feather."

"How did you leave Janet? She hasn't been a bit like herself. You'd never believe that she has one of the sweetest dispositions."

"Anybody would be cheerful with that lovely dress. I never saw anything so perfect as the sash with those artificial flowers."

"You'd think she'd be pleased, but she takes everything for granted."

"That's because she doesn't know what it is to do without."

Mrs. Rowan sighed so heavily that her stiff apron rustled. "I hope she never will. Only sometimes"—her voice quavered—"I wonder if doing things for people is the best way to make them happy."

From the front porch Ada looked back with a kind of stern sympathy. Though she felt sorry for Mrs. Rowan, who tried so hard to please, she distrusted the unbridled mother-love that had spoiled Janet. "Oh, she'll be all right," she said. "When she looks in the glass she'll forget she didn't know what she wanted."

STOPPING where the path twisted away from the churchyard, Ada unfolded the napkin and broke off an end of the gingerbread.

I'll give it to Toby, she thought. Grandmother would like him to have it.

Across the field, she saw Mrs. Waters squatting between the rows of her cabbages. Toby was not in sight, but Ada called to him on the chance that he might be inside the hovel or carrying slops to the hogs. Little pigs were his only companions, and he seemed to grow fond of them.

"Toby!" she cried, and over again as shrilly as she could pitch her voice, "Toby, here's cake for you!"

But the call drifted away on the air, and a sentinel crow, posted over a cornfield on the other side of the road, flapped his wings in suspicion. Caw! Caw! floated after her cry like a derisive echo. Well, there wasn't anything she could do, she told herself, as she wrapped up the gingerbread. It was a pity, because the taste of sweet was heavenly bliss to the idiot.

Grandmother was on the front porch, shading her eyes from the strong sunlight with a palm-leaf fan bound in a rim of black cambric. She had put on a freshly starched calico, and the ribbons on her cap were still warm from the iron.

"Were you looking for me, Grandmother?" Ada asked as she ran up the steps.

The old woman shook her head. "I thought I heard something going by in the road. My right ear has got so bad that every sound seems to come from the left side."

"I wish you could see Janet's dress. It has a pink and blue sash with artificial flowers."

"I reckon your pink gingham is more suitable than organdie in a barn."

"Janet says the Padgetts' new barn is as fine as a ballroom."

Grandmother sniffed. "Who on earth would want a barn like a ballroom? Did you bring anything your mother might fancy?"

"Mrs. Rowan sent you some gingerbread. The sponge cake is for Mother."

"Well, I hope it will put a taste in her mouth. I'm at my wit's end trying to find something she is able to eat."

"The doctor didn't think she was worse yesterday, did he?" Ada's voice sank to a whisper, and she glanced from the porch to the window under the ivy; but her tone was so low that the words were lost on Grandmother's bad ear. "She looks much better this morning," the girl said more distinctly. "What will she have for dinner?"

"A cup of tea, she says, and a soft-boiled egg. I tried to make some tapioca, but the milk curdled in the pan. Dr. Updike sent it early, and it was sweet when your mother had her glass at eleven o'clock. But it must have turned in the spring-house. That worried me." She let her palm-leaf fan fall to her side. "I'm always put out when I can't make something to tempt your mother."

For an instant Ada stared in perplexity. "Effectually called," she thought, repeating the words she had heard on Grandmother's lips, "justified, adopted, sanctified, and saved," was it still possible for one to be upset because a pan of milk curdled? "I wish we could have ice for her," she said. "It must be a comfort to have ice every day."

"On the hottest days I try to get somebody to leave it. But we can't afford to have it left regularly, and usually the spring-house keeps the milk and butter all right. It must have stood too long this morning before Meggie went down with it. I can't recollect that such a thing ever happened when I could get about on my feet." She broke off and cupped her ear in her hand. "I reckon that must be your father."

"Yes, he's calling me. I'll come to help you as soon as I see what he wants."

Ada went into the hall, threw her hat on the sofa beside Horace, and opened the door of the library.

"Do you want me, Father?"

He looked up with his expectant air which seemed to come from something he saw far away. "Yes, I've had a letter from Dr. Ogilvy. He would like Ralph to come to the university before the middle of September. I suppose he can arrange it?"

"Oh, yes. He will be only too glad to go. It is the opportunity of a lifetime."

"Ogilvy seems interested. He may do a great deal for him. Ralph won't be the first promising lawyer he has started on a career."

He was seated at his desk, with the manuscript of his fourth volume spread out before him, while the sunshine from the window illumined his features and left his still figure in shadow. The serenity in his face bore that inner warmth which proceeds less from a state of mind than from a climate of soul. One was always sure, Ada thought, watching him while he pushed the papers aside, of a meaning, a purpose, in whatever he said or did. He had not acquired fortitude, she felt, he was fortitude.

"Oh, Father, it's wonderful. I am so happy."

"Then I am happy, my child, and so is your mother. We ask nothing better of life."

Turning his head toward the window, he appeared to withdraw into the morning brightness beyond. He was silent for so long that she wondered whether he had forgotten her. Persons and objects, even the nearest, had a way of slipping out of his vision. Moving noiselessly to the door, she went out and shut it behind her. Poor Father, she thought, as she crossed the hall to her mother's room, he has had a hard life. If I had had a life like his, I'd ask a better reward than just being able to bear it.

Yes, it was true, John Fincastle reflected, his life would be justified in her happiness. Even his work, which had meant much to him and nothing to the world, would be repaid. There were hours even now, before daybreak or at the close of dusk, when a chill, soundless and swift as the flight of time, brushed his mood, and he paused to ask himself whether this book he was writing had not cost him too dear.

Removing his spectacles, he rubbed his hand slowly over his eyes. As he pressed his tired eyeballs, a light flashed in sparks, and a half-forgotten recollection started out of the dimness. An autumn afternoon in Bloomsbury, and the scent of falling leaves in Bedford Square—or was it in Russell Square? Not that it mattered. What he had treasured across the years was not a scene but a sense, barely more than a distillation of joy. He had been making notes for his book, and his mind was at rest. But while he walked under the yellowed leaves, so pale beside the brilliant colouring of Shut-in Valley, he had determined to spend his life among the poor and the miserable, not as a bringer of good tidings, but as one of themselves with a message of brotherhood. Was this the cause of that strange joy, which had never returned, which he had never forgotten? Other joys more intense he had felt, but not that one again. Never in its own likeness, its own essence. For the life he had lived and the life he had planned had been as far apart as the poles.

Among the poor he might have been useful, but whatever he had to give was not needed, was not even acknowledged, by his well-to-do and self-satisfied congregation. Within, he had been attacked from the first by a sense of futility, and this deepening sense had come at last to signify failure without. Then it was that he had retreated into himself, into solitude, and because his intellect demanded an escape, he had plunged back again, with renewed vigour, into his book. What he had not considered was the simple fact of falling in love. But it was love, he perceived, that had altered everything, great or small, in his life, that had seemed to change the very beat of his heart. Instead of a single self, he had become a double self, and then, with each child that was born to him, he was divided into other and separate selves of his being.

Not until five years after his marriage had he found a publisher who was willing to risk money on a work of philosophy that owed nothing to the dynamo. That the money would be lost was an accepted conclusion. Yet ten years later the same publisher, a Hebrew mystic, had issued the second volume, and three years ago the third volume had appeared. So far as John Fincastle was aware, his book had reached only six readers—an English metaphysical poet, a Scottish philosopher at the University of Edinburgh, a student of Neoplatonism in Alexandria, a French scholar at Lyons, and two obscure German professors. This group of readers, diverse but faithful, had compensated for neglect in his immediate place and time.

Of what was he thinking, he now asked himself, before he had heard Ada's voice on the porch? With his eyes on the level crest of God's Mountain, he groped in bewilderment. Then, suddenly, he remembered. Had pure philosophy, he was speculating, ever advanced beyond the Three Hypostases of Plotinus? Was there a swifter approach to Deity (granting an approachable Deity) than the flight of the alone to the Alone? Perhaps not. Perhaps in some distant future man might turn away, disillusioned, from the inventive mind, and human consciousness might stumble back again along the forgotten paths of blessedness and mystic vision.

Clouds had gathered farther away, and a watery violet light, as fresh as rain, streamed over the summit of the mountain. Blessedness is there, he mused, not only in beauty; it is in the little things also. . . . Though his inner world was builded of thought, not of emotion, he had found contentment in many minor activities. The part of life he had called fragmentary and unfinished had woven the peace that is more lasting than happiness. As for his deeper consciousness, the crystal globe holding the light within the light, this had been always remote and inviolable. Nothing had broken through. Not joy, not pain, not love, not passion, not sorrow, not loss, not life at its sharpest edge, had been able to break or bend this still pointed flame that burned upward.

F LIFE were always like this, John Fincastle thought, while he watched the lovers meet in the hall, there would be no need of religion, there would be no need of philosophy. Ada was looking her best, he observed, though he seldom noticed a change in her appearance. Not so beautiful as her mother had been at her age (no woman could ever again compare with Mary Evelyn), but the girl's face was coloured like ripe fruit and eloquent with emotion. Her eyes, though less striking than her mother's, were large and deep, with something of the same dusky radiance. The bloom of love is over her, he said to himself, and sighed without knowing why. Was it because of remembrance, of some stir that was scarcely more than a breath from the past? Or was it from the old Scottish superstition that life will bear watching whenever it appears simple and well-disposed?

For Ralph, he reflected, he had a different, and perhaps a more understanding, devotion. Like a son, like one of his own lost sons, the boy had grown to be in the past few years. His very faults were the faults that endeared. The stubborn willfulness, the periods of introspection and irresolution, which came and went without evident cause, the recklessness for the sake of recklessness, the disbelief for the sake of disbelieving—all these were flaws of character, but not barriers to affection and sympathy. Born six months after his father's death, and brought up by a mother who had become a religious fanatic, what else, John Fincastle demanded of the invisible Powers, was one to expect? Even to meet Mrs. McBride in the road was like facing the grim doctrine of predestination. A strange marriage that had been, though most marriages appear strange to spectators.

Hearing Ralph's eager voice, John Fincastle was reminded of Barney McBride, whose mother, Molly O'Boyle (people in Ironside still remembered her), had come from Ireland when she was a child. Barney's hair had been redder than Ralph's, and his yellow-hazel eyes had held that same gleam of amusement. His marriage to Rebecca Muirhead, of a dour Scottish family, had been a surprise to John Fincastle's womenfolk, though he himself had never given it so much as a thought. Yet Mary Evelyn, who had an ardent interest in all marriages, had told him that Mrs. McBride had passionately loved her husband. Only in widowhood had she grown rigid with piety. Well, it was easier to pity her than it was to forgive her for ruining her son's childhood and destroying his faith in himself. If any woman could save him from his upbringing and his mother's influence, it would be Ada. Yet there were moments when John Fincastle felt that they were too much alike, Ralph and Ada, for a union of even average success. Joy, perhaps, they might find, but not peace, for joy is a restless thing. After all, Ralph might be saved by work in the end. Never in the young had John Fincastle found such power of concentration, provided the subject absorbed him, or such completenes of assimilation. This much, at least, he owed, not to his father's charm, but to the stern integrity of the Muirheads.

Glowing with delight, the lovers went into Mary Evelyn's chamber, and it seemed to John Fincastle, as well as to Aunt Abigail, who had brought a cluster of moss-rosebuds from the bush by her cabin, that the radiance of youth surrounded them and moved with them.

"Good night, Mother, I hope you will be asleep before we come in."

"Good night, dear. You couldn't look any lovelier. Could she, Ralph?"

"She couldn't," Ralph answered, eager and confident. "Nobody could look any better."

The yellow wagon, harnessed to Mr. Rowan's two stout

greys, had lolled over the grass and sheepmint and was waiting beside the old millstone in front of the house.

"Good night!"

"Good night!"

Voices rang out gaily as Ralph and Ada ran down the steps and sprang into the wagon. Then the wheels turned from the square of light into the darkness beyond, and the glimmer of the kerosene lamp in front of the vehicle flitted through the gate and over the wheel ruts and the broken stones in the road. Standing on the porch, with the scent of crushed sheepmint around him, John Fincastle heard the happy laughter, which floated back, rippled into silence, and began again farther away, like dance music that is played in the memory. Yes, if only life, if only what men call civilization, were not hostile to youth and to joy! Suddenly, a thought surged up out of the past, on that distant laughter, now rising, now falling—I, too, have known ecstasy! For an instant he hesitated, then, turning back into the house, he crossed the hall and entered the chamber.

The lamp was lowered, and the familiar shapes in the room had shifted and altered. At the windows a faint breeze was stirring among the tendrils of ivy, and the night air vibrated with a universe of winged creatures. Mary Evelyn had not moved from the window, but Meggie and Aunt Abigail were turning down the bed and arranging her medicines and the mustard plasters on the small table beside it. In front of the empty fireplace, his mother was thrusting her knitting needles through the rolled stocking before she laid it away for the night. As he looked at her, he remembered the abounding vitality of her prime, when his father had called her "a daughter of earth and sky." He hoped that Ada, who was like her grandmother in many other ways, had inherited that intense relish for life combined with that eloquent response to the things of the spirit. Compared with his mother, he told himself, he had never known the true zest of experience.

"Can I do anything for you, Mary Evelyn?" he asked tenderly, the more tenderly because he was longing, against his will, to escape from the room, from the trail of anguish that quivered through his nerves at the sound of his wife's voice. I couldn't bear it if she were not here, he thought, and then, with a throb of pain, And I cannot bear to be with her. Had he loved her less, it would have been easier to watch her suffer and change and grow, day by day, a stranger in the flesh to the Mary Evelyn with whom he had shared that old ecstasy. For it was true that the passion he felt for her was an agony too great to be borne unless there were hours of release into solitude, into silence, where emotion could no longer survive.

"Nothing now, John, but sit by me till I feel sleepy."

Dropping into a chair at her side, he reached for her fragile hand and began stroking it gently from the wrist, which was so thin that the bones seemed scarcely covered, to the tips of her fingers. Sometimes he would sit like this for hours, not hearing a word that she said, yet never pausing in that soft pressure from wrist to finger-tips and then back again more slowly from finger-tips to wrist.

"Have you finished your day, Mother?" he asked presently.

"Aye, my son. I never like to sit long in summer after the light fades. Your father used to say the cock in the barnyard sets the hour in a village. That was the way you were brought up, but the lamp in your library burns well on after midnight." Steadying herself on her swollen feet, the old woman slipped her work behind a cow in Staffordshire ware on the end of the mantelpiece.

While he looked at her, John Fincastle pondered the history of that cow, which had lost her horns but still preserved a suckling calf at her udder. In some fantastic flare of memory (the laws of the mind, he told himself, are still barbaric), the cow reminded him of India, and he thought of the favourite prayer of Schopenhauer, that ancient supplication of the Hindus, *"May all that have life be delivered from suffering."* Aloud he said, "Has it never occurred to you, Mother, that the night has more room than the day? It is only at night that I can find time to range like the lone wolf I am."

"He gives up so much of his time to me," Mary Evelyn sighed in her breathless tone.

"Not nearly so much as I should like to give, my dear."

"Then there's Ralph and the school until it closes," his wife continued, as if he had not spoken. "Besides that, the work out of doors is enough for two men."

"I have a strong constitution." Her husband was still stroking her hand. "Work in the garden and at the woodpile keeps me active."

"He never had a day's sickness as a child," his mother remarked. "It's fortunate for Ada that she has inherited his constitution."

"Yes, it's fortunate that she did not inherit mine." There was a tremor in Mary Evelyn's voice.

"She will never compare with you, Mary Evelyn," John Fincastle said, while a lump swelled in his throat. "You are too precious for the hard life I have given you."

" 'Tis a miracle that she's stood it so well," Grandmother Fincastle assented. "I've always said that, except for her delicate frame, she's more of a Fincastle than you are yourself, John."

"You're right, Mother. I was a variation from type, as biologists say. Such oddities occur even in the best breeds."

Bending over, the old woman kissed her daughter-in-law's forehead with one of the rare caresses she never bestowed on her own children. Then, leaning on the old-fashioned ebony cane that had belonged to her husband, she limped across the floor and into the adjoining room, where she had slept alone since the beginning of summer. "But for my legs," she muttered, as she went, "I'd be as spry as I ever was."

"Would you like me to read to you, or is it too warm?" John Fincastle asked.

"It is too warm. I'd rather stay like this unless you are neglecting your work. You have so little time."

"All I have is yours. Anything can wait when you need me."

She smiled wistfully and sank back on her pillows, while he sat motionless by her side and listened to the soft whirring of a bat at the window. Meggie, having measured out the dose of bromide, was placing the night lamp, with lowered wick, behind the screen in one corner. Aunt Abigail, who was still active from the waist up, like Grandmother Fincastle, but had stopped trying to stoop, was hanging a knitted shawl on the headboard. In a little while the chair would be wheeled across the room, and he would lift his wife into bed, after Meggie had arranged the pillows in the way that made Mary Evelyn's pain more endurable when she awoke in the night. The first sleeping-draught would usually ease her suffering until three o'clock. Then she would waken him if he had fallen asleep, and he would measure out a second dose and repeat one of the Psalms to her until the sedative had taken effect.

When her preparations were over, Aunt Abigail turned away from the bed. "Good night, Miss May Ev'lyn. Good night, Marse John."

"Good night, Aunt Abigail. Good night."

"Good night, Miss Meggie." Then, opening the crack of Grandmother's door, the old servant raised her voice: "Good night, ole Miss. Sleep well an' wake up peart in de mawnin'."

"Good night, Abigail. If the moon ain't up when you go, be sure to light your lantern. You remember that bad fall you had the last dark of the moon."

"I sho' do, ole Miss. We ain't needer uv us de high-steppers we use'n ter be."

She waddled out, while Meggie went into her mother's room to help her undress.

"Are you in pain, my dear?" John Fincastle asked, as his wife moaned softly under her breath.

"Only a stab. It will pass in a minute. I am so happy about Ada, John. If only life will be good to her."

"It will be. She knows its secret. Shall I give you your bromide?"

"Not until I am in bed. Meggie will come as soon as she has seen Mother settled. When I look at Ada's happiness, it makes even pain bearable. I long to see her with children. She is a born mother if ever a woman was."

"Yes, I remember the way she cared for her dolls, and the time I disappointed her. I failed then as I have so often."

"All I ask," Mary Evelyn continued in her excited voice, "is that Ralph will make her as happy—as blissfully happy—as you have made me."

"My dear, my dear!" If only the spirit could be reached through the flesh! If only he could pour himself into this anguish, this tenderness! "You made your own happiness. I was always unworthy."

"I couldn't have done it without you. As a girl, I wasn't satisfied. Then you came, and that made everything different."

His smile wavered and vanished in the moonlight that was beginning to fall through the window. How little she knew him! How little did any human being know another! "I grew up in a sterner age," he answered. "The world has softened nowadays. Nobody but Mrs. McBride believes any longer that the will must be broken if one is to be saved."

"Yet you have always been happy. In spite of all the struggle, the tragedy, you have been happy."

He pressed her hand. "Happiness is a hardy annual."

"You would live your life over again, wouldn't you? As it is, I mean, taking the good and the bad?"

Without appearing to do so, he evaded her question. "And you, my darling? You have had more to bear than I have." Laughter quivered and died in his voice. "For you have had to bear with me."

"Oh, John, John." Memory shuddered through her, but when she spoke there was a triumphant note in her answer. "I would take it all again with you, the joy and the grief, even this last suffering. Yes, I would take it all with you if I could."

His pain was so intense that, for an instant, the pulse of his heart seemed suspended. "You are a joyous spirit," he said at last. "I have a darker mind, or a less courageous one." Why had he made that answer? It would hurt or at least sadden her.

"It isn't that, but life has meant so much to me. Even now I cling on. I can't bring myself to let go my hold."

Leaning over her, he rested his forehead on her hand. It was possible sometimes when they were alone to break through the reserve he had inherited with his rugged body and embattled mind. "Don't leave me," he pleaded. "I'd be lost if you went."

She lay back again, as if feeling had exhausted her strength, and he sat on beside her, sunk in meditation, until she asked, after a long silence, "What are you thinking of, John?"

"Of nothing, my dear. My thoughts wandered. I was wondering what kind of world we might have had if all the love that has been spent on a personal God and an individual human being had been spread over the whole of creation."

She shook her head. "That will never be."

The door into his mother's room opened and shut. Then a fragment of shadow detached itself from the border of lamplight and floated toward them. As it approached, he distinguished Meggie in her grey wrapper and heelless slippers.

"Do you feel as if you could sleep, Mary Evelyn?"

"Is it time for my bromide?"

"Yes, I've measured it out. You've had a long day."

"But a happy one."

When they had rolled the chair across the room and placed her in bed, John Fincastle stood watching while Meggie gave her the medicine and folded back the sheet over her bosom.

"It may turn cooler in the night," Meggie said, "so I've put a blanket on the foot of the bed. Ask for it, Mary Evelyn, if you feel a chill in the air."

"Yes, I'll ask for it. Is my shawl where I can reach it?" Sinking into the pillows, Mary Evelyn put up a trembling hand for the shawl before she settled down into the inner peace of the sedative.

"The bottle and the teaspoon are here where John can give you another dose." With her capable touch, Meggie rearranged the glass, the medicine, and the small brown jug of water on the bed table. All night the lamp burned very low behind the screen, which was papered in a Chinese pattern of temples and peacocks, sent by a missionary to Grandmother Fincastle when she was a young woman.

"You will sleep now?"

"Oh, yes. I feel that I'll have a good night."

"Shall I sit by you awhile?" asked her husband, with his hand on her pulse.

"No, don't wait. Go back to your work. I'm falling asleep already. Bromide is so wonderful." Her soft, eager voice dropped to a whisper. "You will sit up, John, until Ada comes in?"

"Yes, I'll sit up, and I'll hear if you call."

"Don't have me on your mind. Meggie is going to stay downstairs with Mother to-night."

"I'll leave a crack in the door," Meggie said, "and you know I'm a light sleeper, even when I don't have to be up and down with Mother. She says I can hear a leaf turning."

✻ ✻ ✻ ✻ ✻ ✻ ✻DA would not come home until well after midnight, and ahead of him there were three hours of the loneliness that he loved. He loved his family more, of course, John Fincastle thought, but that was an attachment spun by habit and association and the complex need of human relationships. And, when all was said and felt and thought, human beings were more important than ideas about God—at least in the lot of man.

Before striking a match, he went to the window of his library and looked out on God's Mountain in the light of a moon that had just risen over the house. While he watched the glimmering rays grow brighter and stronger, he felt the external world break up and dissolve, as the shredded clouds dissolved in the luminous sky. Here, apart, withdrawn from the enveloping glow of time, he was wholly himself; he was Mary Evelyn's lover; he was the student in Bloomsbury; he was the scholar in exile; he was the labourer in the potato field. He was all these things, and yet he was none of these things alone.

The moon sailed upward, the mist vanished, God's Mountain receded. Where a mystic presence had brooded, there were only dark masses on the horizon. Turning away from the window, he removed the chimney from the lamp and touched a match to the wick, which sent up a thin blue flame and then began to burn brightly. To-morrow a leak in the roof must be mended, the loosened boards must be nailed down on the porch, and several shingles must be replaced on the eaves of the kitchen. But to-night he had escaped, for a while at least, from the boundaries of the immediate and the necessary. Stillness enclosed him, and over this stillness, near or distant sounds trembled and fell without sinking below the surface, as leaves tremble and fall on a pond—the whispering of a breeze, the fluttering of swallows in the chimney, the plaintive cry of a night bird over the spring, the ceaseless patter of unseen but intimate presences in the ivy or higher up on the roof. During the hours between dusk and daybreak the manse seemed to separate itself from the village, to shed the covering of communal life, and to slip back into the wilderness. And in his own nature, too, the link between himself and the community would be broken. Again and again, his look would fly through the open window, and over the sheep pasture and the stony hill, to the unconquerable solitude. So might old John Fincastle have gazed toward some visionary frontier when he shook the dust of the settlement from his feet and marched away to the savages.

Two hours passed, and he was still writing. Only two hours, he told himself with a sigh, as he glanced at the clock. Then the sound that had disturbed him grew louder. There was the rattle of wheels over the rocks in the road, and a grinding noise as the turn was made at the gate and a buggy rolled over the lawn to the old millstone. Perhaps it was not Ada, after all, but a call from the dying or the bereaved for his mother. No, it could not be Ada. He remembered that she had gone, and would of course return, in the spring-wagon. Then, as he was about to go out into the hall, his daughter's voice floated in from the porch.

"Thank you for bringing me home. Good night."

Immediately the wheels started again, and a minute afterwards the grinding noise began over the rocks at the gate. While he waited, pen in hand, the door in the hall was shut very quietly, the bolt was slipped into place, and Ada spoke in a low voice to Horace before she came into the library.

"Is Mother asleep, Father?" she asked in a whisper, closing the door.

"She took the bromide, and she has not called."

"I hope I didn't wake her when I came in."

"She would have spoken to you if she'd been awake. You are home early."

"Yes, I'm home early."

"That wasn't the Rowans' wagon?"

She shook her head. "It was Ross Greenlee's buggy. He never stays late, because he's studying medicine."

"Where's Ralph? I thought he was studying too."

"He didn't know I'd come away. I had a headache, and I asked Ross to bring me when I saw him leaving."

As she answered she moved from the shadow by the door into the yellow orb of the lamplight, which seemed to quiver faintly and then to lie still again under a wave of emotion—or perhaps only a dying breeze. A strange note in her voice, or something unusual in her look, arrested his gaze, and he remained with his pen transfixed in his hand while an impression stabbed into his mind. Was it true—could it be possible that he had never really known her? With the question, all his theories about life toppled over, like the lofty towers in a dream, and crumbled to dust. Not his philosophy alone was threatened, but all that he had discovered, or imagined he had discovered, about human beings.

"What is the matter, my child?" he asked gently. "Has anything hurt you?"

"Nothing has happened. Ralph was dancing in a figure, and I wanted to come home." Her voice trembled, and she repeated quickly in the effort to steady it, "I do hope Mother hasn't waked." Stooping over, she put out her hand as if to stroke Horace, but the old hound, after following her into the room, had retired to his sleeping-place on the sofa.

"You must not take things too hard, my dear. It is so easy when we are young to make mountains out of molehills."

It seemed to him that her eyes were beseeching, but she made no sound as she stood there in the lamplight, winding and unwinding a crocheted scarf over her wrist and hand. His heart ached for her. He felt her suffering as he felt the inarticulate distress of a child or an animal.

"I know," she assented after a pause. "I do exaggerate things."

"Most of us do when we are young."

She shook her head again, and he felt that she was wrapping her pride about her. Even as a child she had a way of withdrawing into her pride when she was hurt. "I'll go upstairs now," she said. "Our voices might wake Mother or Aunt Meggie."

"Are you sure nothing has hurt you?"

"Oh, nothing. I'll be all right in the morning." Then, after she had turned from him, she stopped and looked back. "Why are we this way, Father?"

"What way, my child? There are so many different ways."

"Why are we always doing things we didn't mean to do and didn't want to do? Why is something always tripping us up when we try to be happy?"

"Many have put that question, my dear, and no one has been able to answer it. Some have said that Nature is the antagonist of happiness. But try to sleep off your headache. Nothing **has** occurred that can't be put right to-morrow."

"Oh, yes. It will be all right to-morrow. Only it tears you inside to be angry. I wonder if I'll ever get over flaring up quickly?"

"As you grow older. But be patient. Ralph has had a hard upbringing, and he needs all the patience you have or are ever likely to have."

"If only I could remember that. I do till something happens that hurts my pride, like . . . like . . . Oh, well, I shan't even let myself think of it. It was mostly my fault, because I didn't have patience."

"Then promise me that you will forget your pride and remember Ralph's mother."

"I promise, Father. Good night."

The door opened and shut softly; he felt rather than heard her steps ascending the worn staircase, and then the slight creak of the boards in the bedroom above. Something had wounded her, he knew, and he knew also that he was powerless to shield her from her own nature. She must fight the conflict alone, as his mother had fought alone in her youth, as his great-grandmother Tod had fought alone in captivity.

With a sigh, he turned his gaze to the window and waited until the shiver of apprehension was over and the life of reason spread its protecting wings in his mind.

N O, N O T H I N G had happened, Ada repeated in her room under the sloping roof, nothing had hurt her. Moonlight fell in flakes through the two dormer-windows, but the side window, cutting into the triangle of the wall, was in darkness. Through the rustling leaves she could see the few scattered lights that still burned in Ironside and, flung far out into the silvery dusk of the fields, a single wavering spark in the hovel by the ravine.

Slipping out of her pink gingham, she said, "Nothing has happened." Carefully folding the skirt before she laid it away in a drawer, she added firmly, "Everything will be all right in the morning." As she dropped her chemise about her feet, and drew her cambric nightgown over her head, she looked down at her strong young arms and high pointed breasts, as smooth as cream in the moonlight. And then, while she let down her hair and shook it in a dusky veil over her shoulders, she spoke aloud in a tone of surprise. "I wonder what it is about Janet?"

What was it? She couldn't answer. She didn't know. It was true that she had not wanted to go with Janet (Ralph, she insisted to herself, had never liked her); yet they had gone; she had had her way as always with everyone. "Even when you like to be with her, you don't like her," Ralph had said. And Ada had not understood. She did not understand now, with her eyes on the lights in the village. One light went out while she watched it—then another, and still another. A few hours before she had been happy, and then something, as dark and mysterious as that mountain spur thrusting out in the moonlight, had broken into her life, into her happiness. If only she could think it over. But she couldn't think. She could only feel this sharp thrust, this twisting pain in her heart.

"It was my fault," she said aloud, while the cloud in her mind became lighter and seemed to evaporate. "I ought to have had patience. Ralph didn't want to go up into the barn loft with Janet. She asked him to go. I heard her." He hadn't wanted to go, but he had gone. He hadn't wanted to drink whiskey, but he had drunk it when they dared him. Yet he was always like that. When he was a little boy and his mother had whipped him for playing with Toby Waters, he had stood it without a whimper, and as soon as it was over, he had run straight out of the house and over the fields to the pigsty. That was what Father called Ralph's need to defend his personality. His whole childhood, Father said, had been warped by forces he did not understand, though he felt they were destructive. But perhaps Grandmother was right when she insisted that she didn't hold with such newfangled ideas and willful children should be made to obey. Then, without effort, as soon as she had stopped trying to think things out clearly, Ada began to live over all that had happened, or had not happened, to turn eager expectancy into vague disappointment.

A few hours before, in the evening, life had been simple and straight, and now, at midnight, it was ruffled and complicated and obscured by this smoky vapour of apprehension. And she had wanted life to be simple. She had asked nothing more than a certain security for her life, for her love, for her happiness. They were on the back seat of the big wagon; Charlie Draper and Willie Andrews were in front; Janet and Bessie McMurtry would be waiting for them on the Rowans' porch. When they started down the rocky road, Ralph put his arm about her and kissed her in the darkness. She remembered the warm pressure of his mouth on hers, and she remembered, too, the roll of the wheels, turning within and without, and the yellow gleam from the wagon lamp flitting over tufts of grass and weeds which stood out illuminated, each blade or leaf separate and distinct, on the edge of obscurity. Later, moonlight would pour down over the hills into the valleys, but while they drove on past the churchyard into the village they were swallowed up in the darkness. It was a tender darkness, soft, warm, clinging, not like this burned-out silver light which seemed to drain the world and her own mind of emotion.

"I had hoped we were going alone," he murmured, as she lived the evening over again.

She laughed from sheer delight. "It was your fault. It serves you right for saying you would go with Janet. Is it true that some of the boys went up to Lightning Ridge to buy moonshine?"

He nodded. "Who told you that? It was exactly like Janet."

"I don't care so long as you weren't one of them," she replied, ignoring his question.

The arm she leaned against hardened slightly. "A man can't be a killjoy," he answered. "That is what you and your father can never understand. It is easy to be noble in the woods, but among other people, it makes you a killjoy."

His tone had roughened, and in some strange way the roughness increased his power over her. She felt ecstasy stabbing through her flesh into her heart, piercing every cell of her body with tiny splinters of flame. Why? Why? She couldn't tell, she didn't know. It was nothing that he had said, only the eager seeking of his lips and the ruffled sound of his voice. All his charm, the thrilling charm of his mouth, his eyes, his smile, his imperative tone and gestures, seemed to envelop her and crush out resistance. Yes, it was true. You could not live in the world and be a killjoy. How she loved him! What a miracle love can make of life! Nothing else mattered, not Janet, not moonshine whiskey, not being alone in a crowd. Then, as they stopped before the Rowans' gate, she whispered, "I hope you will be nice to Janet."

She could feel, and see, too, when a light flashed from the porch, that he was smiling. "Oh, no, you don't," he retorted. "You don't really."

Before she had time to answer, Janet and Bessie were calling to them as they ran down the walk, and the three boys jumped out of the wagon and flung open the gate. Charlie held up a lantern, and the light danced over Janet in her organdie flounces, with the single flaxen curl on her neck. She was so lovely that Ada caught her breath as she looked at her. "Oh, isn't she beautiful? Doesn't her dress suit her?" To her astonishment, Ralph was not looking; he had turned away and was fumbling with the reins that had dropped from the wagon. Even when they had all crowded into the wagon, and were driving up the street, Ralph did not turn his eyes from the broad backs of the greys. He did not speak until Janet leaned over and touched his arm. Then he looked at her and looked away again before he replied to some trivial question. She possessed some power, Ada felt, that Ralph despised and resisted but could neither ignore nor deny. A boy brought up so severely would always retain some secret allegiance to duty, Grandmother said, no matter how far he had wandered. Even if his senses fell into sin, his conscience would always remind him that it was not pleasure but sin. And watching the exercise of this power, which appeared to be rooted more in aversion than in attraction, Ada wondered whether Aunt Meggie had meant this when she called Janet "a born trouble-maker."

Somewhere in the fields a hound was howling. The small darkened light still shone, like a vindictive eye, in Mrs. Waters's hovel. Was the woman ill or in want? Perhaps Toby was sick. To-morrow, she must tell Grandmother or Aunt Meggie. Aunt Meggie had told her not to bother about Mother's salt-rising bread, which had to be put down at four o'clock for a third rising. No matter how early she went downstairs, Grandmother, who never slept a wink after the first crack of day, was sure to be ahead of her. A winged shape flew out of the darkness of an oak and sped through the moonlight into the shadows. There was a swift rush, a startled squeak, and then silence woven of innumerable whispering leaves, of soundless wings, of a multitude of soft-footed creatures that lived only at night.

By the window, with the moonlight streaming over her, Ada

told herself that there had been moments in the evening she could never forget. Yet they were as empty as dried husks. There wasn't anything to remember but that uneasiness, that undercurrent of impulse—or was it violence? And what had brought on the quarrel? It was true that she and Ralph had quarrelled before (they were both easily hurt?), but only about Janet, the trouble-maker. It wasn't his being self-willed that Ada resented. It was something different, something that had to do with Janet, not with whiskey in the loft, but with Janet dancing up and down the floor of the new barn. The more the boys drank in secret (Mrs. Padgett was a leader in the temperance movement), the happier they appeared to become, and the happier they became, the louder grew their attentions to Janet and Bessie. Not that anything was really amiss on the surface. None of the boys had tasted too deeply to mind his steps, and only those who knew of the hidden treasure in the loft were the wiser. The row of watching matrons, who would help presently with the supper, had no suspicions.

But there was a difference. A feeling that she had never known before had come between her and Ralph. Pride? Jealousy? Or only the shyness that made her draw away when she was hurt? Well, whatever it was, she was to blame for it. She wouldn't have been like this, she knew, with anyone else; but love, as Mother had warned her, made people act so strangely, made them do such unbelievable things, that their closest friends did not recognize them.

She wished that hound would stop howling. It sounded as if it were hurt or in distress. Perhaps the moonlight made it feel lonely. To-morrow she would find out why the lamp burned so late and the hound howled. But to-night she could not bother about such things. She must rid her heart of anxiety and impatience.

When had the quarrel begun (think quietly, she told herself) and why had she grown suddenly so angry that she had broken away from the party and come home with Ross Greenlee? For an instant the scene whirled before her eyes in a revolving mass of impressions. A dance had just finished, and the music of another was beginning. She had danced with Charlie Draper and Fred Robinson, and she was waiting for Ralph, while she watched Janet smiling and nodding to him from beneath the Chinese lanterns in the doorway. "I wonder what it is about Janet?" she said aloud to herself and, looking round at a touch, saw Ralph at her elbow.

"What's that about Janet?" he asked in a tone that sounded excited and irritable. Then, before she could laugh away the question, he added in a lowered voice, "Don't let's dance. It's too hot in here. Let's go out into the fields."

That was the beginning, that was the turning-point which cut her evening in two parts. For Ralph was not himself, she saw at a glance. He had been drinking that mountain whiskey because Janet and the other boys had teased him, and when he drank he grew sullen and curiously defiant. She should have had patience; she should have remembered that he needed her now more than ever. But instead she felt that stab of pain in her heart, and her indignation flared up because he yielded to Janet, because he had not kept away from the wilder boys in the loft. "I was waiting to dance with you," she said, "but I don't want to dance with you now. You'd better ask Janet." Why had she said that? She had not meant to reproach him. The words were spoken by some inner voice over which she had no control.

"Don't let's dance," he urged. "It's cooler out in the fields, and we'll be by ourselves."

"Not like this." (She was not remembering; she was living the scene again.) "I don't want to be with you when you're like this."

"Like what?"

"I don't want to be with you when you're not yourself."

"But I am myself, and if I'm not, you're to blame."

At that she should have laughed; it was so absurd that she should have laughed it away and tried to keep near him until his temper wore off. But she flared up again, and they quarrelled— as always, about Janet! They quarrelled for a few minutes as bitterly as ignorant mountain people, she told herself, who did not know how to bear themselves when they were in love. For, strangely enough, love had had a part in it too. Love had driven her into saying things that had never entered her mind, that were uttered straight out of the air, without the slightest connection with either the past or the future. A sob escaped her. "You never know love," Mother had told her once, "till you feel its pain." But it would be over to-morrow. He would come in the morning before he went to work, and the making-up would be happiness. Never again would they quarrel. Never, never again!

What had come next? Was that another screech owl or only the shadow of a moving branch under the trees?

"But you're coming?" he insisted.

"No, I'm not coming. Not until you're yourself again."

He laughed under his breath. She could never forget that laugh, though it meant nothing. A dull ache from the stab it had left was still in her heart. "Maybe you'd rather I asked Janet," he said. "Janet says it's cooler outside."

A sensation she had never felt before, a stinging darkness, swept over her. Was it love? Was it jealousy? Was it anger? Was it Ada Fincastle or some strange girl who was speaking, "If you leave me for Janet, I'll go home. I'll walk home by myself."

"You couldn't at night. It's nearly five miles. But why won't you come out? My head is too heavy for dancing."

"That's because of the whiskey. You let Janet and those boys make you drink."

"Well, you can't be a killjoy. Do you want me to ask Janet?"

A sob burst from her lips. Yet she had not given way; she would not go out into the fields with him. A girl with proper pride did not go off alone in the moonlight with a man who had been drinking. No matter how much she loved him, and even though he wasn't drunk, only just not himself, she could protect them both (Grandmother had told her this) if she stood on her dignity. "I don't care. I don't care what you do when you're like this," she flung back at him.

"Then I will," he said stormily. "I shan't have to beg Janet."

He turned away and walked straight to the open door, where Janet was waiting. They were behaving like two children, Ada thought, two children who ought to know better. While she stood there and watched him cross the floor, it seemed to her that joy was slowly ebbing away from her heart. Yet something stronger than joy, the vein of iron far down in her inmost being, in her secret self, could not yield, could not bend, could not be broken. Then, as Janet smiled up at him with her rose-red mouth, Ada turned away, walked the length of the barn with an unhurried step, and went out of the other door into the road. She would have started to walk home, driven by some force that seemed to be outside her thoughts and yet to have control over her words or acts. But just as she was about to leave, Ross Greenlee came out to his buggy, and after a few meaningless sounds had passed between them, she asked him to drive her back to the manse. It was too hot to stay inside; she was anxious about her mother; she wanted to go home.

He seemed to understand, and made it as easy as possible by talking the whole way, without putting a question. A nice boy, fired with ambition, who would probably go North and become a success in his profession. Men with ability never stayed in a village. That was why Ralph was going to Queenborough.

"But it was all my fault," she said aloud, before the sentence had taken shape in her mind. "It was all my fault because I didn't have patience." As if self-reproach were a blessing, anger and apprehension faded out of her thoughts. A moment later, when she turned her cheek to the pillow, she felt that sleep and peace were closing about her.

T SIX o'clock Ada awoke with a start. What had happened? Why did yesterday seem to be still going on? Jumping out of bed, she stood up in the green tub and washed with Grandmother's strong homemade soap and cold water. She was glad her skin was not fine and brittle like Mother's. It must be dreadful to have everything hurt you, and not be able to wear flannel next you in winter, she mused, while she combed back her hair and wound it in the figure eight on the nape of her neck.

In the kitchen she found Grandmother stirring batter in a big yellow bowl. Already the loaf of salt-rising bread was in the oven, and the fresh smell of baking would presently fill the room. Mary Evelyn ate only this kind of bread, which was fine and close in texture and supposed to be good for an invalid.

"What can I do to help, Grandmother?" Ada asked, tying a checked apron over her blue cotton dress.

"You might slice the bacon very thin. My hands are so bad I can't manage that small knife. I begin to dread the time when I shall have to give up my knitting."

"Aren't those big wooden needles a help?"

"They won't be if my joints get more crooked. And they don't knit right. I've had to pull out the armhole in that sweater I'm making for your father."

The old woman was seated by the table, which was covered with brown oilcloth, and behind her the red geraniums on the window-sill were in full bloom. In winter the family had their meals in the kitchen; but in summer they opened the dining-room and used the walnut table, which had served so many preachers and missionaries and presiding elders when the pastor

lived in the old manse. "It won't cost you a penny more to be
particular than to be slatternly," Grandmother would say. "Even
in the wilderness Scotch-Irish housekeepers seldom become slat-
terns. If you have the proper pride, you may keep nice among
savages." Bending over the yellow bowl, she stirred slowly and
smoothly, taking care not to let the big pewter spoon drop
from her bent fingers. Her massive head had gained nobility
with age, and though she wore the plainest clothes, except for
her lawn cap and cameo brooch, no one, meeting her in the road,
would have mistaken her for a peasant.

"I'm afraid Aunt Abigail is sick again," Ada said, as she
poured a heaping cupful of coffee beans into the iron coffee mill
and began turning the crooked handle. The old coffee mill,
nailed to the wall by the door, had been used every morning and
evening, except in wartime, for the last century. As Ada ground
the fragrant Mocha and Java beans, toasted by Grandmother
and bought with Aunt Meggie's savings, she glanced at the
whitewashed walls and the strings of red peppers and the rusted
dipper hanging above the wooden bucket on the small table.
Ever since she could remember the kitchen had looked like this,
with everything in its proper place and every withered leaf
carefully pinched from the geraniums.

"Little black Dinty ran over to ask for turpentine," Grandmother answered, "but Aunt Abigail is coming as soon as she can
get on her feet."

"She's getting worse all the time."

"Aye, it looks that way. If she's bedridden by next winter,
we'll have to get her daughter Liddy to come and help out. It
will mean one more mouth to feed, and we'll have to stint more
than we do now"—she looked up to sniff the stimulating aroma
—"but of course we can't let Aunt Abigail come to want."

"You ought to be spared, too, Grandmother."

"I don't worry about myself," the old woman replied, rising
to pour the batter into the baking-dish. "I'm old, like Abigail,
and my time has 'most come. I made this batter bread because
your father wouldn't take his buttermilk yesterday, and I didn't

want to throw it away. Batter bread tastes better when it is made with buttermilk."

"There's somebody coming in the gate," Ada said, glancing out of the side window. "I suppose he wants Father to advise him. Isn't it funny the way they come to Father for counsel after they've turned him out of the ministry? They even come before breakfast!"

Grandmother looked up at the stout hands of the walnut clock, which had ticked on for a century above a painted landscape. "It's about to strike seven," she answered. "Can you see who it is?"

"I think it's Mr. Rowan." Ada's voice was charged with anxiety. "I wonder what he can want coming so early. They don't keep as early hours as other people. Janet always sleeps late." She slipped off her apron and rolled down the sleeves of her dress. "Had I better ask him to breakfast?"

"It seems more hospitable. We can't let him go away just as it's ready, and we're having a plenty this morning."

Running out into the hall, Ada unbolted the front door as Mr. Rowan was lifting his hand for a second knock. "Father is in the library," she said, smiling, "and Grandmother hopes you will stay to breakfast."

He looked heavy and fat and overheated from the short walk, which must have been hurried, and his expression, she saw with her first glance, was not so hearty as usual. There were pouches under his eyes, and the congested veins in his cheeks had turned purple. But his thin gray hair was neatly brushed, he wore an alpaca coat without creases, and he was holding a fresh straw hat with a striped band and one of the new narrow brims.

"It smells mighty good," he said pleasantly, "but my wife will be expecting me. I wish you could teach Janet to keep early hours." Though he smiled at her as he entered the hall, she was quick to perceive that his smile was forced and unnatural. "I stepped up the first thing this morning for a word with your father."

Opening the library door, she said distinctly, because it was always difficult to distract her father from work, "Here is Mr. Rowan to see you." Then, turning away while the door was still ajar, she went back through the dining-room to the kitchen, where Grandmother sat in a deep study, with her knees apart, like the headless basalt image on the clock without works in the parlour.

"He won't stay to breakfast," Ada said, trying to speak cheerfully in spite of the hard lump in her throat. Emptying the ground coffee into the coffee-pot, she mixed it with part of an egg Grandmother had kept back, and dropped in the shell before she filled the pot with cold water and put it on the stove to boil up twice. "I hope there's nothing the matter," she continued uneasily, as she opened the door of the stove and thrust in some sticks of wood.

Grandmother glanced up with a stolid expression. "If 'twas sickness," she answered, "he'd more likely come straight to me."

Ada's face was flushed from the heat of the stove, and she raised her free hand to push back a lock of hair from her forehead. "It must be something important to bring him so early."

"We'll know in a few minutes. Tell me when you hear him come out of the library. It ain't likely he'll stay long with breakfast waiting for him at home. Well, whatever he has, it won't be a better breakfast than ours this morning."

"I wish Ralph could come in time for it. He has so little at home."

"His mother has to be sparing, poor woman. Be sure to have the bacon ready to go into the frying-pan as soon as the batter bread is brown on top."

Ada opened the door of the oven and glanced inside. "It won't be long. I wish Father could have become a great preacher," she remarked thoughtfully, "but I suppose he had to follow his conscience."

"It's a poor conscience," Grandmother retorted, "that leads into error."

"I'll never believe that Father ever had a poor conscience."

Grandmother's eyes softened while her mouth hardened. "It

is a trial of faith to believe that a good man can be an unbeliever. All the Fincastles were men of spirit, but not one was ever before an open doubter. They never questioned God's will, not even when it went against them, and they kept their word to Christian and heathen alike. It was told of old John, the pioneer, that he was strung up and half choked by a party of hunters because he refused to give away the hiding-place of some Cherokees who had trusted him. When the men from the settlement found him, he was lying unconscious at the foot of a tree, and as he came to, he cried out in a loud voice, 'What I have said, I have said!' Roaming white men, he wrote down somewhere, were his abomination, and he added, 'Only a God-loving man can be a good hater.' "

"He's going now!" Ada exclaimed, at the sound of chairs pushed back in the library.

Grandmother rose, patted her cap in place, and picking up her ebony cane, went out into the hall.

"Won't you stay to breakfast, William? We are about to have prayers?"

"Thank you, Mrs. Fincastle, but my wife will be waiting for me."

"I hope 'twasn't sickness that brought you."

"No, ma'am, if it had been sickness, I'd have come first to you." Without a change of tone, he inquired after the garden, and Grandmother replied that the turnip salad was about over, but they were getting beets and onions and snaps, and there was a good promise of corn and tomatoes and black-eyed peas later on in the summer. Things to eat occupied a large part in her old age, and she was never reluctant to talk of them.

"Well, you have a fine garden spot," he remarked as she finished. "Thank you again, and good morning."

His departure was too hurried, or so it seemed to Ada, who was watching through a crack in the dining-room door. A moment later she heard the tapping of Grandmother's stick and her imperative voice, saying, "Breakfast will be ready by the time we've had prayers, John."

"What has happened?" Ada asked herself, as her father came out into the hall on his way to her mother's chamber, where he read family prayers every morning. Her heart fluttered and sank as she followed him into the room. "Don't let it be about Ralph," she prayed mutely to her grandmother's God—or to any god, even a heathen one, that would listen. "Anything but that. Oh, God, please, please, don't let it be about Ralph!"

Outside, the morning was fair; sunshine streamed from a sky as blue as the traveller's-joy by the fence; birds were singing in the bright green and gold of the trees. Yet, while she stood there and listened vaguely to her father's solemn tones reading a Psalm, it seemed to her that the world beyond the window was suddenly troubled, as if a storm were approaching. On her knees a moment later, she entreated wildly, "Not about Ralph! I can't bear it if it is about Ralph!"

Through her loosened fingers, as she knelt she could see her father's face, steadfast, inscrutable, confirmed in fortitude. Her mother, in the invalid's chair, was bowed over with her eyes hidden in hands that trembled like leaves. By her side on the rag carpet Grandmother, who had bitten back a groan as she eased herself down, was praying aloud. Near the door, Aunt Meggie listened with half a mind for the sound of Aunt Abigail in the kitchen. "Oh, God, don't let any harm come to Ralph!"

Worship this morning was soon over. Rising with a spring, Ada stooped to help Grandmother to her feet ("You oughtn't to kneel, Grandmother; it is bad for your joints") while her father rolled the chair from the front window across the hall to the dining-room. Ahead of them, Aunt Meggie had darted into the kitchen, and she was already back again with the steaming coffee-pot in her hand. Her father, Ada noticed, with a shiver of apprehension, ate nothing. But then, she reassured herself, he was seldom hungry and could go for a whole morning on dry bread with a radish. Only Grandmother, whose appetite never flagged, and Aunt Meggie, who enjoyed anything she did not cook herself, remarked that the breakfast was better than usual and ought not to be wasted. When at last the meal was over,

Ada left Aunt Meggie to clear the table and went into the library to wait until her father returned from rolling the chair back to the window.

"You haven't touched a morsel, Ada," Grandmother called.

"I'm not hungry. Give it to Horace."

"Do you feel sick? Here, Horace, here's your good breakfast."

"No, not sick. I want to see Father. I'm waiting for Father."

"Well, he'll come in a minute. He's fixing your mother in her chair."

Was it a minute or an hour that she waited? What was time after all? Who had divided it? Who could tell where now ended and for ever began? Perhaps there wasn't any time. Perhaps there was only having or waiting to have. Across the hall she could hear her mother's animated voice, and the sound seemed to pluck at her nerves. What on earth can Mother find to talk about from morning till night? she thought, with a quiver of exasperation. A redbird flew by the window and alighted on the branch of an oak. Then, without waiting, it spread its wings and flew on again. It must be wonderful to fly. That bird could fly away and leave things. But it couldn't fly away from love and pain. An eagle looking down from the sky must see love and pain all over the world.

Her father was coming. He had shut the door of the chamber, and then had opened it a little way when her mother called, "Leave the door ajar, dear, if you're going for good." His steps were in the hall now; he had paused a moment to look out of the front door and exclaim in a raised tone, "Did you see that redbird, Mary Evelyn?" Then he came into the library, walking as stiffly as an old man, as an old woman, and she saw that his face was a grey mask behind which pain burned and flickered. Her mind went blank as a wall, and out of this blankness a single thought flashed: "It is my fault. Whatever has happened is my fault." Not until the words were in the air did she realize that she had spoken aloud.

He turned back to shut the door, and then sat down at his

desk and stretched out his hand, which was shaking a little. "Why, he is old," she said to herself in surprise, "I didn't know he had so many wrinkles." She could hear him swallowing when he tried to speak, and she felt her fear dissolve into nausea. "Poor Father," she thought, but she could force no pity into her voice, only irritation because he prolonged the extremity of suspense. "It is my fault," she said again in an angry tone, as if he had contradicted her.

"I don't know how to tell you, my child," he began slowly. "I shall have to hurt you, and I don't know how to do it."

"I can bear anything. Whatever it is, I am to blame." Between her and desperation there was only this single thought.

"It may be nobody's fault. It may be only the way life has of trying our strength."

"What is it, Father? I can bear anything better than waiting to hear." A tremor had crawled up her spine and was spreading over every part of her body—millions of tiny tremors, like invisible creeping feet.

"I am trying to, Ada, but I cannot find words. It is about Ralph . . . Mrs. Rowan found Ralph in her daughter's room after the young people had come home last night . . ."

"It isn't true. Janet was lying. Janet is always lying."

"It is true that he was there. He says the girl asked him to come in to look at some photograph . . ."

"Then that was true. He doesn't like Janet. He never liked her."

"Whether it is true or not, naturally Rowan is on the side of his daughter. It seems the whole house was alarmed. Janet was in hysterics. Even if Ralph is innocent, Rowan insists that her good name is damaged."

"Her good name! Why, she's never had any. Everybody knows how she is about men."

"Her parents do not. You can't blame them for defending their child."

"I do. I do blame them for not knowing." Her voice rose on a sobbing breath.

"Be careful, my dear. We must keep it from your mother as long as we can."

"Keep what? What are we keeping?" When she lowered her tone it was as hoarse, she told herself, as the "Caw! Caw!" of a crow.

"Even now, in spite of all Rowan told me, I find it incredible," John Fincastle said. Then, without warning, he asked, "Why did you leave the dance last night and come home with Ross? We must try to get at the truth."

A sob seemed to tear her lips apart. "What did Ralph say? Whatever Ralph says is true."

"He has said very little. It seems that Janet has been in trouble for some time. Nobody suspected it. Nobody knows it now except her parents and Mr. Black and Ralph's mother. But she says that Ralph is responsible, and that seems to settle it for her parents. It is the custom," he added dryly, "to accept a woman's word in such cases."

"It's not right, Father."

"I know, my child, but we cannot alter a rule of conduct. No matter how wrong or absurd it may be, it is stronger than we are. Tell me why you came home with Ross."

Somewhere in the trees a bird sang the same note over twice and broke off. Before replying, she turned her head toward the window, as if she were listening for the song to be renewed. "Oh, we quarrelled," she answered presently, "but it didn't mean anything."

"Was the quarrel about Janet?"

For an instant she hesitated, trying to think clearly and wisely. Was it about Janet? Or was it about nothing? "He called me a killjoy, but it was my fault."

Her father sighed and looked down at his papers. "How often I have seen it happen like that in human relationships. You had everything, you and Ralph. All you needed to do was to hold fast to your happiness—but you let it slip through your fingers."

"I know now . . . I know . . . but, oh, Father, I didn't

know then. Why didn't somebody tell me that life was this
way . . ."

"It is something we have to learn, Ada. I did tell you to have
patience."

"And I didn't have. I didn't have patience. I thought being
good mattered. But it doesn't. It doesn't matter to life—it doesn't
matter to God."

"We know as little about life as we know about God, my
child."

"Where is Ralph?" She looked up with a start. "What have
they done to him?"

"He is coming. Rowan has gone to bring him. I told him I
must talk with Ralph. But you must not blame the Rowans for
standing by their daughter."

"I do blame them. They ought to stand by the truth."

"They think they're doing that. But you must try to be brave,
Ada, and face what you have to face."

"What do they mean, Father? What have they done to
Ralph?"

"They are trying to make him marry Janet and take her away
from Ironside. They insist that her future here is impossible.
They believe, or pretend to believe—I think they are honest
about it—that Ralph ought to marry her."

Though her mouth dropped open, no sound came from her
lips, and when she tried to lower her eyelids she felt that her
lashes were plastered back.

"But he won't . . . he won't," she said at last in a strained
whisper. "They can't make him, Father?"

"I don't know, my dear. Everything is on their side, religion,
law, morality, influence, even money. . . . They can release all
the forces of society."

"They couldn't, Father. It would be savage."

"We are still savage, my child. What we call civilization is
only a different and perhaps a higher level of barbarism."

Words! Words! Impatience twitched through her. "Don't

let them, Father!" she cried out. "Don't let them take Ralph away from me."

"Would they listen to me, my daughter? Have they ever listened to me? I may have taken the wrong way in life," he said, with a controlled wildness in his look, in his voice, in his gestures. "There are only two ways of meeting life—one is to yield to it, and one is to retreat from it. I chose the latter, and I may have been wrong. That may be why I am inadequate in dealing with circumstances."

But she was not listening. What did it matter? What did anything matter? She leaned forward, pressing her hands together until the knuckles stood out like white pebbles. Something that had been asleep in her nature awoke, flared up, and quivered into vitality. All the part of her that had been innocent and unawakened to passion became as living as agony. Pain had brought her to life, not pain of the heart or of the mind alone, but of every nerve, every pulse, every cell and pore in her being.

"Where is Ralph, Father? I must find Ralph."

"He is coming, my dear. Try to be quiet. Your look makes me anxious."

"I must see Ralph. If he doesn't come," she started up, "I must go to find him."

"You cannot, Ada. You cannot fight with another woman—not over a man . . ."

"I must see Ralph."

"Will you talk to your grandmother?"

She shook her head stubbornly. "I must see Ralph."

He looked at her without speaking, and his features, while she watched them, seemed to fade and reassemble and fade again into a watery mist. Only his long, fine hands, which were roughened and blistered from the hoe and the ax, did not waver.

"How soon are they coming?" she asked. If only that bird would stop whistling the same call over and over!

"At any minute now. They were waiting to have breakfast."

"To have breakfast!" When suspense was eating into her heart—and into Ralph's—they could wait to have breakfast.

"Can't you leave this in our hands, Ada? If Ralph has been at fault, he must bear the responsibility. There is no way of escape."

"But he hasn't been at fault, Father, not really."

"By our moral code, my dear, an appearance of error is punished more severely than error itself."

"He didn't think. He does things without thinking."

"And he pays with thought in the end."

"If only I'd stayed!" She sprang up and dropped back again. "I ought to have gone out with him when he asked me. What does it matter now whether I did right or wrong? But why didn't you tell me? Why didn't Mother or Grandmother tell me that self-respect doesn't help you when you've lost happiness?"

"In the end it may make all the difference in the world to you. You are too young to look far ahead. But you shall see Ralph. I promise you that."

"I shall see Ralph." As she repeated the words, a faint distant drumming surged into her mind—"What I have said, I have said." Somewhere, miles and miles away, it seemed, she had heard this voice and these words in another place.

"I will send him to you if you will wait quietly. You must be brave. I would give my life to spare you this trial."

Life? But what did he know of life? Even his happiness, she thought, had no connection with the life that was jerking in her muscles and twisting like a knife in her bosom. For she did not want quietness; she did not want to be brave and to suffer. "I can't sit still," she said in a hoarse whisper. "I can't sit still any longer." She could not bear that changeless tranquillity of the old which came from not wanting things.

Turning away, she rushed out of the room; and it seemed to him that the very sound of her footsteps was alive and throbbing with passion. Long ago, in some other existence, he had suffered like that—long ago. Nothing of his old wound was left now. Yet he knew that while a single creature he loved remained alive on the earth his heart could never become wholly invulnerable to fate.

N O, SHE couldn't bear peace, Ada thought, as she ran down the hall and through the open door of the dining-room. There would be time enough for peace when she was dead, and she would be dead then once and for ever.

Glancing into the kitchen, she saw her grandmother bent over the breakfast things, while small black Dinty scraped the grease from the frying-pan. Aunt Abigail, who had had a turn for the worse, had gone back to bed in her cabin, and Aunt Meggie would be feeding her chickens before the door of the henhouse. Usually Ada helped with the work, but this morning it did not matter to her whether the house was clean or stayed dirty. What she could not stand was the look in her grandmother's face. Resignation to the will of the Lord was the one thing more that would drive her wild.

After she had bolted the door of her room, she sat down in front of the mirror over the pine bureau and gazed at her reflection as if it were the face of a stranger. Removing the hairpins, she let down her hair and brushed it until it shone with a dark lustre. "If I am going to my funeral, I may as well put on a clean dress," she told herself mockingly. Slipping out of her crumpled dress and into a fresh blue cotton with a white lawn collar that rolled back, she felt her strength flowing into muscles that were strong and free under the silken warmth of her skin. She would stand firm; she would hold fast to her own; she would not exchange a living happiness for the last refuge of fortitude. Even if that iron cross sustained her father and exalted her grandmother, it could do nothing for her. For she would rather suffer and keep alive than be crucified by God's will into submission. Sweeping the floor, she thought over and over, as if the words rose and fell and rose again on the steady strokes of her broom, I want to live while I'm living. While I'm living, I want to live. After she had made the bed and put the room in order, she emptied the water from the tub into a pail and carried it downstairs to pour over the hop-vines. The pail was heavy, but her arms were hard and firm, and to-day she felt the need to undertake fresh trials of strength. Since they depended on their old well and the spring at the foot of the slope, dry summers had taught the Fincastles not to waste water; and the stern struggle with the wilderness had trained them not to fear effort.

When she returned with the empty pail, three men had entered the gate and were walking slowly across the grass to the front porch. Three men, and one of them Ralph. Ralph with his head held up defiantly, and his boyish figure slouching between the minister and Mr. Rowan. As in a bad dream, while her heart seemed to pause, she watched the three shadows marching ahead into the next minute, vanishing as they passed under the oaks, and then flitting back into step as they emerged into the sunshine. But it was all so vague, she felt, that it might be scarcely more real than a reflection in running water, which rippled on and on and mirrored always, as it flowed away, the same broken images.

"Ada!" her grandmother called in her Sabbath tone. "Ada, will you wait patiently until your father and I have talked over this matter?"

"I must see Ralph, Grandmother."

"Well, I've sent Dinty to the cabin. Wait in the dining-room till we call you."

Grandmother had changed into the alpaca dress she wore on Sunday or to funerals, and had put on her best cap with a bunch of fresh ribbons. Only sin itself, the old adversary, which must be wrestled with and prayed over, could explain, Ada realized, the company dress and the best cap in the morning. But who had told her? Had Father spoken to her while Ada was upstairs in her room? Had Mr. Rowan contrived to let fall a warning? Or had she been granted some special gift of foreknowledge?

Well, however it occurred, she always knew things before any-one else; she was prepared, at any time, day or night, awake or asleep, for calamity.

"Aye, you may see him," the old woman continued, as she shut the door between the dining-room and the kitchen. "I'll send him to you as soon as I can, but he'll feel easier if you are not in the library."

This sounded true. It even sounded fair, which was by no means the same thing.

"Then I'll wait," Ada replied. "I'll wait in this very spot. I'll wait all day if I have to."

What else could she do? she demanded of vacancy, while she watched Grandmother move with a massive dignity, in spite of her stick, down the long hall to the front door. After the usual greetings, more formal because of Grandmother's respect for her pastor, the men entered the house and followed the rus-tling skirt and the tapping cane through the door of the library.

Sitting there at the dining-room table, Ada tried in vain to empty her mind and to fix her thoughts on external objects alone —on the clustering branches of an oak by the window, on the shadow of a hawk as it flew over a brood of chickens, on the fig-ure of Dinty skirting the garden fence on her way to Aunt Abigail's cabin. But the instant she released an impression, the whole pattern of her mind would shift and break up, and sus-pense, which she had driven out, would filter in with the green light from the window.

It would be an eternity, she thought, before Grandmother called her, the worst kind of eternity, without minutes, and en-closed within revolving circles of time. Round and round in circles. What had happened? What were they saying behind that shut door of the library? A power, terrible for good or evil, was offended, and only sacrifice could appease its resentment. The wrath of God, said her grandmother. The law of the tribe, said her father. Well, no matter, since the wrath of God and the law of the tribe both demanded atonement in blood. Suddenly, it seemed to her that she was opposing a phantom. But it was a phantom that would prevail in the end because it was the stronger.

She started back from the window as Grandmother came down the hall and into the dining-room. The old woman was saying something out of a tumult of sound, like the drumming of arteries . . . something about right . . . something about honour . . . something about duty.

"What have they done, Grandmother?"

"You must prepare yourself, my child. You must remember that other women have endured worse things than disappointment in love."

"I don't care about other women. What are they doing to Ralph?"

"You must try not to think of Ralph. You must bridle your wild impulses."

"I can't wait any longer, Grandmother."

"If he has harmed Janet, Ada, he will have to bear the blame for it."

"But everybody knows what Janet is."

"I am not defending Janet. I leave that to her father, who is well able to do it."

"I must see Ralph."

"Your wild heart is speaking again. Try to bring your will to God before it is broken."

"I must see Ralph."

"You must remember that Janet is an only child. Her father and mother are broken-hearted. They insist, and Mr. Black and your father agree with them, that the girl cannot be left to bear the burden alone. You have no share in this, Ada. You must be left out of it."

"I don't want to be left out. If Ralph is made to marry her," her voice was a mere thread of agony, "he will be miserable all his life."

"There are more things than happiness to be considered, my poor child."

"He loves me. He would hate Janet." Ralph's suffering was

harder to bear than her own, because Ralph would never, she felt, learn how to suffer.

"There are more things than love to be considered in marriage." Though the words were uttered in a refrain, the old woman gulped down a sob. "They have been talking since midnight," she said. "I don't see how the older men keep it up. But Ralph, anyway, is worn out. He is sullen and defiant, but he has agreed to marry Janet and go with her to Queenborough . . ."

"But he can't . . . he can't . . . Oh, Grandmother . . ." Misery broke over her in a curved wave.

"William Rowan is not an easy man to oppose. He is an elder in the church and a pillar of the community. He is able to ruin Ralph, and he will believe it his duty to do it if Ralph has disgraced Janet. And Ralph's mother is on his side. Though Ralph does not get on well with his mother, she has a strong—almost an extraordinary—influence over him."

"She loves to make him suffer."

"That is unjust. It is only that she could not let her feeling stand in the way of God's law. You must learn that, too, before life is done with you."

Before life had done with her! "Oh, Grandmother, I can't bear it! I can't bear what is ahead of me!"

"My child, my dear child. I wouldn't spare myself if I could help you."

"What are they doing now?"

"They are afraid to leave him. William Rowan is afraid to leave him to himself. As soon as they are married, William seems to think people will forget about Janet. He doesn't know human nature any better than he knows God, though he is an elder. They will go away, he says, and begin life all over again. Of course Ralph will have to give up law. All his study will be wasted; but William thinks he can do better as an agent for the new automobiles. There's a kind of small car that William has taken the agency for in Queenborough."

"It will ruin his life. Can't you see, Grandmother, that it will ruin his life?"

Grandmother groaned as she sank heavily in a chair by the table. Ada's grief weighed on her mind as a catastrophe that some error of faith could not reconcile with God's providence. All this Ada saw in the stricken old face as she looked at it through the mist of anguish that floated between them.

"I know, I know, my child, but if I were you, I shouldn't try to speak to Ralph while he is with them. Though he is so quiet, he looks ready to fly off the helve." . . . The stick dropped to the floor as she reached out her trembling hand to seize the girl's dress, which slipped from her grasp when Ada turned away and darted out of the room.

While the old woman sat there alone a sudden vertigo rushed over her, as if every object in the room had become menacing and alive. To save herself from falling out of her chair, she clutched the edge of the table and looked up, startled, astonished, incredulous. In front of her yawned the bottomless pit, outside and beyond the infinite mercy. Then, just as the room and the earth were about to give way under her feet, she said aloud: "The Lord has never failed me. I am in the hands of the Lord." While the chant pealed through her mind, equilibrium was restored, faith balanced itself on its throne, a fresh infusion of energy surged through her veins, and her withered heart, she felt, put on greenness. For she had spoken only the truth. The Lord had never failed her. She was in the hands of the Lord.

E HAD come at the sound of her voice. He had broken away from the older men and had followed her through the door and down the slope of lawn to the willow beside the spring. The others had gone without him. She could see them moving in dark smudges over the grass and down the road to the village. On the other side, beyond the circle of love and terror that closed in about them, Aunt Meggie was scattering dough for her hens. But while they stood there in that invisible circle, they were safe, they were alone together, they were still lovers.

With her first glance at him, after they had joined hands and fled out of the house, she felt that something (was it hope?) had died in her bosom. He looked sullen, defiant, and years older since last night, and what was even harder to bear, he looked humbled. They had not only broken his spirit, they had humbled his pride. Worst of all, there was a flickering rage, like a dark fire, in his eyes, and his usually charming mouth sagged downward at the corners in a curve of brooding resentment. Yet never, not even in their happiest moments, had she loved him so much. Never until she had seen him humbled, but still defiant, had she felt that her heart was flaming with tenderness. Nothing could ever change that. Nothing could make her stop loving him. Oh, Ralph . . . Ralph . . . She had again that sense of struggling with an illusion, of being swept away by an invisible current.

"I am trapped," he said hoarsely, as if his mouth had gone dry. "They've got me in a trap. I can't get out. There's no way." He hesitated, swallowed hard, and repeated with smothered vehemence, "I'm trapped." His clothes looked as if he had slept in them, and the knuckles went red and white as he clenched his hands.

"I ought not to have come away last night," she said.

"You were right to come. I was making a fool of myself."

"They've gone back without you." It was like catching at a leaf in a flood.

"I told them I had to see you. I told them I wouldn't budge a step till I'd seen you." His mouth flattened into ugliness. "I told them . . ."

"What have they done to you?"

"They're making me give you up. They're making me marry Janet." He spoke in sharp bitten-off phrases, with a whistling sound in his throat. "They're all against me, even your father. It isn't that they believe anything happened last night. I kissed her, that was all. Anybody could kiss her. We weren't in her room five minutes. She pretended she couldn't find the photograph. Then she screamed at a mouse. But there wasn't any mouse."

"I know Janet. But why does she have to have you? There are plenty of others."

"She thought you wanted me." His laugh curled like a whip round the words. "That would be reason enough."

"Tell them. Let me tell them."

"They wouldn't listen. There're some things a man can't say, not even if he's trapped. Your father thinks I deserve anything. I reckon I do for being a fool."

"Can't we fight them? I'll fight them with you. I'll never give in." Her tears streamed down, and without wiping them away, without lifting a finger to her convulsed mouth, she broke into a sobbing moan, "Oh, Ralph . . . Ralph . . ."

While he looked down at her, violent yet helpless, he began trembling from head to foot, like a tree in a high wind. "Don't, Ada. . . . Don't, my darling. . . . I feel as if I'd like to kill something. But not an animal. I know how animals feel when they're trapped. I want to kill something human."

She clung to him, sobbing. "You're different. They've made you different."

"The difference is that I see what a fool I am. I've always been a fool, but now I know it—and I've dragged you into the mess."

"You haven't. You haven't dragged me into anything."

"Yes, I have, that's the worst of it. I love you. I've never loved anybody but you, and I've spoiled your life." His rage leaped out in a running fire and subsided as quickly into disgust. "It isn't fair. I'm no worse than others. Any boy who wants to kiss Janet can do it. I never did more than kiss her. You believe that, don't you, Ada?"

"I believe it."

She stared through tears at a soaring hawk, which swooped suddenly, flashed downward like a curved blade in the air, and seized a small bird—or it may have been one of Aunt Meggie's chickens—in its claws before it swept upward and onward. And she felt that the same claws had seized her heart out of her breast, and had swept away with it over the sunny land, over the tranquil blue of the hills. Until this moment of anguish, she had felt that she was a part of the Valley, of its religion, its traditions, its unspoken laws, as well as of its fields and streams and friendly mountains. But now her heart was torn up from its place, mangled and bleeding. Only a jagged scar was left in the spot where her life had been rooted.

"I must go," he said. "And you will despise me. You will love someone else. But . . . but we belong together . . . we've always belonged together. Nothing can change that."

"Nothing can change that." She looked round with a wild gaze, as a person looks on the verge of flight. "If only we could go away! But where? There isn't anywhere."

As he opened his lips, a sound between a groan and a sob strangled his words. There was a throbbing pulse in his voice, and when he spoke at last this throbbing made a formless tumult in her mind.

"Will you come with me now—this minute? Will you come up on Thunder Mountain? We could walk over the old Indian

trail to . . . somewhere. People have done things more reckless."
Then the flare of courage died down. "But we couldn't go far
enough. They could ruin us before I found work. The little I've
saved Mother has put away in the bank, and Mr. Rowan was
going to lend me the money to start on."

She nodded while her lips worked to keep back her sobs.
Dumbness had seized her. At the moment when she needed words
most, when she longed to pour out her heart, to utter vows, to
speak prophecies, dumbness had sealed her lips.

"There's no place we could go." The cry might have been
wrung from him by the turn of some inner screw. "There's no
room in the world for a fool." He crushed her to him till she felt
there was nothing left alive in her but the burning sense of that
pressure—nothing but his kiss, which was salt with tears, and the
extremity of her despair. "I love you," he said, and drawing away,
looked at her with that dreadful humility in his eyes. "I've loved
you all my life. I'll always love you. Not only this way, but every
way."

Again her lips worked convulsively, though no words would
come, only that straining to shape syllables. Animals must feel like
this, she thought, when they are trying to learn human speech.

His smile swept away the darkness from his face, and she felt
again that she had never loved him so much as in the moment
when she must lose him for ever. "I ought to fight," she told herself. "I ought to fight for what is mine." But how could she fight?
How could she fight an antagonist that had no reality?

She was alone now, alone with that phantom. He had kissed
her again and said more quietly, "I love you." He had taken her
hands, folded them on her bosom, and kissed them over and over.
While she was still struggling to speak he had turned away, and
then, abruptly, as if the earth had opened under his feet, he was
gone. One minute he had been there, his arms about her, his
mouth on hers, and the next minute she was alone with the empty
day and the shadows moving over the grass.

Far away, across an immeasurable vacancy, she heard the thin
piping call of her grandmother's voice. "Ada! Ada, where are

you?" No, she couldn't bear her grandmother—not now. As the call was repeated, she fled from the willow, past the henhouse and the garden fence and Aunt Abigail's cabin, to the stony hillside where sheep were cropping. But the hill was too near the heartbreaking blue of the sky. She must go away. She must go away from peace—from beauty. Only ugliness could help her—only ugliness that stabbed into her eyes. Only the world's pain could blunt the edge of her own pain. Turning her back on God's Mountain, she climbed the board fence and skirted the edge of the meadow until she came to the old field and the gully of red clay by Murderer's Grave. Here she dropped down on soil where nothing would grow, and stared into bright emptiness. She felt the warmth of the ground stealing over her, but it awoke only repulsion. Pain had thrust her out of the smiling meadow into this unhealed wound in the earth.

The soil fell away, without a blade of green, into the rutted basin of the old watercourse. Nobody knew the spot where the murderer was buried. But somewhere below those reddish furrows, which the rain had worn into grotesque shapes, lay the skeleton of a man who had been hanged because he had murdered a woman—his wife, the old story ran—though Aunt Abigail believed the woman had had her deserts because she had left her real husband to run off with her murderer. Not that it mattered. He was at rest now; his grave had sunk down out of sight. They had cast him out from the churchyard, but for nearly a hundred years he had taken his revenge as a scar on the landscape. That was the way life left its brand upon happiness. Wherever life was, there was evil and ugliness; there was misery.

"It is all over," she said aloud. "Everything is over." Her voice startled her, it was so toneless and grey—a drab voice. "It is all over," she said again, still speaking aloud. But the words meant nothing to her; the syllables were as empty as old wasps' nests. A deep instinct, stronger than speech, superior to knowledge, told her this could not have happened. To someone else perhaps, long ago in that half-obliterated past when savages roamed the mountains—long ago a boy named Ralph and a girl named Ada might have lived through such shame and suffering and bitterness. If it were true, and not merely an evil dream, her heart would feel broken; but now, after that first shock of agony, she felt nothing. There was only a numbness that began in her senses and closed in slowly about that beating pulse in her head.

On the other side of the ravine Toby Waters was crawling on his stomach over the ground. Being an idiot was more terrible than anything in the world. It was worse than death; it was worse than losing your lover. It was so terrible, being an idiot, that she pressed the thought deeper and deeper, like a thorn, into her consciousness. If only the thorn would pierce sharply enough, it might bring relief. It might even separate the old past where such things happened from the new present in which she was dreaming about them. In her dream there was Murderer's Grave; there was the green valley; there was Toby Waters crawling toward her; there were the hovel and the pigsty and the squealing pigs and the chickens scratching among refuse. And, in some strange way, she seemed to deny her own suffering while she dwelt on the dirt and squalor and horror and inescapable misery of life.

An unknown bird with a white breast flew overhead. Was it a dove or a hawk? Her gaze followed it in its flight toward Thunder Mountain, and she remembered the Indian trail on one of the timbered ridges. One might live for weeks, people said, on the berries and roots in the forest. Then, suddenly, like the shadow of a beast, pain sprang out on her, clutching, tearing, devouring. . . . Everything was over. There was nothing to expect, nothing to fear, nothing to dread. Flinging herself on the ground, she bruised her bosom against the hard furrows. All that remained now was waiting—waiting for nothing. Twenty years . . . thirty years . . . fifty years might be ahead of her. The Fincastles and the Craigies were long-lived. She was only twenty now, and she might live to be ninety! And she had not fought for her own. She had yielded without a struggle to this tyranny of opinion, of the way people think about things. It was only air, after all. Words are only stale air—yet they had conquered her.

She had been conquered by a mere mouthing. There are some things a man can't say. Who had said that? Even if a woman is to blame, a man cannot accuse her. Who had said that? Not Ralph? Yes, it was Ralph. It was Ralph who had said he couldn't accuse Janet. He had sacrificed himself, and her also, to a last rag of chivalry, to a tradition in which he did not even believe. And her father! Her father was a martyr to truth, but it was his own truth, not hers, not another's. Oh, Ralph . . . Ralph . . . While she cried the name without sound, her anguish increased until it filled all the hollows. The June meadows and Smiling Creek and Murderer's Grave and the emptiness in her own mind became only stark outlines of pain—mere skeletons of what had once been a living and moving world.

An eternity (or was it a minute?) afterwards a voice whined over her head. Turning on the ground, she saw the idiot's face bending above her, holding out hands that were filled with purple larkspur, torn up by the roots and already beginning to wilt. "Sugar, sugar," he drooled, offering her the flowers. "Toby wants sugar."

Before springing to her feet, she sat motionless for an instant, as if she were only a larger lump of clay, and stared up into the grinning face, where yellow teeth protruded like fangs, and a crooked leer slanted up to the squinting eyes. Almost he had touched her. Never before had she been so close to his filthy clothes and his evil stench. Horror, less gnawing but more loathsome than pain, seized her. Yet he was a creature like herself, she thought, more repulsive than any animal, but born, as she and an animal were born, to crave joy, to suffer loss, and to know nothing beyond. His mother, she found herself thinking vacantly, ought to do something about him. She ought to make him clean himself before he came out to beg in the road. "No sugar to-day," she said sternly, warding off his approach because his acrid odour, like the odour of a bear, sickened her. Then she saw his eyes water with tears and his mouth stutter, and she added hurriedly, "There will be sugar to-morrow. Toby shall have a sugar cake in the morning."

Leering joyously, he held out the larkspur, which scattered and dropped to die on the ground. No, she couldn't touch them. Even the flowers would be tainted by that foul smell. Nothing could be worse than that, it was true. The village ought to take care of him, her father said. Yet his mother had buried two other children, both idiots. Mrs. Waters had a father, an old man, still living in Panther's Gap. He had married an idiot girl from the almshouse, and they had four idiot sons, who worked in the cornfield. Once when Ada was little she had ridden by the place behind her father on his old bay mare, and she had seen three of these boys gathering sunflower seeds for the chickens. They had frightened her so by the faces they made that she had slipped down from the mare's back. If Bess, the mare, had not been wise enough to stop, her father had said, there might have been broken bones for Doctor Updike to set. But people couldn't do anything about idiots. It was God's law, Grandmother said, that married people, no matter whether they were half-wits or not, must bring all the children they could into the world to share in the curse that was put upon Adam and Eve.

Standing there, while Toby ran back to the hovel, she felt the sharp revulsion of her senses deaden for an instant her intolerable heartache. Life was like that. Life contained no security. Horror waited everywhere to pounce upon happiness, as the hawk had pounced upon the small bird. Under her feet there was the sterile clay, encircled by the flower-sprinkled valley which shaded from palest azure to deepest violet. Beyond the smaller valley the light was already changing on the lower hills, where noon hesitated before passing. Ugliness she could bear, even horror, but not beauty. Not the beauty that was like a knife in her heart, the beauty that made her believe in the joy she had lost without ever possessing.

Hours later, when she circled the field, the light had changed

again, and afternoon brooded over the valley. Within its clustering oaks, the old brick house was folded in quiet. The birds were
silent in the trees, the leaves had ceased to quiver on their stems,
and the shadows were so transparent that they might have been
merely darker waves of the sunshine. It looked a place of happiness, she thought bitterly; but the lost harmony of mood and
scene was sarcely nearer to her now than was the girl she had
been yesterday. For that girl seemed as remote and unreal as a
snow image. She had never known pain, she had never known
cruelty, she had never known life.

As she crossed the lawn her father came out of the garden
with a hoe in his hand. "There are times," he said, "when the
pen is heavier than the hoe." Though he was stricken to the
heart, she knew, he could still smile his inward, dreaming, faintly
ironic smile.

"Father, why did you let them ruin Ralph's life?"

"You will understand better when you are older, Ada. But
Ralph's life is not ruined, nor is yours. You are both young, and
to the young nothing, not even ruin, has finality. Don't lose your
courage too soon. The future still belongs to you."

She shook her head. "No, I haven't anything left. Nothing
again will ever make any difference."

Inside the house, she heard her mother's voice, soft, eager, yet
vaguely apprehensive. "Is that you, Ada? I have not seen you to-
day. Where have you been?"

"I've been out in the fields, Mother. As soon as I've washed
my face and hands, I'll come to read to you."

Peering in from the back porch, Grandmother beckoned to
her. "You haven't eaten a bite, my dear. I've saved some cold
buttermilk."

Ada slipped noiselessly past her mother's door and went out
on the porch. "No, I don't want anything."

"Couldn't you swallow a little of your mother's tapioca?"

"I don't want anything."

When she had finished hanging out a dishcloth, Grandmother
turned and looked at the girl from under the horn rims of her

spectacles. There was sympathy in her face, but there was a tremendous power also, the equanimity of unruffled conviction.

"Try not to take this too hard, my dear child. God would not have sent you a trial of faith if it were not for your good. You won't make it easier by taking it too hard."

"I take it the only way I can, Grandmother."

"Pray over it, and try not to be rebellious. The Lord knows what is best for you."

"I'll never pray again. I'll never, never pray again as long as I live."

A shudder ran over Grandmother's massive frame. So she had shuddered in church when Dugald Adcock had turned away from the bread and wine of the Lord's Supper.

"Bend your will, my child!" she cried out in fear. "Bend your will before it is broken!"

For an instant Ada stared dumbly away into space. When her voice came at last it was barely louder than the whimpering moan of a small animal in a trap.

"I don't care," she said. "I don't care what God does to me." While she dragged her body, which felt cold and dead, upstairs to her room, she thought wearily, "It will always be like this. No matter how long it lasts, everything will be nothing."

ARY EVELYN was dying. For weeks she had not moved from her bed, but had lain propped on pillows while she gazed through the open windows, where the ivy had been trimmed back to let in the light. Outside, she could see the light drift on the grass and the sunflowers, heavy with brown seed, sway and bend over the garden fence. In the room her invalid's chair stood empty, pushed into a corner but not put away out of sight. Hour after hour, day after day, week after week, her family listened anxiously to a murmur so thin and soft that it might have been the voice of the stillness. Not only the birds, but even the insects, were hushed in the trees; the wind made no stir as it passed on; only this whisper, rapid, fugitive, yet strangely alive, gushed out from the pallid lips and became a part of the silence. The bed, the room, the house, the whole of life, were saturated with the mingled smell of mustard and camphor. The odour of pain! Ada thought. As long as she lived that smell would always mean to her the odour of pain—of the dying flesh, of the spirit struggling to release itself from the clay, of loss, grief, helpless pity, and heartbreak.

"Is it time for her medicine, Grandmother?"

"I tried to give it, but she can take so little."

"Does she know what she is saying? Does she know when she smiles or frowns?"

"I think so sometimes. Anyway, she is at peace. She has put her trust in her Redeemer."

"She is trying to tell us something. Oh, Grandmother, what is she trying to tell us?"

"I think she is wandering. Perhaps you can catch the words, John."

"Can you hear, Father? Oh, Father, she is trying so hard! It makes her cry, she is trying so hard."

Still clasping his wife's hand, John Fincastle leaned over with his ear close to the fluttering breath. "Mary Evelyn! Mary Evelyn!"

Light broke in her face. Her head raised itself from the pillow and turned slightly in his direction. Then it fell back. Her eyes opened and looked through him, and through the room and the trees and the hills, as if they were all figures of shadow. While she looked, she spoke in a new voice.

"I have been happy," she said clearly.

Grandmother measured out a dose of digitalis and rising softly, held a towel under Mary Evelyn's chin. "She has swallowed a little, if only she is able to keep it down." But the medicine came up almost immediately, and the old woman's hand trembled as she wiped away the stains from the moving lips. "Doctor Updike says there may be no change for weeks," she whispered, "but the doctor from Queenborough was less hopeful."

How often had she heard those words? Ada asked herself. When and where were they first spoken? How long had they sat here, waiting through days that had no hours, through hours that had no minutes, flat, timeless, everlasting, for her mother to die? Was it yesterday? Was it to-day? Was it even to-morrow? Her back was toward the window, and she saw only the rays of sunshine that trickled in through the leaves and settled in a still pool on her mother's face. Near the head of the bed, beside the bottles of medicine on the candlestand, her grandmother was seated with her knees far apart, erect, tireless, watchful. Her grey hair straggled in wisps from under a cap that was now slightly askew, like the wrinkles across her brow, but at eighty-three she was still calm, austere, indomitable. Within the shadow of the headboard, John Fincastle's features seemed to blend with this outline, though the serenity in his face was shattered by grief. To her father, Ada knew, death was a part of life, to be accepted with the animal faith which was nobler than vain conflicts with nature. To her grandmother, death was an act of

God, and so justified. Yet they both valued existence; they had lived more happily because they had believed, each in a different way, that life was something more than mere living.

Her mother was now sleeping quietly, so quietly that fear shot through Ada's mind while she watched. "Is it natural, Grandmother?" she whispered. "She's barely breathing."

"Yes, she's sleeping. You'd better go upstairs and lie down."

"I can't. I can't leave her." In years to come she would reproach herself for every minute she spent away from her mother's side, she would suffer over every remembered neglect. "But you need rest yourself," she urged in so low a tone that the old woman was obliged to guess what she was saying.

"No, I must keep watch. Old people can do without sleep." While her stooping spine sprang upright, she said again, "I must watch. I can bide my time."

Horace, fourteen years old now, if a day, and almost as rheumatic as Grandmother, padded in from the hall, raised his eyes with a wondering glance, and lay down on the strip of rug by the bed. They wouldn't keep him long, Grandmother feared, though a foxhound belonging to her husband had lived nearly seventeen years. It was seldom that he left the house, and then only for an excursion into the unmown grass or to the roots of a tree. "I declare that dog is almost human," the old woman murmured. "I believe he understands every word that we say." She laid her hand on his head, and he thumped his tail so gently that it was merely another vibration.

I wonder whether Ralph knows? Ada thought. But Ralph and her unhappy love were shapes without substance. When she tried to think of him, he evaporated into a mist. She could say to herself, Three years ago he married Janet, and it meant nothing. When she said, My heart is broken, that also meant nothing. The only thing that now lived for her was the slow dying, day after day, of her mother.

"Grandmother, isn't there a change?" Doesn't she seem to know more?"

"She is still sleeping, my dear. Doctor Updike says she doesn't suffer even when she comes back."

"If only she wouldn't frown, if only she wouldn't cry to herself."

So it had been since the beginning of July. So it would be, the physicians thought, for months longer, perhaps into the autumn. But at the end of August she died very quietly, alone in the room with her husband and old Horace. Grandmother was making a fresh mustard plaster, Aunt Meggie was warming a little milk in a saucepan on the kitchen stove, and Ada had slipped out of doors for a breath of the late afternoon. At the door the girl had beckoned to Horace, but he had refused to leave the rug by the bedside. John Fincastle had glanced round and smiled at his daughter, and for an instant it had seemed to him that his wife's fingers played as softly as the touch of a fern over the back of his hand. Then the pale golden light of the afterglow had shone into the room, and somewhere outside, far up in the leaves, there was the startled cheep of a bird. At the call, Mary Evelyn opened her eyes and looked at him with a flash of her old animation. "It will be dark soon," she said in a cheerful voice, before sinking back into a sleep from which she never awoke. For a few minutes he sat there beside her, apprehensive yet hopeful, while he listened to her breathing, which seemed to grow fainter and fainter, like a breeze that is dying away in the distance. Even then, after it had entirely ceased, without effort and without horror of the death struggle, he did not realize that she was dead. Grandmother, coming in with the plaster, found him still holding Mary Evelyn's hand.

"I thought I heard somebody call," the old woman said, "and I came as quick as I could." Then, as she reached the bedside, she pushed her son away, and he saw her hands, knotted and worn with healing, pass over his wife's bosom.

What is it, John Fincastle asked himself, that has enabled human beings to build their indestructible fallacies about death?

Is it hope? Is it fear? Is it the long mingling of both? As a part of life, perhaps, one could accept death without bitterness, as the only part of life that is endowed with finality.

With his mind he had acquiesced; he had triumphed over belief and denial. But one does not believe, one does not doubt, with the mind alone. The heart must be convinced, and the blood stream, and the nerves. "If only I had known," he thought, confronting the universe, where not a gleam, not a flash, lighted the darkness. For there was much, there were so many things, that he had not known, that now he could never know. He had thought of himself as strong; he had thought of Mary Evelyn as weak; yet he felt to-night that, in some mysterious way, he had renewed his strength in her weakness. He had listened so long to the murmurous flow of her voice that he could not think in the silence. His freedom was so vast that he was lost in the midst of it.

Beyond the open window, it seemed to him that the very brightness of the stars was dim and tarnished with grief. "Mary Evelyn! Mary Evelyn!" he cried without sound into a void that was bottomless. There was no answer. He had not expected an answer. Though her going had drained the world of life, she would vanish from his sight and his touch without pausing to look back. "Mary Evelyn!" he cried over again and aloud, trying to reach her while she was still so near, before she had passed entirely out of the universe that contained them both. But there was no return from the abyss that was loss, no stir, no shadow, not so much as a vibration of light. She had left nothing behind her but this intolerable stillness.

Yet in my flesh shall I see God, Grandmother Fincastle was thinking, while a few tears rolled over her eyelids and down on her furrowed cheeks. Even now, Mary Evelyn was beholding the face of God, though her body would wait in its grave, as in a bed, for the Day of Judgment. How could one mourn when one remembered that incorruptible glory? When one remembered the promise that the righteous shall be caught up to Christ in the clouds, that they shall be set on His right hand, and shall join in the judging of reprobate angels and men? A spasm of pain convulsed Grandmother's features. But what of John? What of her son? Where would he stand among the reprobate angels and men? Would Mary Evelyn be asked to judge her own husband? And could she, who had loved him so passionately, be happy after he was judged and cast out? Could she be satisfied even in the company of innumerable saints and angels, "but especially in the immediate vision and fruition of God the Father, of our Lord Jesus Christ, and of the Holy Spirit, to all eternity"? Who could answer? Could even the Larger Catechism cast light into that darkness? But it was God's will, and so one must believe. One must see with the eye of faith, not with the eye of flesh, as her husband had said. And, meanwhile, the work of the house waited. She must leave salvation to God, and remind Meggie not to let her dish of batter bread burn while she laid out the dead.

"If only I had stayed with her every minute," Ada told herself in remorse, for she felt that her heart was breaking over again. "If only I hadn't neglected her because I was unhappy. If only I hadn't let myself think of Ralph when she needed me."

But it was useless to try not to think of Ralph when Ralph was still the very pulse of her thought. If she tore him out, there would be nothing left of herself. He had been a part of her happiness; he was now a part of her sorrow. She could not escape him by wishing. Not seeing him did not alter her love. Mother had wanted her to marry Ross Greenlee, but she could never think of any man but Ralph as her lover. Yet while her mother lay dying her self-reproach was so bitter that she would have married anyone, no matter how old or ugly he was, if only her mother had approved of him. "Oh, Mother, Mother!" she called aloud, biting back the cry before it reached the ears of her grandmother. Nothing, not even Ralph, not even her own faithfulness, would be too much to give if it would bring back her mother.

But life was here, and the will was toward life. Nobody, not even the old, not even the despairing, wished to come to an end in time or in eternity. So her grandmother said, and her grandmother must know. Ada wondered now why her father believed that fear of the end was an ignoble delusion. Surely he also, like other persons, sound or unsound, must still wish to live on. Well, whatever came to her must be borne. "If broken hearts could kill," Grandmother had reminded her, "the earth would be as dead as the moon."

Dressed in ill-fitting black, tearless and composed, Ada stood in the parlour, which was thrown open for the funeral, and thanked the neighbours who had flocked to the manse. The road from the village was crowded with vehicles, and with those too poor to own a horse and buggy who came walking. Many of them had brought mourning garments to offer Meggie and Ada, and closer friends, such as Mrs. Black and the Rowans and Doctor Updike and the Melroses and old Mrs. Tiller, stole across the hall and into the dimly lighted chamber, where Mary Evelyn, young again and indescribably radiant, lay in her coffin. "She couldn't look that way," Mrs. Black had whispered to Ada, "if she hadn't liked what she found over there." "My boy has come to the funeral," Mrs. McBride murmured, softened by death. "I've always told him he loved Mary Evelyn better than his own mother."

In the churchyard Ada saw only the open grave, and heard only the clods of earth falling, falling. Her father's arm felt as fleshless as a bleached bone in her grasp, and it seemed to her that the universe, with all that it contained, was pared down to a skeleton. All the Fincastle skeletons were lying there, within that rusty railing, under the old sycamore. The row of sandstone slabs, as yellow as old teeth and stained with the droppings of birds, stood upright among the periwinkle and ivy. Oh, why did she think morbid thoughts at such moments? Her grandmother, by her side, could keep her mind properly governed and fixed upon the hope of a joyful resurrection. When the last clod had been shovelled in, the flowers had been placed on the fresh grave,

and Ada had driven home in a borrowed carriage with her father, her grandmother, and her weeping aunt, she cried out
wildly that she could not bear the blank horror of loss, the un-
endurable flatness of grief.

CHAPTER 13

✿ ✿ ✿ ✿ ✿ ✿ ✿HE next afternoon, when Ada was in the kitchen
✿ ⎡ ⎤ ✿ ironing a cap for her grandmother, she heard
✿ | | ✿ Ralph's voice speaking to Horace. Handing the
✿ | T | ✿ iron to Aunt Abigail, she went through the din-
✿ | | ✿ ing-room and into the hall as he entered the
✿ ⎣ ⎦ ✿ front door.
✿ ✿ ✿ ✿ ✿ ✿ ✿

"I must see you alone, Ada. I'm going away, and I must see you alone."

"Come into Mother's chamber. Nobody's there."

Together they crossed the threshold, and he helped her unfasten the closed shutters. "Father has slept on the sofa in his library, but I don't like to feel that the room is deserted."

"You know I cared for her," he said.

"I know." Turning away from the window, she looked into his face and saw how much he had changed.

"I had to see you."

"I thought you'd come."

"It's the first time I've been back since . . ."

"I know." She dropped into her grandmother's winged chair, while he paced restlessly from the empty fireplace to the open window, and then back again from the window to the fireplace.

"I sometimes thought your mother understood better than anyone else."

"I know." The word fluttered like a dead leaf from her lips, and she could think of nothing to add.

"I ought to have stood up against them," he burst out. "Janet had to marry somebody, and she thought I was the easiest."

"I know." All this seemed to have occurred in another period of time, when people did absurd things for absurd reasons.

"The child wasn't mine. I want you to know that."

"The child?" The echo floated back from some void that was windless and dark.

"I suppose there was really a child. She said she lost it before it was born. But it wasn't mine."

She bowed her head, weeping. "Nothing seems to make any difference now. Nothing makes any difference but the thought that Mother . . . oh, Mother . . ."

"She would want you to be happy."

"She believed in happiness. Feeling meant life to her. It is only in the heart, she used to say, that anything really happens."

He looked round, startled and attentive, as if he had heard a bell ringing. "Did she say that?"

"Can't you hear her voice?"

"I'll always hear it. Now I must go. But I had to see you."

"Of course you had to see me." As he smiled down on her, she felt that she was slowly coming to life again. "You couldn't have gone without seeing me."

"I've been living in hell," he said, as if the words were forced out by torture. "That's why I couldn't come before. If this ever ends, and it's obliged to end some way, I'll come again."

"It almost broke Father's heart when you gave up the law to sell automobiles."

"And your heart?"

"I didn't care so much about that."

"You've never asked about Janet?"

"No, I'll never ask you about Janet."

"You thought she wanted me."

"Yes, I thought so."

"If she did, it was soon over. We quarrel now all day and the better part of the night. Whenever she finds a man with money, she will leave me and marry him. What fools people are when they think they can make two lives belong together by saying words over them."

"It's funny," she sighed indifferently, for the glow of life had flickered out again, "the things we used to believe in. But you were never bitter before."

"I never had need to be. By the time I am free to come back to you, I may be so hardened you won't know me."

"You couldn't be that. No, you could never be that."

The derision faded from his tone. "You ought to be happy, Ada," he said. "You ought to fall in love with a better man."

"I may be happy again, but there will never be another man."

"If I'm ever free, will you go away with me? I mean go across the world to some other place?" His voice broke, and under the tenderness, she heard for the first time the stifled cry of his longing.

"But for Father and Grandmother, I'd go away with you to-morrow," she said. "I'd go with you anywhere."

"Then it's a promise?"

"Yes, it's a promise."

As she waited for him to speak again, he bent over suddenly, kissed her lips, cheeks, and throat, and then breaking away without a word, ran out of the room and the house.

She heard the flight of his footsteps on the porch, the millstone, the drive, and the road, dying at last into silence. From the echo in her mind, she could not tell whether the footsteps were going or coming. But it seemed to her that she should hear them eternally passing in and out of her life. Then, gradually, while the faint reverberations persisted, she became aware that activity was no longer suspended, that the breath of life was flowing back into the house. A board creaked, a clock struck, a door opened and shut, there was an almost inaudible movement, a slow pulsation, from the cellar below to the closed rooms overhead. As the pulsations grew longer, all the scattered threads of sound seemed to be gathered into a single strand of existence. She heard her father cross the floor of his library and go out on the porch. Ever since the funeral he had wandered about as if he were searching for something. There was the measured fall of his tread, and looking through the side window, she watched him walk over the grass and stoop to pick up his hoe at the garden gate. Why was it, she wondered, that digging in the ground appeared to comfort him more than the wisdom in books? His nerves, he said, not his mind, were soothed by the smell of the earth, or by the even strokes of the ax or the hammer.

The diminishing nest egg he had borrowed from his life insurance was withdrawn from the bank and used to pay the modest expenses of Mary Evelyn's funeral, and before the summer was over another sandstone slab was placed in the churchyard. Even then, Ada felt, something of her mother remained, some unseen presence, or some familiar fragrance of cinnamon-roses in the new stillness. There were moments when this sense of a lingering spirit became so vivid that she would go into the chamber and call "Mother!" in heartbroken appeal. Mary Evelyn, not her way of living, had vanished; and this bond of personality stronger than death held the family together.

Slowly, almost as if it were unwanted or unrecognized, the movement of the house renewed itself and went on again. Unfinished tasks were taken up and completed, work was planned and discussed with interest, meals were cooked and eaten with the old relish. Though they were poor, they were not too poor to wear turned mourning; they were not, as Ada reminded herself, as poor as the poor McAllisters. In September the school term began, and sufficient pupils would provide money for the taxes and the next payment on the mortgage. The garden would yield them a living, even in winter, for Aunt Meggie and old Aunt Abigail, who had to be brought over in a wheelbarrow by her son Marcellus, were wise in methods of canning and drying. Aunt Meggie was always able to exchange eggs or young chickens for coffee and sugar at Mr. Robinson's store, and Grandmother's trembling fingers spun wool into yarn and knitted yarn into jerseys, stockings, and petticoats for the winter. Clothes were scarce, but occasionally there would be money for a bolt of cotton cloth or red flannel or printed calico, and then Ada would make house dresses and underwear. John Fincastle's coats and trousers were turned so often that they had become a problem for the women, though not for him. He had never known what he wore, Aunt Meggie insisted, not even when he was pastor of the largest congregation in Queenborough. Money he required to pay taxes, to meet the mortgage, and to buy Horace a license. For the rest he had never failed, he assured them, to find enough to eat in the ground. But when the need became acute, he would select a few books from the remnant of his library, and set out with Mr. Rowan to sell his precious volumes to a professor at Washington and Lee University. For the first few weeks after Mary Evelyn's death, he had turned to the hoe and the spade as an appeasement of grief; but when autumn came and school was opened in the parlour, he went back to the lonely work of his lifetime.

"I know I could make my way in Queenborough," Ada would urge. "So many girls are going to the city. I know I could find work and help pay off the mortgage."

"Not as long as I last, my child," Grandmother would beg, with a catch in her old voice. "It won't be long now, and I want my children about me when I come to the end."

"What would the manse be like with nothing young in it?" Aunt Meggie would ask wistfully. "I'd rather do with less and keep the family together."

"That's going, too, like everything else I was used to," Grandmother sighed. "Even families don't hold together any longer."

"Well, I'll stay," Ada said, but she said it regretfully. There were moments when she felt the stirring call of the unknown— of anything that was different. I know I could make my own way, she would tell herself, and besides, Ralph would be near me in Queenborough. Then the strong pull of roots in the soil would hold her steadfast. I couldn't leave Grandmother, and if Grandmother were not here, I couldn't leave Father.

When she looked back from a distant time, the years immediately after her mother's death appeared to have flowed into a single year. She could not separate them in memory, or if she separated them, it was merely by the thought, Ralph wrote to me often then, or Ralph came back to Ironside, but I seldom saw him. Or again, That was the spring Horace died, and we buried him in the corner of the garden where the day lilies bloom, or, That was the winter a fox ate Aunt Meggie's Rhode Island Red rooster.

From the beginning, John Fincastle had stood aside while war hysteria swept by in a whirlwind. "A moral pestilence," he had said, "and it will pass as a pestilence." Only when America was wavering, and he refused to sing warlike hymns in his classes and to teach his pupils that God was on the side of the Allies, did the villagers begin to withdraw their children. Not all of them, to be sure, for some who had overlooked heresy were able to regard "pacifism" as merely another mental oddity, but these were invariably the poorer parents, unable to pay the fee for tuition.

On a bright Sunday morning soon after America had entered the war, Ada met Ralph's mother as the congregation streamed out of church and over the flagstone walk to the gate. "That was an inspiring sermon," the older woman said, drawing the girl aside, while John Fincastle passed on with his mother and sister. "I wish Ralph could have heard it."

"Aren't they preaching that way in Queenborough?"

"Not with the same zeal. Churches grow lukewarm in cities. But we are blessed beyond most congregations, even in the upper Valley. Mr. Black is as tender as a father with the afflicted, but his sermons on the war are fiery with the wrath of God. There won't be many skulkers in Ironside after this morning. I am proud to think," she added, pursing her lips, "that my boy will volunteer as a private if he does not get into an officers' training-camp. He applied the very minute war was declared. You remember he always said he would be ahead of the draft."

It seemed to Ada that her whole life—or was it only her heart? —shuddered and sank. But she had known it would come like this, that they would go into the war, that Ralph would be one of the first to volunteer, that he might be killed over in France. Regret was, of course, the wrong emotion to feel. War must be splendid, a righteous war, or Mr. Black, a saint in everyday life, would not be so certain God was behind us. Clergymen seemed to want war more than most other persons, but everybody, so far as she could see, wanted to fight Germany—everybody except her father, who was condemned, it appeared, to be upon the deserted side of every mass movement. "I know Ralph wants to go," she answered, and prayed silently, "Oh, God, let him come back!"

"I hope this will be a lesson to Janet," Mrs. McBride continued. "Janet has not made the right sort of wife. But it won't matter so much now that he has had to give up his career. In war," she rolled the phrase on her tongue, "we are all ready to make sacrifices."

To make sacrifices! How she hated the word, Ada thought, as she slipped out of the churchyard, while tears clouded the spring landscape. Ahead of her, she saw her grandmother, supported by her father and Aunt Meggie, moving, in all the luxury of martyrdom, up the steep road to the manse. Though the walk was torture to the old woman, she could not be induced either to stay away from church or to drive on the Sabbath.

"Somehow, I don't seem able to get excited about this war," she was confessing, as Ada joined them. "War isn't real to me as long as it leaves a window-pane in your house. I recollect as well as if 'twere yesterday the skirmish that shattered every pane of glass in the manse. Well, I'm thankful that General Hunter is safely buried and not on the side of the Germans."

"It is hard to understand," Ada said, "how God can want war." Pressing her father's arm, she added consolingly, "Even if all the children stop coming, Father, you will have that much more time for your book." But she was thinking sadly, "And fewer people than ever will read it."

John Fincastle smiled and patted her hand. "Yes, I'll have more time and fewer readers than ever. Still, my concern is with Reality alone, and I shan't worry if the whole world of appearances goes mad over killing. As long as it leaves my potatoes in the ground, we shall be able to get on without starving. But there are concrete problems that only the hoe can solve."

Around them the meadows were sprinkled with flowers, the fringed willows were silver-green by the brooks, and the tranquil blue of God's Mountain was bathed in a light that refreshed the eyes. Yet here also, Ada thought, hatred and bloodshed, the torch and the scalping knife, the gun and the bayonet, had once raged and passed and were now almost forgotten.

Where was Ralph? she wondered. Had the war taken him already, or would he come back to her? She had seen him seldom and at long intervals in the last three years. Whenever they met, he had spoken of Janet in a kind of sullen fury that reminded her of a brushwood fire. The appeal of the flesh had recoiled into aversion. There was no peace, he had said, they quarrelled like bluejays. Janet was going with other men, and his only hope was that, sooner or later, she would find one rich enough to give her the luxuries she demanded. She was a favourite in the less dignified circles of Queenborough; but Queenborough was a small place, and she craved the excitement of New York or Hollywood. Once she had been photographed for a moving picture, and it was soon evident that the edges of her beauty were too soft for the screen. The mouth and chin of Queen Victoria, even without the royal virtues, had ceased to be an advantage.

"I have learned why men kill women," he had declared vehemently at their last meeting. "I don't mean that I want to kill a woman, simply that I understand why men do it so often."

"After all," Ada had sighed, "she may never find the man she is looking for."

"I've thought of that. If I had proof of what I know without proof, I shouldn't wait to let the grass grow under my feet. But you still have to have evidence in Virginia, and I can't afford to go West. Well, there's one thing certain, if the choice is offered me between living with Janet and fighting the Germans, I'll choose war with a vengeance."

"You sound like Grandmother. We tell Grandmother that she really likes war."

That was five months ago, and Grandmother was becoming more militant. She approved of a righteous war, and what war could be more righteous than the war to defend little Belgium?

For the second time, John Fincastle was snatched by his mother from the outcast company of reprobate souls. A quarter of a century before she had shielded him from the penalties imposed by a God-fearing village. In the summer of 1917, she towered, impregnable as a fortress, between him and the suspicion that he preferred an unrighteous peace. Too infirm to stand, but busily knitting for devastated France, she presided impressively over the first Red Cross meetings in Ironside.

"Ralph is a second lieutenant now. He has his commission," the old woman said proudly one day in September, as she was assisted down from Judge Melrose's buggy. "He wrote to his mother from Fort M——."

To his mother! Suddenly Ada felt that the soft breeze had turned to blown smoke in her throat.

"Your grandmother says she will be eighty-six to-morrow," Judge Melrose remarked flatteringly before he stepped back into his buggy, "but I tell her she has more pith and sap left in her still than many who are yet in the prime of life."

"But for my legs," Grandmother's old complaint slipped readily off her tongue, "I'd be as good as I ever was."

"You used to be a sufferer, I recollect, from lumbago."

"Aye, aye, but I've been spared that. Now 'tis mostly seated in my knees, though in summer I still manage to get about."

"How can I stand it any longer?" Ada asked herself desperately while she helped Grandmother into the house. "How can I stand it?"

The six years since she had lost Ralph seemed to stretch away into a blind alley, and down this alley, strewn with the dust of old summers, she saw her own figure diminishing, as if it were the shape of a stranger. If only I'd known, she thought in despair. If only I'd known what it all meant! If only I'd known what life is!

I T W A S October when he came. The leaves had turned before falling, and the hills were changing their colour. One morning, on her way to the springhouse, she looked back and saw him enter the gate and pause an instant in the walk to the porch.

"Ralph!" she called in a voice that was tremulous with joy, while she ran toward him. Was it the khaki that made him look hard and lean and red-brown and years older? Even his skin and hair had acquired this hardness like bronze. Then, as he reached her and she was enveloped in his disarming smile, she saw that he wore the look, strong, free, happy, of a man who has escaped.

"I didn't know," she cried softly, "that you were coming."

"I didn't know myself till yesterday. What was the good of coming when I couldn't be with you? It's worse seeing you at a distance than not seeing you any more."

"Oh, no, Ralph, oh, no." She was in his arms, her face hidden against him.

"It is for me. I can't help how I'm made."

"Then why did you come?"

"I couldn't help that either. I've only three days of leave left, and I had promised Amory Morgan to spend it hunting with him on Thunder Mountain. He has a cabin a little way up on Eagle Ridge, and he has sent a man from Teesdale to put it in order. Then he was taken ill two days ago. They think it's pneumonia, and he has had to go to a hospital in Queenborough. But the food is all there, and he gave me his key in case I wanted to go up without him. I thought of asking Charlie Draper. Is he home on leave now?" He talked breathlessly, as if he had been

159

running, while he kept his eyes away from her face as she raised her head and looked up at him.

"I don't know. Oh, I wish you could stay here!"

"What's the use? I couldn't be with you without starting a row. What a hell of a world, God!"

"But you'll be free some day."

"Well, Janet has found her man. She wants to be free now as much as I do. But he has a wife, and his wife must get a divorce too. It sounds like squaring the circle. Anyway, Janet is doing her best. She's in Reno at this minute, so far as I know. I believe she's been there for six months. She may have been there when I last saw you. It's no use trying to keep up with her. All I ask," he broke out vehemently, "is not to have her so near I feel the impulse to kill her!"

"Ralph, Ralph!"

"You don't know. You couldn't know the kind of hell another woman can make for the man who is tied to her."

"I know enough." She clung to him in fear and tenderness.

"Well, it can't last for ever." His voice rang out on a triumphant note. "We're going over. We don't know just when. That's a secret. But we're going over." His face was glowing with an emotion that seemed to thrust her away, and for an instant she felt that she was dying of love and despair in his arms.

"And you're glad. You're glad that you're going."

"Who wouldn't be? This war is a great thing. But for you, I shouldn't have a regret. It will be rotten luck if I have to wait for you till I come home—if I ever come home."

"If you ever come home!" His smile had sunk into her heart, she felt, and was drawing out the pain and the bitterness.

"Oh, I'll come home," he rejoined in gay derision. "You'll see that I'll come home." Still laughing, but on a deeper note, he caught her to him again and kissed her lips, while it seemed to her that all living had been distilled into some pure essence of life. It was madness, she knew, but a blessed madness.

When he released her from his arms, she sank on the bench under the old willow, and he stood looking down at her. "I've been thinking a lot in the last months," he said almost shyly, and she realized that the sullen anger had passed out of his mind. "I've an idea—it keeps getting bigger—that we're beginning all over again. This is a fresh start. The war can't last for ever, and when I come home, we'll forget everything that has happened and go ahead just as we planned. You'll meet me at the dock. Maybe I'll be free before I sail, but if I'm not, we'll be married the very minute I'm home again. I'll find that job as somebody's secretary and take the law course at Washington and Lee just as I've wanted to do all my life. We'll make up the six years we've lost. We'll be as free then as we ever were."

How like him that sounded! How careless, short-sighted, splendid, and irresistible to the heart of a lover. For he loved her! Never had she doubted, never could she doubt when she looked into his eyes and heard his voice, that he loved her.

"It must be over soon. And you will write to me?"

"Oh, I'll write, but I can never put anything in a letter. We wasted six years and you don't look unhappy." He stooped over her and plunged his hand into her thick upspringing hair, until she felt that tiny waves of delight rippled after his touch. "I suppose it's the way your features all seem to be expecting something to happen—your eyebrows and the corners of your mouth and that queer hopeful smile, like your father's, that is always waiting to come out. You couldn't look sad if you tried to."

"I haven't been really unhappy for long, except at first, and then when I lost Mother. But I always felt that we belonged to each other, and I began to hope that we'd be together again. In the last two years, I've begun to enjoy living, just as if I'd come to myself after an illness. We're made that way, the Fincastles. Even when we're broken-hearted, we still love life and enjoy it. I mean just getting up and seeing the sunrise, and then all the little things that happen before we see the sunset and go to bed. It isn't much, but it keeps us going. And I like sleeping because I have such wonderful dreams, like Aunt Meggie's, only hers are about Heaven, and mine are always with you following the Indian trail on Thunder Mountain. For six years I've

dreamed, whenever I dream at all, that we were together somewhere in the Indian trail. It isn't happiness exactly," she added,
stroking his sleeve, "but it's better than nothing."

"Oh, Ada, Ada, I can't stand it! Oh, Ada, my darling!"

It was he who had broken down now, and she who felt suddenly stronger. When she withdrew her gaze from his face, all
she had said seemed unreal—but then, the war in Europe seemed
unreal too. Less near than the War Between the States, which
had burned the roof off the manse, and shattered the window-
panes, and killed three of her great-uncles. Almost as far away
as the massacre of Smiling Creek.

"Would you go with me now?" he asked in a tone that was
shy, eager, and yet as deeply thrilling to her as a storm. "I have
two days more before I have to go back. We could go to Teesdale by train, and then up to the cabin on Eagle Ridge. I
have the key. Nobody is there, and everything is ready and
waiting."

Above the drumming in her ears she heard her own voice
speaking, and it sounded far away and unnatural. "Father thinks
this war may last a long time. He says the Germans will not
give up for years."

"A lot of people say that."

"And years last forever." A shiver ran over her. "You might
stay over there always."

"Perhaps." He laughed, and she wondered why he always
laughed when he alluded to death. "After all, the ground makes
no difference. I'd be in France anyway."

"But for ever." Her voice shook with fear. "For ever never
ends."

He held her bare arm against his throat, stroking the inside
curve of her elbow. "When you flare up like that it makes your
eyes shine."

"If you never come back, I'll always be cheated of life."

"They stole six years, and we can get back two days."

"It wasn't fair, Ralph. You were mine. We belonged together."

"I was a fool, and I let them trap me. Even your father wasn't fair to me."

"He didn't understand. There are times when he is too far away to see the things as they are. He's like that about the war. But for Grandmother people would shun him. Mr. Black warned him against going down to the village; but he went just the same to the post office. If anybody insulted him, he wasn't looking. He insists there's no such thing as a righteous war, not even in the Old Testament, and that makes people furious."

"I used to talk that way when I was studying philosophy with him. It seems a million years ago. The world has moved on since then. Or maybe it has only swung back."

"He's never been the same since Mother died. Yet I used to think she sometimes wore on his nerves."

"What was that she said about things happening? I've tried to remember."

" 'It is only in the heart,' she used to say, 'that anything really happens.' "

He was still stroking her arm. "You know, don't you, that there's never been any one else? Not really. Not when it mattered."

"I know now."

"Janet didn't make any difference."

"Not for long. I knew she didn't mean anything."

"Nobody ever meant anything. Nobody but you." He kissed her throat, and she drew back under the willow.

"Grandmother might look out. I saw her go by the kitchen window."

"She wouldn't hurt us. But I wish we had those six years."

"Six years! And it may go on till we're dead. I can't bear it when it comes over me. Oh, Ralph, I can't bear its being for ever!"

"Then come with me now. We'll save our two days out of life."

"If you're killed, I'll never forgive myself. I'll feel that I missed life because I was afraid."

"You aren't afraid, darling?"

"Not of life. I can bear what I have to bear."

"Two days aren't much, but they're something. We could save something." When he smiled at her with his serious eyes and careless lips, she felt that parting was too intolerable to be borne. The swift, exulting tremors of her heart seemed to pass on into a world where valleys were rising and hills falling under a sky that was splintered to pieces. Though she had drawn away and was trying to wipe the mist from her eyes, to think clearly and quickly, she could still feel his hand stroking her arm and the pressure of his mouth on her throat.

"It isn't only six years," she said in a voice that was stifled by joy—or was it pain? "It has been all my life."

"Then two days must make up for all our lives."

The throbbing within ceased suddenly, and she felt that the shock of emotion no longer frightened her. Only this longing for joy, this sense of separation from life, filled her universe. No, it wasn't any use trying. She could never learn, like Ralph, to live in the moment, not even in the burning moment of ecstasy.

"Whatever you do will be right, Ada," he said, "because you do it." His voice had grown husky and there was a white circle about his mouth. "It's like your looking happy. You can't get away from it."

A thin call piped from the house, and he turned to wave to Grandmother, who was leaning out of the window. "It does me good to see a soldier, Ralph. Don't go without coming in."

"I'd sooner go without my dinner," he called gaily, and she answered, "Ours is nearly ready. Won't you stay?"

But he couldn't stay; he had to tell his mother and a few of the boys good-by before he caught the two o'clock train back to Teesdale.

"Are you going on that train?" Ada asked, watching the fluted outline of her grandmother's cap.

"Here's my ticket to Teesdale. If you'll take it and come on that train, I'll join you two stations down the road. Then we can catch another train to Enniskill. It isn't far, but it's a round-about way. There's only a trail from the branch road to Eagle Ridge. The Indian trail is on the other side. I've always promised to take you there."

"I can tell them I've gone to Doncaster." A lie? Oh, what was a lie?

He held out the ticket, and as she took it from him, she saw that his hand was shaking. "I'll take you now, if you'll come," he said. "We may never have a chance after to-day."

"I'll come," she answered in a clear, firm tone. "I'll come on the two o'clock train."

"Then I'll join you down the road. I'd better go now. Can you find a way easily?"

"Oh, I can find a way. It won't matter how. I'm coming."

"I know I oughtn't to let you. I know as well as anyone I oughtn't to let you."

"That doesn't matter. They ought to have known they couldn't keep us apart. We came first with each other. They ought to have known."

"I've thought that too. I'm always thinking it. Being a fool oughtn't to draw a life sentence."

"No matter. We'll be happy now."

"Then I'll go on. Tell your grandmother good-by, and your father too."

"Poor Father, though I suppose his happiness is the only kind that is safe. People can't break in on it."

"And they can't break in on ours after this. I'll be watching for you every minute."

As she looked after him on his way to the gate, she thought, "Two days out of our lives! Two days all our own! And if I'm punished, I'm punished."

Upstairs, in her room, she opened the bottom drawer of the bureau and took out the garments of white china silk that her mother had made more than six years before and had put away wrapped in one of her best towels of fringed damask. Soft and fragile, they seemed to Ada, slipping through her fingers like flowers, and as fragrant with memories. Her mother's eyes filled with that deep radiance! Her mother's lips quivering into a smile! Her mother's hands moving swiftly while the needle flashed in and out and in and out again to the end of the seam!

When she had brushed her hair until it was as lustrous as satin, she slipped into her Sunday dress of navy-blue silk with a white polka dot, which felt smooth and clinging over the thin chemise, and studied her image in the gay little hat of red straw Aunt Meggie had bought for a dollar from a girl who had gone into mourning. Every minute, while she packed the willow basket in which she had carried a dozen eggs to the store yesterday, she was thinking: This is my dream coming true. If only I have something true to remember, nothing that happens can ever hurt me as much again.

Downstairs Aunt Meggie was calling, and when Ada went into the dining-room, only her father's chair was vacant. He was preparing his fourth volume for the press, though it was doubtful whether it would be published as long as the war lasted, and frequently he would take only a glass of buttermilk and a piece of corn bread that Grandmother carried into the library and put on one end of his desk. Energy consumed him and, like her mother's inward flame, it was superior to the pleasures and pains of the flesh.

"Why, you've got on your best dress!" Aunt Meggie exclaimed. "Has anything happened?"

"I want Miss Fanny Hopkins to see it. She may tell me what is wrong with it."

"I can't see anything wrong with it, honey," Grandmother said, raising her horn spectacles. "Navy blue is always becoming, and that hat looks very well on you."

Ada poured out a glass of buttermilk and drank it standing by the table. "I'm not hungry now. I'll eat something later. Has Father had anything?"

"He is so absorbed we don't like to disturb him," Aunt Meggie replied. "I wonder if that book will ever be published now that we've gone into the war?"

"I sometimes hope," Grandmother's voice sank to a husky whisper, "that it will never be."

Refilling her glass, Ada sipped the buttermilk slowly while her thoughts danced like motes in a sunbeam. She couldn't eat—she was too deeply stirred—but the buttermilk, she told herself, would carry her through the day, and in the evening she and Ralph would have supper together . . . far away, she hoped, in the Indian trail. She had written a few words on the back of an envelope, "I've gone to see Lizzie Draper in Doncaster. Don't be anxious," and stealing across the hall, she placed it on the Bible in her mother's room, which they still called "the chamber." Grandmother would be sure to find it there when she went in for her knitting. Then, after slipping on her coat in the hall, she picked up the willow basket and ran down the steps and over the grass to the gate. Once in the road, she stopped and glanced back, as if she heard a voice calling her name. But there was only the silence and the October haze dusted in a powdery bloom over the valley. She had made her choice; she would have her dream come true if she paid for it with all the rest of her life. Swift, light-footed, with radiant eyes and heart, she appeared to be running toward happiness.

She went by the churchyard, where Abraham Geddy (Uncle Beadnell had died last winter) was trimming the ivy. She went by the Rowans' house, where Mrs. Rowan was putting up fresh curtains at the parlour windows. She went by the Red Cross workrooms, where several fiery non-combatants were rolling bandages as grimly as if they were bullets. She went by the harness shop, where kind old Mr. Wertenbaker, who was finding life difficult, smiled wistfully. Then, just as she reached the station, she saw the smoke of the train curling upward where the track wound through the lowest notch in the hills. A little later, when she sprang up the steps to the platform and entered the nearest coach, she saw that it was already filled and that she knew none of the passengers. One seat alone remained empty, and in front of her several young men in khaki were making sounds without sense to a group of girls with fresh, flat, expressionless faces, insatiable for adventure. They might have been going to a circus, she thought, idly listening to a conversation that was noisy, gushing, monosyllabic. But they also were straining toward happiness, though they appeared only flippant and foolish. Withdrawing her gaze, she fixed her eyes on the landscape, which swept by in flashes, glowing with colour. The buzz around her was as meaningless as the chirping of grasshoppers. Maybe we are grasshoppers, she thought, and something bigger will tread us into the ground, and our time will be over. But even then, a voice added within, I shall have something true to remember.

A hand touched her shoulder. She turned, startled, and saw Ralph standing beside her. Suddenly the chirping, the gushing, the near tinkling, and the distant rumbling all died away and left them alone in a place apart with their happiness.

PART
THREE

LIFE'S INTERLUDE

HE car had left them in the branch road, and they carried the few things they had brought up the tangled trail to the cabin. At noon on Monday the same car would be waiting for them in the same spot. Then they would come down the mountain; but there were two days and three nights before Monday, and days and nights are a part of eternity. Beyond the hunter's cabin, which awaited them with food on the shelves and wood under the shed, they could plunge deep into the wilderness and follow the old Indian trail.

At first they walked in silence, clinging together, because the nearness, the stillness, seemed to be fuller than speech. One of his arms pressed her to his side, and looking up into his face, she thought, as she had thought so often before, that never had she loved him so much—not even when she believed she had lost him. What was the meaning of it, this incompleteness, this longing that she had brought into the world? She didn't know. She could never know. All she felt, while his arm held her, was the perfection, the shining joy, of the moment. And this shining joy was mingled with the sharp scents of autumn, with the flame and scarlet and bronze of the trees, with the plaintive murmur, now near, now far away, of the October wind in the leaves.

"Let's rest awhile," he said presently. "I haven't seen you alone for six years. Let's rest awhile before we go on."

But she broke away and ran ahead up the climbing path. "Not till we reach the top."

"We don't go to the top. Only as far as the cabin."

"But the Indian trail is beyond. Except when I'm dreaming, the Indian trail is always beyond."

"There's barely a sign left. The Indians went long ago. Now the bears and foxes are going fast."

"Well, we'll go with the bears and foxes. Isn't that the cabin up there in the clearing?"

When he tried to catch her, she slipped from his arms, sprang over a fallen log in the path, and ran toward the grassy space where all the forest trees fell away in a circle. Her body, winged and tremulous, seemed as light as a swallow's. There was a tumult in her ears, but it was the divine tumult of living. If only it would never end! If only the moment could pause, arrested by its own fullness, and stay with them for ever!

"This is the ridge," he laughed, breathing quickly, as he held out his hands. "Now we may rest."

Within a screen of yellow sycamores, she saw the cabin beside a tiny stream, as bright as quicksilver, which darted over the bare rock. Around them, the wilderness closed in, murmurous, myriad-coloured, inscrutable. Above the wilderness and the violet-blue rim of the mountains, the autumn sunset was throbbing. While she hesitated, without touching him but aware in every heartbeat, in every sense, of his nearness, a single thought shot through her mind and was gone with an arrowy swiftness: I can never in all my life be happier than I am now!

He had put the basket down at the door of the cabin, not hastily, she noticed almost with surprise, but slowly and gravely, as if the act had significance, or the hush of the solitude had sobered his mind. When she took off her hat and tossed it beside the basket, he put his hand on her head and pushed back the waves of hair from her forehead.

"Tell me," she begged. "Tell me over and over, I want to hear it in words."

He shook his head, while his hand wandered from her hair to her face, and then to her throat and the slender curve of her bosom and waist. "I can't say things. You know. You know without my telling you."

"Tell me you love me."

He laughed with a stinging softness, while she seemed to dissolve to air and light in his embrace. "I love you, love you, love you. Haven't I always loved you? Has there ever been anyone else from the beginning?" His swift kisses became harder and deeper, until her restless thoughts were suspended in a universe of pure feeling. All the hunger and the thwarted happiness of the last six years were consuming her with his lips. But it was bliss. Even the hardness and roughness were a part of the ecstasy.

Breaking away from his arms, she gazed into the forest which flamed in the long pulsations of sunset. "Let's find the Indian trail. Before the sun goes down, we must find the real warpath."

"This is enough. Oh, Ada, I've wanted you so! For six years I've wanted you so. And they cheated me. They spoiled my life. Now we've only two days left out of the whole of life."

His outburst died in a sobbing sound, and she caught his head to her bosom, as if he were a child that needed quieting. "I know, Ralph, but we must find the trail. It is as warm as summer. We may stay out in the moonlight."

Drawing him with her, she turned and ran into the forest, where the light was splintered by the coloured branches and scattered like jewels over the brown mould and green moss on the ground—square, round, triangular, diamond-shaped, crescent-shaped. The air was still and fragrant with the ending of day; the only distinct sounds were the crackle of the leaves underfoot, the dropping of acorns near and far, the startled movement now and then of a bird or a squirrel. While they ran on, springing over fallen logs, plunging deeper into the woods, pushing aside the thick underbrush in the hollows, she felt that the pulse of wildness in her heart was at rest.

"This is the Indian trail," he said presently, pausing where the oldest trees were assembled like columns and arched into a roof overhead. "There's a feeling still left—but it's only a feeling." Reaching up, he began tearing down the thickest pine boughs and a covering of brilliant leaves. "I'm making you a couch—an Indian couch. All the Indians have gone, and we're the last of the lovers." He laughed as he spoke, but under the light overtone she could feel the thrill of his longing.

"I think you love me more," she said.

"Don't think. Don't waste time in thinking. We've waited too long."

"I know," she answered regretfully. "I try to stop thinking. But I can't. It goes on without me."

"Are you happy? You aren't afraid?"

"I'm happy. I'm not afraid. Not even if I have to pay for happiness with all the rest of my life."

"You're thinking again, darling."

This was true. Feeling swept over her, but below feeling, thought went on into the next minute, the next hour, ticking steadily, like a clock that could never run down. "I'm perfectly happy," she answered. "Life may take away happiness. But it can't take away having had it."

"Well, I'll be free soon. It can't be long now. A telegram may come to-morrow saying I'm as free as I ever was."

Over a vast stillness she heard the sound of his voice. Against the afterglow on the leaves she saw his auburn head bending over her. She saw the glow in his face, in his eyes, in his smile, which was shy and adoring. She felt his swift, seeking hands, which moved over her with the touch of vision, as if they were the hands of the blind. If only thought would stop and she could become all emotion! Yearning over him, she ran her lips from his eyes to his mouth and his cheek. This was what she had longed for. This was happiness. "Let me feel it all," she prayed. "Oh, God, let me feel it while I have it and do not have to remember. Let me feel every wave, every spark, every flash of the ecstasy."

"This is just the beginning," he said.

"Yes, it is just the beginning."

But it was the beginning of life, she told herself, yielding at last to the tide of emotion. This was life—to give and give until the aching heart and mind and nerves were appeased and asleep.

Gradually moonlight silvered the sky; the still leaves shone like metal; a fox barked far away; and suddenly the wilderness awoke from sleep and gave voice to the solitude.

"I was dreaming," she said, sitting up on the pine couch, "but I knew I was happy."

"We oughtn't to waste time sleeping. It's only for two days."

She shook her head with a smile. "It's for ever. Nobody can take away what is ours. Not even people who think they're right."

The fox barked again from a nearer distance. "I wish they couldn't take you away," Ralph said.

"They can't. Nobody can."

"Well, they'll try, but you mustn't let them. You're mine. If I'm killed over there—that isn't likely, I'm more of the damned sort that gets knocked up—but if I'm killed over there, you're still mine. Those aren't words. They're things. I hate words. But you're mine."

He stood up and held out his hand. With a spring, she rose to her feet, and looked through the opening in the trees, which was so faint that it might have been the vanishing track of the moon. She shivered at his side, and he asked, "Are you cold?"

"No, it was only that the war over there, so far away, brushed my thoughts."

"Remember, you must live without thinking."

"I know. Are you hungry?"

"Starving. It's too late for supper, but we can find something to eat in the cabin."

She clung to him, laughing. This also was happiness, being hungry together, going home together in the moonlight through the wilderness, picking their way over logs, and at last searching for food in the cabin. "I'll cook breakfast before you wake up," she said, and saying it filled her with a glow. "Is this the way? Everything looks so different by moonlight."

"I could feel the way with my feet." He caught her up as she would have slipped over a stump hidden by creepers. "You mustn't be unhappy again. Promise me that."

"I feel now as if this would last always. Anyway, nothing can ever be the same when we have this."

When they came out of the woods, the moon was riding high, and the light illumined the dark rim of the mountains and flooded the brushy hills and the valleys. In the stillness the music of the little stream tinkled like bells. Then, suddenly, it seemed to her that everywhere bells were ringing.

"I never saw the moon so bright," she said.

"I never saw you so lovely. If happiness had a body, it would look like you."

"It's a pity to leave this and go in."

"It's a pity, but I'm as hungry as a bear."

Ada sighed as she turned the key in the creaking lock. Men were like that, she supposed; their thoughts could never stay away long from what they called the necessities of existence. A minute later, she heard the scraping of a match, and the wick of a lamp caught the light and flamed up in the dusk. Reluctantly, while her eyes strained backward to the glimmering world, she followed him into the cabin and through the front room into the kitchen on the side next to the bedroom. Here he placed the lamp on a table and looked round at the shelves.

"We'll eat dry bread and apples. It won't take me a minute to fetch a pail of water."

Seizing the wooden bucket, he ran down to the spring, while she went out on the grass and watched him swim through the moonlight as if it were water. The shadows by the spring sucked him in, and all the bubbling joy went flat in her heart; then he plunged back into the light, and the phosphorescent spray scattered again. This is life, this beauty, her thoughts were singing. This is love, this delight.

After he had returned with the dripping bucket, they broke off the end of a loaf, and sat on an overturned box, eating dry bread and winesaps, which they had found in a hempen bag in one corner.

"It's too late to make a fire," she said, "but I'll cook a wonderful breakfast, and we'll have it out of doors on the grass.

There's everything we need." Raising the lid of the icebox, she glanced inside. "They've left us butter and milk and eggs. Are you as sleepy as you look, Ralph? Your eyes are like chinquapins that are just beginning to open."

"I'm happy. Happiness makes me sleepy."

"Did you ever feel happy and know it when you were asleep?" she asked.

"Only in a dream. Do we ever know things in dreams?"

"Well, you'll know to-night. Let's take the lamp and look about."

There were two rooms, besides the kitchen, which was barely more than what the mountain people called a lean-to. In the back room, built out from the hillside near the stream, she found clean sheets of unbleached cotton, and a pair of red blankets tucked away in a pine chest in one corner. "I shan't wake up," she said, while she unfolded the covering, "not if a bear looks in the window."

"A bear would be better than Mr. Black."

"Or than anybody else. Are there bears left about here?"

"Not many. They're more afraid of us than we are of them."

"Well, they're right. We're more dangerous than they are."

The lamp was smoking on the chest, and he trimmed the wick while she pressed the pillows into the pillowcases and tucked the covering under the thin cotton mattress. Below her careless tone there was a mute supplication embedded somewhere in her unconscious being. Don't punish us, God. We aren't hurting anyone. Don't punish us, God.

"It will be like sleeping in the trail," she said, as she turned back the covers. "What is that rushing noise I've heard ever since we came? It is like wind blowing under the stream."

"That's Cockspur Run. The trees hide it."

"I like to hear it in the night. It sounds as if time were going by and leaving us alone on an island of happiness."

"You've queer fancies, but so have I." He laughed again as he spoke, because the protective reserve he had built up so carefully had broken down. He had hated words as long as words had been weapons of conflict and treachery. But with her, while they strove to reach each other through the veils of the flesh, while they sought with passionate tenderness the reality within realities, words had become as natural and as unguarded as impulses.

"Let's put out the lamp now, and pretend we're in the forest," she answered. "Is that the hoot of an owl? Or is it the ghost of Grandmother Tod's Indian lover?"

Waking in the night, while he lay asleep with his arm thrown across her, the thought flared up brightly in the darkness: This is life. Whatever comes afterwards, I shall always have had life. Then the flare went out, and she drifted back into unconsciousness that was still strangely blissful.

With the break of day, she heard first the rippling murmur of the little stream, and then, farther off, the windy music of Cockspur Run as it dashed over ledges into the deep basin below. The rhythms of ecstasy, the singing pulse in her heart, were blended with the long strokes of light and the awakening stir in the forest. As she looked down on Ralph's rumpled auburn head, a sudden passion without desire suffused her being. In that instant she realized not only the mutability of joy, but the poignant tenderness that might remain after longing was spent.

When the sun had risen over the mountains, she left Ralph still asleep and stole out of doors to bathe in the stream. Running with bare feet across the grass, she plunged into sparkling water, as cold as ice on her skin, and then, after rubbing her body into a glow, put on her clothes and combed her hair behind the screen of the sycamores. With a radiant face, she went back into the cabin, built a fire of lightwood in the stove, and ran down again to fill a pail with fresh water. On her way from the spring to the cabin, she set the pail down in the dew-drenched weeds and lifted her arms in a gesture of pure delight toward the risen sun. Far away the blue mountains were like clouds on the horizon, and high above the blue clouds were like mountains. Below, through webs of iridescent mist, she could see red or gray roofs and the ripe autumn fields in the smaller valleys.

In the kitchen the fire burned well and, moving as noiselessly as she could, she poured water into the kettle and the coffee-pot and prepared the frying-pan for the eggs and thin bacon. The little table was set out on the grass, and the aroma of coffee had filled the cabin, when she turned from the stove at a sound and saw Ralph, with a bath towel over his arm and his hair still glistening from pearly dew. As he bent over her, she thought that his kiss tasted of happiness.

"You were so busy you didn't hear me slip out," he said. "The stream was like ice, but the sun is almost warm and the day is going to be like summer."

"I was thinking of breakfast. It will be ready in a minute. You're dressed, aren't you?"

"Dressed enough." He dashed into the bedroom, jerked a comb through his hair, and returned with a blanket. "You'll need your coat out of doors till the sun is well up."

"Oh, I'm not cold. I'm too glad. Gladness warms. Put the plates on the stove for a minute and fill the cups with hot water while I'm heating the milk. There isn't any cream, but I'm bringing the milk to a froth." Pausing to whisk the batter bread from the oven, she gave it to him on a tin plate. "Be careful how you hold it. The plate is bent. All the cups have lost their handles, and I can find only one teaspoon."

"No matter. We'll use the same spoon."

"I had to hunt for pepper. Why is it people always forget pepper? You'll have to sweeten your coffee with brown sugar."

"That's fun. It's all the sweeter."

Wrapped in a blanket, she smiled at him over the coffee-pot, and thought of the six long years in which she might have looked at him every morning at breakfast. They could never grow tired of each other, she told herself innocently, not in six years, not in six hundred years. It was like being with another and a nearer self. He talked now without stopping, as if he were only thinking aloud, and she felt suddenly that nothing they said or did could make any difference. Merely being together was all that they needed.

"Do you suppose anything was ever so perfect before?" she asked. "I mean for others———"

"Are there any others?"

"Well, they think they are."

"Then they're mistaken."

"It's absurd the way people talk," she said. "Even Father, who was so happily married, speaks as if love didn't last."

"Well, he's old. The old get queer. Ours has lasted, hasn't it?"

"When did it begin?"

"I can't remember, can you?"

"We've grown together." She reached for his cup and filled it for the third time. (Why did little things give such bliss?) "Even if we become like other people and stop talking about love, that won't make any difference."

"No, that won't make any difference," he repeated, but she realized that he had taken in her voice, not her words. His eyes were on the glittering summit of God's Mountain, and a look of startled surprise made him appear young and ardent.

"I wonder if I am too old to begin from the beginning," he said.

A<small>LL</small> that day, it seemed to Ada, she wandered in a pause of time from which she should presently awake to find that the world had dissolved. The autumn wind, like racing sunlight, had shaken down a rain of leaves. In the slanting shower she could see the crimson pink of the dogwood, the purplish velvet of the oaks, the clear gold of the hickories and beeches, the wavering flame of the maples, the fugitive scarlet of the black gum, and the tarnished bronze of the sycamores, walnuts, and poplars—all driven by streamers of mist toward the dark background of pines. The air sparkled like new cider, the pines droned in the wind, the sun blazed on the splendour. Merely to be alive was like music. She longed to run, to sing, to dance over the rustling leaves. And flowing between them was this deeper mood, this effortless harmony of being together. She hadn't known love was like this! She hadn't known living was like this! "Oh, my love, my love," she cried without words, while they walked with clasped hands, seizing the ecstasy before it escaped them. Yet, beneath the wonder and delight, she knew always that parting must come, that anguish waited, as it had waited six years before on that June afternoon. Love brings fear, she thought, trying not to remember. When one has been through that parting, love can never lose fear. Round their island of happiness, there was the ebb and flow of a treacherous universe. For six years she had missed him, as she might have missed a part of herself that had been torn away. Six years of fruitless hope, of long waiting! Yet the wound was healed now, the soreness was eased in her mind.

Lying on the crisp sun-warmed leaves beside a mountain rill, they ate, for lunch, slices of bread sprinkled with brown sugar, and drank water that gushed over a rocky ledge.

"Are you happy?" he asked for the hundredth time, looking through the boughs of a sycamore up into the clouds.

"Perfectly happy . . . if only . . . if only . . ."

"You're thinking again."

"If only I could make myself know that this isn't a dream. It's too good to be true."

He laughed. "This is the only thing that seems true to me."

"Talk to me. I like to hear your voice. Talk about any-thing."

"My mind has stopped. Everything has gone into . . . well, into being happy. That's all there is."

"That's all there is," she repeated, and shivered as she drew nearer to him.

"What's the matter? You aren't cold?" He reached out his arm and pressed her so close that she felt the shape of his bones, she thought with a laugh, and heard the steady beating of his heart under her head.

"No, I'm not cold. I don't know why I shivered."

"That's silly, Ada darling. Any day now I may be free. Janet's trying to get that divorce before her man goes over. Then we'll be married as soon as you can come to me. If I'm killed in France," he continued gaily, "at least I shall leave the widow I want."

"Don't, oh, don't," she said, with vehement reproach. "That doesn't sound funny."

"Doesn't it? Perhaps Janet would think so."

"I wish you would never think of Janet again."

"I wish I couldn't. I think of her now as I think of a toothache on the way to the dentist."

"More than anything," she said passionately, "I wish this could never end. I wish we didn't have to go back."

"Winter would come. Then we shouldn't have anything."

"We'd have everything. We'd have each other."

"Well, we'll have each other anyway."

"If we stayed up here, they'd bring things to us, wouldn't they?"

"Not if they thought we were happy. Don't people try to starve happiness?"

"But we aren't really so far off. We're nearer than we think to everything."

"Nearer than we think," he repeated slowly, "but what is everything?"

"Everything is what happiness needs to live on. That isn't much. Do you remember how we used to play we were escaping from Indians? You always led us back, because you knew the Indian woodcraft. You could tell so many secrets from the side of a tree that bark grew on, and the way moss covered a rock, and even the kind of moss, and how the leaves fell on the earth, and all the tracks of small creatures."

"Well, that wouldn't help us now. We're escaping from worse things than Indians. If I thought I'd harmed you," he said, frowning up at the sky, "I'd want to go away and put an end to myself."

"You haven't harmed me. I shall always be glad. Nothing could ever make me sorry."

"I wonder," he whispered, and she heard the strangling of a lump in his throat. "All the same, I wish I were free."

"You may be. At this minute a letter may be on the way to you."

"If you should need help, and I can't get to you," he answered, "there's a man in Queenborough who would look after you. He is an old man, but my friend. His name is Herbert Bentley, and he lives at six hundred and two Gamble Street. Will you remember that, darling?"

"Yes, I'll remember."

"I'll write it down anyway. It might be useful, and I'll feel easier. Of course nobody knows how long I'll be gone."

"Nobody knows," she echoed faintly, while fear surged through her mind.

"I'm made that way," he continued, with a spark of his old

derisive humour. "I'm always waiting for punishment. I suppose I'm still incurably Presbyterian."

"Or Irish?" she laughed. "Perhaps an Irishman makes a bad Presbyterian."

"Or a Presbyterian a bad Irishman." The cloud had passed from his face, and his quick smile swept the apprehension out of her thoughts.

The wind dropped and died in the valleys; the light thinned and paled over the mountains; the rustling of the leaves, like the stealthy patter of bare feet, sank from a murmur to a sigh and from a sigh into stillness. Only the small hidden lives, the creeping furry shapes, within and without the forest—only the scurrying of mice, the burrowing of moles, the shuffling of toads, the scampering of ground squirrels—had inherited the twilight. With the fainting wind, all the wild earthy scents grew stronger and closer.

"It's time to go on," he said, lifting her from the moss.

"I know. I'll cook supper to-night."

When they came out into the clearing, the afterglow still lingered in streaks, and the visionary light transfigured the grassy circle, the dappled boughs of the sycamores, and the wheeling wings of late swallows. The scene of their happiness was enveloped for her in some changeless air of the mind.

"I wish the cabin belonged to us, Ralph."

"When the war is over, we'll buy it. When the war is over and won, we may have everything we want."

"I have everything now, only I want it to last."

The next morning they walked in the woods again, but there was no running and little speech. All the afternoon they lay in the warm sunshine on the grass by the cabin and talked of their life together after the war had ended in victory. Parting was not mentioned in words, though the knowledge pierced as a mental darkness, as a moving shadow, into their unspoken thoughts. Cheerfully, almost lightly, they discussed practical plans for the future—where they should live, how he could arrange to resume his study of the law, how much money they might save if they were to take a house in Lexington and he worked as a secretary while she made fruit cake and preserves to sell. Yet, beneath the casual words, there was the slow drumming of fear. Suppose he should never come back! Suppose her happiness should be snuffed out as quickly as the flame of a candle! Safe, for the precious instant, within the circle of sunny grass, like a ring of white magic, she drew his head into her arms and looked over the valleys and the mountains toward some hidden antagonist beyond the blue of the heavens. There was a fluttering in her bosom, but her voice was strong and steady when she answered his questions.

"No, it can't be long now. The letter may be waiting for you. Janet isn't going to let you stand in her way. Charlie Draper says he's afraid the war will end before he can get over. He thinks the Germans will give up as soon as they see we're in earnest."

"He talks that way. His head is too big for his body."

"Well, they can't hold out much longer. I believe you'll be disappointed if you don't get to France."

"I don't want anybody else to do my fighting. But for you, I'd be glad to be sailing."

"I'm thankful you aren't."

"It's leaving you I mind. I ought never to have asked you to come away with me."

She stroked the top of his head. "I'm glad you did. Would you have missed our two days?"

As the light faded into dusk, the wilderness appeared to creep nearer, but the solitude could not protect them from the dread of separation and the threatened loneliness of to-morrow. "We're so happy," she said in a whisper, for she had become suddenly afraid of the word "happiness." Through the night she lay with her head on his arm, fearing to fall asleep, trying to keep back the hurrying minutes. "I mustn't lose a second," she told herself. "I must fill my memory so full that it will last me until he comes home." Gazing beyond the open window, she watched the moon, which sailed like a ship in the waste of sky, while her ears were awake to every ripple over the rocks and to every movement or sound in the trees.

Toward morning she fell asleep, and awoke with a new sense of security, a vision of permanence. Between earth and sky, she seemed to be anchored fast in some central radiance, while the hostile universe flowed away from her. The night and the world were moving round her, but eternity had found a place in her heart. Was she awake or asleep? she thought happily. Outside, she could hear the wind rising; the clouds were flying like witches, ragged and dark against a thin moon; the forest was shaken; leaves whirled past the cabin; the very mountains were loosened and flowed away with the universe. "But love is safe," she said aloud, in a pause between sleeping and waking. "I can never lose what is mine."

At noon the next day they put the cabin in order, saw that the last embers had burned out, turned the key in the lock, and taking up Ralph's bag and Ada's basket, stepped over the threshold and stood clinging together. Though tears filled her eyes, they did not fall. Is it for the last time? she thought, but, no, there is never a last time while we are still alive. She felt the deep vibrations of his love and pain, and she knew that he also was longing to bring only happiness, to be true, tender, loyal. They were young, they were lovers, they were parting in a world with which love could never be reconciled. We have done no harm, she said in her heart. We have hurt nobody. We have asked so little beyond ourselves, so little beyond being together.

Then, once again, she felt this inner sense of security. All this is ours, she thought, while her eyes shone through a rainbow mist. We have everything. Nothing can take it away. As long as she lived her will would have a part, perhaps an immortal part, in this place and this moment. She would have this forest enclosing this circle of bright grass. She would have this joy, this autumn sunshine, this stream, this valley, these mountains, even these leaves falling, these birds flying . . .

Once more they clung to each other, while he kissed her

weeping eyes and smiling lips. "Some day," he said, "we'll come back again."

"Yes, we'll come back."

"If I find the letter, you'll join me to-morrow."

"Oh, I hope it is waiting for you!"

"You won't be unhappy? If I thought I'd made you unhappy . . ."

"Don't say that. Oh, don't say it! Ralph . . . Ralph!"

"Well, you know what I mean."

"I know you love me. Nothing else matters. You'll write often?"

"As often as I can. You know how I am about letters. But I'll see you soon. After all, we may not go over till spring. The talk is just rumour."

They drew apart, looking at each other, at the cabin, at the wilderness, at the sky. Then, joining hands again, they turned away and walked slowly down the winding track to where the car waited for them in the road.

PART

FOUR

GOD'S MOUNTAIN

CHAPTER 1

NOTHING had changed.

Can this be real, and that also? Ada asked herself as she walked up the long street in Ironside. Was the cabin still there as they had left it? Or was that only a dream, like her old dream of the Indian trail?

Here was the same trodden dust, the same trash in the gutters, the same beams of sunshine gilding the ragged leaves on the maples; and when she raised her eyes to the mountains, it seemed to her that the same clouds were scudding across an unchangeable sky. Even old Mr. Saunders, the blacksmith, was still shoeing a grey mule. In the store Mr. Robinson was still measuring off a yard of red flannel. Old Mrs. Tiller still peered eagerly after scandal over her window-box of frostbitten geraniums. Farther back in the churchyard, as if he had drifted on with the leaves, Uncle Abraham Geddy was still trimming the ivy. And when she passed the church, she saw that Toby Waters was still carrying slops from the hovel to the hogs in the pen.

But it was the actual world, not the inner vision, that was wanting in substance. The core of life was within her heart. If all this were to break up and dissolve, she thought, the reality, as her father said, would not change; the image would exist for all time, perhaps for eternity. Even Father could not tell me which is more real, she mused happily. Nobody knows.

When she reached the gate of the manse, she met Aunt Meggie on her way to a Red Cross meeting. The round, ruddy face, as soft as old leather, wore a mild beam of astonishment.

"Everything is all right, Aunt Meggie. I hope Grandmother didn't worry about me."

"We couldn't imagine what had got into you. It wasn't like

you to do such a thing. Ada. You might have known we'd be anxious."

"I had to go. There was a chance to drive over." Why, she wondered, did the lie bring no feeling of shame? All her life she had been taught that a lie, like unlawful love, was a sin. Yet she could feel no remorse, only amusement because the words came so readily. After all, it was a white lie, and though Grandmother condemned equally all shades of lying, Mother had distinguished between "black lies," which were evil, and "white lies," which were always harmless and occasionally benign.

"Did you find Lizzie Draper well?"

"Oh, yes, everybody was well."

"How does she like living in Doncaster?"

"Very much."

"Does Henry like teaching?"

"I think so."

"Well, I always thought Charlie was the brightest of the Draper boys and would have made the best professor. Did you hear any news of the war?"

"Only what everybody knows."

"You look as if you'd had a good time."

"Oh, wonderful, Aunt Meggie!" The words sang on her lips, and her aunt, who was passing on, stopped and glanced at her sharply. "I'm glad you had the change. I believe in taking pleasure if you can do it without being selfish."

Without being selfish! Did Aunt Meggie, who had never taken a selfish pleasure in her life, think that Ada had been wicked? Well, perhaps she had been, but the thought did not dampen her gladness. It might be true that God would punish her for two days of joy. But she was not sure that she believed in a God of wrath; and it was strange the way God never seemed to feel it necessary to punish people who did not believe in Him. But it made no difference. She had made her choice, and she was prepared to pay for it with all the rest of her life.

Running up the steps and into the hall, she opened the door of the library. Her father, absorbed in his work, did not look

up, and she shut the door again very softly and went on, through
the dining-room, into the kitchen, where Liddy was ironing
one of Grandmother's black-and-grey calico dresses.

"Is everything all right, Liddy?"

Before replying, Liddy moistened a finger and flicked it
across the bottom or an iron which she returned to the stove.
"Yas'm, ev'ybody cep'n Aun' Abigail. She's done mos' come
ter de en sence you been gone."

"I'm sorry for that. I'll go over to see her. Is Dinty with her?"

"Yas'm, but I'se here all de time now f'um sunup ter sundown. I'se gwineter stay on jes ez long ez ole Miss needs me ter
help out."

Turning back into the house, Ada hesitated an instant, while
she tried to summon an explanation that would sound natural,
before she entered her mother's old chamber. In front of a single smouldering log, which was charred on one side, Grandmother sat in her usual chair, knitting her interminable stockings for the Red Cross.

"Oh, Grandmother, I'm so sorry to hear about poor Aunt
Abigail!" the girl exclaimed as she went over to the hearth,
and after bestowing a hurried kiss, stooped over the basket of
chips.

"No, don't put on any chips," Grandmother said. "I lit the
fire to warm my knees, but we mustn't waste fuel while the
weather keeps mild. Yes, we were up most of the night expecting Aunt Abigail to go. Dr. Updike says she can't last many
days."

"I'll go right over."

"I've just come back because she didn't seem to know anybody, and Dinty's mother, Rhody, has come to sit with her.
Rhody is a good nurse. I taught her how to be useful in sickness."

"Then I'll go up and take off my best dress."

"I hope you didn't hurt it. It looks mussed under your coat."

"No, I didn't hurt it."

"Where have you been all this time, my child?"

"It was only two days, Grandmother. I had a chance to go and see Lizzie."

"You might have told us."

"It was so sudden I didn't have time."

"Did you find Lizzie well?"

"Yes, she is well. They're all well." Fortunately Grandmother's eyes were dim, and her spectacles, though strong, were easily blurred.

"What kind of war work is Lizzie doing?"

"Oh, every kind!"

"Well, she hasn't any children, so she ought to have plenty of time. I saw Mrs. Greenlee at church yesterday, and she told me Ross was already with the French. The day after he received his commission, he was assigned to a division that was about to go over. She hasn't heard from him more than once, but she isn't a bit downhearted. Did you see Ralph again after he left here?"

"Yes . . . no." A sob burst from Ada's lips, and dropping on her knees, she buried her face in the old woman's lap. "Oh, Grandmother, why did you let them do it? Why did you let them spoil our lives?"

Grandmother put down her knitting and laid both hands on the girl's head. "Nobody can do that, my dear. The only way to spoil a life is to take away God's grace, and nobody but God Himself can do that."

"And God wouldn't, Grandmother, not the God I believe in."

"Only as a trial of faith, my child."

Ada sprang to her feet with a laugh that had begun as a sob. "Then I'd better go up and put on something old," she said. "This is the only good dress I have, and a trial of faith would certainly ruin it."

She had turned away when Grandmother's voice stopped her. "What we did seemed best at the time, but more than once it has crossed my mind that we weren't as careful as we ought to have been. I've always liked Ralph, in spite of what the Rowans said of him, and I never had a particle of use for that empty-headed Janet we made him marry."

"But it's too late now, Grandmother!" Ada cried out, as she left the room. "It is too late to give us back what you took from us."

Flying away from the answer, she ran out into the hall and up the stairs to her room. Once inside, with the door shut, fear ebbed from her mind and she said aloud, "But they couldn't take love. When you have love, nothing else makes any difference."

Two days afterwards, when his letter came, she told herself that she had expected too much. What she had expected she scarcely knew, but it was more than this; it was different from this. The surface of restraint, which had thawed while they were together, had frozen over again. "I can never write a love letter," he had said, but she had not believed him. "I can't put down on paper things I have to pluck up out of myself. You know I care. You'll have to understand that once for all."

Once for all! When she was aching to hear it a hundred times, when she found that words, even more than embraces, meant reassurance. Well, it was her own fault. She had hoped for too much. She must be satisfied to know without being told in the future. Nothing can keep us apart, she thought, nothing but death, and even death may end, as Grandmother is convinced, in everlasting reunion. If she didn't believe this, how could she look ahead to the war? If all women didn't believe this, how could they face the long waiting for birth and death?

He had felt so free, so sure of their marriage, he had written early in November, that it was a blow to find the divorce was still hanging over. Janet, he heard, had been ill with pneumonia in Reno, and for a few days they didn't think she could possibly pull through. But she was eager to be free and to be married again before her lover, whose wife had already divorced him, was ordered to France. She had charged Ralph with mental cruelty, whatever that implied, but, so far as he was concerned, she might accuse him of murder and he would not deny it. This meant, he hoped, only a few days or weeks longer of separation.

It was queer how much harder waiting was after you had seen light ahead. There were rumours of going over, but there had been rumours for weeks. Nobody could tell what the next move would be. Orders had been hushed up since the sinking of the *Antilles*. If she did not hear, she must understand that they were going over or had already sailed. All the talk now was of joining the British troops—but it was only talk.

For a fortnight she heard every few days, and in that fortnight Aunt Abigail died and was buried in the churchyard of the Negro church a few miles away. Judge Melrose drove Grandmother to the funeral, and the rest of the family went in Mr. Rowan's carriage, with the Geddy family and the coffin leading the procession in a spring-wagon that was shrouded in black. All the way they talked of the war, and Aunt Meggie recalled Aunt Abigail's pride when her grandson, Marcellus Junior, had enlisted. The next day Grandmother was kept in bed with a return of lumbago, and after she was up and about she complained that the pain had crept from her loins into her legs.

"But my suffering is small compared to the agony in Europe," she would say, as she limped across the floor and slowly eased herself down on the cushions of her winged chair. "Lying there in bed, my mind went over what we endured in our own war. Many and many a time, with your grandfather away in the army (and he wasn't the only minister who took up arms in defense of his State), I've gone out and chopped and sawed wood for a fire, not knowing where I could find a scrap of food to cook when the fire was made. And all the time the children were clinging to my skirts and crying from hunger. Yes, many and many a time I've done that. We thought we'd surely starve, all over the Valley, after Hunter and Sheridan. I had a baby born the worst winter, with only old Aunt Jerusalem to take care of me and the children, because Abigail had taken it into her head to run off and have a look at the Yankees. I named the baby Elijah after the prophet, but he lived only long enough to be baptized by a minister who came over from Doncaster to preach. His father never saw him, poor lamb, until they met in the blessed Resurrection."

Sometimes she would pause in exasperation, raise a flushed face from her work, and inquire suspiciously, "Did I name him Elijah or Elisha, Meggie? I don't seem to recollect clearly."

"Elijah, Mother, because you had prayed the Lord to send ravens."

"Yes, Elijah was the name, but what about that general? Was his name Hunter? Are you sure? It doesn't sound right somehow."

"Yes, that was General Hunter. He burned Glenburnie."

For a few days Grandmother's memory seemed to desert her. She would ask the same questions over with a peevish and acrimonious expression, while her face flamed out in angry splotches.

"She's not herself," Aunt Meggie said, wiping her eyes. "It's not like her to be so irritable."

"Why doesn't her faith help her, Aunt Meggie? Is faith, like everything else, at the mercy of the body?"

"I don't know, dear, but she was never this way before."

Then, suddenly, just as they feared the general breaking-up of age, her will triumphed over the flesh, and she collected her faculties. One morning, as she finished breakfast, she asked Liddy and Aunt Meggie to have her room ready for her and a fire burning as soon as she came in from the porch.

"I need a breath of air," she said. "I haven't had a breath of air for a week."

Going out on the porch, she hobbled up and down with the help of her cane until Meggie ran out to tell her that her room had been made ready.

"Is there anything you want, Mother? Can I help you?"

"Nothing, my child. I must get command of myself. When you're old, the fight is on between the will to live and the nature to die. I'm beginning to break, but it must be a long beginning before I let go."

Taking her Bible from the table, she went into her room and shut the door, though they could hear the sound of her voice, strong and composed, as she read from the Scriptures or prayed aloud on her knees. Once or twice, a groan reached them, but when she came out at dinner time, in response to a knock on the door, her resolution had conquered. She ate with her usual robust appetite; her temper had recovered serenity; the purple flush in her face had subsided; even her memory seemed to have been restored by a miracle. From this time her infirmities appeared to decrease, and her only allusion to her weakness was when she said, " 'Twas those apple dumplings upset me."

For a week in November, Ada heard from Ralph every day. Then, just as she had become accustomed to brief notes which told her nothing, not even that he loved her, there came a long letter, written in dejection, that seemed to tear at her heartstrings.

"I have been sitting here alone, thinking of our first night in the Indian trail and the way I held you in my arms, and the way we loved each other, and all that happened to us up there by ourselves. If I had known how things would drag on, that we might sail before I saw you again, that I might even have to die without seeing you, I would never have urged you to come away with me. I see now I ought not to have done that. It was not fair to you. I thought I loved you then as much as I could ever love you. But I know now that was just the beginning. I love you more to-night than I have ever loved you. If I thought I had made you unhappy or brought you harm, I'd rather put an end to myself than come back from France. This sounds like a weak fool. I never could write things I feel. But if you were here to-night, I could make you feel how much I love you. Did you know that the memory of happiness could turn into a torment?"

After this there was a long silence. Though she wrote cheerfully every day, there was no answer to her letters, and she might have told him, had she been able to pierce a void, that silence can be a worse torment than memory. But she still wrote on, in the hope that her letters might follow him to France and even, if it were necessary, into No Man's Land.

"I can never forget, not for a minute, that we have been perfectly happy. Only for two days. But how many people in this world have been perfectly happy for two days? No matter what comes in the future, we shall always have that, and I shall always be glad we have it—no matter what comes."

When still another fortnight had passed, the long suspense became almost intolerable. One afternoon, when the weather was bright and mild for the end of November, she went into Ironside to ask Ralph's mother if she had known of his sailing. Even if Mrs. McBride had had no word, she would still be eager to talk of her son, and her perpetual complaint might act as a counter-irritant to anxiety. "Anyway, I can't stay in the house," Ada told herself. "I'd rather go anywhere than help Aunt Meggie in the kitchen, or sit by the fire and watch Grandmother doze over her knitting."

As she descended the road to the church, she turned to look back over Shut-in Valley, which was powdered with sunshine. The more brittle leaves had all fallen, and were scattered in wind drifts against the wall of the churchyard, but sheltered boughs of the oaks still held a few russet or pale maroon-coloured patches, which might hang on until April. No living thing moved in the landscape. Only the long shafts of sunlight were alive with the stir of doomed insects—or was it the thin drift of pollen?—not yet overtaken by winter, a vibration so faint, so fleeting, and yet so close, that it seemed scarcely louder than the humming within her ears.

RS. McBRIDE was in her small front yard, watching Uncle Abraham Geddy pile manure and straw about the roots of her rosebushes. Since Ralph had been able to send her a monthly allowance, she had made the cottage more comfortable and had taken a destitute cousin to live with her. Years of toil and self-denial had bowed her shoulders and crippled her slender hands, but she had found it impossible to break away from severe habits of saving and drudgery. Her fine eyes were brooding and secretive; the wrinkles in her face were so deep that they might have been bitten in by an acid; and to look at her, one might have imagined that her piety, like her patriotism, was rooted in hatred. What could Ralph's father have been like? Ada wondered. It was not from his mother that he had inherited his disarming smile and the amused gleam in his eyes. When she kissed Mrs. McBride, the withered cheek seemed to leave a bitter taste on her lips.

"You weren't at church yesterday," the girl said as she entered. "We were sure you wouldn't have stayed away without reason."

"No, I came down the night before with one of my bilious headaches. Did you have a good sermon?"

"Everybody seemed to like it."

"Was your father there?"

Ada shook her head. "Aunt Meggie and I went alone. Grandmother had to give up at the last moment."

"Is it true that Mr. Black warned your father not to come into the village?"

"He hinted something. But Father never gave it a thought. You know how he is."

"Yes, I know," Mrs. McBride assented, as she led her visitor into the front room and seated herself stiffly on a sofa upholstered in horsehair. ",You heard, of course," she said, "that Ralph had sailed."

"I thought so."

"Everything was very secret. No one was allowed to mention the name of a port."

"How long have you known?"

"Only a few days." The bluish lips quivered. "I expected to see you at church yesterday." There was hostility in her fixed gaze and in the cutting sound of her voice. "I am glad he has gone. I am glad I had a son to give to the cause."

"He wanted to go," Ada said. "Nothing could have kept him from going."

"I was afraid your father might try to influence him."

"Father never tries to influence any one. He believes in leaving people free."

"Too often they are left free to work out their own destruction," Mrs. McBride observed dryly.

As if the thought choked her, Ada swallowed a lump in her throat and looked away to the figure of Uncle Abraham stooping over the rosebushes. Yes, religion could be a bitter and a terrible thing! As a child, she had known that Mrs. McBride enjoyed punishing Ralph. Now she felt, with the same aversion, that the older woman found a thrill of cruelty in the Christian symbols of crucifixion and atonement. She had wished him to marry Janet, Ada realized indignantly. She had wished him to be hurt. Even if she doesn't know it, the girl thought, she really hates him. Something deep down in her, perhaps an embittered love for his father, perhaps the crying blood of persecutors, was gratified when she thought that any one, even her own child, would be punished by God.

"I must go," the girl said, moving toward the door, because she felt that she could not breathe in the heavy air. "I hope Ralph will be safe. If you have any news, will you send me word by Uncle Abraham?"

"I'll be glad to." Mrs. McBride rose and stood looking at her with a wintry smile. "I know you and Ralph never felt we did right by you. He took it hard when he was forced to marry Janet. But it was right. He had to do it because it was right."

"But it wasn't right."

"A girl wouldn't have lied about such a thing, Ada."

"Hasn't Janet always lied for what she wanted?" (Well, she had lied, too, Ada's conscience reminded her, but hers wasn't a bad lie.) "Why were you willing to believe Janet instead of Ralph?"

"I wasn't willing. I had to do what was right. But why did Ralph give in if he hadn't been in the wrong?"

She has never liked me, Ada told herself; she has never really liked Ralph. But no matter what she does to me, I shall tell her the truth. A shiver ran over her, but she answered steadily, "Because you had broken his will, and he couldn't resist you. You had broken his will when he was little."

"All I did was for his good. He was a headstrong child, and he had to be disciplined. He had to have his feet set in the right road. I never cared about myself. It was of him I was thinking." Mrs. McBride turned away her face, and when she looked round again, her eyes were misted with tears, and a tiny dewdrop twinkled without falling on the reddened tip of her nose. "He is my son," she said. "He is the only thing in the world that is mine. Don't I lie awake till dawn wondering if he is sick or cold, and whether he will be killed over there or come home crippled for life?" She raised her worn hands and let them fall with a despairing gesture.

"I am sorry," Ada murmured, "I wish I could help you." But her voice was cold, and she was thinking, It was your fault that our lives were spoiled.

"There isn't any help except in the Lord. I found that out long ago. I've gone through worse things. Even my own family never suspected. But trials taught me that there is no help in this world."

"Well, you have God left anyway."

"There are times when He seems to leave you in darkness. I thought for years that I could never find the light—that I was lost for eternity. Then suddenly one Sunday morning, after the long night of repentance, during a missionary sermon, I felt that I was called and regenerated. After that, I had a new heart and a new spirit."

"Did they bring happiness?"

"I didn't think of happiness. Happiness is a small thing beside salvation."

No, she couldn't understand, Ada told herself, she should never, no matter how long she lived, be able to understand religion. Ralph's will had been broken and his life ruined because his mother had discovered that salvation was better than happiness.

"I know how anxious you must be," she remarked, and perceived immediately that Mrs. McBride was offended. How could one be both anxious at heart and convinced in mind that everything, even war on land and sea, was in the hands of the Lord? "If I can do anything for you, let me know," she added, from the doorway. "Grandmother sent her love."

"Tell her I've been wanting to come to see her. There aren't many women like your grandmother."

"That will please her." Then gathering her courage, she asked boldly. "Did Mr. Rowan tell you anything about Janet?"

"Why, hadn't you heard? It was in the paper yesterday."

"We never see the paper on Sunday. Has anything happened to her?" A wild hope shot through her heart.

"Mr. Rowan came to tell me. It was on his conscience, he said, and he didn't try to defend Janet. The divorce wouldn't have been so bad—though he blames her for that—but she stepped off the train the very next day and was married at some little place in the West."

The room rocked, and beyond the window Uncle Abraham and his piles of straw and manure were caught up into the clouds. "Janet married! But how could she? I didn't know. Ralph didn't know . . ."

"It has all happened since Ralph sailed. She wasn't free but one day. She won her divorce on Friday, and on Saturday she was married. I don't remember even the man's name . . . something like Hawkins . . . something like Horley. . . . Her father had never heard her mention him, but it seems that he is well off. I'd have told you, but I don't like to think of her, and, besides, I thought you would have heard of it. I have always felt strongly about divorce. Separation may be tolerated, but remarriage is simply living in sin."

"I wish Ralph had known! I wish Ralph had known before he went!"

"He told me that you and he would be married as soon as he was free. But he knows how I feel about it."

Ada's cheeks flamed to crimson. "That doesn't matter. Nobody could come between us a second time."

"Well, he is in France now. All we can do is to pray that he may come safely home."

"I don't dare think of it—of his not being safe."

"God is with us. Our cause is just."

"I don't know about God."

"You are a member of the church."

"Isn't everybody a member of the church"—Ada laughed defiantly—"everybody, except poor Toby Waters, who needs religion more than any of us?" Why had she said that? Why did things slip out before she could stop them?

"If you have hardened your heart, I must pray for you," Mrs. McBride said, with a kind of cold pity, as they parted.

So Ralph was free! He was free. He was in France. He might be killed. He might, even now, be lying shot to pieces in a hospital, or under foreign soil among hundreds of others. I must pray, she told herself passionately, but prayer wouldn't come. Yet praying couldn't do any harm, and it was on the safe side, as Aunt Meggie used to remind her when she forgot to kneel down at night.

The sun had dropped behind the darkening summit of God's Mountain, and the deep bowl of the valley was filled with the hazy blue of Indian summer. When she walked up the road past the churchyard, a suspicion, more an anxiety than a question, floated up from her unconscious mind, like a face under water. Did it mean nothing? Did it mean everything? Ever since the days and nights on Eagle Ridge, it had seemed to her that the wonder—or was it expectancy?—had lain there out of sight, out of thought, and yet urgent and vital. In the sky above the sunset a small white cloud streamed back like a golden fleece—like the golden hair of a child. Her heart shuddered in fear and was still again. It was only her fancy. Or it may have been some fragment of an old wives' tale she had heard from Aunt Abigail Geddy. But it was too soon to know, she told herself; it was too soon to suspect. In a few days everything might be right, and the danger well over. Anxiety for Ralph may have disturbed not only her mind, but her body. And the streaming fleece, the golden cloud, was already dispersing. Yet such signs, Aunt Abigail had once told her, were not uncommon, and they were usually good signs. Though there was a legend, Grandmother had remembered, of a Mrs. Morecock, one of the frontier women, who had seen the head of an Indian in the sunset before her eldest baby was born, and two years afterwards a Shawnee brave had dashed out the brains of the infant in the massacre at Smiling Creek.

But I mustn't think of myself, she thought. That is the way fear comes into the mind. What I can't help, I shall be able to bear. In the morning I may wake up and know it was merely my fancy. And, whether it is true or not, if Ralph is killed over there, I shall be glad his child is mine and not Janet's.

❋ ❋ ❋ ❋ ❋ ❋ ❋N the brow of the stony hill, Ada said to herself:
You can bear what you have to bear, as long as
you don't let fear push into your mind.

O

Her look swept the April landscape, looping
an invisible chain round the mountains, the sky,
the valley, the sheep pasture, the three sheep and
the one lamb, the house, the road, and the sloping roofs of the village. But she turned her eyes away from the village. She had not
been there since she had known how it was with her—since any
one who glanced at her figure could tell how it was with her. If
she saw people whispering about her, she might begin to be sorry
for herself. And she did not want to feel sorry. She wanted to be
glad, because there was safety in gladness.

It was tragic the way Grandmother had taken it. Her father
had been different, but her father was always different from
every one else. He had said only, "I blame myself most of all. I
should have known better. You have prepared a blow for us, my
dear, but I blame myself most of all." Then her grandmother had
been terrible. . . .

Dropping on a flat stone, she tried to think plainly in words
of one syllable, thrusting away every image that was not linked
to a fact. For she had needed all her courage then, and she
needed it now. The sin was carnal, Grandmother had said, with
a stricken look, flinging out her hands, which had always been so
tender in trouble. There was no hope but in repentance, in a
broken and contrite heart. Still, Ada could not repent, not even
when her grandmother moaned like an animal in pain, sinking
her proud old head on her chest.

"I am sorry I hurt you, Grandmother. We thought it would
all come right. We hoped we could marry before Ralph sailed.

We never dreamed . . . But if he is killed in France, I shall be glad of it all—glad that we took those two days for our own out of life."

"What does Ralph say?" Grandmother had asked suddenly, lifting her head with a distraught air.

"He doesn't know, Grandmother. I haven't told him." Was it thunder in the sky or only the hammering of her arteries?

"Not told him? Why, you've known for months. You must have suspected . . ."

"He couldn't help me, Grandmother. They wouldn't let him come home, and he might try to do something rash. It would be more than he could bear to feel he had brought this upon me."

Grandmother's face had turned to stone. "He should be made to feel remorse. He should be made to suffer for his sin."

"He is unhappy enough without this. At first, when I was in a panic and thought I couldn't go through with it, I wrote to him. Then when I heard how miserable he was, and the way war sickened him to death, I tore up my letter. If he could help me, I'd send for him. But I don't want to make him feel remorse. I want only to spare him."

"To spare him!" Grandmother's voice had cracked and broken with anger.

Then it was (as long as she lived, Ada told herself, she would remember this, she would be grateful!)—then it was that her father had put his arm on her shaking shoulder and said gently, "You are a good woman, my child. True goodness is an inward grace, not an outward necessity."

Grandmother had not understood. She would never understand now. Her faith was watered with the strong blood of martyrs. Lying sleepless at night in her mother's chamber, which her father had given up, Ada would hear the floor creak in the adjoining room as the old woman rolled from the bed and her knees bent in prayer.

"If only you would repent, Ada," Aunt Meggie urged. "Mother could find it in her heart to forgive you if only you would repent. She is grieving so that it may be the end of her."

"Oh, Aunt Meggie, what can I do for her?"

"You can tell her that you repent of your sin, and you can write to Ralph as she wants you to do."

"I will when it's over, Aunt Meggie. If I live through it, I will write to him the first day I can sit up."

As the weeks had dragged by and she had grown heavier and more shapeless, Ada reminded herself again and again that she must have given way to despair but for Aunt Meggie's devotion. A dozen times a day the older woman would spring out of a corner with a jug of cream or milk that she had brought up from the village, or a pot of tea and a plate of buttered toast on a tray. "I noticed you didn't touch a morsel at breakfast, Ada, so I've fixed a little snack for you. It's bad for you to fast, and you mustn't let yourself mope." And once she had burst out impulsively, "You look so well to-day I can't take my eyes off you. I was just telling John that there is a light, a kind of starriness, in your face."

Resting there on the hillside, Ada felt the sudden stir of the child, of a strange life knit to her own and thrusting up from the depths of her being toward a destiny that would be separate and different. Women have been through worse things, she thought, while her glance brushed the sheep pasture and lingered on the willows by Smiling Creek, which rippled with broken lights as the leaves turned in the wind. Whenever her thoughts slipped control, she felt that dark fear clutching her bosom, and in the effort to balance her mind she gazed steadily down on the sunny stream and the whitening willows.

Those men and women on Smiling Creek had endured the worst, yet the will toward life had not failed them. Mrs. Morecock had seen the brains of her baby spatter her skirts; she had been famished for food as a captive; she had eaten roots; when she reached water, she had knelt down and lapped it up like an animal. In the end she had had the courage to escape, she had crossed trackless mountains on her way home to Ironside. For months she had lived on berries and the bark of black gum or sassafras. Though she was a walking skeleton when she reached

Ironside, she had had the spirit, or the folly, to begin life again. How was she able to forget? Ada wondered. How could they drop the past so easily, those pioneers, and plunge into the moment before them? They were hard, it was true, but it was the hardness of character. Unlovable they were, but heroic. Had they been soft to the touch of fate, the exiled Shawnees would still be roaming their lost hunting-grounds.

Was the past broken off from the present? she mused, or did that vein of iron hold all the generations together? Sitting there, in touch with the land that had been won from the wilderness, she braced her own strength against that endurance, that hardness. How had her Great-great-grandmother Tod felt when she bore her child in the wigwam of a savage? What was her own plight to that?

Oh, but the wilderness! If only she might hide away and have her child on a bed of pine boughs! A matronly ewe with an inquisitive face stared at her over a stalk of mullein, and she said gravely, "Don't pity me, Martha. I can't bear it if you pity me." She must not feel sorry for herself, not if it killed her. Self-pity, her father had told her, was the most primitive form of sentimentality. Wait till the worst comes. When the worst comes, you will be dead, and that will be the end of it. Aunt Meggie, who had gone soft in spots, was fond of saying that human nature can stand only so much and no more....

The sheep had turned away, cropping the young weeds. Was that old tragedy still lying there in Shut-in Valley, underneath the tender bloom of the spring? Had it left an eternal outline somewhere in the universe? Or had it melted as a vapour, a breath, into emptiness? Suddenly, without reason, the meaning that sometimes starts out of life and seems to make everything clear and simple flashed back at her from the valley, the stream, the mountains, the sky. An instant only, and then it was gone, like the flight of an eagle. Struggling to her feet (would she ever be quick again?), she walked slowly down the hillside and across the narrow pasture to the garden fence, where her father and a small coloured urchin were spading together.

"Side by side," she exclaimed, "and it doesn't make the slightest difference to the earth that one is a philosopher and the other a piccaninny!"

At the sound of her voice John Fincastle straightened his shoulders, as if he were easing himself of a load. "It must be time to go in. Where have you been, my dear?"

"Up on the hill with Martha and Mary and the lamb Minnie."

"It was Mary's lamb that died, wasn't it?"

"Nobody knows, not even Mary. But they are both mothers to Minnie. Send Tommy home, Father."

"Run home, Tommy!" John Fincastle called over his shoulder. "You may come back after dinner. What it is, my child?" he inquired, as Tommy trotted away.

"I'm afraid of fear. It comes over me in a panic."

"But it mustn't come. You must fight it off. Wouldn't you be easier if Ralph knew of it? It doesn't seem fair to him. And then your grandmother feels very bitterly."

"Not yet, Father. I'll write as soon as the worst is over. If I don't come through, you can write for me."

"Still, I think he should know . . ." Then, as she broke down and wept, he yielded the point. "It's hard to decide what is right. You have chosen your own way, and life has a habit of compelling us to abide by our choices."

"Well, I'll write soon. Not to-day, but some day just before the time comes. We were driven into this," she cried, with sudden passion. "We wanted to be right. We meant well. It wasn't as if we had been strange, or wild, or bad, or dissatisfied with goodness. We might have been good and happy all our lives if only people had let us alone."

"Many of us have felt that, my dear. But try not to think about life. The only way to live happily is not to think about life. There may be much for you in the future."

"I know. If Ralph comes home, I'll look back on all this as a nightmare. It's over now for the moment anyway—the fear of fear. I shan't let it come back if I can help it."

"Try to be active, and take care of yourself. I shouldn't, if I were you, go into the village. Not yet, anyway—not for the present."

"Aunt Meggie says Mr. Black and Doctor Updike are keeping it secret. For Grandmother's sake, Mr. Black told her, he hopes it won't be known till . . . till . . . Poor Grandmother! The one thing she dreaded even more than sin was disgrace, and I've brought it upon her in her old age."

"And I in her prime. That is the greatest injustice in life—we cannot suffer anything alone, not even disgrace. Well, I'd take Mr. Black's advice, and walk with sheep instead of human beings for the next few months. There is something companionable about animals, even about sheep, that human beings lack. I discovered that when I was expelled from the ministry. That's why I've a sneaking fondness for Martha and Mary."

"And we're so near the village we could almost throw a stone into the street. But I won't go again for a long time." She pressed his arm, clinging to him to save herself from a plunge into the void. For the meaning (it may have been only a sensation) she had found on the hillside had been wiped out as utterly as if a brush had swept it away.

"Aren't you coming in with me?" he asked, when she released his arm at the front steps.

"I'll come later. It distresses Grandmother to see me."

"She wouldn't wish you to go hungry."

"Aunt Meggie won't let that happen. She's always bringing me something between meals. But I want to spare Grandmother as much as I can."

"It's her love for you that suffers. Love is a terrible power, and it's more deeply rooted in the old than in the young. When it's torn up in age there's nothing left but decay."

"I never thought of that, Father. Grandmother never entered my mind. My life was my own, and I thought I'd be the one to suffer if I made a mistake."

"And all the time you were taking the lives of others into your hands. When one starts a forest fire one seldom looks beyond the match in the hand or the ember in the pipe. But the blaze doesn't discriminate."

They parted at the door, and she circled the house until she reached the bench under the willow tree. Here she waited until she saw first Liddy and then Aunt Meggie come out on the back porch, and knew that dinner was over. But a few minutes afterwards she met her grandmother in the hall, and drew aside to make way for her. Without glancing at her grandchild, without quickening her step, without the flicker of an eyelash or the quiver of a muscle, the old woman swept on, supported by her stick, to the closed door of her room.

She will never, never speak to me again, Ada thought, with a pang. Slipping into the dining-room, she shed tears into the bean soup Aunt Meggie had kept hot for her.

FOR the next few months Ada did not go down into the village. Every morning, when the work in the house was finished, she would pick a book from her father's library and go up, through the little pasture, to the hillside. Here, with the friendly sheep browsing around her, she would lie flat on the earth and fold her impatient hands under her head. Martha and Mary and sometimes William, the ram, would walk delicately at a safe distance; but Minnie, the lamb, was quite tame, and would sidle up to butt a woolly head against her shoulder or knee.

The book she seldom opened. There was cold comfort to be found in books. How had her father escaped, she wondered, into that bloodless republic of the spirit? Ralph, too, was separated from her by the space of the universe. He was somewhere in a far country, fighting in a war that seemed as remote as the battles in history. Would the broken rim of the world ever mend? Would he ever return to her out of the shattered circle of life, out of the wheeling fragments of time, out of a universe that was destroying itself? For nothing else really mattered. All the vacancy, all the death and dying in the world, meant only that one shape was missing, that one fragment was lost among the multitudinous shapes and fragments of being. So her father told her, reminding her of the world's agony, and she knew that it was true. Her fear was merged into a larger fear; but it was still for her own. There were hours when her courage seemed to flare out and leave her supine and indifferent. Then fortitude, which lies beyond courage, would renew itself from some inexhaustible spring of vitality.

Lying there in the June sunshine, between the fruitful earth and the clement sky, it seemed to her that a sense of the past would overflow and obliterate her actual share in the present. Well, no matter. . . . What she must face, she could face. But suppose—the blue was spinning overhead—suppose it was at last over! Suppose the war had ended suddenly, Ralph had returned without warning . . . Rising with the thought, as on the crest of a wave, she would stand erect and stretch her arms to the loneliness. As she picked her way, followed by the two ewes and the lamb, through tufts of mullein as grey as stones, she would find again, for the moment, at least, that her old faith in the goodness of life was restored.

On a Sunday morning in July, when she had felt unable to make the climb to the hillside, she came in from an hour's rest on the grass under the willow and saw the figure of Mr. Black pass through the gate and disappear down the road to the village. What could have brought him in his crowded hour between the morning service and the midday meal? Once only in recent years had he been known to visit on the Lord's day, and that was when he had denied himself his frugal dinner in order to comfort a widow whose son had fallen in France. Then, while she stared after his retreating shape, motionless because her legs seemed to give way under the leaden weight of her body, the back door opened and Aunt Meggie came hurrying to meet her.

"You look frightened, Ada. What is the matter? When I saw you out of the door, I thought you were going to fall down."

"Why did Mr. Black come? I was afraid Ralph had been killed."

"No, he missed us all at church, and Mrs. McBride told him Mother was sick in bed. He wouldn't even come inside the hall, he was in such a hurry to get back to his dinner. You mustn't let yourself be upset about nothing. 'Tis bad for you."

"I thought you'd gone to church, and when I saw Mr. Black, something like a shooting pain ran all over me."

"Your nerves are unstrung, and I don't wonder, I stayed at

home because Liddy wanted to go to the first big meeting over at Sugar Spring. Mother is ailing, though I couldn't make her stay in bed. You're gasping for breath. Come right in and get something to eat. Mother has just finished her dinner."

"Suppose Ralph never comes back! Oh, Aunt Meggie, I can't bear it if he never comes back!"

"I know, Ada, but you mustn't give way to your fears. Have you written to Ralph yet?"

"I'm waiting till it's over. As soon as I can sit up, I'll write to him."

After she had struggled into the house, she stood staring about her mother's chamber with dazed eyes, as if she were still feeling the shock of her terror.

"You don't look right, Ada," Aunt Meggie said. "Don't stand there like that. There's only a cold dinner, but I've made you some hot coffee, and there's a pitcher of rich milk Mr. Rowan sent Mother. She won't touch it. Since she's turned against milk, I don't see how she's going to keep up her strength on that diet for lumbago."

"I'll come in a minute, Aunt Meggie. Wait till I settle down and can swallow." Going over to the winged chair, she picked up a baby's wrapper of pink flannel Aunt Meggie had left on the table. "You do such lovely scalloping," she said softly.

"If it weren't Sunday, I could finish those sleeves in no time," Aunt Meggie replied. "You don't see fine French flannel like this now. Mary Evelyn had it put away in camphor ever since she lived in Queenborough. She always bought the best when she could afford it, but think of her keeping it all these years."

For the first time Ada's tears, which had felt like stones behind her eyeballs, melted and ran down. Poor Mother! Or was it fortunate Mother? She had liked nice things, yet she had known how to be gay in calico dresses and red flannel petticoats.

In looking over the boxes Mary Evelyn had never unpacked after leaving Queenborough, they had found piles of little garments, some yellowed by time, and dropping apart when they touched them, others fresh and unworn, which she had saved from Ada's infancy, or had prepared for her last baby that came stillborn the year after she moved to Ironside. There were long dresses of sheer lawn, too fragile for country wear and now out of fashion, wrappers, sacques, and bands of pink wool scalloped in silk, and even one of the streaming sky-blue veils which had floated, pinned to the shoulder of a coloured nurse, over every well-born baby in Queenborough. After spreading the garments in her lap, Ada had selected the plainest and strongest slips and a few soft flannel bands. The others she had folded again and given to Aunt Meggie to hide away from Grandmother's eyes.

"Is Grandmother in her room?" she asked now, putting the wrapper aside.

"No, she's on the back porch. She insisted on helping with dinner. It keeps her mind occupied, she says, to use her hands."

"That's why I like to sew. Do you think she'd mind if I took a few stitches?"

"I shouldn't, if I were you, Ada. She's proud of the fact that nobody has ever mended a break or knitted a stitch in this house on the Lord's day. Won't you try to eat something? The coffee won't be fit to drink if you wait any longer."

"Yes, I'm famished. I've been famished for an hour without knowing it. Only I can't bear to see Grandmother."

All day she kept occupied, and late in the afternoon she wrote to Ralph and tucked the letter away in a drawer. She would send it as soon as she was able to sit up and add a postscript. Or if she died when the child came, Aunt Meggie would find it when she went to look for something to put on her.

Whatever happened seemed to be taken out of her hands, and not greatly to matter.

"I am cheerful," she wrote, "and everything goes well with me. There is no need to be anxious. By the time you read this, I shall be sitting up, perhaps walking about, and thankful anyway that the long waiting is over. Nothing in this world is so bad as waiting for it. That is why I couldn't bear war. But nothing else matters if only you will come back and we can all be happy together in some other place. Everybody is kind, and Aunt Meggie is taking the best care of me. You would think I was a prize chicken from the way she stuffs me."

As she laid down her pen, she felt that the summer stillness and the random green lights at the window were quivering with surprise. But this cannot have happened to me, she thought. Ralph and I love each other. Yet we parted and went on as strangers might pass on a road, and he does not even know I am going to have his child and may die when it comes into the world. And he may be dead now, at this minute, while I am writing to him. He may be dead, but I should not know. I should go on just as if a stranger had been killed and nothing had happened that did not happen every day of my life.

The door of her grandmother's room was shut fast, but occasionally she heard the creaking of boards and a monotonous supplication winding in and out of the smothered sounds. "Poor Grandmother," she said to herself. "She is praying that I may be brought to repentance." While she listened, a superstitious dread shot through her mind. Suppose the punishment should fall not on her, but on her child! The sharpest anguish she had to bear was the fear that her baby might be born deformed or disfigured, or even an idiot, like poor Toby Waters. "Not that," she implored in breathless horror. "Whatever happens to me, don't let Grandmother's anger fall on my child!"

At midnight, after broken dreams in which she was wandering in search of Ralph through an eternity shaped like a tunnel, she awoke, drenched with sweat, in a terror that seemed to be half nightmare and half real. When had it begun? How long could it last without killing her? Fearing to call out, she sucked in her breath while the pain seemed to be grinding the flesh away from her bones. Then, suddenly, it was over, and she felt at ease and almost asleep. It couldn't have been so bad as she imagined. But do you ever, she asked in surprise, feel so sharp a pang in a dream? Just as she was distracting her mind, another coil of pain unwound in those long spirals of agony.

"Aunt Meggie!" she called softly. "Aunt Meggie, are you awake?"

There was a rustle in the darkness sprinkled with moonlight. A match was struck, the lamp on the table flared up, and in a minute, Aunt Meggie, wearing a calico wrapper over her night-gown, was standing beside her. "I'd just gone to bed," she whispered. "Ever since you told me about the way you felt this evening, I've been worried. Are you worse?"

"Not much." But the words ended in a sobbing moan.

"Couldn't you get up and walk about? I've heard Mother say 'twas easier if you kept on your feet."

"I've tried, but I can't. I give way."

"Are you afraid to stay by yourself while I run into the kitchen and light a fire? I want to fill all the kettles and have things ready before Doctor Updike comes."

"No, I'm not afraid. Not unless it gets worse."

"It may be hours yet. I'll send your father for the doctor. He's still at work in his library."

"You won't be a minute, Aunt Meggie?"

"Not more than three minutes. Just long enough to tell your father and start a fire."

She melted into the dimness, and Ada waited in terror for the return pain, watching a shadow, shaped like the head of a beast, which the screen threw on the wall. Would Aunt Meggie come back before the pain seized and tore her? Was she racing with pain? One, two, three, she began counting slowly. One, two, three ... Footsteps passed rapidly through the hall, and she knew that her father had started on his way to the village. A sense of unutterable degradation, more vehement than physical nausea, rushed over her! Where could the soul hide itself when the body was degraded and tortured? What reserve, what defenses were left? A thought throbbed in her mind: This is life, this hideousness! This is love, this horror! Then, before the words had died away, a moan of anguish burst from her lips, "Aunt Meggie! Aunt Meggie!"

Suddenly arms were about her. She was pressed to a bosom

as stout as oak, as sustaining as fortitude. A hand, large, strong, knotted, healing, pushed the damp hair back from her forehead, and looking up, she saw her grandmother's face bending over her. The old woman must have risen at the first stir; the bunch of black ribbon nodded over her left eyebrow, the cameo brooch pinned her collar together.

"Hold tight to me, Ada," she said. "Hold tight as you can. I won't let you go."

"Grandmother! Oh, Grandmother!" The steadfast life of the house, the strong fibres, the closely knit generations, had gathered above, around, underneath. She might sink back now, cradled in this blessed sense of security. "Now pain may have its way, and I may give up. Grandmother will know what to do."

All night she saw familiar figures moving through a red mist. She saw Doctor Updike come in at the door, his black bag in his hand. The tall, stooped shadow that brought in a fresh lamp and took away one that smoked was her father, though he seemed to have turned into a stranger. Aunt Meggie hopped like a rabbit, she thought with a queer twist of humour, knotting sheets at the foot of the bed, or carrying steaming kettles between the door and the empty fireplace. A strong sweetish odour filled her nostrils and floated upward into her mind as if it were flying. What bliss! she thought suddenly, and then, Am I really here? Is Ralph over in France? Is the cabin still where we left it?

The winged odour ascended, and everything shifted and broke, even the agony. All the figures round her bed, all the objects in the room, were swimming in this elastic fluid, which seemed to contain light and blessedness and oblivion. Only the arms of her grandmother remained as firm as the roots of an oak.

Then, at last, through a watery haze, she could see the darkness paling to lavender and a red tongue of fire licking the eastern range of the mountains. From a million miles away, somewhere beyond life, beyond death, a whimpering cry wavered, and above or below the sound, a voice exclaimed, like the startled cheep of birds in the trees, " 'Tis a boy! Well, all things considered, I'm glad it isn't a girl."

I am here, and not here, she thought. Part of myself is lying on this bed, and part is off in another world, in another life. Or am I divided into two separate selves, leading two separate lives? And has all this happened to that strange self I have never known?

FTER the baby's birth Grandmother Fincastle failed rapidly. While Ada was kept in bed and Ranny, the baby, needed her care, she refused to break down and forced her tired bones to obey her commands. But as soon as her grand-daughter was well again, the old woman's grasp upon life seemed to relax. Her mind would slip into strange spells of wandering, and she would sit for hours and stare at the child with a look of bewildered astonishment, as if she wondered when and why he had dropped into their midst. Once she called Aunt Meggie to her, and asked in a querulous whisper, "Where did that baby come from, Meggie? Does it belong to the poor McAllisters' brood? Speak up. I can't hear when you mumble." She now used two sticks whenever she walked without help, because her husband's ebony cane, a gift from his congregation, was not stout enough. Then, on the afternoon before her eighty-seventh birthday, when she rose to put down a bowl of peas she had shelled for canning, she staggered and fell to the floor of the kitchen. Her son had driven to Doncaster with Mr. Rowan, and Grandmother was alone with Aunt Meggie when she was stricken. At the first sound Ada hurried across the hall, and then, without waiting to summon Liddy, ran on to find Doctor Updike in Ironside. Not until she had passed the church did she remember that she had not been into the village since months before the birth of her child. But it was too late to turn back and send Liddy. Grandmother was in danger; an instant of delay might be fatal. Even if she were to meet Mrs. McBride, what would it matter? She can't kill me, she thought, and nobody else will take the trouble to snub me.

Doctor Updike was not at home, but his sister said she could reach him over the telephone, and that he would be at the manse by the time Ada returned. "He's at old Mrs. Morse's, and that's the last house on the way. Yes, he says he'll go right over," she added, replacing the receiver. "It's fortunate that Mrs. Morse's daughter put in a telephone last week. She was beginning to worry about what she'd do if her mother had an attack in the night. You'd better rest, Ada. You look as if you'd run every step of the way."

"No, thank you, Miss Amy, I must hurry home. Grandmother hasn't anybody but Aunt Meggie with her."

Still struggling for breath but spurred on by anxiety, she left the house and started at a run up the steep street. It was the running, she realized afterwards, that set the pace of disaster. Why does every frightened and fleeing creature awaken a deep-seated instinct of cruelty in the minds of children and savages? Had she walked slowly, no one, not even the children playing rowdily in the street, would have noticed her. But because she ran, flushed and frightened, they stopped playing and pursued her toward the churchyard, as they had so often in the past pursued Toby Waters. She had barely reached the church when the shrill cries pierced her nerves through the fog of distress. Half in malice, half in sport, the children were romping about her, pelting her with bits of red clay or tufts of weeds with the roots still attached. Already she had passed beyond the sight or sound of the shops, and of the busy mothers hanging clothes on lines in the back yards. Up the road to the manse, the throng pressed about her, while a few of the bolder boys thrust themselves between her and the easiest way of escape.

"Go home!" she commanded in a tone of fear that thrilled them with delight. "Go home, every one of you!"

"Go home," echoed the little girls, forming a ring as they danced round her. "Go home, every one of you! Go home to your piggie—pig—pigs!"

While their eyes gleamed and their foolish mouths dribbled, a vivid memory crossed her mind of the day when she had chased Toby Waters, and had suddenly felt herself fleeing in the skin of the idiot, as she had fled once before in the skin of the hare. So this is what it means to be human, she thought, swerving out of the road into the track that wandered over the fields to the ravine. Was all life divided, she wondered while she ran on, between the pursued and the pursuers? Did fate compel one, sooner or later, to take part? But Father wouldn't have seen. He wouldn't have seen they were chasing him. A lump of soft clay struck the back of her head; behind her the voices of children—or were they idiots?—were babbling. She had reached Murderer's Field, her foot had almost touched the slippery edge, when the gate of the hovel burst open, and Mrs. Waters and Toby rushed, amid a swarm of pigs, along the rim of the ravine. Stopping with a hysterical laugh, Ada watched the woman fling the hogwash from her pail into the flock of tormentors.

"Varmints!" she screamed. "It ain't often ye come within throwin' distance, or I wouldn't waste my good slops on ye! Take that thar broom to 'em, Toby. You won't git a better chance to pay back what you owe 'em."

The children had scattered, still shrieking, on the way to the village, and Toby stood leering over his broom with the air of a benevolent conqueror. Though his features were fantastic, his little bloodshot eyes contained hollows of shining darkness. "Sugar, sugar," he begged, stroking a fold of her skirt.

"Not now, Toby. I'll bring you some next time."

"He's never forgot the way you used to keep maple sugar in yo' pocket. Toby's a man now, but he ain't never lost the sweet tooth he had when he was little. I declar' you're all blown. Hadn't you better set down and get yo' breath?"

"Thank you, Mrs. Waters, but I can't stop. Grandmother has had a stroke, and I ran for the doctor."

"Yo' Granny? Now, ain't that too bad! She's one of the Lord's own."

"I must hurry back to her." As the sudden fright passed, she was assailed by her old moral antipathy to Mrs. Waters. A shiver of aversion stung her like frost. Suppose some one should come up from the village and see them talking together! "I must run home," she repeated, blushing from mingled shame for Mrs. Waters, who had rescued her, and embarrassment over her own humiliation. "Is the road safe?"

"Yas'm, Toby has rid us of 'em, the varmints! They used to pester him near to death when he was small, though not the same bunch. But he's grown so big now that they're feared of him."

"Good Toby," Ada said, while the idiot nodded and leered with pride. "I shan't forget your stick of candy the next time I come."

Hurrying along the track to the road, she entered the gate of the manse as the sun scattered the first westering beams over God's Mountain.

At the sound of her step in the hall, Aunt Meggie opened the door of Grandmother's room and looked at her with eyes that were disfigured by weeping. "She passed away a few minutes after the doctor came. Don't come in just yet. The doctor and Rhody are helping me to have everything as she wished. She always said she wanted to go to her long rest wearing her cap and her cameo brooch. No, she never gave the slightest sign that she was conscious. I've been trying so hard to think of the last words she spoke before she was stricken. But they have gone out of my mind, like everything else."

"They will come back," Ada answered. "Isn't there anything I can do?"

"No, go and look at the baby. I thought I heard him cry awhile ago, or it may have been a bird outside. There's one comfort," she continued earnestly, "Mother didn't need any time to prepare. Her whole life, as Doctor Updike said of her, was a preparation for the end."

Grieving but consoled, she wiped her eyes and turned back to the dead. If only she could believe! Ada thought while she hastened into her mother's chamber, where she had left the baby asleep in his crib. Picking him up, she held him close against her bosom and hushed him to silence. At seven weeks, he was a fair baby, the colour of ivory, with a golden down on his head, and the bright blue eyes of his grandfather and his great-great-grandmother, Margaret Graham. Though Ada tried to be sorrowful, and to keep her thoughts fixed on Grandmother lying dead in the next room, she could not entirely banish the suffusion of hope in her heart. The day after the child's birth, Aunt Meggie had posted her letter to Ralph, and only that morning an answer had come.

"If I had had to look ahead to it, I couldn't have borne it," he wrote, "but now that the worst of it for you is over, I'll put my mind on the future when we'll all be together and happy—if there's such a thing as happiness left in a rotten world. If you should find living in Ironside unbearable, go to Queenborough and take my name and wait for me. It will save us the trouble of explaining when I come back. But, fine as you are, you can't live on air, darling. I am writing to my friend in Queenborough, and he will send you as much as you need."

There was a step in the hall, and going out as noiselessly as she could, she found her father slipping out of his greatcoat. How worn he looks, she told herself, how tired and old! At last he is beginning to stoop in the shoulders.

"I saw the doctor's buggy," he said.

"Grandmother was stricken." For the first time the fact of death penetrated to the core of her mind. "She fell down in the kitchen when she got up out of her chair, and she passed away a few minutes after the doctor came."

She saw him shudder once, and then stand very still, as if he were collecting his faculties. "Was she alone?"

"No, Aunt Meggie was with her. But Grandmother didn't know her. She never came to herself. She said something just before she fell. Poor Aunt Meggie is distressed because she hasn't been able to remember the words. Oh, Father!" Ada choked for a moment and then burst into tears. "I killed Grandmother!"

"You mustn't think that, my child. She would not wish you to think that."

"But I did. It came over me then for the first time."

He patted her shoulder, and she clung to him. "You must not let yourself brood."

"I wanted to be good, Father."

"You are good, Ada. Not in your grandmother's heroic way, perhaps, but in your own way. There are many kinds of goodness, my dear, but there is none that does not spring from the heart alone. Now I shall go in."

"They want us to wait a few minutes."

He sighed under his breath, and it seemed to her that his thin arm was braced with an indestructible strength. "I have held on to the manse as long as she lived. Now it must go. Nobody is willing to take another mortgage, and when the place is sold, as it must be soon, there will be little left after the debts are settled. Yes, she had had a splendid life, and she has been spared a great deal."

"What will become of us, Father?"

"We may find work in Queenborough. The war has made work plentiful, even for men of my age. It is hard to tear up the roots of generations, but I have few tendrils, and by the time Ranny is old enough for school, you will probably feel at home in the city."

"I shall be glad to go. Since Grandmother has gone, I want to go too. I am not happy here. The children ran after me to-day in the village and called me names. They could only have got them from their mothers. Oh, why are children like that?"

"You should not have gone alone into the village. Yet, even then, I had not thought . . ."

"It was because I ran. When Grandmother was stricken, I was so frightened that I ran as fast as I could for Doctor Updike. On the way back the children stopped playing and chased me."

"That chase began many millions of years ago, and it is still going on. It will stop only when the human race becomes civilized."

"Perhaps the world will be better after the war."

"Perhaps. But I have little faith in the theory that organized killing is the best prelude to peace. Well, we must do the best that we can till Ralph comes back to you and the child."

"That is why I want to leave Ironside. In Queenborough nobody will know about us. I am strong, too, and the papers say there is plenty of work."

"We shall know by the end of the year. But whatever happens, life will go on. Life must go on in one place as well as another."

PART

FIVE

THE DYING AGE

SNOW is cleaner in the mountains, Ada thought, raising her umbrella as she passed from the store into the midwinter evening. A scudding wind, laden with sleet and mud, whipped her back into shelter, and lowering her umbrella again, she flattened her tall strong figure against the glass of a window. In a little while, perhaps, the gust would blow over, and walking in the slush on the pavement would be less difficult. Even if she waited for a street car and was fortunate enough to find a seat vacant, she would be taken only a few blocks nearer home. Mulberry Street, where they lived in a small dilapidated house, had once belonged to a prosperous quarter of Queenborough, but that was before the tide of fashion and business alike had turned toward the West End and the new Granite Boulevard.

The walk from Shadwell's department store was not long, and in fine weather Ada was glad of the exercise. After two months, she was astonished afresh whenever she remembered the abundance of work and the ease with which she had found a position in the autumn of nineteen hundred and eighteen. The prejudice against women as workers had not survived the economic urgency of a world conflict. There had been no eager preference, immediately after the Armistice, for returned soldiers. Women in industry would always be cheaper than men, and since the war was won, prosperity was more agreeable, if not more important, than patriotism. The first place she had sought in November was hers for the asking. Now, at the end of January, she felt secure at least until Ralph's return, or as long as she needed security. Her father, too, had found work, and was teaching history and languages in Boscobel School, a fashionable academy where the daughters of the best families were instructed in all that was necessary. The salary was small, only a hundred dollars a month, but with her twenty dollars a week added, they had been able to live and to pay the cost of moving and settling. Yet she had never imagined that food, even the simplest, and clothes, even the plainest, could bring such high prices as were asked in the shops and markets of Queenborough. Their joint income, which would have represented fabulous wealth to her grandmother, was barely sufficient to keep them properly clothed and fed in a neighbourhood that had seen better days.

Well, since the war was over and right had triumphed again, life might begin to be easier. There might be room for every one, even for a scholar, Aunt Meggie exclaimed hopefully, in a world that had been made safe for democracy. For Aunt Meggie's serenity was unruffled. After her first grief for her mother had subsided into regret, she had regained her cheerfulness without effort. "Mother is happy," she had said. "You could tell by the way she looked how much she liked Heaven." And when the manse was sold at auction over their heads, she had rebuked Ada for weeping. "Maybe the good Lord doesn't want us to love a house more than our heavenly mansion."

As soon as the furniture was unpacked, she had set to work making a new home. Life may be a pilgrimage, Ada had thought, while she cleaned and scrubbed, but a home is something more than a house. Yet, in some intimate fashion, material links still held the seen and the unseen together. The cheerful hand-woven rugs were spread over the floors; the speckled engravings nobody would buy were hung on the walls, over which John Fincastle had spread a pale cinnamon-coloured wash; and the treasured remains of his library were placed on shelves he had made from old timber. There were two stories to the house, with three rooms on each floor, and an additional bedroom under the red tin roof over the kitchen and laundry. The living-room, which opened on a balcony of wrought iron above Mulberry Street, looked, even when it was bare, Aunt Meggie had remarked, as if it had been lived in not by nomads, but by civilized people. A coal fire was kept up all day in this room, and the baby's crib stood in one corner. Fortunately, the child flourished in any air and on any diet, from mother's milk to patented prepared food. Once even, attracted by a delighted gurgle, Ada had surprised the charwoman, who came to clean every Saturday, feeding him strips of broiled bacon skin. Though the other rooms were insufficiently heated by gas stoves, it was only when they reminded themselves of the log fire in Mother's chamber that they paused to regret the lost glow of the flames. When John Fincastle came home from his classes and tied his old brown jersey about his neck, he would remark jestingly that the stove made him sleepy, but the still cold invigorated his mind. With a pot of coffee on his desk, he would work long after Aunt Meggie had piled quilts on her bed and dropped asleep in a bleak room with tightly closed windows.

But they were happy. They were waiting. The war was over, and a new world was beginning. Ralph was coming home, and nothing else really mattered, Ada's heart assured her, while gladness poured into her mind.

"If it weren't for you, I shouldn't care," he had written, "but with you and the boy, I begin to think there may be something ahead. The war didn't scratch me. I haven't so much as a shell shock to bring home, and I can never leave you a pension. But you come too close to human nature in a war like this, and when you are through, all you want to do is to forget you're human. Disgust is the only feeling I have left, and that's not much worse than the way I felt when I left Ironside after that rotten deal. I'd like to go off somewhere with you two alone, but I suppose I'd better try to pull through where I can find a job. I don't give a damn for law any longer. It's too old, and so am I. I've been living for a thousand years, and I'm as dry as a husk. And God knows I'm sick of women—except you. But you aren't a woman. You're Ada, and that's different. There's been no lack of women in this war. They've rushed for every horror as straight as ducks

Vein of Iron

for a puddle. I'm sick of women, and God knows I'm sick of mud. All I want is to get away. Never to speak of it. Never to think of it . . ."

Round the electric light at the corner a million tiny globes of sleet circled, like frozen moths in an eddying swarm. The wind hurtled; signs rocked; bells clanged; horns shrieked; voices brayed; wheels skidded; chains rattled; and overhead lights blazed and faded, as if the dissonance were threaded on flashes of brilliance. Within the shelter of the doorway, she watched the throng slipping, sliding, spinning, slouching, through the slush and the watery reflections. Under the glare of electricity, broken by ice-green splinters of light, the scene wavered and passed before her eyes, like a procession in a delirium. In the window at her side her own image turned and glanced back at her. She saw her shabby coat and her ungloved hands clutching a cotton umbrella. Then, looking more closely, she met the fearless gaze beneath the dark winged eyebrows, the wine-red in the cheeks, the glow of sanguine vitality. They're different, these women, and they're all alike, she thought. . . . A rush of rain dashed against her. "Ah, ah, ah, ah," moaned the wind, speeding by, and below the storm, through the driving gale, she heard the shrill, thin, metallic song of the human stream. "I, I, I, I . . ." Never an end. Always the bright, blank current, eager, empty, grasping, insatiable. . . .

The cold touched her with icy fingers. Here she stood detached, solitary, self-rooted, while throngs of human beings plunged by her toward some catastrophe they both feared and desired. In Shut-in Valley each separate individual had projected above, or aside from, the community. The bold outline of the frontier had not flattened to a uniform level. But this mass movement of living seemed to threaten that precious identity she called her soul. There's no use waiting, she told herself; yet she still waited, with her gaze on the crowd which scurried, in the shape of a gigantic insect, through currents of wind and rain. They were all alike, she thought, especially the women—all wore that stare of bright immaturity, all moved with flat bosoms, with narrow hips, with twisting ankles on French heels. Her thoughts drooped with fatigue, and the blur of faces spread before her, like rows of shallow saucers filled with slopping idealism. Hundreds of women—of women trying to look like boys and to fill the places of men! Would the swarm seize her at last and distort her outline into a caricature of male adolescence?

But youth that had saved the future for itself was now setting out blithely to dismember the past. To begin again without a foundation. In Ironside, poor as they were, they had built upon rock. Now in Queenborough, it seemed to her, life was an air plant, springing up out of the emptiness. Vapour it was yesterday, and vapour it would be again to-morrow. All that she had thought of as enduring for ever had apparently melted away.

Without putting up her umbrella, she pushed out into the storm, and her image in the lighted mirrors pushed with her, strong, erect, undefeated. Ahead of her, she saw the warm room, where the baby waited in his crib, and Aunt Meggie set the table for supper in front of the open fire. It would be like this, only better, far better, when Ralph came back to her. Then they would find each other again in a world that had mistaken sensation for happiness. They would build a home in the wilderness of the machines as their forefathers had cleared the ground and built a home in the wilderness of the trees.

Suddenly the wind lulled, the glare darkened, the discord receded into a rumour. From Broad Street she had turned into Mulberry Street, where the sunken brick pavements stretched dimly away to the terraced hill presiding over the canal and the river and the iron furnaces that shot up flame and smoke into the twilight. A few of the more spacious houses had been turned into flats and supplied with the modern necessities of steam heat and electricity. A few others had become boarding-houses for the clerks and stenographers in the near factories and the saleswomen in shops. Over these places, one and all, a kind of skin-deep prosperity had broken out in a rash. When every man, black or white, who could wield a hammer was able to command from six to eight dollars a day for driving a nail, the earliest war wages had been transformed by magic into pianolas and Nottingham lace curtains, just as the later and still higher wages of the post-war period would change automatically into radios and electric refrigerators and the newest model of Ford cars. Though the wind had died down for a moment, it seemed to her that she could still hear the shrill human wail, "I . . . I . . . I . . . I . . ."

A DARK star shone out in the snow, and Ada thought, Aunt Meggie has put the lamp near the window. Every winter afternoon that lamp with the red shade flashed a welcome when she looked over the way from the beginning of the last block. Suppose Ralph has come! her heart sang. Suppose Ralph is waiting for me! Other lights twinkled from the closed houses, and it seemed to her that these lights were suddenly fused with the star in her own window. In Ironside they had lived more or less withdrawn from the community, because the road and the fields and the church separated them from the village; but in the last two months they had settled into a strange neighbourhood, and Aunt Meggie at least had earned a welcome for herself in every house in the quarter.

A boy in a rubber coat, his face shining with sleet, joined her at the crossing. She knew his name, Bertie Rawlings, and Aunt Meggie had told her that he was the son of a dressmaker who lived on the first floor of the yellow house at the corner. Every day when she went to work or came home, Ada could see Mrs. Rawlings stooped over her sewing-machine, and she wondered whether the woman, who was a widow and frail, ever paused to draw breath. She had seen better days, and she had determined that her son, a wide-awake handsome boy, should have every advantage his father had known in his youth. "It will be time enough to rest when Bertie is able to take care of me," she had said to Aunt Meggie above the ceaseless whirring of her machine. "I shan't begrudge any sacrifice if only Bertie can make a success of his life."

"Does your mother ever stop, Bertie?" Ada asked.

He laughed gaily. "When she goes to bed. She never stops except when she's in bed."

"Well, you must make it up to her."

"When I'm a man, I'm going to be rich. Then we'll have a fine car and plum pudding every day."

He darted over the slippery pavement, and she pushed on against the wind until the sound of dance music floated from the boarding-house next to her own door. Beyond her iron gate, light flickered up from the basement, where Otto Bergen, a cabinet-maker of German descent, had his neat workshop and kept his green and red parrot and his family of tame white mice with pink eyes. A stout, round, genial man, with a pleasant smile and hair like beaver fur, he had already formed a friendship with John Fincastle, from whom he rented his basement rooms. With his thrifty homekeeping wife and his two little daughters, he lived in the adjoining house, and he had transformed a grimy back yard into the only flower garden in Mulberry Street. Usually, when she came in Ada stopped for a word with him, or to exchange a greeting with the Hamblens, an elderly couple of faded gentility who occupied the second-floor front rooms of the boarding-house; but this evening she shut the gate quickly behind her, and ran up the steps to the balcony of wrought iron, where the mellow lamplight splashed like wine on the snow. When she entered the dim cold passage and paused to leave her soaking umbrella, the door of the living-room opened and Aunt Meggie called, "You must be wet through. Change as quickly as you can, and give me your things to dry."

"Is the baby all right? I shan't go near him till I'm dry and warm."

"He's had a good day. That infant's food seems to agree with him splendidly. I never saw such a healthy baby. Rub your feet well before you put on your stockings."

"I'm warm now, and so hungry." Her spirit fluttered upward and fatigue melted away. All that meant home and peace seemed to close in about her and to defend her from the malice of circumstance. The red heart of the fire, the shadow of flames on the ceiling, the old walnut table with its thread mats and worn silver, and the flushed baby breathing as softly as a butterfly in his crib —all these things were swimming in a miraculous fluid, in an extraordinary delight.

When she came back from her bedroom, after smoothing her hair and slipping into the old dress of crimson wool that she wore in the house because it looked and felt warmer than black, Ranny awoke and cried, and she picked him up in her arms and sat rocking him to sleep again in front of the fire.

"I wish we had a telephone," she said to Aunt Meggie, who was preparing supper. "Every footstep seems to be Ralph's."

"He'll be sure to telegraph. We don't miss a telephone in town as much as we did in the country."

"I can't help feeling he has landed."

"We'd certainly have heard." Aunt Meggie was placing the worn Sheffield candlesticks beside the blue bowl, which was filled with winter leaves and berries John Fincastle had picked. "Anyway, he is safe, and I keep thinking of poor Mr. Midkiff, out yonder in that old kitchen next door. He has just lost his only child. She was a fine trained nurse, Mrs. Hamblen says, and Mr. Midkiff, who had never had any education because he was born in a county almshouse, worked his fingers to the bone trying to give her the kind of start she needed. It seems dreadful— doesn't it?—that he wasn't taught even to read and write when he was little. His father was disabled in the war, and the whole family (there were five children before Mr. Midkiff) had to move to the almshouse. Then his father and mother died, and all the children were put out to work. His daughter had always said she would look after him, and she didn't go over with the Red Cross because he was in a charity ward for an operation, and she was all he had to depend on. She nursed all through the epidemic. Then, after Christmas, she went out on a case of flu and caught it and died in three days."

Ada shivered and drew nearer the fire, while the baby clutched her and whimpered. "I've been haunted by his misery. He was a good carpenter, and now he is too weak to go back to work. How in the world will he manage?"

"Mrs. Maudsley lets him live in that tumbledown kitchen, and she always has enough left over to feed him. Her boarders are very particular, she says, and she has to be careful not to feed them on anything that looks like scraps from the last meal. As soon as he's well, Mr. Bergen is going to give him a real job doing over old furniture. He's a steady worker and has a knack for treating old mahogany. If these good times keep up, he'll be able to make out, I reckon, with what the neighbours can do for him. Ever since he began to get on in life, he has cut railway ties at fifteen cents, or twenty cents, if he was in luck. Nobody ever told him what year he was born in, but I doubt whether he's more than forty-seven—though he looks older. I wish you could see that kitchen he lives in. It's no better than a rat hole, but Mrs. Maudsley says she's never seen anybody with such a horror of the almshouse. He says calling it the City Home doesn't take the shame out of it."

"He has a good face. That thick grey beard makes him look like a prophet. Has Father been over to see him?"

"He was there right after breakfast. But he says it isn't easy to help people who have nothing to live for. Your father has his own worries, I know, though he never complains. I can tell just by the way he looks when he comes home how those girls torment him at school. They do everything they can to get rid of him, because he is old and they want a young man they can flirt with to teach them. Nobody need tell me the world is going to be any better because the young have taken it over."

"I am sorry about Father. Where is he now?"

"Upstairs at work. I tried to make him light the stove, but he said he'd rather put on his greatcoat. He had a letter from a Scottish professor this morning, and that pleased him. Now that the war is over, I hope the next volume of his book will be brought out as soon as it's finished. This man at the University of Edinburgh thinks it is the greatest work of the last twenty years.

Isn't it queer John should say he'd learned a great deal from the war when he spent most of his time in the manse?"

"The work is everything to him. I suppose he trusts to the future, but I'd feel better if I could give those girls a piece of my mind."

"I know that feeling. What troubles me most is that children are growing worse every day."

Ada shivered at a recollection. "There were bad children in Ironside. But I hope the world will have settled by the time Ranny grows up. Did you ever see such a skin? His hair is the color of honey, and his eyes are like blue flowers."

"Yes, he's a handsome baby, and a good one so far. You'd better put him down and let me bring in supper. I don't want the omelet to fall. There's one thing to be said for living in the city, butter and eggs aren't so scarce in wintertime."

"And there's money to buy them," Ada replied lightly, while she tucked the baby in his crib, where he fell asleep almost immediately. If only Ralph could see him, she thought, and turned with a start of joy at the sound of steps on the porch.

Before the bell rang she had flung the door wide and was drawing him to shelter from the thrust of the wind. "Ralph, Ralph," she breathed over and over, on a note of quivering ecstasy so faint that it was lost in the dim passage. At last she was in his arms again; her whole being was charged with this precious sense of recovery, fulfilment, completeness, perfection. "Oh, Ralph . . . Ralph . . ."

"You came so quickly," he said, "you must have been waiting."

"Ever since the Armistice." Her voice faltered and drooped, as if she were running. "We've expected you for weeks. Aunt Meggie was sure you'd telegraph."

He shook his head. "There were things I wanted to see about —things like getting a job. Well, anyway, it's good-by to war. You aren't sorry to lose a soldier?"

"Sorry?" Inside the living-room, they fell apart and looked at each other.

"You're still yourself," he said. "You haven't changed."

"No, I haven't changed." She reached out her hands, stroking first his face and then his arm, as if she needed to be convinced by a touch. He looked thinner, harder, older, and his fresh skin had coarsened. It struck her as swiftly as a blow that he had forgotten how to smile. "No, we haven't changed, have we?"

He drew her into his arms. "Why did I come back?"

"Then you're happy? You're happy to be back?"

"Happy?" He laughed without merriment. "When you've been in that muck and got out of it, you don't know the meaning of happiness. But I'll be happy. Soon I'll be happy. I can do almost anything when I make up my mind to it. Only have patience and let me get clean again."

"I'll have patience." Her voice broke. "But you love me? You're glad to be back?"

"Of course I love you." He glanced round him. "You're like your mother. Wherever you are becomes home." Then his lips trembled. "Where is the boy? Let me see him first when we are alone."

"Look at him now. Aunt Meggie will come in a minute." Seizing his hand, she drew him to the crib and watched while he bent over and touched the baby's hair as delicately as if he feared that it might crumble to powder. He was silent for so long while he stood there that she spoke again in a whisper.

"They're coming, Ralph. Aunt Meggie is calling Father. But isn't it wonderful? Just the three of us together."

"He's a fine boy. I hope his life will be less rotten than mine."

"Less rotten! Oh, Ralph, isn't this something?"

"It's everything, only"—his smile flickered and went out—"I've almost come to believe that everything is nothing. No, I don't mean that, Ada. This isn't the first time I've talked like a fool." He turned away from the crib. "Would they rather not see me till to-morrow? We can be married the first thing in the morning. I've arranged it with a clergyman a little way out of town. Nobody need know when it was."

"Father and Aunt Meggie understand, but Grandmother never forgave me. I killed Grandmother." How far off, how dim and unreal, remorse now seemed to her as it sank into the past!

"You're wonderful, Ada," he said, and though he spoke with feeling, it seemed to her that the feeling and the words were all part of something he had learned long ago and was repeating with tenderness but without passion.

Was it only the pulsing fear in her mind or did he turn with a look of relief to Aunt Meggie? There was a choking sob in her throat, and she put out her hands again to grasp reality before it turned to a shadow.

"You've come at the right moment," Aunt Meggie exclaimed, while his face lighted up at her welcome. "Ada will pour the coffee, and I'll run back and broil the ham I was saving for breakfast. Sit down by the fire while I beat up another omelet."

"There's nothing I'd like better." For the first time he was speaking without constraint. "Every time I tasted chicory in France I remembered your mother's coffee."

As John Fincastle came in and took off the greatcoat he had forgotten to leave in the hall, Ralph sprang up and went eagerly toward him.

"So you're back, my boy?"

"Yes, I'm back to do the best I can for you. Ada can stop working and give me a chance. She's been wonderful . . . but she mustn't be too wonderful. . . . I shan't talk about it, but I've made all our plans for the future, and they begin early tomorrow."

"Well, I'll be glad," John Fincastle said. "I'll be glad to have Ada stop working."

At the head of the table, with her arm bent over the coffee-pot, Ada felt that the walls of the room were breaking up and reassembling in curves and arabesques of firelight. Was this the way things came after waiting? Always in a new design. Never again with exactly the same perfection? There was pathos in his look, and a pathetic wistfulness in his anxiety to do right.

Even his pleasure in his supper, and the flicker of expectancy in his eyes while he watched her pour his coffee, seemed to her boyish and touching and in some queer way unnatural. Of what was he thinking? she asked herself, while she raised her free hand to brush a mist from her eyes. Had the long separation, and all that he had seen and suffered while they were apart, opened an abyss between their lives that nothing, not even love, would be able to bridge?

"Oh, Ralph, is it true? Are you really here?" she exclaimed.

"Sure!" The russet colour flowed under his skin, and he straightened his shoulders as he smiled back at her. "That's the only thing I'm sure of to-night."

"Well, the rest is over," John Fincastle said quietly, but there was a dazed look in his eyes, as if he were still inhabiting the world of ideas in which facts are as fleeting as symbols.

The door into the hall opened and shut, and Aunt Meggie brought in the omelet and a dish of broiled ham. "But you must be glad," she protested in her sprightly tone. "You must be glad, Ralph, that you helped to save civilization."

"I am not so sure as I once was." Ralph took the dish from her hands and placed it carefully in the centre of the thread mat on the table. "I'm not so sure civilization is worth saving."

"But, my dear boy, you were splendid. Ironside is so proud of your record, especially of the time you killed all those German soldiers single-handed."

"Lord, Lord, was it as bad as that? Well, it's news to me, like most war news."

"Why, the church wall has a tablet with the names of all the young men of the congregation who went into the war. Mr. Black is so proud of it. He never fails to point out your name and to tell about your exploits."

"Worse and worse." Though he laughed pleasantly, there was an overtone of derision. "Well, I hope he won't begin to tell me. Ever since I landed three weeks ago I have been trying to keep my mind on automobiles."

"You landed three weeks ago!" John Fincastle exclaimed, while Ada watched breathlessly.

Ralph flushed. "I know it seems queer, but it wasn't, not really. It was like shedding a dead skin and growing a new one. If I'd been wounded or gassed or shell-shocked, I might have known what to do. But I was as sound as I ever was. Nothing had touched me. Yet for a week after I landed I walked the streets of New York in a blue funk. I had to forget what I'd seen in France—oh, I know some men enjoyed it!—before I could start selling cars in Queenborough."

"Well, the killing is all over," Aunt Meggie persisted. "And the world will look better when you've had a third cup of coffee."

"It looks better after a second."

When he smiled the drawn muscles of his face relaxed and the moody stillness in his eyes sparkled to humour. His eyes, Ada noticed, were darker, as if a shadow from within retarded the light. He loved her, he had come back to her, yet something was missing. A faint chill crept over her gladness. Would it ever return, that lost radiance? They could not, he had said then, look back. They must go on—but to what? If they had waited for love, would they be happier now? Or would they have missed forever that intensest joy in terror of parting? She didn't know. Who could answer that question? But she would have patience as she had promised him. It isn't merely loving that matters, she thought. It is belonging together.

When supper was over, she helped Aunt Meggie clear the table, while her father and Ralph sat by the fire and talked of the future. Never of yesterday. Always of tomorrow, of next year, of the years after. Life was renewing itself. The past had faded and vanished, and everything would be different. Moving from firelight to shadow, which seemed to mingle with the rhythm of voices in her ears, in her mind, she heard the two men speaking in subdued tones of the years ahead.

"Every one is expecting an after-the-war boom," Ralph was

saying. "You must let me take care of the household. I'll have a salary of three thousand dollars besides a commission after I sell a number of cars. I'll be sure to sell cars. Everybody who has money is buying, and the Duncan makers are going to put out the best cheap car this spring."

"I'll be glad to have Ada stay at home," John Fincastle replied. "But the habit of independence is a stubborn one. I'd rather keep my classes as long as I am able." He had aged since coming to Queenborough, and it seemed to Ada, as she watched him, that his features were chiselled down almost to the bone.

"If you like," Ralph said, glancing round, "we can move into a bigger house and a better neighbourhood."

"Not yet," Ada answered before her father could speak. "Not until next year, or the year after. There is nothing the matter with this neighbourhood. It's quiet, but so are we, and we like it."

"Yes, they're simple folk like us," John Fincastle agreed.

"If only you could have a fire, Father, instead of a bricked-up grate and a gas stove."

"We'll have all the fires we want," Ralph said, eager and wistful to please, and so strangely appealing. "At least we can be warm if you'd rather not move."

Ada laughed happily. Oh, how beautiful life could be after suffering! "Let's save a little before we begin to spend. If we save enough, we may be able to buy the manse for a summer home. Nobody is going to pay a good price for that out-of-the-way place."

"But I thought you wanted to come away. Would you like to go back to Ironside?"

"In a few years when we're older. I've a feeling that I've left a part of me, perhaps only a root, in the Valley." For this had been her secret dream ever since she had lived in the city. To go back, not now, but some day when they had prospered and saved, and all the children in Ironside had grown up.

"Hasn't Ada any kin here?" Ralph asked. "Where are her mother's people?"

"If I have any, they aren't thinking of me," Ada replied. "And I'm too proud to remind them of Mother."

"I pass the Blands' house every day," John Fincastle said. "They were Mary Evelyn's cousins, and she was visiting them when I met her. She had come to town for the winter."

"It is a beautiful house. I'd like to go inside." Ada's tone had grown pensive.

Ralph was looking steadily into her eyes, and she leaned over him while her enkindled features reflected his gaze. Though she did not speak, she knew that her smile told him everything. What joy, she thought, while the burning sweetness saturated her being. Was this the end of long patience, of sleepless anxiety?

Starting up, he pushed back his chair. "Everything is ready for to-morrow, even the license. I went out to see Mr. Berry this morning, and he is expecting us—the four of us—at ten o'clock."

"Well, it's Saturday," John Fincastle said gravely. "There are no classes on Saturday."

For a minute Ralph hesitated. Then he looked at Ada and asked, "Will you wear this red dress?"

"Who ever saw a bride in a red dress?"

"I don't care. I like it."

"Then I'll wear it." For it was bliss, and he knew it, to have everything, even the colour of her dress, taken out of her hands.

Everything is ours now, she told herself, everything we had hoped for. Yet a moment later, when he stooped to kiss her good night, reserve had closed in a mask over his face, and she looked in vain for the romantic gleam in his eyes.

S IT because I'm old, John Fincastle asked himself, that the world seems deranged? Had the
dregs of violence churned to a froth on the surface? Or was the thing called civilization now
dying in spasms after a victory over nature?
Not that it mattered— One must keep an open
mind toward the future. If one waited long enough, froth would
settle and dregs would sink again to the bottom. Meanwhile, he
had finished his book; the fifth and last volume would see the
light (or so his publishers assured him) as soon as the post-war
world had found itself; and life as a spectacle was never more
amusing, perhaps, than in the autumn of 1925. He was old, and
he would presently pass away, but his work, all that was important in his existence as a human being, would live on as thoughts
in the minds of a few scattered and lonely thinkers. If he were
remembered by others, it would be either as a dangerous skeptic,
or as a man of simple faith, who believed that God is essence,
not energy, and that blessedness, or the life of the spirit, is the
only reality.

As he descended the steps of the finishing school, he pushed
onward through a thicket of flaxen legs and blank flowerlike
faces. Not until he had passed beyond the rosy knees and the
red mockery of the lips (even schoolgirls painted their lips) did
he slacken his pace and pause to draw breath amid the purring
of ceaseless dynamos. He could never escape from that mechanical vibration, which seemed to him not only the pulse, but the
very soul, of the machine. Yet he had resolved that as long as
his strength held out, he would earn his keep and pay the premi-
ums, as they fell due, on what was left of his insurance. After
that, when the infirmities of age overtook him, there would still

be the good end ahead. For, whatever else he had missed in life, the good end he could never miss.

But the young? Would the young always and everywhere confuse change with progress? Did every new age evolve from a ferment of centrifugal forces? Had it been like this in his youth? He tried to look back, but the view was too far and too faint. Still, it seemed to him that his generation had held, however loosely, to some standard of living. Nobility of motive had not then become a lost issue. True, then as now, the world was inhospitable to the lover of wisdom, though it had remained for the age of invention to make him an outcast. Nowadays, he mused, with a glance at the scattered clouds in the November sky, whatever could not feed the machine was discarded as rubbish. Everything, from the aimless speeding of automobiles down to the electric dust in the sunlight, appeared to whirl on deliriously, without a pattern, without a code, without even a centre. Yet he was an old fogey, of course, and youth, with its cool, resentful stare, mocking and insolent, was rebuilding the world.

Only that morning, on an early walk, he had seen front yards littered with empty bottles, and three drunken boys sprawling on the grass after a dance at a club. A few weeks before he had stumbled upon one of his own pupils, a girl of seventeen, locked in an embrace in a parked car down a country lane. All this, he reminded himself, was merely the foam of transition, and would disappear as it came. But would the perpetual flux and reflux of individualism reduce all personality to the level of mass consciousness? Would American culture remain neither bourgeois nor proletarian, but infantile? Would the moron, instead of the meek, inherit democracy?

While he walked on, towering above the crowd, with the scholar's stoop in a spine that had once been erect, and the ray of otherworldliness shining through his deep eyes and transparent features, persons who passed him hurriedly turned, with a backward glance, and said to themselves, That tall old man must be a stranger. But he was thinking, There is something in me that is still young, that will stay young if I live to be a hundred. It was this something that loved life and would live it over again in its wholeness, mingling the good with the bad, that had never valued an effortless heaven, that sympathized with youth even while he condemned its unimaginative cruelty, its pitiless egoism.

As he reached the corner, an old Negro peddler rolling a pushcart was knocked down, and from the speeding car that struck him, several bright young faces stared back with a look of indignant astonishment. "They are just young things out for a good time," remarked a middle-aged woman in the maternal tone. "All the same there ought to be a law," protested a moody bystander. And a traffic policeman, who had strolled over from the middle of the street, observed cynically, "Well, as long as they'd rather risk a killing than slow down, what is anybody going to do about it?"

In the old Negro's face there was neither astonishment nor indignation; there was only perplexity. He lay on his back, in the midst of his scattered vegetables, onions, beets, carrots, turnips, potatoes, wrinkling his forehead as if he were trying to recollect something he had forgotten. One bluish hand, on which the knuckles gleamed pallid, still clutched the turnip he had reached out to save. Then the group closed in about him, a passing physician stopped his car and stepped out, and the old Negro was dragged aside to wait for the ambulance.

When John Fincastle turned into Washington Street, a flock of sparrows scuttled like brown leaves over the pavement, and for a moment he stood watching them, while his soul was swept by a wave of nostalgia. The Great Valley might be upon another planet, so distant, so luminously green and springlike did it appear in his memory. Always in spring he now saw it, never in autumn or winter. Yet there were times when the thrilling blue of God's Mountain seemed to exist only within his mind, and to melt into his being. And there were other hours when he felt that he was wandering on a vast plain, treeless and dead, where all the peaks had been leveled and twilight was flowing down in a sultry, impalpable tide.

Every afternoon, rain or sun, he walked several blocks out of his way for the sake of passing the Bland house in Washington Street. It was there that he had first seen Mary Evelyn, as she came down the steps between the white columns and paused for an instant under the elms on the terrace. Sometimes, toward sunset, Ada and he would stroll up the street, with Ranny running between them, and for a little while they would watch from the opposite pavement to see the Bland family come in or go out. It was the one romantic image now left in their lives—the old yellow house, with the Doric columns, the grassy terrace, and the look of ancient nobility that had fallen on vulgar times.

"It must be beautiful to live like that," Ada would sigh. "In that house they must have kept dignity. I suppose things still move with ceremony, and they think romantic thoughts as people used to do when Mother was a girl."

"I wish you knew them, my dear. They are your mother's people."

"I'd love to see them, but not now. I want to feel as dignified as they are before I claim kinship."

Usually, he would pause for an instant as one might pause by a grave or a memory; but this afternoon he hurried on because the face of the old Negro floated before him in the shadows under the elms.

Like himself, he mused whimsically, as he turned into Mulberry Street, this neighbourhood was decayed and forgotten. The people who lived here were quiet folk, stranded in some slow back current of time. They worked hard, enjoyed simple pleasures, and asked only a reasonable security. His first feeling of strangeness in the community had worn off, and in the past seven years he had fallen into the habit of dropping in on one of his neighbours at the end of the day. He had grown attached to the Hamblens, an elderly married pair, who had denied themselves in youth for the sake of a peaceful old age together in two front rooms of a boarding-house. Both were devout in the Episcopal faith, and though they had always been

poor, they prided themselves upon being, as they would have
said, "well-born." In the old-fashioned spacious rooms, with
high ceilings, they now lived in the way they had admired in
their laborious youth. Mr. Hamblen was a slight, frail, asthmatic
man, dry and brittle, with a pointed grey beard hiding his
chin, and eyes that were a little guarded but quick and kind
when you took them by surprise. His wife was so much like him
that Meggie was sure they must have been cousins. Her figure
was tall and spare, with nervous, willowy movements, and there
was a look of anxious solicitude in her face that reminded John
Fincastle of an aging Madonna. All about them, around, below,
above, industrious young persons who had escaped the post-war
contagion of wildness, slept and dressed and ate sober meals before they set out to spend the long day in steam-heated factories
or shops. Many of these young people helped to support families, and most of them asked as little of life as their patient elders
had asked in their youth.

But the neighbours he liked best were the Bergens, who rented
his basement and lived in the small house with the iron balcony
on the right. Otto Bergen had inherited a magic touch with furniture, and he could bring out the secret lustre, like a shining
heart, in old walnut or mahogany. He had, too, the German
friendliness for animals. His workshop in the basement sheltered,
to the delight of Ranny and other children on the block, a
variety of pets he had rescued from ill-treatment. Not only was
there his superb parrot on its stand, but the big cage contained a
whole community of trained white mice. He was never seen
apart from his slender little dachshund, Hans, with a coat like
brown satin and a long wise head, as flawless and fine as a cameo.

In the middle of the block an alley ran through to Hill Street.
This was the favorite playground of the neighbourhood children, and as he approached it now a little boy in a knitted suit
dashed out, with a toy gun, crying, "Uppity! Uppity!" in an
excited treble. Immediately behind him, a young mother bore
down proudly upon her offspring. "He means you must put up
your hands!" she exclaimed. "He says he's going to be a gangster

when he grows up. And he was just five his last birthday!"

"But suppose I don't put up my hands?"

"Oh, of course, the gun doesn't go off. But he'd make believe he was holding you up."

She beamed, and John Fincastle chuckled, but it was not a chuckle of merriment.

When he went by the Bergens' workrooms to-day, he glanced in without stopping. Was it the fluting presence of canaries that made the basement so cheerful? Was it the fire of coals in the grate, and the rapturous gloating of Otto Bergen over a table by Duncan Phyfe? Or was it the animated coming and going of Mrs. Bergen and her two pretty daughters? Though Otto was not disposed to piety, his wife was a German Catholic, and she lived and moved in the serene order of ritual. She was still very pretty, and John Fincastle admired her neat blue or pink cotton dresses, and the wreath of fair plaits she wore like a coronet. Both daughters resembled their mother, though Rosa, the elder, was a silvery blonde, and Minna, a forward girl of sixteen, had borrowed her sister's pure features and enkindled them with a personality that was already defiant and dashing. At eighteen, Rosa was engaged to be married. Her hands were usually filled with linen she hemmed or embroidered, and the old man enjoyed watching her while she sewed with her pensive gaze on the damask that streamed over her knees. There was something exquisitely touching in these blissful preparations for a future that might be different from the one she anticipated.

He had never seen, he reflected, so happy a family. Though the ties of kinship were strong in the Fincastles and Craigies, the moral climate of Calvinism was not favorable to effervescent emotion. At Ironside, anniversaries were ignored or neglected, but in the Bergens' family circle every festival, even the birthday of Hans, was celebrated with a kind of wistful remembrance. For three generations the Bergens and the Hartmanns had lived in Queenborough, yet Mrs. Bergen, who had made only one visit to Germany, still observed many of her grandmother's customs. Occasionally, when John Fincastle would drop in on a wet afternoon, she would summon the two men into the oddly furnished living-room next door, and give them coffee with thick cream or hot frothy milk, and slices of light sugary coffee cake. Only during the past weeks had the old man surprised a brooding anxiety in her smile, and a note of exasperation in her husband's whistle as he worked. Was it possible, he wondered, that Minna was so soon beginning to cause her parents uneasiness?

W******HILE John Fincastle ascended the steps to the balcony, Ranny dashed across the street from a vacant lot and climbed the steep flight beside him. At the age of seven he was a well-developed and vigorous boy, with thick chestnut hair, a ruddy skin that was not sensitive, and bright blue eyes which were clear and direct, without the dreaming inward gaze of his grandfather.

"I want my skates, Grandfather," he said. "I got to go out again."

"It's time to wash your face and hands." The old man glanced at his watch. "When did you come home from school?"

"At one o'clock. I had to do over a sum, but it didn't take me a minute. All the other boys are older'n me, and I got through the first one."

"Well, I'm proud of you, my boy. You're manly for your years. But have you forgotten what I said this morning about rowdy speaking?"

Ranny squirmed. "I can't talk like you, Grandfather. I can't. The boys don't know what I mean. They say it's just baby talk. I can't, can I?"

"Perhaps not. By the time you're grown we may all be saying 'older'n me.'"

"Did you know Aunt Meggie was making apple dumplings?"

"Then you'd better come in. She doesn't like to be kept waiting."

"Do you have to go to school most of your life, Grandfather? I mean most of the time you want to have fun?"

"Some people have to. That depends on how quickly you learn."

Yes, he was a fine boy, the old man reflected. Tall and strong for his age, and brimming over with energy, he was already a leader among the neighbourhood children. Though he lacked the Irish charm of his father, he had been born with that effortless magic which subdues circumstances.

When John Fincastle came downstairs he found the table set for dinner at three o'clock, after the custom at Ironside. While he watched Ada bring in the dishes, he regretted that her figure was losing its girlish outlines, though years had given her the noble bearing that men of his generation had admired more than slenderness. Her smoky blue eyes, so like her mother's in expression as she grew older, held the darkened radiance that proceeds from within outward. Wherever she went she would carry her way of life with her, as the pioneers had carried their Bibles beside their flintlocks and shot pouches. She must have felt, he told himself, that there was something missing in her marriage, but she had felt it in silence. We made a mistake when we tried to separate them, he conceded. You may separate lovers, but not human relationships. On rare occasions, it is true, he had heard her quarreling with Ralph over a trifle; and once at least the marriage had been ruffled by a brief flare of jealousy. Strange, that he should have studied his daughter so closely and yet have believed her incapable of making a scene! Yet this proved only that one human being could never completely understand another. He had learned, though, that anger and jealousy are spasms of the nerves, not of the heart. Vehemence had blown over, like a storm on deep water, leaving the still depths untroubled.

"You may as well sit down," Ada said, bending over to rearrange the berries in the blue bowl. "Ralph telephoned he couldn't get home to dinner. I'm sorry, Ranny, but Aunt Meggie is saving the apple dumplings for supper. After to-day, I think we'll begin having dinner in the evening. Ralph so seldom comes home by three o'clock. Have you washed your hands nicely, Ranny?"

" 'Cep'in' one finger, Mother. I dyed that blue 'cause I was

Dick Blue-Finger. We were playin' pirates. Jimmy Wheatley says his Ma never makes him wash his hands lessen they're real dirty. And the only time he has to wash all over is on Sad'day night." He spoke with spirit, holding his own because he felt that there was reason, if not right, on his side.

Ada regarded him doubtfully. "I sometimes wish we lived in a better neighbourhood."

"Do you suppose children like to wash in another neigh-bourhood?" her father inquired. "Anyhow, Ralph was eager to move seven years ago."

"I know. I was the one who wanted to stay here. But Ranny was a baby then, and now he is so knowing for his age that it makes me anxious about him." Her gaze passed from her father to her son, and she thought proudly, Any mother in the world would want to give a son like that every advantage. I can under-stand the way poor Mrs. Rawlings has worked until she looks as if she had a hump on her back.

"If we save the apple dumplin's, Mother, I want some mo-lasses and corn pone."

"I'll tell Tillie. She's bringing the scalloped oysters."

"I don't want oysters. If I can't have an apple dumplin', I want molasses."

"Did you ever imagine we'd be so well off?" Aunt Meggie asked, with a sigh of contentment, while she sat down with her back to the fire and threw her little crocheted shawl away from her shoulders. Though the lines in her face had deepened with age, they were still sanguine wrinkles. After all, John Fincastle meditated, if Meggie's happiness is the gift of faith without imagination, then Ralph's unhappiness may be the bitter fruit of imagination without faith. Aloud he said, "Yes, Ralph has done well by us."

"But you won't let us help you, Father," Ada protested in a hurt tone. "There is no reason now for you to teach in that girls' school."

"I know, my dear, and I appreciate it. There was never a more generous heart than Ralph's, and generosity is an agreeable virtue. By the way, have you heard anything from Midkiff?" Old Midkiff was always more or less on his mind. In the past seven years John Fincastle had suffered from the strange sensation that he was becoming gradually a part of a street, that his individual unity was a cell in some organic whole.

"We had him mend a broken chair this morning, and he told us he was working steadily for Mr. Bergen. The trouble is that he won't eat enough because he wants to save every penny he makes. He is ridden by the fear of dying a pauper."

A faint quiver crossed and recrossed John Fincastle's features. "Many of us have known that fear."

"His mind has never been quite right since his daughter died," Ada said. "We try to give him one good meal every evening. That is the only way we can make sure he is not starving himself."

"As long as we lived at Ironside," Aunt Meggie murmured regretfully, "we knew at least where we'd be buried. Somebody told me the other day that the manse had been sold again to pay the taxes, and Dr. Updike had bought it in for a song."

"If we do better and better, we may go back some day," Ada answered. "I wonder how Ironside would receive us."

"Oh, everybody would be glad," Aunt Meggie insisted. "They're so proud of Ralph's war record, and folks haven't as long thoughts nowadays, in the midst of all this machinery."

Ada laughed. "It's a pity Ralph is the only person who isn't proud of his war record."

"He will be," John Fincastle retorted, "by the time he is too old to fight. Yes, I like to think I may end my days in the manse."

"Anyway," a shiver crawled down Ada's spine, "the children there will be grown up before we go back."

"Do you feel a draft from the door?" Aunt Meggie inquired anxiously.

"Oh, no." Ada shook her head impatiently. "Ralph says the people let the house go after they found the new highway wouldn't come to Ironside. It went to Teesdale because there were some politicians on that side the mountain. Yes, it would be nice if we could buy the place and go up there for the summers. Summer never seems real in the city."

Suddenly, while she spoke of summer in the Valley, it seemed to John Fincastle that he felt the upward springing and downward seeking of fibres. Was there a physical weakness within? Or had his heart tightened again in the last loop of the road round the hills? "Well, we may yet live to end our days there, Meggie," he said in a quizzical tone.

Ada pushed back her hair as if she were brushing away a stinging recollection. "In a few years we may be able to buy it again, but of course we must think first of Ranny's education."

"Oh, no, you mustn't, Mother, you mustn't. I don't really need one. Lots of people haven't an eddication, old Mr. Midkiff says."

"That's true, my son, but you're going to be educated."

"But why, Mother? Why must I be eddicated if I don't want to be?"

"Because it's the most important thing in the world. Because you must make your way."

"Do I have to be eddicated to play football? I'd rather play football than be a lousy . . ."

"Ranny! Ranny, where did you learn that word? Father, did you hear what he said?"

"I heard it, my dear. I'm used to hearing it."

"Everybody says it, Mother. Father says it." Ranny sounded subdued but unconvinced.

"Well, you shan't. You must never use it again. You aren't old enough. Your father was in the war," his mother replied, with more sincerity than logic. "He may use bad words because he was in the war. Now, if you're going to be good and talk nicely, you may get your skates and run out. The daylight goes so soon, and you simply must not stay in the street after dusk."

As he ran out eagerly to join his playfellows, she said in a whisper, though he was well beyond the range of her voice,

"I sometimes wish everything did not come so easily to him. He's too far ahead of his years."

John Fincastle smiled. "He is only seven, my dear. When he is a little older he will not seem so far advanced."

"We ought to be thankful in this age that he isn't a girl," Aunt Meggie remarked briskly. "Minna Bergen is giving her parents a great deal of trouble. Mrs. Bergen—she is such a nice woman—was crying about her this morning. Rosa is so gentle and good, but Minna has got entirely out of hand. She's only sixteen, but when they reprove her, she tells them she is living her own life. Last night she went out in a roadster with a young man she'd picked up at a movie a few days before, and she didn't come home until almost four o'clock. When Mrs. Bergen asked Father Tallyman to speak to her, she was just as impertinent to him as she is to her parents."

"Well, it takes character to stand being as pretty as that," John Fincastle observed charitably.

"Nobody knows how pretty she'd be if she washed her face," retorted Aunt Meggie, who was without malice but disliked paint and powder.

Ada's features, so eloquent with feeling when she was happy, hardened into a frown. Even as a child, Minna had seemed to her selfish and wayward, with an unchildish arrogance in her manner. There was something about her, Ada had once remarked to Ralph, that resembled, or at least suggested, Janet Rowan; but Ralph had only laughed and denied that he had ever noticed the likeness. And even her father, with the singular lack of reason in the reasonable, was now defending Minna simply because she was pretty.

When Ralph came home that evening, she told him that both her father and Aunt Meggie were homesick for the Valley. "They try not to let me see it, but the note of homesickness sounds in their voices."

"Do you want to go back, Ada?"

"I'm not sure. That depends . . ."

"Everything depends upon something else."

He was standing beside her, and before she answered him, she searched his features with a look that was bright and startled. She knew he loved her; yet in their closest embrace this uncertainty would drift between them, this sense of something intimately dear she had lost without wholly possessing. Everything but the gleam, she had told her troubled heart over and over. No one, of course, could expect that to last. It wouldn't be the gleam if it lasted. For the change went deeper than love, she understood while she accepted it; the flaw was inherent in the very structure of living.

But how she loved him, she thought, though this deep and quiet tenderness was so different from the flaming ecstasy of her girlhood. A better love, perhaps, but not the same love. Just as his face, red-brown, weather-beaten, with the hardened crease round the lips and the defiant reserve in the eyes, was not the face of his romantic youth. He looked more vital than ever; and he was still young, though he was no longer romantic. At moments his touch and voice held the old power over her senses— but only at moments. Yet these instants were still worth to her all the tranquil hours of her happiness.

"Do you really care as much?" she asked suddenly, instead of replying.

"Why do you ask things like that?"

"Because you never tell me so. If only you'd sometimes tell me."

"You ought to know without my having to tell you."

"I do know, but I want to hear it."

He laughed softly. "Well, you'll never get an answer by asking."

No, she couldn't understand. "You used to—I mean when we were younger."

"That was different. That was before we knew anything about life."

She choked back a sob. "No, that was when we believed love

was the best of life and Eagle Ridge the whole world. I can't see," she burst out impulsively, "why the war should have changed you."

"It wasn't the war." His face turned to a mask, she thought, and the amusement in his eyes cooled to derision. "Everything flattened out and went dead on me. But I get a lot out of life as long as I take it on the surface. It's only when I punch through the surface that the world seems to go rotten. Of course I care for you, but it sounds silly when I try to be sentimental. That part doesn't seem to mean anything. When I look about me, in spite of all the good times, misery is the only thing that is real. Hunger and cold and disease and physical agony and meanness and rottenness inside and out human nature. . . ."

"But these things have always been in the world. . . . These things were around us at Eagle Ridge. . . ."

"They hadn't got under my skin . . ." He broke off with a laugh as if he were ashamed of his outburst. "I'll brush up a bit before supper. Would you like to go to a movie?"

She shook her head, and after he had gone into the bedroom she sat alone on the hearthrug and looked through tears at the firelight, which wavered and melted and wavered again into a new pattern. No, it would never come back. After his return, she had hoped for years that the dark mood would wear out. But now she knew better.

She was still sitting alone when he bent over her, with the burnished glow on his hair, and put his hand on her shoulder. "Are you all right?"

"Perfectly all right."

For an instant he stood looking down on her. Then, suddenly, he dropped on his knees by her side and laid his head in her lap. While his arms closed about her, she understood that he was telling her in his own way what he could never put into words. But she knew; she realized without speech what he was trying to say. She felt his hardness and strength; and through the flesh and bone and muscle, she responded to an inner rhythm that was like music. Yes, there was a love that went with you, she thought, while this harmony of mood flowed on into deeper vibrations. A love that came and went with passion, and was over for ever. And there was another and a stronger love that stayed by one if only one had fidelity. But fidelity, she found herself thinking an instant later, is even rarer than love.

HE was almost, if not wholly, glad that she had no daughter to bring up, Ada thought, while she shielded her eyes from the May sunshine and watched Minna Bergen flirting with a strange young man over the black iron gate to the next yard. Last winter, for a few weeks, the girl had become engaged to Bertie Rawlings, while he spent the Christmas holidays with his mother. Then, as soon as the boy returned to his studies, Minna had resumed her casual happiness-hunting. Not only Mrs. Rawlings, but the whole of Mulberry Street, was proud of Bertie Rawlings, who had distinguished himself at the university. Though his mother still bent her rounded back over her sewing machine, her features were wreathed in the smile of a martyr whose martyrdom has been crowned.

Girls were wilder than boys, it seemed, and more troublesome in this spring of 1928. Poor Mrs. Bergen, so good, gentle, and unselfish, had mingled many tears with her prayers. Yet Minna was extraordinarily alive, and that, Father said, appeared to be all people asked. Glutted with its orgy of death, the modern world was now famished for life. For life in any form, even in paroxysms of inflamed egoism. But Ada disliked everything about Minna. She disliked the small, flat head, with the boyish bob, as smooth as butter, pasted in dampened rings on strawberry cheeks; she disliked the large, round, light eyes, like the challenging eyes of a bad baby, staring upward from beneath eyelashes fringed with soot; and, most of all, she disliked the wide insatiable mouth, painted as red as a wound, and the flaunting bare knees above rolled stockings. Cheap, that was the trouble. "A puny breed," was the way her grandmother would have dismissed the whole post-war generation. Though the old woman was safely dead, Ada could hear her strong snort of disgust: "The Evil One Himself cannot stomach a puny breed."

Why was it, she found herself thinking abruptly, that her grandmother, more than her own mother, seemed to live on in her mind and nerves, awaking whenever a bell rang from the past? And the stranger part was that the place Grandmother had filled on earth appeared to grow larger and more empty. A terrible old woman in some ways—yet immortal. "The empty hiccough of lust," she had once said in horror.

Ada's name was breathed in a muted tone, and turning her head, she saw Mrs. Hamblen climbing the flight of steps to the balcony. Aging, though not yet old, she was still slender and upright in carriage, with the refined manner and the sober apparel of discredited gentility. Yet Grandmother, Ada suspected, would have classified her also as "puny."

"I was just admiring your aunt's fine Rhode Island Red rooster," Mrs. Hamblen was saying.

"Oh, Henry VIII! Yes, and he has six handsome hens."

"They have a nice place to scratch in your back yard. I hope it isn't true that you're planning to move in the fall." As she put her hand to the edge of white at her lean throat, Ada saw that her joints were swollen and inflamed, and that she winced when she tried to straighten her forefinger.

I am glad they have enough to live on, the younger woman thought, with an ache of pity. It must be dreadful to be growing old without a sense of security. Aloud she said doubtfully, "We'd like to move next year if this prosperity lasts."

"Every one says still better times are ahead."

"It's hard to believe that. Ralph is selling more Duncan cars now than the factory can turn out. Everybody appears able to afford a car. Even the scissors-grinder told Aunt Meggie he was trying to buy an old Ford."

"What I can't understand," Mrs. Hamblen replied, with an anxious frown, "is that nobody seems to pay for anything he buys. It is all on the installment plan, buying and selling. The coloured maids in our boarding-house buy silk stockings by installment. They wouldn't be caught wearing cotton stockings or lisle thread like mine."

Ada laughed. "I never saw a pair of silk stockings in Ironside, except on Janet Rowan."

"We were taught to practise thrift," Mrs. Hamblen sighed, "but when I see how easily people live without saving, I sometimes wonder whether we made a mistake. My husband and I never had any youth. We were too afraid of having to ask for charity when we were old."

"That kind of fear seems to have passed away."

"The sad part of it is that the young people aren't happy. They aren't even," Mrs. Hamblen murmured pensively, "as happy as we were, saving for something better to come. But that's the trouble, I expect—none of them believe there is anything better to come."

"If they're happy, they don't show it," Ada assented. "Maybe they plaster their faces to hide the discontent in their look. I was just watching Minna Bergen and wondering why she jumps up and down all the time."

Mrs. Hamblen pinched her nose into rimless glasses. "All the girls of her age twist their hips. They appear to have an idea that it is attractive." Her prim, pale lips tightened. "In my day, when we cultivated the Grecian bend, it was thought vulgar to jerk the hips."

"Well, they seem to fall for it now," Ada laughed.

"It's a pity about Bertie Rawlings. He might have done better."

"How does Mrs. Rawlings like it?"

"She thinks it won't last. Bertie is working for his M.A. at the university, and then he's going to try for a scholarship. It will be a long time before he is ready to marry."

"I hope Mrs. Rawlings will live to see him succeed."

"I doubt if she holds out much longer. Ever since Bertie was born, a few months after his father was killed, she has sacrificed everything to his future. She's at the sewing machine by daybreak, and people tell me she works every night till midnight, cutting and basting. Poor woman! My mother used to say she could always tell a mantua-maker by her back."

"Yet she isn't unhappy. I met her going to church with Bertie on Easter Sunday, and her face was shining with happiness. He's nice with her too. He was trying to make her wear a black felt cloche instead of that big hat with the brim."

"If only Minna would let him alone! I heard her speak very pertly to his mother, and he only laughed. Well, I hope you won't feel that you have to move in the fall. Mulberry Street has come to seem like one big family."

"Yes, we're at home here, but I'd feel safer if Ranny could get farther away from those gangs of boys on Oregon Hill and in River Bottom." That was the truth, she told herself, but was it the whole truth? Well, it couldn't be helped . . . The unfinished thought turned in her mind and plunged down into darkness. "If good times keep up, we hope to buy back our old home in the upper Valley. When we do, you must both come to see us one summer."

"Oh, how lovely! We've never been west of the Blue Ridge. We've never had a glimpse of the Alleghanies."

Alone once more, Ada turned her eyes to the street, where billows of dust rose and fell and settled, like waves breaking. There must be room somewhere, she thought, for quiet people who wanted to live apart from the delirium of an ailing world. For it was spring again, and the long shafts of light were ranging over the Valley. With time softening her vision, she watched her own image as it stood, walked, ran, stooped, rose, and at last vanished, in its dim blue dress, a shadow among shadows, within the hyacinth-coloured circle of mountains. That vanishing image was herself. Yet, this also was herself, here, now, in this point of time, this single cell of experience, warm, eager, expectant, still waiting for the lost gleam to flash out of life.

The strange young man had gone on his way (her gaze dropped back to the yard next door), but Minna, touching her orange lips, was looking for someone else. It seemed to Ada that whenever she glanced out of the window, the girl, always with the tiny gilt mirror flashing in her hand, was going out, or coming in, or simply looking for something or somebody. She was like a blaze that may run wild, dazzling, restless, dangerous to watch.

A primrose curtain was blown out from the window behind her, and sucked in again as a door opened and shut. She thought happily of the room at her back, with its soothing colours and the mellow tone of old furniture. The last home-lover, Ralph called her teasingly when she refused to go out at night.

She was still standing there, on the balcony, when she saw that Ralph had jumped out of his car, which he had parked lower down on the block. Every time he came back after parting, it was just as if life were beginning all over again. Though he set out eagerly in the morning, he was always glad to return before the afternoon was far spent. His head was bare as usual, and she watched, with a sense of ease, of complete well-being, the way the sunbeams picked out the auburn tints in his hair and the bronzed ruddiness of his face and throat. He was so near that she could almost see his smile as his eyes searched for her. Then, as he swung on (she liked him in that nut-brown suit matching his eyes), Minna Bergen called his name and reached out her thin arm, without a sleeve, over the gate. At the sound of the girl's voice Ralph stopped and, with her hand still in his, began talking. Of course, it meant nothing. How could he have done otherwise? The girl ran after him, it was true, but then, she ran after any man. Yet it seemed to Ada that all women ran after Ralph. What was there about him that made them, young and old, feel that he attracted them? He never apparently went out of his way; he had been, as he once said lightly, "fed up with women in France"; yet this very indifference appeared to act as a challenge. Few of them meant anything serious. Not one in a hundred was as designing as Minna Bergen—but, oh, that sudden, short, sharp, burning sting of jealousy!

"Ralph!" she called, without thinking, and leaned over the balcony. It was unreasonable, she knew, but she knew also that this impulse of unreason was stronger than her will to resist.

"I'm coming in a minute." He looked up with a laugh. "Has anything happened?"

Turning away quickly, she went indoors and through the hall and the kitchen to the back porch. No, she wasn't, she could never be really jealous. She despised women who were suspicious and nagging. Jaundice-eyed, her grandmother had called them. If that had been anyone but Minna, she told herself, she should not have cared for a minute. But . . . oh, well, all men liked flattery, and as long as Ralph was faithful to her in his heart, nothing else mattered.

CHAPTER 6

N THE kitchen Tillie, the light mulatto maid, was
singing softly while she prepared supper. Now
and then, she would pause, with a big yellow
bowl in her hands, and gaze dreamily through
the back door, over the dandelions and blue-
bottles in the grass, to the poultry yard where old
Midkiff was mending the wire. He was a silent, brooding man,
who worked slowly and diligently. Since the loss of his daughter
he had become slightly unbalanced in mind, but he was honest
and faithful and a good worker. All his life he had turned his
hand to whatever came, and bit by bit he had saved enough to
keep his little girl out of the factory and to buy, when his wife
died, an edge of stony ground overlooking a dump heap in the
poorer part of Rose Hill Cemetery.

Beyond his grizzled head, as he nailed up the chicken wire,
Ada could look into the Bergens' back yard, where the climbing roses were in full bloom. In the centre of the garden there
was a small table, under a Silver Moon rose on an arbour, and
the whole family, except Minna, sat on two grape-leaf iron
benches, which Otto Bergen had picked up in a junk shop and
painted to match the soft green of the leaves. Rosa and her husband, William Ruffner, with their year-old baby, Otto and his
wife, who looked almost as young as her daughter, were all
gathered round Otto's birthday cake and some cups and plates
of brightly flowered china. On the grassy plot, between the
benches and a bed of sweet-william, Hans, the little dachshund,
was sitting in a watchful attitude. Even the parrot and the cage
of canaries had been brought out to enjoy the flowers and the
sunlight driven by shadows.

In a little while Ralph joined Ada, and in the next yard she saw Minna run out and cut a slice from the cake.

"You're home early, Ralph."

He bent over to kiss her. "I'm going straight out again. Will you have supper a little late?"

"We'll wait for you, except Ranny." Her voice dropped to a whisper. "The Bergens look so happy. I like to watch them."

"Think of making all that fuss over a birthday."

"They enjoy it—all but Minna."

"Doesn't Minna enjoy it?"

"She's too discontented."

"Well, she's a live wire."

"Did you see Ranny when you came in?"

He laughed. "Yes, he's watching a ball game between the Oregon Hill Cats and the Mulberry Street Bats."

"I wish you'd brought him in with you. He's too little to play with those big boys."

"He wasn't playing. But he'll have to take his knocks and stand up under them like the rest of us."

"He's too small to begin."

"Not if he knows how to hold his own. Anyway, we shan't have to lie awake worrying about a boy like that."

"But he's the chief reason I want to move. He picks up the most dreadful words."

"Nobody uses nice words any longer. The world's gone roughneck."

"You don't expect it from a baby." Slipping her hand through his arm, she turned back with him into the bedroom. "Did you have a good day?"

"Middling. I've sold two cars since three o'clock. Minna is trying to persuade her father to buy one."

"He hasn't any idea of it. They're too careful. He told me this morning he was putting aside everything he could spare for a rainy day."

"Minna hadn't been after him then. She has a way of getting whatever she goes after."

"I know she has." What had started that pricking sensation in her nerves? "And Rosa is so much nicer."

He assented. "I like her better. She keeps up with life, and she isn't dumb like Minna. All Minna can do is wriggle and make faces."

"What did she want with you?"

"I told you it was about a car." Questioning always made him impatient. "There's no harm in that."

"No, there's no harm in that." Perhaps she had said too much already, yet something stronger than prudence prompted her to ask, "Is she going out with you?"

Annoyance flickered in his eyes. "Is there any other way she can see the car?"

"Why does she have to see it? Otto has no idea of buying one."

"Now, you're going to nag . . ." he began on a note of irritation, and broke off with a laugh. "If you haven't anything more than Minna to worry you, you don't know your blessings."

"But I do know my blessings!" she retorted gaily, clasping her hands over his arm.

She wanted to say more, to assure him that she knew her blessings because he was one of them; but Ranny came rushing in at the moment, and it was always difficult to put love into words when the boy was listening. Strangely enough, with all the opportunity in the world for confidences, they had never recovered in marriage the complete freedom they had known in the Indian trail.

"Mother, may I go out again?" the child asked breathlessly.

"What are you doing, Ranny? I don't like you to be with those big rough boys."

"I'm just watching the game, Mother. It won't last much longer."

"Well, if you promise not to go down into the Bottom."

"I promise. All the smaller boys are looking on from the hill."

"Run along, then, and remember to come in soon. I'll give

you your supper on the back porch, and I'll help you with your lessons if Grandfather isn't ready."

The boy started out and then turned back to join his father. "Are you going out, Father? I'd rather go out in a new car than watch the ball game."

"I can't take you to-day, Ranny, to-morrow perhaps." As the child scampered off like a young puppy, Ralph looked after him with a quizzical smile. "He's a stout little chap."

"It's wonderful how he gets on, but I wish we had other children. I wanted a large family." It seemed incredible that a few moments before she had felt almost thankful because she had no daughter to bring up.

He shook his head. "In this age they take too much providing for. But I shouldn't mind one more. I'd like a girl."

"That's just what I was thinking. Girls are lovely to dress. I want a girl with my eyes and your hair." After all, she reminded herself, Minna's way was not the only way to be modern.

"Well, we've time enough ahead of us." He was smiling again, and when he stooped to kiss her, his mouth felt warm and eager and searching. "Tell Aunt Meggie to pray!" he tossed back over his shoulder.

When she went into the living-room she found that her father had come in and was talking to Aunt Meggie. He had grown so gaunt that his clothes hung on his figure as on a pole, but his faint autumnal smile, like light that is ebbing away, softened the carved severity of his lips. The fifth and last volume of his work had been published in April, and it seemed to her that he had broken since his long task was finished. So far as America was concerned, the book might have dropped into a well. In a month or more, no doubt, he would begin to hear from the few philosophers exiled, out of their time, in obscure places. But the work was completed. To John Fincastle, nothing else was important. He had loved wisdom; he had sought truth; he had set himself to the task of a lifetime. Almost happily, he now asked, What is left for one to do when life has been lived?

"Have you been to the Bergens', Father?"

"Yes, I stopped to congratulate Otto, and then Mr. Hamblen and I strolled up Washington Street. We were trying to decide whether human beings are better off nowadays than they were in the past. I am inclined to think that they are, and that the best age of the world is the age in which the sum total of happiness is greatest. Hamblen dislikes the levelling process, and still has faith in the heroic mould for mankind. He can see little hope for civilization, he says, as long as the lowest common denominator is the popular hero." And a little later, "But it is too easy to forget that philosophy is not a reform, but a consolation, that it is still what it has always been, the only infallible antidote to life."

How frail yet indomitable he looked, Ada thought, as her gaze followed him. Next year, she knew, his classes would be taken away. The principal of the school had been regretful but positive. Modern youth required modern instructors, and the girls, she felt, would respond better to younger teachers. "Of course, Mr. Fincastle has great learning," she had sighed, "and has written a monumental work of philosophy." But the parents of her pupils, without exception, felt that science was more important than metaphysics, and that history and languages might be taught by a more advanced method, which exacted less effort from youthful minds.

Yes, he is a failure in his age, she thought, watching him proudly, but he is a splendid failure.

Her father and Mr. Hamblen would have interminable discussions, with Ralph or Otto Bergen occasionally joining in. Mr. Hamblen, who knew his Bible, personified every principle, even Original Sin. He favoured government by the superior, and complained that all the oaks were cut down and only the scrub was left. Ralph, on the contrary, had lost his old eagerness to excel; he appeared even to take pride in a pose of vulgarity. He enjoyed, or so it seemed to her, the popular baiting of superiority in any field. Yet egoism, whatever mask it wore, her father insisted, was still triumphant. Each man wanted an individual prosperity. Only when he had not eaten or was empty-handed had he ever endured total immersion in the common good. While the Stock Exchange stood, individualism would stand also; when the Stock Exchange fell, individualism would fall with it. As for immersion in humanity, Mr. Hamblen would retort: Well, if a man could not suffer a single fool gladly, how was he to suffer all the fools in the multitude? Then Ralph would begin to argue about the lot of the average man in a republic, and the general uselessness of the past, composed entirely of experiments that had failed, as a guide; and so on and on, until he wound up with his opinion that the age was in a bloody flux and democracy was going lousy. . . . It was pathetic, she felt, to watch the pleasure men seemed to take in saying at the top of their voices words that bad little boys had once written with chalk on back fences.

Her father and Ralph were still close and devoted friends. Only, it seemed to her, Ralph was splashing easily in the surf of his age, while her father was becoming more timeless, if there could be a degree in the absolute. Who was right? Who was wrong? She did not know. She could not choose between the old and the young. Still, if youth must fight, why couldn't it fight for something worth having?

Ranny rushed in and threw his arms about her. "It's over, Mother. The Cats beat."

"I'm sorry, darling, for your sake. Tillie will have your supper for you on the porch by the time you've washed your hands and brushed your hair."

While she waited for him on the back porch, arranging his bread and milk and strawberry preserves on a small green table, she glanced into the Bergens' yard, where only Hans and the parrot and the canaries were left of the party. The afterglow was fading, and the shadows on the grass had overtaken the faint sunshine. After nosing vainly about the roots of the rose-bushes, Hans raised his eyes to the sky, shook his refined and melancholy head, and trotted over the flower borders into the house.

"They've all gone in," she said, as Ranny slammed the screen door behind him. "Hans has just followed them. He knows perfectly well what it is about, Mr. Bergen says, and he barked his thanks when Aunt Meggie took them a coconut cake."

"Did she make one for us too?"

"We'll have ours next Sunday for your grandfather's birthday. He will be seventy-one."

"That's awful old, Mother. Was Methuselah any older'n that?"

"Fifty years from now you won't think much of seventy, my dear. You'll learn that age knows all youth knows, and something more besides."

"Fifty years from now." He drew a long whistling breath, and asked abruptly, "Are you going to give me a radio for my birthday, Mother?"

"I don't know, Ranny. Don't you want us to save our money to buy the manse?"

"That's where I was born?"

"I was born there, too, and your grandfather and your three great-grandfathers."

"But I want a radio, Mother. Almost everybody has a radio now and a car too. Jimmy Bangs says they're still paying for theirs, and they've had both a year. What does installment mean, Mother?"

"It means buying what you can't afford, Ranny," she replied as tonelessly as if she were hearing a lesson. "Now, drink your milk, because Tillie wants to go to a prayer meeting as soon as your grandfather and Aunt Meggie have had their supper."

"Will you have yours too?"

"No, I'll wait for your father. It won't be long now."

But after the others had had supper, and she had washed the dishes and tidied the kitchen with Aunt Meggie's help, she sat straining her ears for the first sound of approaching footsteps. Ralph would leave his car in the garage at the shop, as he did every night, and walk the few remaining blocks down Mulberry Street. When Ranny had finished his lessons, she followed him upstairs to see that he washed his hands and brushed his teeth before going to bed.

"I wish we lived on Oregon Hill, Mother. Then I might join the Cats when I'm bigger," he said while she tucked him in.

"Oh, no, Ranny. I've enough trouble as it is."

"But I've got to get on, Mother. I'm going to be something when I grow up."

"Well, there're better ways, dear."

"Not like Grandfather. I don't want to stay at home and think. I want to go out and do something different."

"There's time enough. We'll see when you're bigger. Did you brush your teeth well?"

"Well enough," Ranny replied stubbornly, and turned his cheek to his pillow.

Downstairs in the living-room John Fincastle closed his book and rose from his chair. "That's ten o'clock striking. Would you like me to wait up, my child?"

"No, go to bed, Father. You had a long walk, and I know you're tired."

"I doze easily; but I'm apt to wake before light."

"It's hard to sleep with those radios next door," Aunt Meggie said. "That jazz kept up till after midnight. Yet those girls have the impudence to complain of my cock's crowing."

Ada frowned. "I thought Mrs. Maudsley had got rid of them. They've never paid any board."

"These are others. But they're worse, if anything, she told me this morning. They have wild drinking-parties every night in their rooms."

"Well, I'm glad we don't have to let rooms. If it isn't one complaint, it's another. Good night, Father. You go, too, Aunt Meggie. It's still early, and I'm not sleepy."

"Maybe Ralph joined somebody and they went to a roadhouse," Aunt Meggie suggested.

"But he told me to wait for him."

"Well, something must have stopped him. He's always careful to telephone."

"Yes, he's thoughtful," Ada assented. "There aren't many men as easy to live with as Ralph. There's that jazz beginning again. How can the Hamblens stand it over their heads?"

"It's driving Mr. Hamblen distracted. But of course it's worse on Mrs. Maudsley, who is trying so hard to make a living and pay her rent. These girls have bought radios, though not a single one of them has paid for her board and lodging." Aunt Meggie turned away and then looked back with a sound that was between a laugh and a groan. "It's funny the way people mind noise, unless they make it themselves. You won't believe it when I tell you that I like jazz even when it keeps me awake. It seems to let out something that's stopped up inside of you."

"Oh, Aunt Meggie, who would have thought it!"

"Well, things just cross my mind, Ada, but I reckon that's the way young people feel. There's mighty little to cling to when you've lost your convictions. And even convictions don't fill up your time somehow."

"But you're happy, Aunt Meggie. We've loved you and valued you, and you're always so cheerful."

"Oh, yes, I'm as happy as anybody, I reckon, but I sometimes wonder why people struggle so hard for so little. It's the Lord's will, I reckon. That's what kept Mother going, and I s'pose it keeps me going too. When that leaves you, it looks as if you had to take to wild doings. Well, I'm kind of drowsy, and I'll go to bed if you don't need me."

As she went out, Ada followed her with her eyes and the thought, I wish it were easier to show affection. She wanted to run after Aunt Meggie and put her arms about her, but she said only, "You know we couldn't possibly do without you, Aunt Meggie."

An hour later, as the slow strokes of a bell chimed over the city, she put out the light and went on the balcony to watch the length of the street. Twelve o'clock! Never before had he stayed out until midnight without telephoning. A good husband, Aunt Meggie had called him. It was true, Ada thought, gazing into the pallid wash of electricity. Even if love had ceased to be an emotion in his life and become a habit, still a habit of the heart would often outwear the flying ardours of the blood. And passion lived on, she felt, lost and waiting for them between the sky and the mountains. Raising her eyes above the smokestacks on the horizon, she saw again the tall trees on Eagle Ridge and the flight of leaves colouring the air.

While the image was in her mind, a voice spoke from beyond a Wistaria vine on the next balcony, and she knew that Otto Bergen and his wife must have lingered there without suspecting her nearness.

"I did speak to her, Otto. I spoke to her this morning, but you know how she is."

"Well, I'll talk to her myself to-morrow. This thing has to stop. She may chase after all the other men she pleases, but as long as she lives under my roof . . ."

"Hush, Otto, you're raising your voice."

Then, just as they were about to go inside, a car dashed round the corner of Mulberry Street, speeded along the block, and stopped in front of the Bergens' house. A man and a girl jumped out, opened the gate, and ran up the short brick walk to the steps. It isn't Ralph, Ada thought. I may as well go to bed. He has his key anyway.

She had entered the house and was about to begin undressing when the bell rang twice, and hurrying to the door, she heard Mr. Bergen say to somebody outside, "She is still up. I saw a light in her room." Then, as she opened the door, his features seemed to float toward her, like a drowned face out of shadows. A foolish thought shot through her mind: Something must have happened or he would have buttoned his collar. Aloud she asked quietly, "Is it about Ralph?"

"There's been an accident. He is in the hospital."

"Is he dead?"

"No, oh, no. We hope it isn't serious. Minna came up to tell us."

"Minna?"

"He was showing her the new model. They were on the Hanover turnpike when a hit-and-run driver knocked them off the road into a ditch. Another car brought them to the hospital—to St. Giles. Minna has only a few scratches."

But Ralph? Ralph? What did it matter about Minna? Who cared about scratches? "We mustn't stop to talk. Oh, we're losing time while I ask questions!" She had started down the steps toward the car at the curb. "Is this car waiting for me?"

"This is Mr. Hill. He picked them up and brought Minna home."

"Thank you, Mr. Hill," she said, and then to Mr. Bergen, "Aunt Meggie and Father may wake and miss me. Will you leave a note without waking them?"

"I'm going too," Otto Bergen said. "I'll stay with you." He put his friendly hand on her arm, and she thought, I always knew he would be a friend in trouble.

As they were about to start, Mrs. Bergen ran out of the gate and slipped a necktie into her husband's hand. "Put this on at the hospital," she said, "and be sure to fasten your collar."

A wailing sound followed them. Minna, who was not hurt, was having hysterics over her scratched face. Well, I'm glad of it, Ada told herself sternly. I only hope the scratches are as deep as she deserves.

A s s h e looked down on his bandaged head, the light carved grey hollows in his face, which appeared wooden. He was still unconscious, but the doctor had told her the skull was not fractured. One hand was hidden beneath the bedclothes, and the other was turned palm upward on the folded sheet. Years had passed, it seemed to her, since the afternoon, when he had left her to go out with Minna, and she felt that she had grown old and haggard from watching.

"Is he asleep?" she asked the nurse, who answered in a rapid whisper, as expressionless as a breeze, "Yes, he came to, and they gave him an opiate. His head was hurting him." Shielding him with her arms, Ada touched the ashen cheek under the bandage. His mouth was open, and his breathing, slow, heavy, listless, was as unfamiliar as the breath of a stranger. A fantastic idea spun round in her thoughts. Suppose this is really a stranger! Suppose he doesn't know me when he comes to himself!

"He doesn't look natural," she said.

"That's the bandage and the shock. You ought to be thankful it isn't more serious."

The nurse tripped silently across the floor in her white canvas shoes with rubber heels. As she went she put up her hand to straighten the cap on her bobbed hair, which was bronze at the ends and dark brown at the roots. In a few minutes she came back and whispered, "A friend is at the door—Mr. Bergen."

Turning from the bed, Ada went out into the passage and shut the door softly. "How do you find him?" Mr. Bergen asked, but his voice was so low, in deference to the sleeping patients, that she had to make him repeat the question twice over.

"I don't know. The X-ray didn't show any fracture, but he looks queer and unnatural."

"Well, he would after that blow. He was thrown over a bridge."

"I wish I had Dr. Updike. I don't know any doctor in Queenborough. The one here is so young."

"I'll get in touch with Dr. Bradford. He's the best, and he'll know about specialists. It's all right till morning?"

"The doctor thinks so. I always imagined," she whispered, shaking her head, "that everything was perfect in a big hospital."

"Not when politics has a hand in it. But you won't be here long, that's one comfort. I'll see your father as soon as he's up, and telephone Dr. Bradford."

When she went back to the bedside, Ralph stirred and groaned faintly. "Is that you, Ada?"

"Yes, Ralph. Do you want anything?"

"Is Mother dead?"

"She's been dead for two years. Two years from next July."

His mouth twitched at the corners, and she thought for a moment that he was going to smile. Then he said slowly, "For two years. That's a pity. She would have enjoyed this."

"Oh, Ralph, how can you?" But he had slipped back again into unconsciousness. She longed to draw close to him, but she knew that if he came to himself, he would resent any outward show of affection. Never when he needed sympathy would he submit to it.

All night she sat there in the small, hard chair by the bedside, while the soft breeze, laden with scents of spring, floated in through the window. Far away, very thin and clear, she heard bells ringing or clocks striking. Once a young doctor looked in, and a little later the nurse, who was also young, with pouting red lips and thick ankles, went downstairs to supper. Their attention had been amiable but casual. Ada had felt when they leaned over the bed that only death could have divided their interest from youth and spring and each other. But it made no difference. Nothing made any difference as long as Ralph was alive. Minna might run after him as much as she pleased. Ranny might speak all the bad words, old or new, he could pick up.

A shiny black beetle scurried out from under the slop jar, and she watched it make its perilous journey across the floor to the wardrobe. She had believed that hospitals were cleaner than sickrooms at home, but there was a lump of stale chewing-gum stuck between two white iron spokes of the bedstead, and when she looked under the bed she found some dried grapeskins that had been swept out of sight. Perhaps the private rooms were neglected, but the wards provided by the city were well looked after. The queerest thing in life was that nobody wanted to work the right way simply because it was the right way, not even for the sick and the dying. The people in a hospital, like people everywhere else, were interested only in themselves and in what they could get out of the world.

Presently, between waking and sleeping, she lost herself in a dream. Through this dream, which was a familiar one of her childhood, she was running from Indians up the stony hillside at the back of the manse. As a Shawnee in war paint pursued her, she dodged behind big grey rocks, up, up, up, always with her heart in her throat and her breath whistling from terror, springing, stooping, bending, crawling, fleeing, until at last a tomahawk whirled down at her from the other side of a stone, and while she waited for the crash into her skull, the painted face of the Indian turned into a sheep—into the benign features of the old ewe that had gazed at her over the stalk of mullein.

With a start, she opened her eyes in the wan glimmer of daybreak. The nurse sat prim and straight in her chair. From the street below, she heard the rattle of milk wagons and the honking of motor horns at the corner. Then Ralph stirred and groaned under his breath, and looking down at him, she saw that he was returning slowly to consciousness. The nurse sprang up without a sound and moved to the bedside.

"Ada! Ada, is that you?"

"Yes, I'm here. Do you want anything?"

"Where are we? This isn't home."

"We're in the hospital. There was an accident. But it wasn't a bad one, and you may go home as soon as you feel well enough."

"Yes, I remember. What rotten luck!"

"Are you in pain?"

"My head is pounding like hell. It's like an army of elephants. The thunder in my head makes my feet feel as if they didn't belong to me."

"It won't be long," the nurse said soothingly, "before the doctor comes. Then he will give you something."

"I want something now. I want coffee."

"It isn't time yet, but I'll try to get you some in a little while. The doctor left some medicine for you if you complained of your head."

As he looked up at the nurse, his smile twitched and was gone. "Well, I'm complaining, old dear. My head sounds so loud that I don't seem to know my own legs. And I don't like the idea of paying to suffer. I suppose this ward must come high."

"This isn't a ward," the nurse replied in an indulgent tone. "It is a private room."

"Did you ask the price, Ada?" How like him that was! He would squander money on pleasures, but it annoyed him to pay for anything he did not enjoy.

"Don't worry about that, Ralph," Ada pleaded. "It's only for a few days. We may go home to-morrow."

"Oh, I'm not worrying," he answered touchily, and then, after a minute, "I wish you'd go, Ada, and bring me my things. Tell your father I want to see him as soon as he's had breakfast. This is Saturday, isn't it?"

"Yes, this is Saturday."

"Then he won't have any classes. Tell him I want him."

"He's coming, dear. I don't have to go after him."

"But I want you to go. I don't want to be fussed over."

Tears filled her eyes. "I'm not fussing."

The nurse looked at her warningly. "He'll be all right as soon as he's taken his medicine. It will be better for him than coffee."

"I want you to go home, Ada," Ralph repeated, as if the nurse had not spoken. "I want you to go home and take a nap and get dressed. You don't know how you look."

She tried to laugh off his bad temper. "Nor do you, my dear."

"I have a right to a long face. But bring my things out of the bathroom when you come back. Where is your hat?"

"I didn't wear any."

"Well, go home and get it."

"I'd like to be here when the doctor comes."

"I don't want anybody."

"I'll send Father in a little while." She turned away, hesitating, and then came back to take the hand he stretched out.

"Well, I don't mind him. But I like being alone. Is it thundering outside?"

"No, dear, that's from the shock."

The nurse gave him the opiate, and then settled his head on the pillow before she followed Ada out into the hall.

"They're always touchy when they first come round," she said. "We had a man here last month who wouldn't let his wife poke her nose in the door for a week."

"It isn't a bit like him."

"You never can tell. Sometimes the one they like best they try the hardest to keep out."

"I'll be back by the time the day nurse comes on."

"It won't matter. He'll be quiet now. But you're sensible to go. It's always best to humour them."

"The doctor says it isn't serious."

"Oh, it isn't, not really. But a thing can be pretty disagreeable without being serious. He's feeling both the shock and the opiate, and he doesn't know half he's saying."

Walking bareheaded in the street, Ada told herself that the accident of leaving off her hat had made her a part of the morning crowd. There were no taxicabs in sight, and if she took a street car on Main Street, she would be spared only a few blocks. Besides, the walk would do her good, and Ralph (her eyes were misted) did not want her at the hospital. Even at this early hour, the happiness-hunters were still on the chase, speeding by in the wan light through waves of dust and blown papers.

While she waited at the crossing, an amiable dark face flashed a triumphant grin at her. "Lady, I'se done made a heap uv money. I'se done made mos' twenty dollars in stocks yestiddy." A coloured bootblack, his box slung over his shoulder, was standing beside her.

"That's nice. How did it happen?"

A w'ite gent'mun I shine fuh, he done hit. I'se gwineter shine fuh 'im dis mawnin' in de hotel ovah yonder."

"Well, take care, and don't lose it." He had an honest face, and she hoped he wouldn't let the money slip through his fingers. But the gambling fever ran through everything, from the top to the bottom. Even Ralph had been touched by the strange contagion. She had had to plead with him before he would put away a share of his earnings. How thankful she now felt that they had waited to move! The nine thousand dollars they had saved (five thousand safely invested and the rest in the savings bank) would be something to lean back on in case of an illness.

The old houses in Mulberry Street were unshuttered, and women in cambric mobcaps were sweeping off the porches and pavements. From their gate Ranny darted out to her with the news that his grandfather had already gone to the hospital. "I've been up a long time, Mother. I washed before there was any warm water."

"Well, I'm glad you washed. But I'll have to tie your tie over."

"I put on a clean shirt because I thought you might let me go down to the hospital. I've never been inside a hospital." He was excited and eager and had forgotten to ask after his father. All children were like that, she supposed, and it was useless to try to make people over.

In the kitchen Aunt Meggie and Tillie were making fresh coffee. Mr. Bergen had come over as soon as it was light, and John Fincastle had snatched a mouthful of breakfast, Aunt Meggie explained, and gone straight to the hospital. "He must have got there soon after you left. He said he'd call Dr. Bradford and ask him to come before he went to his office. Somehow Otto Bergen didn't seem satisfied."

"I didn't want to come away," Ada said, with a catch in her voice. "But Ralph didn't want me."

"Well, you mustn't take that to heart. He doesn't like a fuss made over him."

"I wasn't making a fuss."

"You remember his mother always complained he wouldn't tell her when he was sick."

"That was different. Who would want to tell Mrs. McBride anything?"

"Well, sit down and drink your coffee. You'll feel better as soon as you've eaten something. I was perfectly certain I heard Ralph come in last night, but it must have been Mr. Bergen. With those radios going on in that room next door to mine, I sometimes think I couldn't hear Gabriel's trumpet." Her busy hands paused a moment. "Ralph must have come to, or he wouldn't have known you."

"The nurse said he wasn't himself. He was suffering terribly with his head. As soon as I've had breakfast and dressed, I'm going right back again. But I must change my clothes." She laughed and wiped her eyes. "He told me I didn't know how I looked."

"You look all right to me, but you'd better lie down."

"Not now. Not till I've heard what the doctor says this morning. The one last night was so young I couldn't feel any confidence in him."

"They all seem young now, or it may be because I'm getting on. I suppose I'll always miss Dr. Updike."

After breakfast and a bath, Ada tried to lie down, but her mind was a cage in which anxiety darted round and round like a squirrel. In a flutter of apprehension, she jumped up and reached for a hat on the top shelf in her wardrobe. There were two, a red felt cloche and a black straw with a narrow brim, and she chose the red cloche because it gave her a jaunty air, which had always seemed to her out of character. As she pulled it down on one

ot happened.
The flush in her cheeks had not faded, the shadows beneath her
eyes had not deepened, the startled expectancy of her gaze was
as fresh and young as it had ever been.

A T THE hospital she found her father and Dr. Bradford, a slow, heavy, pompous man, who diffused an air of authority. When Ralph had complained that his legs felt stiff and numb, as if they didn't belong to him, both the hospital surgeon and Dr. Bradford had suspected that there was an injury to the spine. A second X-ray, her father said, had failed to show a fracture or dislocation of the vertebrae (the words droned on in her ears like the memory of the sea in a shell), though there had been a sprain and a severe bruise. The symptoms pointed to a haemorrhage, but it was possible that this might clear up in twenty-four hours.

"I can't understand, Father. Do they mean that Ralph may be paralyzed?" She had followed him from the room, and they stood facing each other in the passage while they spoke in strained whispers.

"They don't know, my child. The stiffness may pass almost immediately. Both Dr. West and Dr. Bradford have looked at the plates, and they can find nothing serious enough to explain the symptoms."

"And his head?"

"That was a bad blow, but he escaped with concussion of the brain instead of a fractured skull. However you look at it, he had luck on his side when he went over that bridge. The accident wasn't nearly so bad as it might have been. But as soon as Ralph became conscious, he knew, he said, what it meant to feel as if his feet were attached to somebody else."

"Why didn't he tell me?"

"He was trying to keep it from you. He wanted to send you home before the doctor came in."

"Oh, Father, and I thought . . ."

"He wanted to spare you, but I suspect, too, he found courage in being alone or with strangers. Some men are like that."

"It's terrible to see him suffer with his head. Mother used to say she could stand anything if it wasn't in her head. Can't they give him something to stop the pain?"

"It might be graver if he knew nothing about it. Try not to talk to him when we go in."

Lying on his back, with his head slightly turned on the pillow and the corners of his mouth twitching, Ralph listened resentfully to the two doctors. Though he was not an agreeable patient, his bad humour and the grotesque bandanges seemed only to throw a fresh slant on his curiously erratic charm. Was it because he was always himself? Or was the attraction she felt even now merely the old incalculable power over her senses? As soon as Dr. Bradford had reached his bedside, he had demanded to be told the whole truth about his condition, and after the doctors had spoken, he had asked gravely, "Well, is there any rule against being shaved in a hospital? If I'm going to be paralyzed, hadn't I better prepare for it with a bath and a shave?"

"He was whistling to keep up his courage, I know," the day nurse observed to Ada, when she carried out the basin and towels, "but I must say I like it better than when they're so down in the mouth. He does look fine, too, now we've fixed him up. I don't wonder you were scared about losing him."

All that day and the next they watched anxiously for the first sign of improvement. The injury to the spinal cord had not been sufficient to cause paralysis; yet he grew no better, and his legs, as he insisted mockingly, "had gone dead on him." Though the cut on his head healed quickly, the inflammation of the nerves had altered his disposition, and he became, as the weeks passed, more resentful than despondent. He had had, as he asserted sullenly, "a raw deal," and all the particulars of the accident, including the company of Minna, conspired to make him a laughing-stock. When they attempted to argue with him, he grew angry and bitter. "If I had to be smashed up, why couldn't it have been in France instead of on the Hanover turnpike?" The nurse had gone down to her lunch, John Fincastle and Ranny had just left, and they were alone in the room. "Anyway," Ada urged soothingly, "it is easier on me to have you here than in France."

As she leaned over him, he caught her hand and pressed it over his inflamed eyes. "Did you ever think that Minna mattered?" he asked.

"Never. I never worried about Minna." Like the shadow of a wing in her mind, a question turned, flashed, and vanished. If there had been no accident, how far would they have gone, where would it have ended?

"Well, she didn't matter. I wouldn't give your little finger for all the other women in creation."

"I know that, Ralph. I've always known that." But before Minna, had there been others that mattered as little? Again the thought turned and flashed out of obscurity. Long ago there was Janet. . . . What had really happened? asked a small malicious voice from the depths below the depths of her consciousness. What had really happened with Janet?

"If I pull through, it will be because of you." Then he laughed softly, and beneath the crooked bandage she could see his eyes, tender, amused, and tinged with irony, as if he were trying to turn the jest upon life. "It's rotten luck, though, for that girl baby."

She breathed quickly. Why should a little thing like that make her heart tremble? "Well, she'll have to wait," she said quietly. "There's still plenty of time."

He dropped her hand as the knob of the door turned. "Has the nurse come back already?" But it was only Aunt Meggie bringing a bowl of chicken jelly, which she called "nourishment."

Then, as the weeks dragged on and he was still unable to leave the hospital, Ada and her father and Aunt Meggie divided the nursing among them. After Boscobel School had closed, John Fincastle would sit in the sickroom through the long sunny afternoons when all they could see of summer was a distant cloud of green over the roofs. Ralph's early reverence for the older man had returned, and he seemed to prefer his companionship even to Ada's. For hours at a time they would talk of subjects that were remote not only from the accident and the hospital, but even from the age in which they were living. "It's easier to stand things," Ralph would say afterwards, "when you measure them against all time." Ada and Aunt Meggie and the neighbours when they came would talk of the present. Only John Fincastle would sit in silence, with his visionary gaze on the triangle of blue sky, and listen with wordless patience to outbursts of angry despair. "He's found something," Ralph would muse aloud to Ada. "I don't know what to call it. Invulnerability is as good a name, I suppose, as any other."

"He feels for people, Ralph, as much as anyone."

"I know, but not for himself. He's got beyond himself. That's the secret."

"I want to take you away from here," Ada answered after a pause. "If you can't go home by the end of June, Dr. Bradford will let us move you to the West End Hospital. He's on the staff there, and he says it's more cheerful."

"It will cost a lot."

"Well, we can pay the difference. I'm thankful we have our savings."

"We shan't have them long if this goes on."

"Oh, you'll be well and at work again before we see the bottom. Dr. Bradford and that new specialist are both sure you will be as well as you ever were."

"That's one of the things I can't stand. All these specialists with their stuffed shirts and fat fees."

"I shan't begrudge a penny if they put you back on your feet."

"If they don't . . ." His voice broke with helpless rage, while the nervous twitching she dreaded began again in the muscles about his mouth.

"Don't think that, dearest. They will . . . they must . . ."

No, she couldn't bear this hospital another week, she decided. It wasn't only the discomfort for Ralph. He had a private room, and she could bring clean sheets and pillow-cases from home, but whenever she came or went, the relatives of poor patients would join her in the street and describe the public wards down below. There was dirt; there was neglect of the simplest decencies; there were, some complained, vermin in the mattresses and the bedsteads. Yet they dared not protest to a bureaucracy that was founded on a political rock. And the cost of dying, like the cost of illness, made death the last extravagance for the poor. The highest wave of prosperity had merely engulfed, it had not abolished, the potter's field.

"Everybody seems to think that only people who can afford them should have feelings," Ada said one day when Ranny had brought in a story of destitute dying in the midst of luxurious living.

"It's a hell of a world!" Ralph exclaimed. "But we're in it, and there's nothing to be done about it."

Ranny stared back at him with his candid child's eyes, clear, critical, without mystery, even the mystery of innocence. "Why can't you do something, Father?" he asked. "When I grow up, I'm going to do something about everything."

On a hot morning toward the end of June, Ralph was put into an ambulance and moved to the West End Hospital, which was encircled by a garden planted in roses and dwarf evergreens. True, the roses were past blooming and the blighted evergreens had turned rusty, but from his bed he could see the broad glossy leaves of magnolias, and breathe in the deep fragrance. The food, too, was better, and Ada could leave him at night, or for an hour or two in the day, with the knowledge that he would not be neglected.

In a few days he had begun to improve, though he was not yet able to move his feet, and he still grumbled over the cost of his illness.

"What are we to do when we've spent all we've saved?" he asked fretfully.

"By that time you will be well and can make more. Dr. Bradford is very hopeful."

"He isn't hopeful for nothing. Professional hopefulness is expensive. Nothing comes free in a hospital, not even the nurse's smile."

"I know, but we can't help it. As long as our money lasts, we must spend it on getting you well. There's a new specialist coming down from Washington in August. He's from Vienna."

"Good Lord! Are there any left in Vienna?"

"Dr. Bradford wants to consult him. He's a neurological surgeon."

"What are they trying to find out?"

"They can't see why you don't get better. Isn't it funny," Ada retorted, "that I used to be the one who wanted to save?"

"It isn't that I want to save, but that I dislike to pay for the wrong things. If I'd kept on, we might have bought a house in a few years. Now, I'll have to begin grubbing all over again."

"Oh, my dear, you can so easily make up what you've lost. And I can always go back to work. I got the very first place I tried for."

"I don't want you to work. Your father knows how I feel about his teaching."

"Yes, he knows. He'll lose his classes next year, but he is hoping something else will turn up. It's terrible to have spent a lifetime on a great work and yet not to have it yield you a living."

"If I once get on my feet, I can look after him."

"But he won't hear of our providing for him. He insists he can live on a crust and independence."

"Why should he mind? He's old."

"He doesn't feel old. Ranny enjoys him more than any one else since they've taken those long walks in the woods. It's amazing how the boy has developed."

"I hope he'll turn out all right, but I don't expect much from precocious youngsters. I was one myself."

"Well, we had to break with tradition, and the war came at the wrong time for us. But I have faith in the next generation."

"We always have faith in it, my dear, while it's the next generation. Disappointment belongs in the present tense."

Ada leaned down to kiss the bitter smile on his lips. "Well, I don't ask any better than you, Ralph," she said gently. "Only I do wish that you weren't quite so grumpy." If only she could look into his mind and know what he was thinking! If only she could look into his heart and know what he was feeling!

The strange physician, when he came during a cool spell in August, was discreet and sanguine, without committing himself to an opinion. Patience, not an operation, was necessary, patience and perseverance and a cheerful outlook on life. These obscure maladies were tedious in treatment, but there was every reason to hope that recovery would be permanent. Everything was in Ralph's favour, except perhaps temperament, and the probability was that, with time and care, he would be as well as he had ever been. Meanwhile, it could do no harm to send him home in an ambulance. With proper nursing, the change might be beneficial rather than otherwise.

"Rather than otherwise . . ." Ralph drawled, while the supreme authority, round, rubicund, inscrutably suave, departed softly down the corridor between respectful rows of doctors and nurses. "How soon can you get me away, Ada?"

"Just as soon as Dr. Bradford will let you go. I'll telephone Aunt Meggie to have your bed turned down and everything ready." Without stopping to talk, she began to fold up his clothes and pack them into bags, while he watched her with eyes that were bright and impatient.

In the afternoon they brought him home and settled him in the big bed by the window that looked out on the Bergens' back yard, where borders of asters and scarlet sage were in bloom.

"There's Hans," he exclaimed, "and the parrot! I never thought I'd be glad to see a parrot. Are Minna's scratches all healed?" he asked scoffingly.

"Except the tiny scar by her mouth. She's proud of that now, because it makes a dimple when she smiles, and she always wanted a dimple." But while she answered, Ada was thinking, They don't know what is the matter with him. Though they call it paralysis, none of them really knows what it is. And it may drag on for years. He may be helpless for years.

"She got off too easily," Ralph replied. "Is that Rosa out in the yard behind the crêpe myrtle?"

"Yes, she comes every day with her little boy. William has done so well in the stock market that they've bought a nice house on Hill Street and are having it done over. Rosa is expecting another baby in October. She's looking so happy, I hope she'll run in to see you."

"Well, you look happy, too, and for less reason." The mockery had left his voice, and his hand fluttered toward her in a nerveless gesture that seemed to pluck at her heartstrings.

"Oh, I have reason enough." She stroked his hand as it lay outside the sheet. "I'm thinking all the time that I didn't lose you."

"I'd rather die any day than be a burden." A frown darkened his face. "Your father and I feel alike about that."

"Oh, Ralph, we've just come home. Try not to say that again. You're going to get well, and besides, you know it isn't a burden for me to take care of you."

"I know you're a good sport." His fingers closed over hers. "And I don't mind telling you that a good sport is a long sight better to have for keeps than a perfect peach. Does Ranny know I've come home?"

"No, we're going to surprise him. It's Aunt Meggie's birthday, and we've saved her cake for supper. Mr. Bergen brought over a wonderful watermelon. He said William had a tip yesterday and has made money on Girdlestone Copper. He thought maybe we might buy some copper stock."

"I wish I could. This doctor from Vienna will clean up our savings, I suppose. We'll have to sell the securities we own, and it wouldn't do any harm to put a thousand or so in copper. It's a great game to get something for nothing."

"William didn't put down much money, he said. It was all on margin, but Father thinks it's little better than gambling."

"Oh, he's old. I don't mean that he isn't fine, but it's the fineness of the past. People don't bother about moral quibbles nowadays any more than they discuss the nature of reality. Anything that clicks is real and all right."

"Well, Ranny is a child of the new age if there ever was one. He's so modern I can sometimes barely understand what he says."

For a moment he looked at her without speaking. Then his mood changed, and the smile of his eager youth flashed from his lips into his eyes. "He'll have to try hard before he's more modern than his mother. Didn't you break away from the past before he was born?"

"That was different. We were fighting against injustice. But Ranny believes in noise, size, numbers. Even when he was a baby he wanted only toys that wheeled or buzzed. Father says he's making the funniest kind of flying machine. Isn't it odd?"

"Not nearly so odd as that I should have a child who knows how to get on. He'll grow up, I suppose, thinking cogwheels in action the most beautiful sight in the world. But even then he'll have his worries."

They were still talking, and the August sunlight still flamed on the scarlet sage, when Dr. Updike, who was spending a few days in the city, dropped in to see them. Though he had grown fat and flabby, with pendulous cheeks and a paunch like a bag of flour, he had lost neither his genial disposition nor his keen zest for living. Even now, Ada could not see him after a long absence without wondering whether he had really fancied Aunt Meggie when she was a girl and, as people said, very pretty. He had always been one of their closest friends, and when trouble came he had been the first to place his means at their disposal. There were not many friends like that in the world, and they valued the old man accordingly. For years they had seen little of him, but since Ralph had had to stay in the hospital, Dr. Updike had looked in on him whenever he came down to Queenborough. Always he brought news of the Valley, and on his last visit he had told them that Janet was to be married for the fourth time, and that her pearl necklace had been stolen in a hotel in New York.

"It's years since I thought of her," Ada said. Janet and all the anguish she had caused seemed to belong to some secondary life.

"You did the best thing to bring him home," the doctor remarked as he sank back in his chair. "I always say that hospitals are for the homeless. We'll have him on his feet again in a jiffy."

Ralph shook his head, but his laugh had a natural ring. "You'd think from the way Aunt Meggie and Tillie welcomed me back that I was doing them a favour when I let myself go to smash."

"Well, you should thank your stars you aren't married to a scatterbrained flapper. Not that Ada isn't handsome enough for anybody," the old man hastened to add, "but it's just as well for you that her complexion isn't the most important thing about her."

"Yes, Ada's all right." There was an accent of pride beneath the chaffing tone of Ralph's voice. "I've never seen a face yet I liked better."

"It's my belief," the doctor continued regretfully, "that in the next fifty years a woman who sits at home in the evening will be as extinct as the dodo. I nursed a teething baby last night while the mother and father went to a moving picture and stopped for drinks on the way home. Never laid eyes on them before in my life. But they'd have gone anyhow, and left the child alone in the apartment, even if old man Noah hadn't heard it crying and offered to look after it."

"You may look after Ralph now," Ada said. "I don't like to take my eyes off him for fear he'll vanish while I tell Aunt Meggie you've come to supper." Glancing back as she ran out, she saw the doctor push his chair to the bedside and lay his heavy hand on Ralph's wrist.

In the kitchen Tillie was busy at the stove, while Mr. Midkiff, as gaunt as ever, was cracking ice to pack round the freezer. Though his last teeth, as he said, "would not stand for ice cream," he would be glad of a few scraps of chicken and a slice of chocolate cake. "Poor old soul," Aunt Meggie had remarked that morning. "What has he got that keeps him clinging to life? He can enjoy nothing but soft food, and he has that only in scraps."

When Ada went back into the bedroom, the two men were cheerfully discussing the manse. Several years before, when the Valley turnpike had gone to Teesdale from Doncaster instead of coming to Ironside, the old house had changed hands again at a forced sale, and a few months later Dr. Updike had bought it from the purchaser. If the turnpike had come by Shut-in Valley, the owners of the manse had expected to make it into a tourist camp, but more and better politicians controlled the right of way round the flank of the mountain. For a while the flourishing values in land continued (he had never seen such prosperity, the doctor said; even the mountaineers, or so he heard, had bought roadsters and radios), but prices were already beginning to drop, and when the new highway failed them, the people who had invested in more acres than they could afford to keep were unable to sell them. He knew because he himself had invested a little too heavily. Not a great deal; his head was screwed on too firmly for that, but he had happened to turn his hand now and then to a bit of trading, and almost before he was aware of it, he had taken over the old manse. With taxes mounting every day, he was eager to get rid of it. There was, of course, nothing to bring tourists to Ironside. All the village could boast of was an old Indian massacre, and plenty of other places had massacres and fancy views and other things added. But so long as there was no hope of turning a penny on the house, with only a bit of garden and that stony hill, he would be willing to let Ralph take it back for precisely what it had cost him.

"Like all vacant houses, it looks pretty dilapidated. A part of one chimney has given way, and the roof leaks in holes. Some gypsies tried to camp there last summer, and once a dark-skinned foreigner with a bear slept on the back porch . . ."

"Oh, Mother, a bear!" Ranny exclaimed in ecstasy, dashing in from the hall while the doctor was talking. "Did they let the bear stay?"

"Ranny, don't you see Dr. Updike? And your father is home again. Isn't that fine?"

"Oh, fine!" He held out his hand to the doctor and then kissed his father hastily on the cheek. "But what became of the bear? Didn't they let him stay on the porch?"

"No, the bear went on, youngster, but his place is still waiting for you. If there was a stick of furniture in the house, you might run up for September. Ralph will need a change as soon as he is on his feet again. And I'll say this much, there isn't a better garden spot anywhere in the Valley. Abraham Geddy and Toby Waters plant the garden every year on Good Friday. I put by enough seeds from one year till the next, and my sister was saying the other day that we still get our best corn and tomatoes out of the manse garden."

"Oh, Mother, couldn't we go?" Ranny sighed. "You wouldn't need a bed for me. I'd every bit as soon sleep on pine tags, if you'd let me have a foxhound, like old Horace, to sleep with me."

Ada shook her head. "Not now, dear. Some day, after your father is well, we may be able to have the manse for a summer home. That's been my dream for the last few years," she explained to the doctor.

"After your father is well," Ralph repeated slowly, "he will have to work to pay for all the fun he has had in hospitals."

"And your mother, too, is going to work," Ada said. "She is going back to Shadwell's the first of October."

While she looked at the two auburn heads, framed in the window against a background of deep-golden sunset, she told herself that working to help Ralph and Ranny would be a new kind of happiness. But it isn't a bit like the feeling I used to call happiness, she thought in surprise.

O MATTER how tired she was, Ada told herself, she felt rested as soon as she saw the firelight in the window and the outline of Ralph's head between the thin curtains. Every week-day in the year since she had returned to Shadwell's, she had quickened her steps, with a sigh of contentment, when she found him watching for her over the rusty iron flowers on the balcony. She was so used to expecting him that it seemed to her her heart would fail to beat if she were to come home and find an empty space in the window.

From the first minute in Mulberry Street, he had begun to grow better. After a few months, he had been able to move his feet and to roll himself in a wheel-chair; and she could never forget the afternoon in early spring when he had taken his first walk, with the help of her father and her grandmother's ebony stick, to a bench on the terrace of Mulberry Hill. Since then the paralysis had disappeared, and gradually he had recovered his health and the look of agile strength that had always delighted her. By the first of November, Dr. Bradford had said, he might take up his work, and since nobody was satisfied with only one car in the garage, it would not be long before he regained all that his illness had cost him. Though his old place had been filled, the shop could easily make a new opening if the automobile industry continued to flourish. Wall Street may or may not have been apprehensive; but in the late summer and early autumn of 1929, Mulberry Street looked ahead to years of undiminished prosperity. Even the Bergens' son-in-law, William Ruffner, had built a better and bigger house than he had planned.

"But don't forget," Ralph would insist moodily, "that it took the savings of ten years to put me on my feet again."

"I can't think of that. I'm too happy."

"It's no fun to me to see you working. I didn't marry you to be supported."

"I don't mind working if only you'll get well. But I wish I could make more. Since Father has lost his classes, it has been harder to manage. I hope we shan't have to touch the money we put by for Ranny's education."

"If we do, I can make it up to him. It's only a thousand dollars."

This was one of his cheerful days, but it was harder and darker in his resentful moods. Last night, when he could not sleep, she had only exasperated him by trying to quiet his restlessness.

"The worst is over now, Ralph. In a week you'll begin to work again. Have patience for a few days."

"I've had patience. I'm tired of patience. This has taken ten years out of my life."

"No, it hasn't, not really. And there must be a reason," she had continued without thinking, because the catchword flitted into her mind. "There must be a reason why we have to go through such things."

"If I thought that . . ." His voice had trailed off on a despairing note. "If I thought any God had made this crazy world, I'd go out and shoot somebody."

"Oh, don't . . . don't . . ."

"Then stop talking like Mr. Black. The only way I can bear it is by believing there isn't a reason."

"Try to lie still. Try to stop thinking, and let the medicine put you to sleep. I wish I could bear it in your place. It is harder on you."

For an instant he had lain so quiet that she knew he dared not trust his voice to reply. Then he had reached for her hand. "If it wasn't for you, Ada . . ."

That strange happiness which seemed always to mean something more than itself flared up suddenly like a torch in her mind. As long as he depended upon her, she could face anything, she said over and over; she could face even the strain of sleepless nights and exhausting days, even the stubborn pain of his misery.

Her work at Shadwell's had been easier when she was employed upstairs in her old place with the dresses. But gloves had returned to fashion, and she was now kept standing all day at the glove counter, where she smoothed, pulled, and stretched kid over too plump or too thin fingers. When six o'clock came at last, she gathered up the split gloves left for repair and brought them home to mend in the evening. Ralph boiled with indignation while he watched her mending the gloves of strange women, but the extra task was required, and she needed employment too much to refuse. Yet that was nothing, she told herself, compared to the blistering pain in her feet. After standing most of the day on the French heels she was expected to wear, her feet felt as if red-hot needles had been thrust into the joints. Gradually they had hardened, but in the beginning she would take off her shoes as soon as she entered the front door, and hasten to plunge her feet into a tub of hot water and Epsom salts. "There ought to be a law," Aunt Meggie would protest, "against wearing silk stockings and French heels in shops."

The ripe October day was closing in, but the far dome of the sky still shed a mother-of-pearl lustre, more a broken vibration than a light, over the grey steeples and red chimneys. A minute before she had ached with fatigue. Then she had come within range of the window, and suddenly she had ceased to feel tired while her thoughts were swept forward on strong waves of expectancy. If only Ralph had had a good day after the restless night that had kept them awake! Now that he was so nearly well again, his moods of tortured indignation were more frequent. Did he ever suspect, she wondered, how completely drained of vitality she found herself after hours of vehement despair and troubled sleep? But it's worse on him than on me, she would think. Everything is worse on him than on me.

From the yellow house at the corner Mrs. Rawlings peered over her machine, with her foot still working the treadle. On the porch of the boarding-house Mrs. Maudsley was stubbornly reasoning with one of her lodgers, while her features jerked up and down in a futile effort to please. Then, as Ada opened the gate, William Ruffner dashed up the curving brick steps from the basement.

"Why, William!" she exclaimed in alarm, for his pleasant face, usually so fair and fresh, looked ashen and withered, and he hurried past her as if he were driven by wind. An instant later, while she gazed after him, Otto locked the door of the workroom and ascended the steps.

"I hope Rosa hasn't had a bad turn," she said anxiously.

"No, Rosa's all right. The baby was three weeks old yesterday. But William's wiped out."

"Wiped out?" She stared at him with dazed eyes.

"In the panic today. Most of the little speculators were thrown over."

"I heard Mr. Shadwell talking about it, but I thought it was a panic in New York, not in Queenborough. Is it worse than the break in September?"

"It's the worst that ever was for us. William has been rushing all over town trying to borrow. Then, after he put up everything he had, he couldn't hold his margin, and the brokers have sold him out. They carried the big traders—or some of them—but the little fellow didn't stand a chance when the bottom dropped out of the market."

"Poor William." There was a tremor in her voice. "I know what it means to him."

"He'd gone in too deep to draw back. Even Rosa didn't know that he was still plunging in oil and copper. Of course, if stocks had soared instead of dropping, he'd have made a fortune. Did Ralph ever buy that Girdlestone stock?"

"No, we put the thousand dollars away for Ranny's education. It seemed too little to risk."

"That was a queer way to look at it, but it turned out to be the best way."

"I suppose William will have to rent his house now and move into a smaller one."

"The house went with everything else. He had mortgaged it to try to save something. I know," he added, with a rueful laugh, "that this sounds as if William were a fool. But he isn't a fool. He has as good a mind as you'll meet any day."

"No, I don't blame William. I'm too sorry about it. Rosa is so fine."

"You'd think that if you saw the way she's standing by William. If all modern girls were like Rosa, they'd be a long way ahead." His face clouded, and Ada knew he was thinking of Minna. "I tell her mother that when she feels the blues coming on, she ought to pull herself together and think of her splendid daughter." He looked at her with a smile that tried to be sportive, and she thought that the plump contour of his cheeks had grown haggard since yesterday. "The trouble is," he continued, "that people, even the best of them, have forgotten how to deny themselves. All they think of is having a good time, and they aren't willing to make sacrifices even for their own children. Rosa wasn't that way till she was married, but she can't bear not to give in to William. Well, I know you're tired, and I mustn't keep you."

Wherever you looked, there was something waiting to destroy happiness, Ada thought as she turned away. No sooner was a shelter found for the mind or the heart than the savage elements of cruelty and injustice swept up and demolished it. Shelters and systems and civilizations were all overwhelmed in time, her father said, by the backward forces of ignorance, of barbarism, of ferocity. Yet the level would steadily rise, little by little; in the end other unities would emerge from the ruins; and the indestructible will of the world was toward life.

With her first questioning glance at Ralph, she saw that the dark cloud had not lifted. "You must be tired to death," he said, as he kissed her. "This life is killing you, Ada."

"Oh, no, it isn't." She tried to laugh away his anxiety. "I can stand worse things than this. Wait and try me."

"You didn't get any sleep last night."

"I slept whenever you did."

"I know it was my fault. But I feel as if I'd been buried under a rubbish heap of wasted time and money."

"Well, whatever happens, I must sit down. If I stand another minute, I'll drop in my tracks."

Pushing her into a chair, he knelt in front of her and took off her shoes, rubbing her swollen feet gently. "I meant to have your slippers waiting, but I forgot after I heard about William." Looking down at him, she thought with that vague part of her which seemed only a second self: Yes, he can be gentle, he can be tender. If he hurts anything, it is because he has been hurt.

"Give me your hat and coat," he said, and taking them from her, he carried them into the closet and returned with the soft old slippers she wore in the house. "Do you want me to turn on the hot water?"

She shook her head. "I'll wait till bedtime. All I want is just to lie here in this easy-chair in the firelight. I believe I could drop to sleep without shutting my eyes." Like a tired swimmer, she felt, her mind floated outward on a shadowy stream. Then, starting up, she said, "I am so worried about William."

"So am I. He spent the whole day trying to borrow. I wish I'd had something to lend him."

That was reckless, and it was like Ralph, yet she had always found such recklessness more endearing than prudence. I couldn't be like that, but I love it in him, she thought. Only, I suppose, for Ranny's sake, one of us had to be prudent, or we should have saved nothing.

"Your father has gone to see Rosa. She sent word that she wanted to see him."

"People always send for him when they're in trouble. That used to surprise me in Ironside. Though he lacks everything that they have, he seems to have something they've lost—or perhaps never had." Turning her head, she spoke to Aunt Meggie in the passage. "Yes, I did bring home some gloves to mend. Ralph must have taken them." With a sigh, she stretched her arms over her head and withdrew her floating self from the shadows. "Did you look in the pocket of my coat?" she inquired a minute later, as she followed Aunt Meggie into the bedroom.

"Yes, I found them, and I'll do them tonight. I didn't like the idea of your bobbing your hair, Ada, but it does make you look younger."

Picking up a comb, Ada ran it through the grey lock that waved like a silver feather straight back through her thick shingled hair. "This is the way I'll look when I'm old," she said abruptly; for it seemed to her, while she gazed at her reflection in the mirror, that the firm contour had broken up into sagging lines.

"That's just because you didn't get any sleep last night, and you're tired out."

"I'm thirty-eight, and I feel as if I were fifty." She smoothed out two deep furrows between her eyebrows, and turned away from the glass. "I didn't have anything for lunch but an apple. A woman from the country had to be fitted."

"You'll feel better when you've had supper. There's a Sally Lunn in the stove."

"You work too hard, Aunt Meggie. I'm so sorry we had to let Tillie go."

"There wasn't anything else to do. We couldn't have managed on what we have. And besides, I never minded working if people like what I do. I'm like Mother in that. It isn't the work that kills, but the complaints, she used to say."

"You know we like what you do, but that doesn't ease the strain. Old Betsey comes only once a week now."

"Your father helps when he can. He never had any false pride about a man's work. He takes Ranny off my hands, too, as soon as the child comes from school. And Ralph isn't any real trouble. He's always had a way with him that makes people want to do things for him. Even when he complains, you don't mind, because it's sure to be about something so big you can't help it."

"Well, you mustn't mend these gloves to-night. It won't hurt them to wait."

"Then things will begin to pile up on us, and we'll get behind in the mending. And I'm not real tired yet. Old Betsey was here washing this morning, and Mr. Midkiff helped tidy up when he stopped by to fix a bench for the washtub. No, I didn't have a bad day. It seemed just like every other day to me."

CHAPTER 10

✻ ✻ ✻ ✻ ✻ ✻ ✻ANNY and I were in the woods," John Fincastle
was saying. "As long as we didn't know of the
R crash, it hadn't happened to us."
Looking at him on the other side of the fire,
Ada thought, It's true that he is unreal. That
makes him so lovable.

But what, he would have asked, is reality? Do we know that
the idea is less real than the object? That the Stock Exchange is
more real than Plato's Republic? His features, worn down to
the spirit, were charged with light, with a singular clearness.
"Yesterday I tried to find something I might do in the library,"
he continued. "A public library, one imagines, might become the
last refuge of the aging student, but there also they demand
youth, they demand inexperience."

"You mustn't think of that, Father." Ada glanced round from
arranging the cups and saucers. "We owe you a great deal more
than we can ever repay."

"It worries me that John eats so sparingly," Aunt Meggie said.

"I eat enough, my dear. You may give my share to Midkiff, or
to some one else who is hungry."

"Isn't there a plenty, Mother? I mean a plenty for everybody?" Ranny asked.

"A plenty, darling. Your grandfather is thinking of the very
poor."

"We aren't that?"

"Oh, no." She laughed, remembering the poor McAllisters.
"There are many people worse off than we are."

"If we're ever very poor, Mother, I can sell newspapers. I
know a boy, Jimmy Brackett, who sells papers. It's a lot of fun.
I'd rather do that than go to school."

"You'd rather do anything than go to school," Ralph said. "But it won't be long before your mother sits at home and I look after my family."

Why did the word "family" on his lips bring a sense of peace to her heart? Only yesterday he had said that they were clinging to the roots of the old order, that the family as an institution was as antiquated as slavery. Yet glancing now out on the lights in Mulberry Street, she thought happily, Behind those rows of windows there must be other families like ours, holding together through success and failure, through good times and bad.

"I saw William and Rosa." John Fincastle looked troubled. "They will have to begin again from the bottom."

Ranny squirmed with curiosity. "The bottom of what, Grandfather?"

"The bottom of the world," Ralph replied impatiently. "I only hope it isn't the bottom of the hill to the poorhouse."

"Oh, don't put that in his mind!" Ada exclaimed. "He will never forget it."

"Why not, Mother? Why can I never forget it?"

"Haven't I always told you," Ralph asked dryly, "that the inquiring mind in a household is not an unmixed blessing?"

Although Ralph had come out of his illness with a strong zest for activity, she soon saw that he flagged easily, and that he had lost his earlier interest in buying and selling. His natural bent, from which he had been twisted in youth, was toward what her grandmother had called "the learned professions," and he was irritated by modern methods of advertising. As long as the business had provided a livelihood and he had been able to divert himself with the hope of success, he had found it possible to drive his mind into an occupation that irked him. But after the frustration of illness, new fears had displaced his old hopes for the future. That strange fantasy of impotence, of failure, so startling to her and so familiar to Dr. Bradford and the neurological surgeon, had built its nest in the lower levels of consciousness.

"The truth is, they don't need me," he complained one day

in the early spring. "They're waiting for the first chance to fire me for good. And you can't blame them. Trade is dull, and they've more men hanging about the place than they know what to do with."

"Things are obliged to pick up."

"Everybody's waiting for that. Stocks are up again, but business is dragging. Every other man you meet is trying to sell you a cheap car."

"I thought they expected a great deal from their tractor plow?"

"They did until the drought."

"But there's always a drought. A flood and a drought were the first things I remember."

"Well, people aren't buying. Or perhaps I've lost the knack of making people want to buy."

"Oh, no, you haven't. It will all come back to you." Merely to say this was not enough; she must believe it. All her strength was poured into an act of faith, into a glowing affirmation of life.

"I've worked for four months, and I haven't made enough to keep us going."

"You will when business is better. Everything will improve now that spring is here. And I shall hold on to my job just a little longer."

"I hate your doing that. It makes me feel that I'm not more than half a man."

"But think how well we were doing before that accident. If nothing had happened, we'd be in our own home by this time, and we should have put by enough for a rainy day." For she must find and give back to him what he had lost, his pride in himself and his masculine vanity. She must pass on that act of faith, that glow, that affirmation which was more to him than the thing it affirmed.

The next day he sold two cars, and returned in a sanguine temper. "It looks now as if better times were coming back. Every one expects a good summer."

Was the worst really over? she wondered as the summer advanced. People said there was a firmer tone in the market, and that it was the best time to buy if one had anything left. Even William Ruffner, who had brought his wife to live with her family and gone to work repairing old furniture in his father-in-law's shop in the basement, was eager to begin speculating all over again. But there was more play and less cheerfulness in the Bergens' back yard. Though the elder grandchild toddled across the grass, there were fewer flowers and they bloomed less profusely. Sometimes, it seemed to Ada, the tunes Otto whistled over his work sounded almost dejected, and even Hans waddled more soberly, and gazed at his master with the look of a tragic poet in his deep, velvety eyes. Minna, who now spent whole nights away from home, confessed that she was bored to death by the crowded house, the crying babies, and the endless discussion of the best way to make two short ends meet. Nothing had come of her engagement to Bertie Rawlings, and there was a smouldering blaze under her fringed lashes. For several weeks she had worked in a hat shop, but early risings and long hours had been too much for her, and she declared, at the end of a hot day in August, that she would rather die than go back the next morning. Rosa had taken her place, and Mrs. Bergen, who was a born mother, but had the cooking and the housework on her hands, was obliged to look after the two babies.

"Otto is the one I feel for," Aunt Meggie said. "His wife has her church, and she can shoulder a part of the trouble on that, but he hasn't anything but his own goodness to fall back on."

"This is only the beginning," Ralph replied. "Wait till next winter."

"But you said in April that things were picking up."

"That was in April. This is August. I suppose some things are picking up, if you mean speakeasies and cockfights and craps."

"When you're in the street," Ada said, "you'd imagine that nobody stays at home except in a coffin."

"Yes, I was thinking to-day," Aunt Meggie sighed, "that I'd

never seen the world look so flighty. It does seem hard that the sensible people have to be sacrificed to the foolish."

Ada tried to speak lightly. "I'm glad Ranny isn't grown yet. There may be worse things ahead of us than gangs of hoodlums."

"Well, we'll have to take our punishment," Ralph said angrily, "and the chances are that we'll have to take it lying down. You can't expect common decency from a bad system."

"No doubt," her father assented, with his tranquil smile, "but until we have common decency we shall never invent a system that is not bad."

Nothing, not even established disaster, Ada told herself, could be so terrible as the rootless poverty of the streets. Aloud she said only, "Where is Ranny? Has anybody seen Ranny? Since he is big enough to fight, I never dare take my eyes off him when I'm at home, and I worry all day long about the company he keeps. He has sworn vengeance, he told me, against the Oregon Hill crowd."

"That's because some of them tried to steal Henry VIII," Aunt Meggie explained. "Before I could get him back, they had plucked out his handsomest tail feather. Otto says he never lets Hans out of his sight for fear they may do him a mischief."

"Here I am, Mother." Ranny appeared with blood oozing from a cut on his lip. "I got him!" he cried triumphantly. "I broke his head!"

"Ranny, you promised me you wouldn't fight."

"But I had to, Mother. I had to."

"You know you oughtn't to fight."

"Yes, I ought, Mother. I ought."

"Good boy!" Ralph said approvingly.

"Tell him, Father, he mustn't fight," Ada begged.

"Violence is the spirit of the age, my dear. You wouldn't have him out of touch with his time."

"Wouldn't you fight, Grandfather, if they plucked your rooster?"

"I don't know, my boy. I've never had that decision to make."

If only they could move! But how could they? she asked herself in discouragement, and where could they go?

"Ranny, do be careful," she begged. "Those gangs are too rough."

"I'm not afraid of 'em, Mother. I'm twelve, and I can throw straighter than they can. Besides, Jimmy Brackett and I are forming a gang of our own. We're going to join with the Bats and the River Bottom Spiders against the Oregon Hill Cats."

"I declare, there goes that rowdy now," Aunt Meggie said from the front window. "Of all the impudence! He has dared to stick Henry VIII's feather in his cap."

"Do you want Jimmy and me to get it back, Aunt Meggie? We can get it for you."

"No, Ranny, oh, no," Aunt Meggie answered quickly and flatly. "That feather isn't a bit of use to me as long as it isn't in my rooster's tail." Her voice changed, and she peered under the old mulberry tree with a sympathetic expression. "Bertie Rawlings is a nice-looking young man," she said. "I wonder why he can't find a place to teach?"

Ada went over to the window and smiled down on Bertie's tall, thin figure. Yes, he was a well-favoured youth, with his deeply tanned skin, his glossy brown hair, and his sparkling eyes between brown and black. "I don't see how his mother makes enough for them both. Everybody is wearing ready-made dresses."

"She's having a hard time, I know, but Bertie hopes to find a job by the fall. He spends his days watching for the postman. I can see that he's worried, though he tries to keep a brave front. All the colleges are turning away men, he says, and a Ph.D. doesn't mean any more than a war decoration when you're hunting a job."

"If nothing better turns up," John Fincastle said, "he might do well in my academy for young ladies."

"But he's tried Boscobel School," Aunt Meggie replied. "They did like him, and Miss Curran would have engaged him if he'd applied a week sooner. If the young man she selected doesn't suit, she has promised to give Bertie a chance."

"Well, the other young man will see to it that he suits," Ralph said. "Suitability is a merit that no longer goes begging."

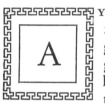 YEAR later, two years later, Ada was still working in Shadwell's, and Ralph was still having his good or bad days, his good or bad weeks, his good or bad months. What had they meant to her, those days, weeks, months of time? Were they spun to endure out of the deepest substance of living? Or were they as brief and brittle as circumstances?

There was, among other recollections, the memory of a particular evening, after the noisy elections were over and done with, in the autumn of 1932. Isolated in its own unhappiness, yet without the moral grandeur of tragedy, it stood alone in her thoughts. Misfortunes never come singly, her grandmother used to say, and on this day of slanting rain and slopping streets, it seemed to Ada that a brood of accidents alighted upon her. In the morning a water pipe had burst, and she had sent Ranny to the Bergens' for a bucket of fresh water. Then, just as she was starting for the shop, Aunt Meggie had tripped over a loosened board in the kitchen floor, and Ralph had bandaged her swollen ankle, while John Fincastle set out to summon old Betsey from her bleak cellar in Jackson Ward.

When Ada finally reached Shadwell's, she heard that her salary had been cut from twenty to eighteen dollars a week; yet she felt only a sense of relief because she had not been discharged with the mournful women and girls she found in the cloakroom. Nobody, she realized, was to blame, not the departing President, not the arriving President, not even the Kaiser. An economic disaster was as impersonal as an earthquake. It overtook, like the rain or the wrath of the Lord, both the just and the unjust, the diligent and the idle. There was nothing to be done about it, unless she could succeed in making eighteen dollars as elastic as twenty. Besides, there was always the chance that Ralph might earn an unusually good commission. Last month he had done better, and the Duncan car appeared to be recovering its old popularity. This, of course, was the sensible, as well as the sanguine, view of their difficulties. But all day long, while she fitted gloves on fingers that seemed to wilt in her grasp, she was wondering how she could possibly buy Ranny the new overcoat and the pair of shoes he needed for school. What could she sell or pawn? All the good pieces of old walnut had gone for a meager sum; the clock with the landscape and the painted tray had brought almost nothing; the scattered books left in John Fincastle's library were such as few persons would read and nobody would buy. Only the blue bowl, which had acquired an ethereal value, as if it were the symbol of some precious bowl of the spirit, stood in its old place and shone with the radiance or the darkness of firelight.

"I wonder if we could get anything for this?" Ralph had asked one day, picking up the bowl in his hands.

Like a fragment of God's Mountain, the blue had deepened to violet as the sunbeams flashed over it. "Oh, no, that was Mother's bowl!" Ada had cried, seizing it from him. "That must go last of all."

"I spoke to Mr. Milliken about it," Aunt Meggie had confessed, "but he said it would bring very little. People aren't buying ornaments any longer."

In the street this afternoon, hurrying home under her raised umbrella, it seemed to Ada that she was stalked by the grim spectre of poverty. So many scarecrow figures, with lean arms protruding from tattered sleeves! So many gnarled dirty hands begging! So many putty-coloured faces hag-ridden by fear! And at lunch time, when she had gone out for a sandwich, she had seen the breadlines forming before an empty warehouse, where a charitable society dispensed stale bread and potato soup. All over Queenborough such lines were forming and such places were opening. Three blocks away from their home in Mulberry Street, rows of hungry men, women, and children, in the cast-off

but still fashionable garments of the rich, waited, with tin cups
in their hands, on every Monday, Thursday, and Saturday. And
this world of visible wretchedness was hemmed in by an area as
unreal and fantastic as a nightmare. Distraught, chaotic, grotesque, it was an age, she told herself, of cruelty without moral
indignation, of catastrophe without courage. Movie-minded
children pounced in bands from the alleys. The nimble wits and
legs of bandits were matched against the sluggish law and the
heavy-footed police. Every class, every period of life even,
demanded more freedom and stronger excitements.

Through the sheets of rain a drunken man lurched against her
as he tossed a pint flask into an alley. On the other side, close
under her umbrella, a woman was shrieking with hysterical
mirth, "He asked me if I'd wear an old-fashioned nightgown, and
I said, 'Never except in my coffin.' Then he said . . ." The
shrieks died in chuckles, and the wind swept on from the
river.

This was a crowded quarter of the town, but in Granite Boulevard, where the very rich were safely buried beneath the last
pyramid of high finance, there were still teas without tea, she
had heard, and motion-picture faces without a film, and endless
gin-drinking, and hastily bitten-back hiccoughs, and stories just
a little funnier that went just a little farther than last year, and
much talk of prize fighting, which was Puritanically forbidden,
and of fox-hunting, which was Cavalierly allowed, and ardent
prophecies that the next legislature would permit horse racing
and gambling and pari-mutuel betting. How long ago had she
waited in an imposing hall, on an errand after Shadwell's had
closed, and listened as if she were at a play to the ribald chatter
of the younger married set that called itself the Underworld?
But people aren't like that, she had thought. People aren't really
like that.

A beggar touched her arm under the umbrella, and after a
glance into his eyes, she stopped and gave him a little money. I
suppose he'll buy a drink, and I hope he will if it helps him to
forget. The dimmed stare had reminded her of Mr. Midkiff.

They were feeding him every night, since he had been without work for a year, and Mrs. Maudsley, who had become sour and slovenly and tight-fisted, poor creature, was trying to push him into the almshouse. But they were beginning to wonder how much longer they could scrape together bread and meat for his plate on the kitchen table. Every penny had to be counted twice over, and the cost of bacon alone, Aunt Meggie complained, would drive any honest skinflint into his grave.

At home she found Aunt Meggie in the kitchen, and a pot of bean soup on the gas stove.

"Yes, I'm all right, Ada. As soon as the swelling went down, the pain stopped. I'm making soup with that old ham bone."

"Did the plumber come?"

"He mended the pipe, but he said it might burst again any day. In a ramshackle house like this something is always the matter. I brought your clothes in here to warm them. You mustn't wear your one black dress in the house."

"It doesn't look as if we could keep on this way." As Ada replied, she peeled off her wet stockings. "Mr. Shadwell has cut my salary to eighteen dollars."

"That means eight dollars less every month. Well, we'll have to see how we can manage."

"Where's Ranny? I'm always uneasy when I don't see him."

"He went over to the Bergens' with your father. They both get restless in bad weather. There they are now. Or maybe it is Ralph."

"Yes, it's Ralph's step," Ada answered, and flying into her bedroom, she changed into a flowered dress which was worn but bright, and hastily dragged a comb through her dampened hair. "Even in my coffin, I should hate to look dreary," she said to her face in the mirror.

In the front room Ralph was standing before the fire, and when she entered he turned to look at her with an expression of hopeless defiance. Rain was dripping from his overcoat, and she saw, with a start, that he had forgotten to take off his hat, which was as soaked as a wet sponge.

"I'm dog-tired," he said in a dull voice. "I'm dog-tired of living."

"I know, Ralph, I know. There are times when I feel that way myself. But take off your coat. Give it to me, and your hat too. They're dripping wet."

While she hurried to the kitchen with his wet things, he sank into a chair and sat motionless until she came back and bent over him. "We all have our blue days," she began, and stopped suddenly because it seemed to her that her heart had turned over. He had been drinking. For the first time since that night of their old estrangement and Janet's triumph, she knew when he kissed her that he had been drinking. I shouldn't mind, she thought helplessly, if he could stand it, or could even afford it, but he can't. He can't, and he is doing it from sheer desperation. And this, she had learned from watching the streets, is the worst of all drunkenness. To drink for pleasure may be a distraction, but to drink from misery is always a danger. What could she say or do? What did other women say or do with men who were not sober enough to listen?

"I'm fired," he said, without turning.

She dropped into the chair facing him—her grandmother's chair with wings. "But . . . but that's ridiculous."

"It's true too. There aren't sales enough to divide among so many men. Two men can handle that part of the business, and the rest of us were turned off. I've seen it coming for six months. As soon as sales pick up, and the farmers begin buying tractor plows, we'll all be taken back again, if we haven't given in to starvation or old age. . . ."

The words rustled in vacancy. "I can't understand," she answered. "There must be a mistake."

"I've spent six hours looking for a job. I must have tramped miles in and out of buildings. Good God! I never realized till now what men are up against when they're out of work. Then, when I was too tired to move on, I stopped at a bootlegger's." He drew a flat pint bottle from his pocket and held it up. "There's mighty little left. It took most of this to get me home, and it cost a dollar and a half. A dollar and a half for a pint of filthy stuff that doesn't touch the moonshine on Lightning Ridge."

"Some men can stand it," she said, "but you can't."

While she stared into his face, it seemed to her that something within (was it pride? was it self-control?) had recoiled like a wave, had curved, ascended, and shattered itself against life. "I can't bear it!" she cried out wildly. "This is the one thing too much. I can't bear anything more." A storm of sobs choked her voice. Flinging herself on the rug, she wept bitterly, without shame, without covering her eyes, without wiping away the tears from her cheeks or the salty taste from her lips. Utterly abandoned to fatigue, beyond restraint, beyond humiliation, beyond effort, she felt only that resistance was hopeless and despair might wash over her.

"But, Ada!" he burst out, suddenly sobered. "But, Ada!" When she did not look up, he knelt beside her and lifted her from the floor. "It isn't like you to break down. You're too good a sport to break down."

Her tears stopped as suddenly as they had begun. With the stains still on her face, she felt for the winged chair and dropped into it.

He gazed at her in bewilderment. "I'm not drunk, you know, if you mean that."

"It's for Ranny. You couldn't put that on Ranny."

"I was worn out, and it went to my head a bit. But I won't again. If you feel like that about it, I won't ever again."

She laughed, fumbling for her handkerchief. "Something snapped inside."

"Well, I promise." His voice was toneless. "You have enough to stand without that."

"Remember Ranny too."

"Yes, Ranny too." He patted her shoulder while he dropped the bottle into her lap. "If it isn't too near supper, I think I'll take a nap on that sofa."

As he lay down on her mother's old sofa, and she covered him with a knitted robe, she said, "We'll manage somehow. When things are so bad, if they change at all, they have to change for the better. We can rent out the rooms upstairs, and that will split the rent almost in half." But her heart was shivering, she felt, like a frightened hare. How are we going to live? it panted faster and faster. How in the world are we going to live?

She had dreaded having to break the bad news to her father and Ranny, but the old man merely nodded in sympathy, and Ranny treated the general calamity as a new kind of lark.

"Now, I can sell papers till Father gets back his job." His round fresh face, with the clear blue eyes, looked manly and eager.

"No, Ranny, you have that scholarship to work for. Everything depends upon your going to Meadow Brook School next year."

"Oh, I can do that too, Mother. All the boys in my class are older, but I keep at the head." Sometimes he was almost too assured, she admitted, too sanguine and self-reliant. She wondered what Ralph thought of such boastfulness, but when she glanced round, she read in his look only pride and a dazed kind of admiration. Well, that was the way, no doubt, to succeed in life, but if the boy was so cocksure at thirteen and a half, what would he become by the time he was twenty-one?

The next instant she told herself that she might have misconstrued Ralph's expression. Never could she surmise what he was thinking. He was still, as he had always been, a mystery to her. Had he found happiness in his marriage? Had he found happiness anywhere? Only when her muscles ached and her nerves quivered like harp strings under an awkward hand did these aimless questions flock into her mind and settle over her thoughts.

Rather than lose his tenants, the owner of the house consented to reduce the rent, and immediately they agreed to let out all the second floor, except the small rooms over the kitchen, to a family from the country. By the end of the week John Fincastle had moved his desk and his books into the back room under the tin roof, and Aunt Meggie had arranged her few possessions downstairs in what had once been the laundry. Ranny, to his intense delight, was to sleep on a cot behind the screen in the living-room.

"In some ways, it will be more convenient," Aunt Meggie said. "I'll take fewer steps next to the kitchen, and it will be easier to keep warm."

In another era, Ada thought admiringly, Aunt Meggie might have been merely commonplace, but she emerged as a heroine from this particular moment of history. Her small weather-beaten face had not aged; her thin grey hair still straggled in curly wisps over her trusting brown eyes.

"When she gets to Heaven," Ralph had once remarked to Ada, "what will she do there? How could she find enough little things to keep her happy?"

"I wonder," Ada had whispered back, "but without her religion, I don't see how we'd make out on earth."

"All the same she works too hard. You ought to stop her."

"I've tried, but I can't. She won't give up. But have you noticed how absent-minded she is growing?"

"Who wouldn't be? And your father too. There's that queer stillness in his face."

"I know. It comes over him, I sometimes think, like twilight on a pond. His heart is somewhere else. Perhaps it is in another age or another world."

HE first lodgers in the rooms upstairs were a retired country clergyman, his second wife, and two stepdaughters just old enough to crave excitement. From Aunt Meggie, in whom they confided, Ada learned that the country church was too poor to struggle on any longer, and had suspended its pastor after a bitter drought and the failure of crops. The man himself had a tortured look, with cavernous eyes, and appeared crushed in spite of his piety, but the wife and daughters were spiteful and quarrelsome. "They blame me because I am a failure," he confessed to Aunt Meggie. "But how could I live on people who have nothing, even though I have nothing myself? The girls want to enjoy themselves, and they think it is my fault because they can't."

At the end of the week, when the rent was paid by a sharp-nosed young woman with a notebook, Ada discovered that the family was supported by charity. It seemed too dreadful when one thought of that nice old man, who looked as if God had ordained him to rescue the perishing. Whenever she saw the impassive countenance of the social worker, like some wooden symbol of philanthropy, she felt a vague resentment against society, against the world, against God, but, most of all, against human nature. A mere slip of a girl, without tact or experience, but armed with institutional methods and possessing a diploma that covered all deficiencies, the investigator classified, tabulated, registered, and summed up with a yellow pencil in her small black notebok held together by a stout band of elastic. Every week, with the inconvenient regularity of a machine, she darted into the hall, without ringing the bell, and tripped up the staircase. For twenty minutes or more, she would remain closeted with her victims in the front room upstairs. Then the door would open; she could be heard piping good advice in the metallic tone of patronage; and a little later she would flit down and disappear as rapidly as she had come. But in the room overhead the quarrels and recriminations would again break out in a torrent.

"I can't see how that old minister lives through those scenes," Aunt Meggie would sigh. "It's a pity he didn't have too much sense to marry that nagging woman. Of course she's years younger than he is, but youth isn't everything."

"They're poor sports," Ralph said one evening when a string of whining complaints dripped through the ceiling. "One thing you can count on in Ada," he continued chaffingly. "She'll never let anybody down. Even if she'd married an old minister, she'd have stuck by her bargain."

Ada smiled as she threaded her needle to patch Ranny's trousers. "I like getting the better of life," she tossed back gaily, "and I'm not ashamed that I do."

It was amazing, she thought, knotting the thread and smoothing the triangular patch on her knee, how many things one could find to laugh at on the brink of disaster. If only one took the world as one found it, and did not sit down and wait for something to happen!

"Please put the patch where it doesn't show, Mother," Ranny begged. "If you put it in the seat, the boys will call me Bottom Patches."

"I can't find a place, darling, that doesn't show when you stoop over. But I'll do my best to hide the stitches where it's put in."

Her gaze left the scrap of cloth and wandered over the living-room to the screen covered with Chinese wallpaper they had brought from the manse. Though little was left in the room, it was still homelike and cheerful when the lamp was lighted at dusk and the firelight rippled over the faded cinnamon-coloured walls. I've held on to my blue bowl, she thought, just as Great-great-grandmother Tod held on to her cameo brooch among savages. We held on because they were symbols.

Now and then, Ranny earned a little money by running errands after school. Earlier in the winter, he had tried to deliver newspapers, but after getting up before day and starting out at a quarter to five every morning, he had found at the end of a week that he was the richer by only seventeen cents. The trouble was, he explained after much earnest figuring, that he had worked under another boy who collected the money and pocketed the entire profits. A green-grocer in market was more dependable, but he needed an errand boy only for a week or two in December, when his regular delivery man was knocked down in the street and had to go to the hospital.

Life that autumn and winter was drawn out into a single aching nerve, Ada felt, a slowly gnawing anxiety. Ralph was walking the streets, and the echo of his wearied footfalls was like a thudding pain in her heart. Sometimes she would dream that a long reverberating roll of drums had marched over her grave, rat-a-tat, rat-a-tat, rat-a-tat. Then she would start up, strangled by fear, while the echo escaped from the nightmare into her waking mind, and she remembered that the thudding sound (the devil's tattoo, her grandmother would have called it) was the monotonous tramp of homeless men in the street. Always they passed on to Mulberry Hill and the shelter for transients, one, or two, or three, or occasionally a straggling row with its dreary passage from the delusion to the actuality. In that grey army all the faces were arrested in a death-in-life immobility, as if the blood in the veins had stopped and frozen. It was the familiar look of long patience, which had carved her father's features into graven serenity, which would presently chisel bluish hollows in Ralph's cheeks and temples and beneath his still amused and defiant eyes.

A shiver like creeping frost would steal over her. Under the strain of tense nerves, would Ralph at last lose his mocking courage and become apathetic, humble, defeated? Suppose conditions should change from bad to worse before the winter was over! Suppose she were to fall ill, or Ralph's paralysis were to return (though the doctor said this was not likely), or suppose she should be obliged to stop work before Ralph found steady employment. Far into the night, after Ralph had tormented his mind into unconsciousness, while Ranny slept snugly on the lounge in the living-room, while Aunt Meggie, drugged by fatigue, dozed in snatches beside the tubs in the laundry, while John Fincastle wondered ceaselessly how he could pay the next premium on his insurance—far into the chill, blank hours of approaching dawn, a multitude of anxieties, featureless, grotesque, repulsive as bats, would pour out from the corners and crevices of the house and swarm over her bed. And she would ask herself, in the clutch of an old fear—or was it remorse?—Is God punishing me because I killed Grandmother? Yet, even in the winter darkness, the idea seemed ludicrous. She was sure that Aunt Meggie, safely anchored on the rock of predestination, would consider such vengeance excessive. If I had my life to go over, I suppose I'd do differently, she thought, but nobody knows . . .

The dark troubled her, but strength returned with the deep vibrations of sunrise. Then she would slip out of bed, without waking Ralph, and steal into the kitchen to find that Aunt Meggie, who awoke with the first crow of Henry VIII, had lighted the gas stove and put on a kettle of water. Glowing and tingling from an icy dip, Ada would hurry into her clothes and help Ranny dress, before the table was set in the living-room and the soft-coal fire fanned into a blaze. "Even if you stint yourself on your other meals," Aunt Meggie would say, as she fried bacon, or scrambled eggs in season, "it is always well to start the day with a good breakfast. Anyhow," she would add with a twist of dry merriment, "Anne Boleyn will never lose her head if she begins to lay an egg every morning."

"If it's hard on me," Ada said to herself, "what must it mean to Aunt Meggie, who works her fingers to the bone and comes first with nobody?" And she wasn't the only one! All over the world there were nameless wives and mothers still baking and scrubbing and washing in the hope that imperfect human ties might remain linked together.

"I'm not easy in my mind about your father." Aunt Meggie lowered her voice while she put the coffee-pot on the table. "I never saw so little flesh on any one who wasn't mortally ill."

"Yet he looks happy."

"That has grown on him since the doctor discovered there was a general breaking-up. He has serious kidney trouble, and his heart, too, is bad. But he wouldn't follow any treatment. . . ."

That was late in January, on the mild, silvery day when the Queenborough Central and Savings Bank, the largest bank in the city, closed its doors. Ada, fitting a glove over stiffened fingers in Shadwell's, listened incredulously to an account of the disaster.

"Why, that's where we have the last of our savings!" she exclaimed.

"I wish we'd known about you," the customer answered regretfully. "My husband says so many people chose that bank because it looks so substantial and the president is considered a monument to integrity. A rumour reached us yesterday that things weren't exactly right there, and my husband went down and withdrew the greater part of his deposit. Early this morning there was a run on the bank, and the doors didn't stay open longer than half an hour." She lifted her pretty face and settled her elbow in the centre of the small velvet cushion on the counter. "There are a great many stories going about, but nobody knows, of course, whether or not they are true. My husband doesn't believe that the directors of the bank knew it was obliged to fail and that several of them had sold all their stock weeks before. Of course, it's dreadfully hard on the small depositors. My husband says they are the people who always pay in the end. He telephoned me just before I started to market that he was having the most trying day of his life, and to send him down some aspirin for a headache. Men and women had come to him in tears and told me they had lost everything they had in the world."

"Everything they had in the world," Ada repeated, with dry lips, working mechanically over the kid fingers.

She remembered the Hamblens, who had invested all their

savings in stock of the Queenborough Bank because it represented power and solidity and financial security. She remembered old Mr. Midkiff, with his hoarded nest egg wrung from
more than forty years of hardship and self-sacrifice. She remembered Mrs. Rawlings and Mrs. Maudsley, and the whole of Mulberry Street in a procession; men, with sagging shoulders in
shabby coats, trudging out to work in the first pale fingers of
light; women, with corded necks and knotted hands, sweeping
porches and pavements; the old and tired; the young and restless; white and black; children and animals—all hurrying by,
caught up in waves of blown dust, from toil into idleness, from
hope into failure. These were not the spenders and wasters of a
false dawn of prosperity. These were the simple folk, the little
people, who had had the gospel of thrift preached to them from
the hour of their birth, who had feared charity more than death
and a pauper's grave more than eternity, who had trusted their
pitiful independence to a name, a promise, a reputation.

"I'm afraid I gave you a shock," the customer was saying.
"Isn't there a place you can sit down?"

No, she wasn't supposed to sit down. "That's a perfect fit,"
she said, smoothing the ivory glove on the soft, plump hand.
"I'm glad gloves have come in again for the evening."

"Yes, it's perfect. I was obliged to have them for the concert
to-night. Perhaps things aren't really so serious as they look now."
She smiled and nodded as Mr. Shadwell, appearing upset but
benevolent, paused to speak to her. "I'm afraid I gave this nice
Mrs. McBride a blow. She hadn't heard that the Queenborough
Bank had closed. Is it really as bad as they say, Mr. Shadwell?"

"It looks very serious," Mr. Shadwell replied, for he also had
suffered from too blind a confidence in solidity. "Hadn't you
better go to the rest room for a while, Mrs. McBride?" he inquired sympathetically. "A dose of ammonia might do you
good." Then, as the customer went out, he continued gently,
"After all, the depositors may be protected, you know. The
doors may open again to-morrow."

While he bowed and walked on, she thought, How rapidly

he has failed! She had never before realized that he was infirm, though she had heard people say that he was too scrupulous in his dealings to contend with sharp modern methods of business. He was the last merchant of dignified tradition, and when he passed out of Queenborough, it would mean the doom of the old-fashioned shop. Buckman, who owned the biggest department store in town, was watching Shadwell's, she knew, as a cat watches a mouse hole. Suppose Shadwell's should go under, she found herself thinking. What would become of them if she were to lose her place and her salary? For all the other shops were turning away older women (only that morning she had told herself that she looked every day of her age), and picked only the tender, the blooming, and the ornamental to decorate counters.

That afternoon, for the first time in her memory, she dreaded to leave the shop and go home. What had they heard? Perhaps they thought that she did not know, and would try to spare her as long as they could. As she turned into Mulberry Street, her steps faltered, suspense pulsed through her thoughts, and it seemed to her that a tumult had broken out in her ears. Had the look of the house really changed? Or was it only that Ralph's head was missing from the front window? Between the parted curtains the firelight glimmered and darkened on the vacant panes, and it seemed to her that both the glimmer and the darkness were reflected from the anxiety within her mind.

CHAPTER 13

AT THE sound of her key in the latch, Aunt Meggie opened the door.

"You've heard, Ada?"

"Yes, I've heard. Where's Ralph?"

"He's found a job for two weeks. A man named Blakely Sands has had to go to a hospital for an operation, and he has employed Ralph to take charge of his repair shop and filling station. He will pay twenty-five dollars a week. That's a help."

"It's a godsend! Is Ranny still out?"

"He went with his father. You know how he enjoys anything that has to do with machinery. Ralph has to go early and stay late, but he said he'd send Ranny home in time for his lessons. The boy is bent on getting a job in a filling station next summer." A grating note ruffled her voice. "Do you reckon Ralph will get back any of the money in the bank?"

"Nobody seems to know. Mr. Shadwell was just as much in the dark as any one else." She sighed as she followed Aunt Meggie into the kitchen. "It takes the heart out of you."

"Everybody in Mulberry Street seems to have suffered. All the women were crying, and the men looked half dead with worry. People say that some of the officers of the bank drew out all their deposits in the last few weeks."

"I heard that, but it may not be true. Mr. Shadwell says the doors may open again to-morrow."

"Well, maybe things will have to get better."

"Maybe. But I'm not going to lie down and let trouble walk over me. When I think I might have lost Ralph and didn't, I feel I can stand whatever I have to stand. But the poor Hamblens! They're so old and tired."

"And they haven't a cent left." Aunt Meggie wiped her eyes on the hem of her apron. "Not even the money to pay their week's board and lodging. Mr. Hamblen meant to draw that much out of the savings department day before yesterday, but something prevented him. They had taken the advice of one of the directors, a man who belongs to their church, and sold all their Liberty Bonds and put everything in bonds or stock of that bank. It looked so big and substantial they never imagined it could fail."

"They may get everything back. All this is just talk. Have you seen them?"

"Only for a minute. They look stunned, just as if they had had a blow on the head. All they do is to sit and stare at each other, and say over and over, 'There must be some mistake. It couldn't be true.' I had a long talk with Mrs. Maudsley about them. She's terribly upset, too, poor soul, because she had all her money for rent in the bank. So many people have been behind in their board, and the agent had already threatened to turn her out. I suppose it's the depression that makes everybody so ready to believe the worst."

"Well, I wish they'd wait to give up hope till the directors have had a chance."

"The trouble is that people have lost confidence in everything and everybody, from the government down."

"I wish the Hamblens hadn't trusted too easily."

"I know. Then there's poor Mr. Midkiff. He had six hundred dollars put away secretly to cover the cost of dying and burial. He drew out three dollars a month to pay Mrs. Maudsley for his kitchen, after she stopped letting him have it for nothing, and then he would have gone hungry if we hadn't helped the Bergens to feed him. For the last two years he has made nothing but the few cents he got for his pickings on the cinder dumps. When he scraped up a piece of old iron or a little tin, he would sell it to a junk dealer down by the river. Somebody gave him that broken wheelbarrow. If it had been a horse and cart, he told me yesterday, he might have done better collecting waste paper."

"Has anyone seen him to-day?"

"Your father went over there, and he came back more upset than he's been for years. Mother used to say that he took other people's afflictions harder than his own."

"When everybody is that way, there may be less misery around us."

"Mr. Midkiff is a strong old man," Aunt Meggie said, still wiping her eyes. "He's a good carpenter and handy with his tools. I asked him once what his Christian name was, and he said if he'd ever had one, he'd 'disremembered' it. He thinks his mother named him 'Mister' when he was born in the almshouse, and they called him that even when he was little. They gave him a number, he said, and he answered to the name of 'Luke' in the roll call. But somehow 'Luke' didn't stick to him."

"Well, I'm going straight over there. I'm going before I take off my hat."

"You look real tired, Ada."

"There're worse things than being tired."

"Won't you wait till you've had a cup of coffee? It's 'most ready."

"Not now. I feel as if I were choking."

When she opened the gate and went out, she stopped for a minute to look through the smoky light and the flying papers. The whole of Mulberry Street seemed to her to be watching and waiting, as if the windows and doorways and even the forlorn basements exhaled the odour of fear. It looks exactly as if a funeral, or a plague perhaps, had gone by, she thought, as she entered the boarding-house and went up the fine old staircase to the Hamblens' sitting-room on the second floor.

At her knock Mr. Hamblen opened the door and ceremoniously ushered her into the presence of his wife, who was seated in a carved rosewood chair (it was once prized, but would now bring nothing, Ada said to herself) before a small coal fire, which glowed with a steady beat, like a living heart. She was dressed as neatly as usual; the brooch of twisted gold fastened her collar; the gold chain was looped over her flat bosom.

"It can't be true," she said, as she looked up from the fire. "There must be some mistake."

Ada bent over and kissed her cheek, which felt soft and dry and wilted. "It may not be so bad as it looks now," she answered.

As she glanced round her, she saw that they had been less inactive through the long day than Aunt Meggie imagined. On the marble top of the centre table a few heirlooms had been carefully arranged: a bracelet woven of hair with heavy gold clasps, several small old pictures of no value, an antiquated watch with a heavy seal attached, an elaborate wreath of wax-flowers, a mourning pin with the design of a tomb under a weeping willow, and a chessboard bearing a set of ivory chessmen, which had belonged to Mr. Hamblen's Uncle John, a famous chess-player, who had fallen at Seven Pines. While she looked at them a wild idea darted like a minnow below the surface of Ada's mind. All their treasures might just bury them and no more.

"We've been looking over our relics," Mr. Hamblen explained formally, avoiding what he would have considered the low comedy of pathetic cadence. "A dealer in antiques has just examined them. He would buy nothing but the old gold."

"If it is necessary, I can add the brooch and chain I have on," the old lady remarked. "Unfortunately, the demand for relics has fallen off since the depression. And they tell me that common walnut or maple, or even pine, brings a higher price than carved rosewood."

"Something may turn up," Ada said hurriedly, fearing that she might break down beneath the strain of their unnatural composure. "I do hope you won't have to give up these rooms."

Though a quiver convulsed Mrs. Hamblen's mouth, her voice was without the note of self-pity when she replied, "I feel that there must be a mistake. But if it should turn out to be true, we shall be obliged to make other plans. We don't know just yet. . . . We don't see our way. . . . We shall have to make shift with what we have. Only," she concluded primly, "that seems to be very little."

"Of course if we were younger," Mr. Hamblen said, "it would

mean only beginning over again. When I was a small boy after the war, my parents began again from the bottom. But at seventy-seven," he smiled at his wife, "that does not appear practicable."

They were wonderful, Ada thought, with a clutch in her throat. They belonged to an age when vehemence was still regarded as vulgar. All their fine qualities, industry, veracity, self-denial, were as antiquated as the linked chain Mrs. Hamblen draped on her bosom. Nothing could stay young for ever, not even the cardinal virtues.

"I'll try to think of something and come back to-morrow," she said quickly. "There's plenty of time."

Oh, yes, there was plenty of time, they assented politely. It was true that Mrs. Maudsley had not been so kind as they would have expected. Fear was whipping her on, no doubt, and fear, as Mr. Hamblen had once said, was the blood brother of cruelty. Still, it was incredible that they should have lost everything. Everything down to the money for the week's board and lodging. But charity . . . no, that was out of the question. To be sure, the world appeared to be rapidly losing its horror of charity. Even the almshouse, once regarded by white and black alike as the final descent into ignominy, was now trying to improve its social position. The very young spoke of it lightly as the resort of the profligate, but for the Hamblens, as well as for old Midkiff, it remained the ancient antagonist of the poor and proud.

Downstairs, she went out of the back door into the cluttered yard, which was used as a trash heap for tin cans and empty bottles and broken crockery. Factories used to buy rubbish like that, she had heard, but Mrs. Maudsley said it wouldn't now bring enough to pay for hauling it down to the river bottom. Even Mr. Midkiff had to find better pickings.

At the end of the slippery walk, surrounded by piles of junk and furnished with baited rattraps, she saw the wreck of an outside kitchen. "Nothing ought to live here," she thought in horror, "not even rats." Near the door, which swung on a single hinge, Mr. Midkiff's wheelbarrow stood half upset, with the refuse spilling over the ground, as if it had been overtaken by the immense futility of cinders. As there was no response to her call, she skirted the vehicle and gingerly ascended the outside wooden steps to what had once been the cook's room in the loft. The door above was not shut; the damp wind was pouring into the vacancy; and she saw that the old man was seated, apparently sunk in a stupor, on the pallet he used day and night as a resting-place. It would be too much, she told herself, to expect him to want to keep the room clean or to notice the stench of old rat-traps.

"Mr. Midkiff!" she called, and was compelled to repeat the cry before he heard her voice and looked round.

"I was just studyin'," he said apologetically, as he shuffled to his feet and stood gazing at her in an attitude of oxlike resignation. If only he were not so patient, so confirmed in that terrible humility of the old! If only he would rebel, strike back, blaspheme against the inevitable! For the pathos of life, she felt, was worse than the tragedy.

"Have you had anything to eat?"

He shook his head. "Naw'm, I ain't felt the want of nothin'."

"You must come over to our kitchen. Aunt Meggie will have your supper ready." Before he came into Aunt Meggie's kitchen, she knew that he would wash himself and put on the cleaner one of the two blue cotton shirts Ralph had given him.

His face was muffled in his wide grey beard, worn long and full, like the beard of Moses in her grandmother's illustrated Bible. She could see only his eyes, as bright and still as rain puddles hidden in dried grass, and the strong curving beak of his nose. "I ain't felt the want to eat to-day," he said. "I was jest settin' thar studyin'."

"Everything may be better to-morrow." The sanguine note in her voice reminded her of the chirping of a doomed cricket. "Your money may be given back to you."

"Yas'm, that may be."

"You know we'll always help you as much as we can."

"Thank you, ma'am."

"It won't do you any good to sit and brood."

"I warn't broodin', ma'am. I was jest studyin'. I'd calc'lated that what I'd put by would last me for rent as long as I had to live and see me through to a good burial. I ain't no pauper, and I don't want no pauper's burial. But it ain't likely I can make more'n a few cents a day by scratchin' on dumps." He held out his big gnarled hands and looked at them with a kind of slow wonder. "I ain't wore out yet. Thar's a good piece of work left in me still."

"That's true. You are strong for your age. Aunt Meggie was saying a little while ago that you know how to handle tools." She couldn't tell him that Mrs. Maudsley objected to him because she said he was dirty.

"Well, I ain't real old. I calc'late that I'll be sixty-three come next March. I'm pretty spry, too, even if I ain't as peart as I used to be. But I was studyin' jest now that I ain't never had half a chance to git on. When I was born in the po'house down the Jeems, nobody took a notion to teach me readin' and writin' and addin' up. But I learnt the whole Catechism by heart befo' I was set out as a hired orphan. I can say parts of the Catechism now right straight off, but it don't git you far in these times."

"You've always done the best you could, I know. Father will tell you that. But don't worry any more than you can help, and be sure to come over for a bite of supper."

As she turned away, she saw, without glancing round, that he had dropped back on his pallet and was sunk again in a stupor of resignation. She felt faint, and slightly sickened by an intolerable pity, as if she were bleeding within. Faceless, dismembered, a brood of half-forgotten recollections surged up from the shaken depths of her mind. Hills tumbled about her. Leaves scuttled. A tower rocked in a pale sky. A crow and its shadow flashed over the barren fields. Then, suddenly, her skin seemed to change, while her identity turned and doubled upon her. Once again she was living two separate lives in two separate places. Was she an idiot fleeing over a twisted path? Was she something soft, warm, furry, with eyes like small, terrified hearts? Or was she merely Ada McBride, who was once Ada Fincastle, clutching the rickety stairway as she descended with a sensation of nausea from the rat hole Mr. Midkiff called home?

ROM the kitchen floated the familiar fragrance of Aunt Meggie's coffee, and Ada asked if she might fill the small tin coffee-pot and take it over to Mr. Midkiff. "I can't bear to think of him over there in that cold loft."

"I'll take it right over myself, and some pork and beans too. They're filling and nourishing and go farther than anything else. I can go through the alley gate. It's only a step, and I feel as if I needed a breath of air." While Aunt Meggie added sugar and milk to the coffee, and put a corn pone on the tray beside the plate of pork and beans, she asked abruptly, "Has it ever crossed your mind, Ada, that you might get help from your mother's people?"

Ada started. "Not for myself, Aunt Meggie. I'd rather starve."

"I wasn't thinking about us. We'll manage somehow, and if Ranny wins this scholarship, he'll earn his own education. But I was wondering if they would do anything for the Hamblens."

"That's different. I hadn't thought of the Hamblens."

"Your father still goes by the Bland house every day. Ranny has made up his mind that he is going to live in it when he grows up."

"Well, making up his mind won't do any harm. I suppose he inherited the feeling from Father and me, but neither of us has ever set foot inside the door."

"They might be glad to see you if they were fond of Mary Evelyn."

"But they gave her up after she married Father. And besides, I am too independent to stand patronage."

"I know how you feel, but the idea just came to me. You look as if you'd drop. Why don't you sit down and drink a cup of coffee while I take this through the alley?"

As she disappeared, Ada poured out a cup of coffee and sat down to drink it. Between sips she found herself saying aloud, "I wonder if it would do any good? I wonder if they would be willing to help?" Breaking off an end of corn pone, she ate it slowly while a resolution sprang into her mind and assumed shape and energy. I couldn't ask help for myself, but I might ask for the Hamblens. I will ask help for the Hamblens. Through the window she could look over the board fence into Mrs. Maudsley's yard, where a lean and rusty cat, with a twitching black tail, was stalking a sparrow. Then Aunt Meggie slipped in through the alley gate, holding her tray carefully, and went up the steps to the loft. It's strange how people, even the most miserable, cling to life, Ada thought, and a small satirical voice in her mind answered, But it isn't so easy to die. Starting up, she washed her cup quickly and put it back on the shelf. I'll go now while my mind is made up. I'll go before Aunt Meggie and Father and Ranny come in to distract me. Hurrying into the bedroom, she smoothed her hair under the cloth beret, fastened the high collar of black fur on her coat, and drew on her only whole pair of gloves. A perfectly good face, she said to herself, with a smile, warranted to wear, but not to remain youthful.

As she passed through the gate, a squat shadow detached itself from the darkness under the old mulberry tree. For an instant, while it approached her, the figure appeared hunchbacked, and she said to herself, That is the shape of depression. Then she saw that it was only Mrs. Rawlings, more bowed than ever beneath her heavy cape and the drooping brim of her hat.

"Is your father at home?" she inquired nervously. "I ran over just for a word with him."

"He hasn't come in yet, but he may be back any minute. Will you go inside and wait?"

"No, I just wanted to ask him what I'd better do about Bertie. It's going on three months since I heard from him, and I'm beginning to worry."

"Why, I thought he was well placed at that college in Texas?"

"Yes, he's well enough placed, I reckon, but they keep him so busy moving about teaching and lecturing that he hasn't been able to get home for nearly two years. It was splendid when they picked him, he said, out of a hundred teachers. We'd just come to the bare end. There wasn't a scrap left to eat in the house, and I hadn't had any work for a month, when he told me he'd met a professor from this Texas college who offered him a place if he could go right away. At first he wrote regularly, though the address was always changing because they sent him to speak in schools all over the State, and he'd asked me to send my letters to the post office. But for the last year I've only had a card now and then, and three months ago he stopped writing entirely. I was wondering if your father knew anybody down there he could ask about Bertie."

"I know he'll do what he can. Why don't you wait with Aunt Meggie while I go out on an errand?" It seemed to her that she was suddenly entangled in the complexities of Mulberry Street.

"Well, I will, and thank you, if you don't mind."

Mrs. Rawlings entered the gate with her stooping walk, while Ada turned away as if she were driven, and hastened up the three long blocks to the once elegant and now faintly malodorous Washington Street. Toward the West End, where the Bland house stood withdrawn behind its Doric columns, the street retained a measure at least of its dignity; but it could never recover the lost opulence, the flowery scents, the vanished illusion. From east to west, there were flying papers in the windy dusk and the forlorn aspect of deterioration.

Through the bare elms the lights of the house glittered, and when she ascended the steps of the terrace, the door was opened before she had reached the porch and put out her hand to the bell. Inside, music was playing, and beyond an arched doorway she caught a glimpse of bright dresses and flowerlike heads swaying and bending. They can't know the misery, she thought. They don't know what life **is**.

"Do you mean the elder Mrs. Bland, ma'am?" inquired the

old coloured butler. "She doesn't come downstairs, but you might see her if you'd like to go up."

"Tell her it is the daughter of her cousin, Mrs. Fincastle."

As he turned away, she moved under the arch in the hall, idly watching the slender shapes winding in and out of the intricate maze. Out of the variegated blur a voice fluted, "But sex has gone out. We've changed the name of our club from the Underworld to the High Flyers." Glancing round, with a start, she smelt the odour of rum, and saw a slim girl, with a face like an artificial carnation, in the arms of a youth who looked vapid, undeveloped, and swaggering.

"Oh, I say, will you go to that cockfight up in Goochland? The police may raid it, you know."

She giggled in rapture. "Not really! Oh, what a thrill to be raided!"

"Mrs. Bland will see you, ma'am," said a voice at Ada's elbow. "Will you please come upstairs, ma'am?" How, she mused, as he ushered her up the distinguished staircase, had he been able to imitate the ceremonious presence and the superior manner of slavery? I wonder, she found herself thinking, if he remembers Mother? Behind her the girl's voice was still fluting over the music, "Not really! Oh, how exciting!"

When she entered the long front room, drenched with the smell of lavender salts, she felt that she was dazzled by firelight. A woman lying on the couch in front of the fire appeared first as a study in mauve that was shading to purple. She seemed merely middle-aged, but when Ada drew nearer she saw that the features were those of an old woman—older than her mother had ever been, almost as old as her grandmother had looked in her coffin. There were mauve tints in her piled white hair, and her sunken eyes, beneath heavily veined lids, were like dead lilacs.

"I have sciatica," she said. "I can't get up. So you are Mary Evelyn's daughter?"

"Yes, I am her daughter. My name is Ada McBride."

"Ada McBride? Did your husband come from the mountains?"

"From Ironside. The McBrides have always lived there."

"Ironside? That must be a small place. I never heard of it. Will you draw up that low chair and sit close to me?"

As Ada pushed the low chair nearer the couch, she thought, She's strong like Mother, in spite of her frail look. No matter how much you bend her, she'd never give way.

"Tell me about Mary Evelyn," Mrs. Bland said gently. "I was very fond of her when she was a young girl, but we lost touch with each other many years go. Is she still living?"

"No, she died before we left Ironside."

"When did you leave? And why?"

"We left before the war ended. Everything seemed to go down, and we couldn't hold on to the manse."

"The manse? I remember she married a clergyman. He was a Presbyterian minister, wasn't he?"

"He was until he left the church and wrote books."

"Books? Well, I don't read. Nobody that I know ever opens a book." As she winced from pain, the hand holding the bottle of lavender salts dropped to her side. "Will you take this? Put the stopper in and take it away. Was Mary Evelyn happy?"

"Yes, she was happy."

"I heard that she had a hard life, that she was living in poverty."

"She was, but she was happy."

"I'm sorry we drifted apart. I'd like to have seen her again before she died. She might have been a celebrated beauty, but she never knew how to make the best of herself."

"She didn't care. Other things seemed to her more important."

"Other things. What things?"

"Well, being happy."

"I wonder," Mrs. Bland murmured below her breath. Then her face changed while the hollows seemed to deepen and to suck in the puffs under her eyes. Her lips tightened as if they were drawn by an elastic string, and beneath her heavy eyelids a startled fear flashed to the surface. "Why did you come after all these years?" she asked stiffly. "I hope you didn't come because you're in need."

"No, I'm not in need. I thought you might help two of our neighbours who lost all they had when the bank failed this morning."

The fear leaped again. "I can't help. For two years my son has been warding off failure. We have tried to keep up to the last. I oughtn't to speak of it . . ."

"I won't say anything. I promise you I won't say anything."

"I know I'm too garrulous, but I feel I must talk to somebody. If I don't talk to somebody, I shall break down. My son is one of the directors of this bank. He has stood by it. He wouldn't draw out and leave the others to bear the responsibility. Even when he saw before the other directors what was coming, and had an opportunity to save a little for himself and for us, he would not sell his stock or even withdraw his account. He is down there now—he has been there day and night—trying to save the bank and to protect the depositors. . . ."

Her voice broke, while a door downstairs opened and a wild strain of music rippled into the room. "This is my granddaughter's birthday. The invitations to her party had gone out long before, or we shouldn't have sent them. It is only for the afternoon, and when it is over, I may be able to quiet my nerves. She's nineteen, and she's coming out this winter. We're trying to give her one happy winter before she knows what has happened. If it takes the last cent we have, we mean to give her one happy winter. Then everything may have to go. The house and everything else. It isn't a secret, except to the poor child, that my son may be ruined—that he is holding on by the last margin." A sob strangled her and, gasping for breath, she sank back on the couch and veiled her face with her hands, which were weak and tremulous, yet still clutching at shadows. "I can't help anybody," she moaned under her breath. "I can't help my own family. We need help ourselves."

What could she say? Ada asked herself. What could any one say or do before the ghastly spectacle of age in defeat? Bending above the prostrated figure, she covered it gently with a robe of violet satin edged in lace and artificial rosebuds. "I'll come to see you again," she said. "We don't need anything. We can always manage somehow."

When there was no response, she turned away from the couch and went out of the room and down the stairs, treading as softly in the violet music as if she were following the burial of a lost hope through a carnival. That is spoilt too, she thought. I wish I hadn't come. I wish I'd stayed away and kept my faith in the romantic life. As long as I believed in it, it was mine. And maybe nothing is real, not even money or the want of it.

The wind shivered in Washington Street. Patches of vapour were blown here, there, everywhere. In the thick dusk the electric lamps bristled, shooting out sharp quills of light. Suddenly a jagged pain clutched her feet and galloped as madly as a living thing up her legs to her waist. She oughtn't to have come. No good ever came of expecting people to help. Each human being lived in its own cell of clay, confined within an inert speck of creation, and indifferent to the other millions of cells by which it was surrounded. A whole world of mud-daubers! Like the red-winged insects, less stinging than wasps, that built their nests in the old stable at Ironside. But I won't tell anybody where I've been, she resolved wearily. I won't tell anybody but Father.

An omnibus stopped at the corner, and she dragged herself to the platform, groped her way inside, and dropped into a seat next to a woman holding a green wicker basket. I was too tired, she reflected, justifying the price of the fare. That long walk was too much for me. But it wasn't the walk that had tired her, she knew. It was the surprise, the disappointment, the death of an illusion. While the bus plunged into darkness, scattering the wisps of vapour, splintering the frosty light on the pavement, it seemed to her that her inmost self, the hidden core of her personality, had been violated by fear. But this isn't true, she insisted. Nothing has really touched me. Nothing has happened that I mightn't have known. Yet she knew that something had happened. She knew that life had lost a sense of permanence, of continuing tradition. What does it all mean? she thought, dazed with weariness. Does it go on for ever, round and round in circles without beginning or end?

That night when Ralph came home, very late and soaked with fog, his first words were, "You'd better call it a day, Ada. You look all in."

"Who wouldn't, my dear? Some days are like this one. Everything comes in an avalanche, without space to breathe, and then it sinks in with the rest. But I'm thankful you found work."

"It's only for two weeks. Still, another and a better job may turn up. We've struck the bottom so hard that it looks as if there must be a rebound."

"Maybe the new President will work out a way," suggested Aunt Meggie, who held a strong political faith.

"It would take more than a new President, it would take a new God," Ralph retorted, "to make over human nature."

"But not to make over human behaviour," John Fincastle said.

Ralph's tone was less sullen, Ada observed thankfully, and he looked animated. Only idleness and the sense of dependence on circumstances sharpened the edge of his temper. Now, though he regretted his own loss and was sorry for the Hamblens and old Midkiff, he was cheered by the news that none of the Bergens had suffered. William had told him, he continued, that they had not heard from Minna for months. She had gone away one evening with a strange man from Baltimore, and had never come home again. They had thought of calling in the police, and Mrs. Bergen had been almost distracted with shame and anxiety. Then an old friend, returning from a business trip, had told them that he had seen Minna at a play in Baltimore, and that she appeared in high spirits and was wearing a mink coat and orchids.

"The uniform of ill fame," Ralph said sardonically. "But she's like those women upstairs. There was always a yellow streak somewhere." He was savage toward Minna, Ada remarked, not without a flicker of pleasure, and entirely lacking in the lip-homage of chivalry.

"There's real trouble upstairs," Aunt Meggie responded. "The

Welfare League doesn't want to keep on paying the rent. I wonder what we'll do when those people stop being helped."

"Well, we can't take them in," Ralph protested. "We have enough to look after as it is. I'd rather take care of old Midkiff if I could. Maybe I can some day. Maybe when the tractor plow is put on the market I can build up the Dungan agency in the Valley."

"If that time ever comes, we will go back to the mountains," John Fincastle said, and Ada noticed, as she watched him, that his shining vision pierced inward.

"Then we'll take Mr. Midkiff to help me with my chickens and the garden," Aunt Meggie mused happily. "Aunt Abigail's cabin is better, anyway, than Mrs. Maudsley's old kitchen."

"Yes, we'll go back if that time ever comes," Ada assented. Then she asked abruptly, "Father, did you see Mrs. Rawlings? She was going to wait for you. There was something she wanted to ask you about Bertie."

"I couldn't help her." He rubbed his hand over his eyes and then looked at it as if he expected to find the image he had seen. "The only address he gave was a post office wherever he lectured. I don't know of any travelling college in Texas. It seems queer. Perhaps she misunderstood."

"He may be sick or in trouble. At least he might have written, even if he couldn't send money. Poor woman, she's dreadfully worried."

"Would it do any good to advertise in Texas?" Ralph asked, suddenly interested. "There's a chance for him now at Boscobel School. Miss Curran brought her car to the shop to-day, and she asked me for his address. Their English teacher died last November, and the substitute she put in his place has resigned to go abroad as a tutor. Bertie always had a winning way. She told me he had made a very pleasant impression."

"If we wait long enough," Aunt Meggie said, "he may come back."

"I have a feeling," Ada answered sleepily, as she rose from her chair and put her work-basket aside, "that, if we wait long enough, everything will come back, and we shall all be happy again." It was like speaking in a dream, she thought, as she crossed the floor with a slight limp, because her legs ached when she stood up. It was like moving in a dream that stretched on and on, and led nowhere. "Well, I'm going to stay in bed, no matter what happens, till to-morrow's troubles begin." Nothing ever lasts, she told herself, but the thought broke away and whirled on without her. It wasn't the right moment, some obscure instinct warned her, to turn round and try to look life in the face.

In Mulberry Street this day of disaster was followed by quiet. On the surface at least living resumed its familiar monotony. After the first shock, men who had lost everything began to hope, men who had escaped loss began to forget, and women, sweeping pavements and trudging to market, echoed the faint hopes or the increasing forgetfulness. Then one evening in February, when Ada came home from work in the early dusk, she found Aunt Meggie shedding tears of indignation and pity. The visitor from the Welfare League had come to see the Hamblens that afternoon. Aunt Meggie had found her with them, investigating, classifying, recording. "I thought it would embarrass them if I stayed," she said, "so I slipped out while she was asking them the most intimate questions, and putting every word down in her notebook. Just as I was going downstairs, I heard her call, and I hurried back to find that Mrs. Hamblen had fainted. In a minute, Mrs. Maudsley rushed in with a bottle of camphor, and one of the boarders, a nice, common man named Smithson, brought a flask of brandy from his room and made the old lady swallow a good drink. She'd never so much as tasted brandy before, but it acted like magic."

"What had the girl done to her?"

"Nothing, she declared, absolutely nothing. All she had told her was that the best place for them was the almshouse. I reckon she called it the City Home, but Mrs. Hamblen knew what she meant. The girl was dreadfully upset. She was trying, she explained, to remove the old-fashioned prejudice against the City

Home. All the charitable organizations have combined, she said, and are trying to place their work upon a scientific basis and to overcome antiquated ideas. They seem to think they can do away with a prejudice just by reasoning with people."

"What will become of the Hamblens?"

"The girl didn't know. I'm not sure she knows how to think for herself. The habit seems to have been squeezed out of her by a system. She was flustered because she couldn't make up her mind what to put in her notebook."

"Oughtn't I to run over and see what has happened?"

"There hasn't anything happened. As soon as the girl went, the old people began to figure out what they could sell, and how little would keep life in them till they recovered some of their money. They didn't talk as if they were low-spirited, but Mrs. Maudsley says they will be obliged to go to the City Home in the end. All their things together would do no more than bury them."

"I thought that when I was over there. But I feel as if I must talk with them."

"Wait till to-morrow. I hate to see you wear yourself out. You are getting real hollow-eyed."

"I know." Ada raised her hand to smooth out the two fur-dows. "Something tells me that Mr. Shadwell is going to cut my salary again."

"Again?"

"It isn't his fault. I can tell that he is failing every day. Sooner or later, he will be ruined."

"You get only eighteen dollars now."

"By next week I may get only fourteen."

Aunt Meggie sighed and threw out her bony arm as if she were feeling for a support. "Well, we'll have to make out, but I wish Mother had left me more of her trust in the Lord."

Ada bit back a smile. "We'll have to manage with what we have. Yes, I do feel too tired to go to the Hamblens'. I'll wait until supper is over."

But after supper she sat in her old dress by the fire and mended gloves for the shop, while Ralph read the newspapers, and her father and Ranny worked out problems in arithmetic. The room was immersed in stillness that trembled and whispered, broken now and then by John Fincastle's cough, by the scraping of Ranny's feet on the floor, by the falling of an ember that crumbled as it dropped through the grate to the ashes. Not a word had been said; yet it seemed to Ada that a voice suddenly called her name and, raising her eyes from her needle, she found Ralph gazing at her with a look that made her heart beat more quickly and the silken thread knot and break in her fingers.

"Tired out?" he asked softly.

"Tired and happy, too—happy in spots down below all the unhappiness."

"Try to stop thinking. What we've lost, we can make up."

"I know, but the others. The whole of Mulberry Street . . ."

"That's the worst. That's why you must stop thinking for to-night. Spring is nearly here. If we can only make out till spring, I'm sure I can get a job, and then everything will be better."

She smiled into his eyes, while his gaze sank into her heart and drew out the pain. It had been years since they had smiled like that, with a look as tender and intimate as an embrace. "The winter might have been worse," she said. "After all, we've been happy together." She had trusted herself to the moment, and it was still here between them, holding them closer. Even speech had not startled it into flight.

"Yes, we've been happy together." A tremor softened the embittered curve of his mouth. "You're easy to live with."

"Well, you're not easy, but you're interesting," she tossed back.

Never again, she felt, flushing under his steady gaze, would she ask if he loved her. It was different, but it was love. It was different, but it was happiness. We couldn't have felt this when we were young lovers, she told herself. What we felt was more glowing, more vehement, more light-hearted and joyous; but it lacked this peace, this completeness, this security against time and change. His smile still held her, and she thought, he doesn't see that my hair is streaked with gray, that my skin is weather-beaten, that my forehead is disfigured by two wrinkles.

For the rest of that night the troubles of Mulberry Street were forgotten. Not until the next morning did she remind herself of the Hamblens, and determine that she would drop in to see them for a minute on the way to her work. But just as they were beginning breakfast there was a frantic ring at the bell, and one of Mrs. Maudsley's boarders burst in before Ranny had had time to open the door.

"A terrible thing has happened, Mrs. McBride! The Hamblens are dead."

"But I saw them yesterday!" Aunt Meggie exclaimed, as she put down the coffee-pot with a shaking hand.

"Bessie, the maid, found them. They didn't come down to breakfast, and Mrs. Maudsley sent her upstairs to tell them. They were never a minute late for a meal. She thought they might be holding back because they couldn't pay her. When Bessie knocked, she smelt gas. Then she went in and found them both lying on the floor of the bathroom. It isn't much bigger than a closet. They had stuffed towels in every crack, and under the door . . ."

"But I saw them yesterday." Aunt Meggie glanced about in dazed perplexity. "They didn't complain. They didn't say a word that . . . that . . ."

"They seemed to be in high spirits at supper. Mr. Hamblen told all his old jokes, and everybody was laughing to keep up courage. But I reckon they couldn't stand the thought of the City Home."

"If only they'd said something—" Ada began. But what could they have said? There wasn't anything to be said that could have made any difference.

"They left a note asking Mrs. Maudsley to sell their relics, as they called them, and keep the money. Only they hoped there would be enough left to bury them in their old plot in Rose Hill Cemetery. But there won't be enough for funeral expenses," she continued, rolling her handkerchief into a ball and mopping her eyes. "We're taking up a collection."

"We'll help," Ralph said eagerly. "I'll give half of my week's salary." How like him that was, Ada thought, with love in her eyes as she looked at him. How like him, and how completely lacking in prudence!

"I'll go over." John Fincastle had come in while they were talking. "I'll go over and see what can be done."

"Drink this hot coffee, Father." Ada filled a cup and held it to his lips. "You must eat something. You are shaking."

"I felt a chill. A thing like this brings a chill." Obediently, as if he scarcely knew what he was doing, he seated himself and drank the coffee and ate the buttered roll she put on his plate.

"You aren't well enough to go out, John," Aunt Meggie pleaded. "Let me go in your place. It is so terrible."

He shook his head, and the empty outline of a smile wavered across his lips. "I'm not sure of that, my dear. A timely end is a good end."

So this had happened last night, Ada thought. This had happened while she sat by the fire and mended gloves, and told herself that the winter had not been so bad, after all, and they were fortunate to have a whole roof over their heads. This tragedy had happened only two walls away while she and Ralph were smiling into each other's eyes and thinking they had been happy together.

CHAPTER 15

"I F HOMER begged," John Fincastle said, "Why should we be ashamed?"

Old Mr. Midkiff, who had never heard of Homer, but had his suspicions of philanthropy, straightened his stooped shoulders and tried to look proud and hopeful, as if he had been ushered as an equal into fine company. That dry humour on Mr. Fincastle's tongue never failed to put the courage back into his bones. It was a way of speaking, and of smiling, too, as if everything, charity included, wasn't worth making a fuss about, because it didn't really matter a straw. "There's one thing they can't take from us, and that's fortitude," he would say, with his laugh so low and far off that it brought back to Mr. Midkiff an echo of the sea he had once heard, as a boy, when somebody put a shell to his ear. That's the sea. I've heard the sea, he had thought, though he had known even then that he should never lay eyes on it. Well, well, those were fine, heartening words. Whether they made sense or not (and not much that Mr. Fincastle said seemed to make sense), they had a power to brace up a man's spirit. Even waiting like this, with a tin cup in your hand, wasn't nearly so humble when you told yourself that it was fortitude.

The March wind had a biting edge. John Fincastle shivered and pulled the collar of his greatcoat (a fine bottle-green, Ada called it) high up to his chin. "Delivered from suffering," he said suddenly, and discovered to his horror that he was speaking aloud, after the bad habit of old persons. The words had blown through his mind. Somebody had prayed that prayer ages before—somebody had prayed: *May all that have life be delivered from suffering.*

Yes, he was old now. He couldn't remember. He couldn't

see clearly. There were times when the world receded into a vast humming. At other times a sudden clutch in his heart would leave him gasping for breath until the sweat poured down on the coldest nights. A general breaking-up, the doctor had called it. When one got on in years, one must not expect too much of the heart and the kidneys. Well, he was glad that the end was in sight. He had lived out his life to the full circle. His work was what he had wished to do, and now it was finished. Whenever he looked back, the way he had come appeared far off and beautiful. He would not like to give up that backward vision. But, for all the world could offer, he would not go over that steep road once again.

In front of him the breadline stretched in two separate rows, one white, one coloured, to the door of the dilapidated dwelling house which had been turned into a soup kitchen. The sagging iron gate was flung wide. An icy rain dripped from the bare boughs of a crooked paulownia tree in the street. No, he had not wanted to beg, John Fincastle thought. After he had been told of that general breaking-up, he had eaten as little food as was needed to keep one alive. He was not deliberately starving himself. Only, since the pangs of hunger had left him, and that strange exaltation had flooded his mind with light, his body had offered less resistance to the advance of mortality. But Mr. Midkiff, who found the cinder dumps scraped bare, could not keep up his strength on the lean scraps Meggie was able to put by after supper. Ada's salary had suffered a new cut. The value of every penny must be stretched out when fourteen dollars a week provided for a family of five. And yet that wasn't the worst, John Fincastle mused. Beneath Ada's brave smile he could see the haggard lines of anxiety. Always, he knew, she was struggling against the fear that Shadwell's could hold out no longer. When the crash came, as come it must, unless Ralph had found work they would be turned out penniless into the street, driven at last to accept the picked bones of charity. And knowing this, Ralph had divided a week's salary with the dead Hamblens. Well, he wasn't sorry. He was glad the boy (he still thought of Ralph in his middle forties as a boy) was still capable of a magnificent folly. It was the Irish in him, Ada had said, with that shining wistfulness in her eyes. Older eyes they were now, tired and older, but still shining.

If only I can die, my insurance will help them a little, John Fincastle told himself. Not much, but a little. Enough, perhaps, to tide them over until better times.

The line wavered, and to steady himself he rested his hand against the bark of the tree, which felt slimy and cold. He had expected to see famished faces and shrunken figures before the soup kitchen, but most of these hungry persons, waiting with tin cups to be filled, were warmly clad, in garments from the Red Cross, no doubt, or other charitable organizations. Many of the women, particularly the younger women, wore bright coats trimmed with the fashionable collars of cheap fur. Never had he seen so much rabbit fur, not even on rabbits. None of the girls seemed depressed or even subdued, and few of them, as Meggie would have said, had spared the rouge pot or the lipstick. Well, scarlet lips helped one, he supposed, to keep up one's courage. Had the homeless men resorted to such embellishments, they might have looked less dejected. For, oddly enough, the men, not the women, appeared to have suffered the most. Flinching, nervous, hollow-eyed, unwashed, unshaven, and bowed with that dreadful humbleness of the down and out, he watched them falling into line, as he might have watched spectres in some grim caricature of existence.

Turning his head, he looked beyond the gate to the coloured row, which reached the corner and swept in a stream round the side of the house. What was there in the nature of the Negro, he wondered, that enabled him to squeeze the zest of life out of husks? A steady murmur, as of bees swarming, drifted from the crowd of brown and black and russet faces. The sound was not gay, nor was it sad; it belonged, with the dripping of the rain or the sighing of the wind, to the natural cadences of earth. Though the Negroes had had a harder time, they had suffered less, he thought, or perhaps they had learned how to suffer. They also wore the cast-off finery of the well-to-do, but they wore it with pride. There was submissiveness without humility in their sleek smiles and soft droning voices.

But Mr. Midkiff . . . Mr. Midkiff, who had scratched rubbish-heaps and lived among rat holes, still feared only one thing more than charity when he was alive, and that was charity when he was dead. "I don't feel no call to eat," he had protested. "I ain't a big eater at no time. I was al'ays scrawny like this." Meggie, however, had insisted that his scant supper could not keep out the cold. "That old man," she said, "is too bony to live on pickings." It was then that John Fincastle had borrowed two tin cups from her, and had begun to ramble on, in his tone of whimsical irony, about the poets and prophets who had begged for a living. Not Homer alone, but many others, many of the very greatest, had begged, without shame, in an abundance of the spirit. Christ had not rejected charity, he reminded Mr. Midkiff, and Buddha, the Compassionate One, had walked the roads of India with his yellow bowl. Then the philosophers . . . He was still harping on the philosophers and the merit of begging in the right spirit when Mr. Midkiff, who had missed every word but was as much impressed as any literary critic by wind humming through syllables, accepted one of the tin cups, and consented to stand and wait with him at the door of the soup kitchen.

From the ragged clouds a light flurry of snow whirled suddenly, and before the flakes had melted in the air a pale finger of sunshine pointed over the housetops. The line shivered as if it were strung on a single wire. Ahead of him, a man raised his arm in a ragged sleeve to turn up the collar of his thin coat. Beside the gay clothes and cheap or imitation fur on the women, the men were like scarecrows. Did well-to-do men, John Fincastle wondered, never cast off old clothing while it still kept the shape of a man? In the street a handsome limousine passed on its way from the lower station. He heard a girl gasp, "Don't I wish that was mine?" and turning quickly saw a woman in the car bending over a little boy. She had taken off her glove, and a single ring on her finger flashed out like a star, and was gone.

There was envy in the faces about him, a physical envy, without the sting and smart of an insurgent idea. Well, the bleating of sheep doesn't make a revolution, he told himself, while the familiar pain struck in his chest. A revolution might end in the shambles, but it must begin in the stars. There must be bliss in that dawn, he thought, remembering Wordsworth, and the tranquil poverty of Dove cottage (stone floors and dampness, and swallows building in windows, and a birch tree like "a flying sunshiny shower," and a beggar with two sticks, and a tall gypsy woman in multicoloured patches), and then the tragic peace of the long evening.

No, one couldn't make a revolution, one couldn't even start a riot, with sheep that asked only for better browsing. The door opened, and the two separate rows swerved abruptly, and then crawled slowly forward while he wondered how a country unable to handle a breadline, or to curb the Stock Exchange, could find a successful way to plan and manage a world. There was a sensation of closeness, a sound of shuffling feet, and for a minute he felt that he was suffocating in the smell of dirty clothes, the stale sweat of unwashed bodies, and, now and then, a whiff of cheap scented powder. Then, as he approached the Negro line at the foot of the steps, his nostrils were assailed by the earthy and more acrid odours of Africa. A wisp of satire revolved in his mind, "The sense of smell remains the greatest obstacle to the parliament of mankind."

As the crowd pushed behind him he tottered, and Mr. Midkiff put out an arm to keep him from falling. Glancing back, he saw rows of vacant eyes, as cold and glassy as the eyes of codfish. Hunger surrounded him. But was it merely a physical hunger? Could the human race, glutted with horrors of its own making, survive upon a material basis alone? . . . Suddenly a voice piped out of nowhere into his ear. "If I hadn't lost my week's pay in that damn slot machine, I'd bet my last dollar on a chicken fight." "You oughtn't to," a second squeak answered. "You oughtn't to, when the baby has to have medicine, and I haven't been able to get to a movie for a whole week."

In waves of elasticity that strange lightness poured into his mind. His body seemed to exist merely as a shred of vapour attached to a mood that was ethereal, swift, and exalted. It can't be long now, he thought, with an exquisite sense of release. "All right?" he inquired of Mr. Midkiff over his shoulder.

Yes, Mr. Midkiff was bearing up, but ashamed. His muffled voice vibrated with humiliation above the thin squeaking about him. Was it another sphere, or simply another tradition, that he inhabited? Inside the house, where the only sounds were the inarticulate scurryings, the jingling of tin cups, and the gulping of pale liquid in which a few coffee grounds swam about, he received a cupful of fluid, a baker's stale roll, and some scraps of stringy meat stewed with potatoes. Well, a warm stomach, however you looked at it, was an advantage. While they swallowed their coffee, Mr. Midkiff riveted his abashed gaze on the floor. When all was said, he pondered gloomily, the man named Homer must have lived in the olden time, for modern paupers, even in the cast-off clothes from the Red Cross, cut a poor figure.

A shabby spectacle, John Fincastle assented. But it may be, he mused ironically, more to himself than to his companion, that poverty, like incest, requires Grecian apparel. In that noonday of a planned to-morrow, when science has bared the last mysteries of the human entrails, and the closed cells of spontaneous generation are opened in public view—in that morning brightness of knowledge will men have found a better world than human nature provides?. . .

"Well, we've had enough," he said aloud, and thrust his arm through Mr. Midkiff's, while a touch of vertigo sent the room spinning round him. Then the dizziness passed, and he discovered that he was in the street again, with the chill wind and the sullen clouds overhead. An icy lump in the pit of his stomach dissolved into nausea when he attempted to walk.

"Lean on me," Mr. Midkiff urged, grasping his shoulder. "I reckon this here charity's done upset your stomach."

But it wasn't that. John Fincastle reflected gratefully that he was dying. The sparks before his eyes would settle into a vast nebula . . . or perhaps into nothingness. It no longer mattered. The end would come slowly. It was a question of weeks, or it might be of days. Whenever it came, he would welcome it. Yet he was not defeated. Life had given him the thing he had wanted most. He had had his moment of victory, and he could look serenely ahead beyond the vanishing-point in the perspective.

"It is over now," he said, pushing his way through the huddled flock, which still reminded him curiously of sheep let out of a pen. The vertigo had left him, but his body felt as inanimate as a dead tree dragged on by a machine. The tatters on Mr. Midkiff's elbow were as much alive, he told himself, as his own clutching fingers.

At the corner running footsteps overtook them, and Ranny's voice asked breathlessly, "Did they give you something to eat, Grandfather?"

"Yes, we had half a mind to sample that fare."

"Are all those people hungry?"

"I suppose so, my boy, or they wouldn't come for what they receive."

"But didn't they have anything at home? Where did they get all those fur collars?"

"The garments of charity are cut thicker than the bread—at least for the women. But it is never safe, you know, to judge by appearances."

Ranny looked puzzled. "But, Grandfather, I went by the market yesterday, and I saw a man dump a whole cartload of potatoes in the mud and trample them down because nobody would buy them."

"That's the way of our world, my boy."

"Can't anybody stop it?"

"Enough people could. But that would require thinking about things, and most people find thinking too difficult or too painful. Give them enough for themselves, and they're satisfied. There is only one force stronger than selfishness, and that is stupidity. But, remember, the man with the potatoes wasn't to blame. He was merely a cog in the wheel that had destroyed the fruit of his toil. I think, on the whole, he is the one we should pity most. Nothing eats the heart out of one so rapidly as wasted toil."

Ranny threw back his head. "I'm almost grown up," he replied stubbornly, "and I'm going to do something about it."

"Sixty years ago I said that, too, Ranny, but you may succeed where I failed."

"I'm going to do something. Grandfather, a stranger is waiting to see you. I came out to find you, but I went too far up the street. Aunt Meggie says he's a German philosopher."

"Well, what does he . . . what does anyone want with me?"

"He was telling Aunt Meggie. One of his reasons for coming to America, he said, was to talk with you, but he has been the whole morning long trying to find you in Queenborough. When he asked about you at the hotel, they thought he meant Mr. Mountcastle who had that burglary at his house last week. You remember," he added in a solemn tone, "his wife lost thirty thousand dollars' worth of rings and things."

"Then I'll be gittin' back to my wheelbarrow," Mr. Midkiff said, with embarrassment. "I feel less set agin that soup kitchen since you took me thar."

"That's only to stay you till supper. You must come over as usual. Did the stranger tell you his name, Ranny?"

"Hardenberg. Dr. Hardenberg, Aunt Meggie called him. He's old, Grandfather. He must be over fifty. But that's not so old as you are."

"No, that's not so old as I am." He knew the name, for it was one of the important names in modern philosophy—the name of perhaps the last great German Idealist.

"Run on ahead, my boy, and say I'm coming." John Fincastle's voice trembled as if it were too tired to take up the burden of speech. While he leaned against a tree for support, he felt that his skeleton more than his flesh was animated by pleasure. It occurred to him that Hardenberg had lived out of Germany, lecturing at an English university, for less than a year, while he himself had been born in the land of exile, where all tongues are alien. And now at last, before he stepped down into his grave, he might, for an hour at least, speak and hear spoken the native language of his thoughts. Impetuously, still wearing his shabby greatcoat and holding his tin cup, he rushed into the house.

CHAPTER 16

T HE strange philosopher, a small, impressive figure with an erect carriage and a pleasant face half concealed by a fawn-coloured beard trimmed square at the end, was discussing Rhode Island Red poultry with Meggie. As John Fincastle entered, he broke off without haste, and murmured his greetings in perfect English with a neatly clipped accent. He had come out of his way, he explained, since his lectures would not bring him to the South, in order to do homage to one of the greatest among living philosophers. He brought also, he continued, in the impersonal tone of metaphysics, and with a gesture that seemed in some curious way (or was it only a return of his vertigo? John Fincastle asked himself) to be linked to the imponderable—he brought also respectful felicitations from a small group of German Idealists.

While he stood there, listening to the smooth, deferential voice, John Fincastle felt the glow of anticipation dissolve at a touch. In one instant, it seemed to him, the expectancy had slipped away, had vanished, was over. Had he lived too long among shadows to renew his grasp on reality? Or had he lived too close to reality to feel at home among shadows? Not that it mattered. The revolving sparks before his eyes might be the rays of eternity. They might, also, be vertigo. It's too late, he thought. I'm too far off to be reached.

Meeting his dazed eyes, Meggie said, "We've a very homely lunch, but we hope you will share it with us." Never had she appeared so natural, and yet so dignified. The mountain poise had not deserted her. His mother had never lost it, and beyond his mother—how far beyond!—he remembered the noble bearing of that grandmother who had been Margaret Graham, walking on her bare feet through the drenched grass. The frontier, for all its savage impulses and brutal habits, had created, if only now and then, characters that rose superior to destiny.

He put his tin cup on the mantelpiece, and said hospitably, "I'm just back from lunch, but I should like to sit with you while you have yours." Meggie would find a way, he knew, to spread the butter thin on her own bread and add a cup of hot water to her own soup. But the stranger would find her coffee better than the flat chicory blend of Europe. And in her grey cotton dress and ample white apron she would remind him of an older and a lost Germany. For he was talking with her, John Fincastle realized, as if he had known her when they were young. While he ate his bean soup, which had not been watered, and broke and buttered his stale roll, their visitor was completely at ease and apparently enjoying himself. Even Ranny, heartily consuming a double share of lunch, paused only once to make trouble.

"Grandfather, the next time you and Mr. Midkiff go to the free lunch kitchen, I want to go with you. When I'm older, I'm going to do something about all the hungry people."

A mauve flush mottled his aunt's cheek, but the stranger, who was praising the coffee while he helped himself to sugar, appeared not to have heard. A most hospitable country to scholars, he remarked, so long as they did not happen to have been born here. Even in the midst of the depression, America provided a living for hundreds of foreign lecturers, and it not only paid them for speaking, it sat quietly in rows and listened to what they said.

After lunch was over, while Meggie was clearing the table, the two men went upstairs to the room over the kitchen, where the few books left from John Fincastle's library filled a shelf in one corner. There was nothing to smoke, until Dr. Hardenberg observed that he had been persuaded to try Virginia cigarettes, and drew out a package. Then, as they settled themselves in the two pine chairs with rush bottoms, John Fincastle realized that the power of speech, as he had once known speech, had deserted him. He was out of touch, it seemed to him, with two hemispheres. Downstairs, he had completely missed the idiom of facts. Up here, alone with a visitor who spoke his own language, the streams of metaphysics sounded as vague as the lapping of surf on a beach. Beyond time and space, nothing that men thought of eternity was either important or unimportant. Speculation? Philosophy? Had these realities failed him? Or were they at last resolved into the only element that endures? He was more at home nowadays with the humble folk, like old Midkiff or Otto Bergen, who spoke neither the hollow idiom of facts nor the dead tongues of the schools, but the natural speech of the heart.

Gradually, as the hours wore on and the sunlight faded from the window under the red tin roof, he heard happily the rise, the curve, the breaking, the thunderous fall and murmur of waves on that invisible shore. There is an understanding deeper than words, deeper than sound, he thought, below consciousness. Time had renounced him. He was a shell, or less than a shell, washed up and left by the tide. Yet the tide had flowed and ebbed over him, and he remained himself; he had endured; he was alone.

"Well, I shall remember this," the stranger was saying out of a fog of light. "It makes life easier and death harder. I am obliged to confess," he continued, with his foreign smile, "that I have no message, not even the simplest, for my age. I exist, that is all. And perhaps I ask myself without expecting an answer: 'After James and Bergson, what now?' "

A flash of irony quivered over John Fincastle's face. "God, maybe. It is true that under a miscroscope God may be only a cluster of cells. But, then, who has ever put God under a microscope? The intellect has survived Bergson. Ultimate truth will outwear James by an eternity. It is possible that God is more than motion. It is even possible that modern man is more than glandular maladjustment. You and I can afford to wait."

"And the wheel turns. For myself, at least, the end is better than the beginning."

Walking after his visitor, John Fincastle descended the stairs very slowly, because the sensation of swiftness, of flying out of himself, had returned. Alone by the gate, when the other had passed through, he stood looking on an earth and sky that seemed to be bathed in some fluid quality of mind. Pure philosophy, he thought suddenly, is a wordless thing.

"A strange country, America," the German philosopher was thinking aloud in his clipped accents. "A race as indistinguishable as the Chinese." While he waited at the corner for the lights to turn, painted faces drifted by him as aimlessly as toy boats drift and pass on a stream. Undoubtedly, a strange country, with its watered psychology, its vermin-infested fiction, and its sloppy minds that spill over. A whole civilization scourged by masochism! Well, one must not expect too much of a people so recently savage and still raw under the skin. In a thousand years or so, when Americans have learned that religion did not begin with Christianity and did not end with the Great War, they may discover also that this queer old man with the tin cup is their greatest philosopher. Still practising the way to think clearly in two languages, while he tried in vain to separate uniformity into features, the stranger again wondered silently, paused an instant to watch a speeding car rock through a safety zone, and at last passed on his tranquil way.

"But hunger is vital," John Fincastle thought, staring ahead at the breadline. "One couldn't, no, not in a million years, think hunger out of the universe." This was the second time he had walked with Mr. Midkiff to the soup kitchen, and he would stand and wait outside while the old man went in for his lunch. A cold spring sky, uncertain, remote, shone through the bare trees. Then he saw that needle points of green sprinkled a branch overhead. "This is the last week," a voice neighed at his side. "The first of April, rain or shine, we'll be turned out to graze."

"I'm studyin' how we'll make out," Mr. Midkiff muttered under his breath.

"We'll find a way." John Fincastle discovered, to his surprise, that he was laughing. After all, a sense of the ridiculous was as stout a prop as one needed. It helped even more than philosophy when one matched one's wits against the universe. Or was all philosophy simply an ultimate sense of the ridiculous?

A man pushed against him, dodged into the moving row, and then pushed again. Seizing a limp arm, which struggled in his grasp, John Fincastle drew away from the throng, beyond a tree by the curb. "What are you doing here, Bertie Rawlings?" he asked in a whisper.

"Nothing."

"Where are you going?"

"Nowhere."

"I thought you were in Texas."

"I was once."

"When did you lose your place?"

"I never had one. Not for more than a few weeks. Just what I could pick up."

Clutching the boy's arm (for he was still scarcely more than a boy), John Fincastle looked at him as he had looked at the points of green on the tree, seeing not the buds alone, but the whole vision of time. Bertie's face was grey, his cheeks were hollowed, his eyes were reddened from cinders, his nostrils might have been pinched in by dirty fingers. He was shabby, unwashed, unshaven—but these things were trifles. What was worse, what mattered most, was that dreadful humbleness, the stain of inward defeat. I know what it is, the old man thought, with a flash of insight as sharp as a blade. I know what it is because I've been through it. A space was cleared in his memory. Pure vacancy closed round him. Nothing lived there, not even an outline, not even a shadow; but in the centre a wing turned, and he saw once again that sudden light on reality. "Yes, I know," he said aloud. "You don't need to tell me."

"I never had a place in Texas," Bertie gasped out, as if he were retching. "But Mother couldn't feed us both. She was beginning to starve herself. I found out that she saved her dinner and gave it to me at night. The streets were filled with teachers looking for jobs. If I'd been a day labourer, I might have had a chance. It's easier in a country like this if you can handle a spade. I tried taking off my collar, only my hands gave me away, and I wasn't husky enough. Once I fainted when I was digging. . . ."

"How did you keep alive?" As Mr. Midkiff went through the gate and into the soup kitchen, they turned away and sat down on the lower step of a neighbouring house. "Did you go as far as Texas and back again?"

"I went to Texas. I went to Florida. I went . . . oh, anywhere. I bummed. I hiked. I panhandled. I've eaten with bums. I've slept with bugs. . . . But I'm not going to talk about it."

"Why didn't you write? We wanted your address."

"I didn't have any address." His voice rose tauntingly, and then strained and broke under the weight of despair. "Whenever I could manage, I'd send a postcard to Mother. Sometimes, if I knew where I'd be, I'd tell her to write to the post office. That's how I heard they wanted me at Boscobel School. I started that night. I bummed my way back as fast as I could. Then as soon as I got here, the first minute my eyes fell on that steeple"—he pointed to a grey spire—"I knew it was no use. I couldn't come back again. I was down for good. I was out and ended. . . . Besides, I'm dog-tired. . . ."

"You ought to have told us."

"What could you have done? I couldn't come home to sit down on Mother. Look at her back."

"She's better off now. She's had help."

"I know, charity. But I went by there, and she was still sewing."

"She hasn't changed as much as you have. You'll have to brush up a bit before she sees you."

"Oh, she shan't see me. I'll take care of that. I'll hop off again on the first freight."

"The head of Boscobel School liked you."

Bertie's laugh sank into a sneer. "I know. She thought I looked as if I might be trusted."

"Well, you may, mayn't you?"

"May what?"

"Be trusted?"

"I'll be damned if I know. But I've never stolen, if that's what you mean."

"No, that isn't what I mean. That isn't at all what I mean."

"Maybe you mean a cigarette. Have you got one?"

John Fincastle shook his head. "No, but I have the price of one." He was still laughing, he discovered, with that deep inward irony. It wasn't easy to surpass the Ancient of Days in a burlesque of mortality.

"You're just my height," he said carelessly, almost gaily. "My clothes would fit you."

"Well, you're not an old-clothes man." The sneer had returned. "I know I look a bum, but a suit of clothes and a pair of shoes can't build up a man from the bottom."

"Maybe not. Still, my clothes would fit you. But you need a bath. There's plenty of hot water to-day. Old Betsey is washing clothes, and she's kept the kettles filled on the stove." While he shivered slightly in the brisk wind, he stared into Bertie's sullen face without seeing it. He had meant to wear that one good suit of clothes, that one whole pair of shoes, back to Ironside. When he came to die, he had intended to spare the pride of Meggie—of his mother—of Mary Evelyn. Women had queer ideas about burials. They wanted a man to look spruce when he entered into eternal rest. As if worms could discriminate between homespun and broadcloth. As if there were fashions even for the incorruptible.

"What's the use?" Bertie was scoffing. "They don't begin school in the spring."

"There will be a summer term. They are moving out of town, and they need an English instructor to keep on. Since the substitute teacher resigned, the English classes have been divided among the others. It's your only chance, and you're going to take it. Think of your mother's back. Think of all those years bent over that sewing machine."

"I do think of them, but it's no use."

"Anyway, you're going home with me now."

The boy jerked away. "No, I'm not. I'd be ashamed before that old coloured woman." He dropped back on the step. "I'll go to those public baths up the street, if you can let me have the money to rent a towel. I can still remember how it feels to be clean. Until a few weeks ago I washed regularly. Sometimes in a place for transients, when I could stand charity. But the best place to wash, when it isn't too cold, is a park fountain at daybreak, before the police are about. A woman gave me a cake of soap—good soap, too—" he chuckled at the recollection—"scented with lemon verbena, and I hoarded it as if it were money. She dropped the package in the street and a cake rolled out. When I picked it up, there was a little mud on it, so she gave it to me. A nice woman. She'd have given me the price of a cup of coffee if she'd had any change in her purse." For the first time he smiled, yielding his will to a sensation of pleasure.

"Miss Curran remembered you," John Fincastle rambled on, as if he were thinking aloud. "It was easy to see, she told me, that you had kept your standards . . ."

"Standards? Good Lord!" Bertie groaned. "You can do anything with standards except eat them."

"Besides, your professors all thought well of you. She had never read recommendations she liked more."

"Professors? What are they?"

John Fincastle stood up and fumbled in the depths of his pocket. "I can manage just enough for that rented towel, and perhaps a shave and haircut. Did you get a roll here?"

"I'd just eaten it when you caught me."

"Well, come straight to us. There isn't anybody in the house but Meggie. Ada is at work, Ralph is looking for work, and Ranny took his lunch to school. I'll have a cup of real coffee for you, if nothing else, and while you're getting clean, I'll telephone Miss Curran, and look over my clothes. It's lucky that you're tall, with a stoop, and haven't put on an ounce of flesh."

"I can leave my shirt at the bath."

"Yes, it's only a few blocks. Button your coat tight after you get warm. I'll lend you my greatcoat when you go out to Boscobel. It's green with age, but of good quality, and you may leave it in the hall if you don't show the lining. You won't disappoint me if I wait for you? Here's Midkiff coming now."

"Oh, no, I'll come. I'll come whether there's any use or not. I'll think of that coffee." He stretched out a shaking hand. "God knows I'm grateful."

A smile that was barely more than a quiver of the muscles tightened John Fincastle's lips. "Don't worry, my boy. You won't be by to-morrow." Turning away, he slipped his arm through Mr. Midkiff's, while he added dreamily, "The eternal verities are few, Midkiff, and gratitude is not among them."

"I reckon that's so," Mr. Midkiff assented, "but I'm studyin' about how we'll manage next week."

"Something will turn up, my friend. Let us hope it may be better bread." Would Bertie Rawlings keep his word? he was wondering. Ought he to have gone with him to the public baths and the barber? Could the boy be saved, or was it too late? Was he even worth saving?

In Otto Bergen's shop, where there was a telephone, he picked up the receiver with a trembling hand and called up the head of Boscobel School. Until her composed voice reached him, he had a moment of doubt, of suspense, of perplexity. Then, abruptly, he heard himself speaking in thin, clear tones across a tumult of reverberations. "So the place is still vacant? Yes, he has come back. I have just seen him. What? No, your letter did not reach him till a week ago. He has had an illness. What? Oh, no, nothing like that. All he needs is building up. A doctor? That would be a good idea. The school doctor might examine him, and give him a tonic. Don't be shocked when you see him. Young people pick up weight rapidly. Good food and work he likes will be the making of him. The professors? Yes, I'm sure they were right. He is a born teacher. You liked what they said of his character, and he looked . . . what? . . . oh, yes, I hear . . . he looked innocent. Well, I'll send him up this afternoon late, as soon as he has seen his mother. . . ." While he turned away from the telephone and went out into the street, it seemed to him that the earth rose with him when he stepped higher and higher into space. Things don't happen this way, he thought, but there are times when life surprises one, and anything may happen, even what one had hoped for.

The house was so quiet when he entered that he wondered whether Meggie had gone out. Could she have run over to chat with Mrs. Bergen, or to do an errand at the apothecary's on the corner? Then he saw a flutter and change in the light at the end of the hall; the kitchen door, which had stood ajar, opened wider; and Meggie called softly, "Is that you, John? Do you want anything?"

"I want you. I want you to help me."

"Well, I'm right here."

"Have you any coffee? I mean the kind of coffee Mother used at the manse?"

"I have a little Mocha and Java put away for sickness. We use a cheaper blend in Queenborough. Everything is so dear. The poorest coffee beans cost more now than we used to pay for the best."

"I know, but I want the best, and I want it strong."

"What is the matter, John? Are you feeling faint?"

"No, I'm all right. Did you ever hear of a soul saved by coffee?"

Meggie shook her head. "No, I never heard of it, but I can believe in it. Have you brought the Hamburg steak?"

"I gave the money to Bertie Rawlings."

"Bertie Rawlings? I thought he was in Texas."

"He wasn't. He was in the soup line when I went there with Midkiff."

"Where did he come from? How did he look?"

"He'd just come off a freight train. That's how he looked. I gave him the money to have his hair cut and a shave. He's coming here from the public bath."

"Then I'd better begin grinding that coffee. I'm glad I saved the shell of Ranny's egg after breakfast."

"Can you scrape up something else? Hope, Mother used to say, doesn't settle on an empty stomach."

"I'll send Aunt Betsey out to buy some middling. Otto Bergen sold one of those old pine corner cupboards this morning, and I was saving the money. The people wanted it, he said, because it's early American, and was made by hand in the Valley. They may buy the table, too, but he wants us to hold that for better times."

"Well, we'll hold what we can. But we've got to do more than this for Bertie."

"What more can we do, John?" She looked worried. "I don't see what we can do for ourselves. If Otto hadn't sold that cupboard, I don't know how we'd have managed till the end of the week. I'd have put off old Betsey, but I knew she'd come down to her last crust. By next month, she'll most likely be in the City Home."

For a long pause he looked at her in silence, while the edge of a smile flickered and died and flickered again. When at last he spoke, it seemed to her, as she said afterwards, that he had taken leave of his senses.

"Do you remember, Meggie, what dress Mother was buried in?"

She started as if she had seen a mouse. "Why, what in the world, John?"

"Well, do you remember?"

The start of fear passed off in a shiver. "Of course I do. She was buried in her best dress of grosgrain silk. You gave it to her for your wedding, and she kept it pinned up with camphor to be buried in. She'd never worn it but three times."

"A whole generation! I didn't know silk lasted that long."

"Silk like that lasts for ever, she used to say. It was the best quality, so heavy and stiff that it would stand alone, and yet as soft as a pigeon's breast. I don't believe anything ever gave her more pleasure than the knowledge that she had that one good dress to be laid out in, and we shouldn't have to worry about how she looked in her coffin. It has always distressed me," she added, with a sigh, "that I have never been able to remember her last words."

"Poor Meggie," he said gently. "I wish I'd given you a dress for my wedding."

Her thin cheeks were stained with a lavender flush. "But you did, John. It's funny the way you forget some things and remember others. You gave me a silk dress. It was the colour they used to call ashes of roses."

"Did you put that away?"

"What else could I have done with it?" she sighed softly. "But it hasn't held together as well as Mother's did."

All those years they had treasured that silk! It was incredible; it was ridiculous; it was profoundly and mysteriously moving. He had a vision, vague, fleeting, fringed with light, of his mother's brave old body lying at rest, beneath billows of black grosgrain silk, in her coffin. That was not defeat. That was a triumph over death, he thought proudly.

"You must have my best clothes put away somewhere, Meggie," he said in a cheerful tone. "Everything from the socks up, neatly mended and darned."

She shook her head. "I've always kept something nice for you, in case you should begin to teach again . . . or . . . or . . ." her voice quavered, "be called back to the ministry."

There was now no effort in his laughter. "That isn't likely, my dear, but I want my good clothes all the same. Life is more important than death—at least to the living."

"It doesn't seem right, John. I wish you wouldn't." As she turned back to the kitchen she added briskly, "They are all pinned up in that unbleached cotton cloth on the top shelf in your closet. Now, I'd better put on the coffee if you want it good and strong." A minute later he heard her composed voice saying to old Betsey in the kitchen, "I'll have to send you to the corner, Aunt Betsey. I'm sorry, but Mr. Fincastle forgot to buy that Hamburg."

"Yas'm, I knows. Dey sho do furgit whut you tell um."

Beyond the red tin roof of the next house, where sparrows

were quarrelling, a dispassionate sun blinked mildly through the shredded clouds toward the west. Strange, how the weakness of the morning had left him, he thought, as he pushed a chair into the closet and groped back in the dark corners on the top shelf. Was the bundle there? Had Meggie, who forgot so few details, forgotten where she had hidden it? Then his hand touched it, and he drew it out, a little dusty, but neatly wrapped and pinned with safety pins. As he unfolded the cloth, a whiff of moth balls stung his nostrils. Camphor, like everything else, Meggie said, was too dear nowadays. Prepared to meet his Maker, he thought, with that irrepressible humour, while he looked at the clothes on his bed. He was glad the suit was grey and not too old-fashioned in cut. Ada and Ralph had given it to him when they were prosperous, and he remembered that Ralph had chosen that dark tweed because it would keep its shape and stand wear. "But it's better to meet life," he said aloud, picking up the blue tie (Meggie had always had a fancy for polka dots), though he observed, after a quizzical glance, that she had included a black tie in the bundle. Yes, women were kittle cattle, as he had so often, in the past, heard his mother remark of men. Meggie was an honest soul, yet she had tried to make him believe she had saved a grey suit for the ministry. Or perhaps she had forgotten that it was not black. Even women forget sometimes.

Standing there beside his bed, in the pale flakes of sunshine, he gazed down on the clothes he had once worn, and thought, I am giving them a new lease on life. Then his amusement faded at the touch of anxiety. Suppose Bertie never came after all! Suppose the boy had not really meant to come back when they parted! To distract his mind, he went into the closet and brought out a pair of shoes he had had half-soled a few weeks before. Nothing to boast of, he decided, as he examined each shoe, but they would wear a good while longer if one were careful to watch where one walked. Bertie's feet were shorter, he suspected, but it would do no harm to fill in the toes with paper. Shoes, he had discovered long ago, were the major problem in poverty. Good shoes—he had begun to smile again—never went begging. But no man, not even at his burial, could ask for a better shirt. When it came to shirts and socks and woollen underwear, Meggie's instinct was infallible. Her needle could be trusted, not only with a nightshirt, but even in the more intricate pattern of pajamas.

From the kitchen below fragrance ascended. Meggie's coffee was already beginning its benevolent mission. "There is a spirit in coffee like the spirit of to-morrow," he said aloud to himself. "But I wish I felt easier about Bertie." Opening the door, he glanced out into the hall and down the staircase just as Bertie entered the house and a minute later waved a hand in his direction. Even in his ragged clothes he looked young and clean and eager to begin something and start somewhere. While he came up the steps with the long stride of youth, John Fincastle thought, Give the young half a chance and they will create their own future, they will even create their own heaven and earth.

"I'd forgotten how it feels to be clean all over," Bertie said.

"Well, strip and change. There're your things on the bed. Put your old suit in this newspaper, and we'll give it to Aunt Betsey to take away."

"I hope she'll burn it. I want to get that smell of bumming out of my head."

Yes, he was worth saving, the old man told himself while he watched the boy strip and change in the middle of the room, standing on newspapers he had spread over the rag carpet. A decent chap, as they used to say, before decency had been discredited. And after all, though it had become the world's scapegoat, there were more dangerous virtues than decency. But that bluish pallor was not unattractive, and the sunken darkness round his eyes lent a wistful pathos to his expression. Women would find him more appealing than ever, and it would not matter in the least that he was a rather commonplace youth at bottom, with more behaviour than brains. In a democracy, and perhaps anywhere else, it was safer to be average.

"As soon as you've had something to eat and spoken to your mother, you are to go out to Boscobel School," he said. "I've called up Miss Curran, and she is expecting you."

Well, that was over, though he had a curious feeling that he had turned back his own funeral when he saw the grey figure neatly tie the blue tie in front of the mirror, and then swoop down on the newspapers and quickly bundle the old clothes out of sight.

CHAPTER 17

A S THE days drifted by, it seemed to John Fincastle that he was resting in some timeless reality. With his failing body, the sense of immobility deepened, until at last, after a lifetime of speculation, he attained the inarticulate certitude of animal faith. And like a dying animal, fearless of death or dissolution, he remembered and longed to return to the places he had known when he was happy. Looking over the smokestacks by the river, he would say cheerfully, "Spring is coming in the Valley," while his heart would quicken with the new pulsing life in the earth. He would feel the swift stirring of the sap in his veins and taste the bitter sweetness of April showers on his lips.

This secret way alone, interwoven with nature yet derived, in some deeper sense, from the source of all wisdom, was real and vital, and as close to the life of reason, he felt, as the stem to the fruit. All the rest, whatever happened on the surface, was unimportant and fragmentary. The noises of the city, which had once tortured his nerves, now dwindled into an immense distant humming. Beneath the thunderous silence, so remote and yet so oppressive, like an approaching storm in the sky, he strained the ear of his soul for a whisper that was still inaudible though he felt its vibrations. Whenever it reached him, day or night, he would know that the last bell was ringing and it was time for him to seek solitude.

Then, while he still waited, Ada told them one evening that Mr. Shadwell had barely averted failure by selling his entire store to a new firm of Jewish merchants. The old staff would, of course, be discharged. Few of the older women would be retained, and she would not be among them.

377

"But I've a week ahead." Though she laughed as she spoke, her feet throbbed and the smile twisted on her pale lips. "I've a whole week with a salary. Anything may happen in a week. Wasn't the earth, with all its unnecessary inhabitants, created in less time than that?"

"Yes, anything may happen and occasionally does," her father assented.

"I heard today of a job I may get," Ralph said, and there was the old protective note in his voice, "but it depends on business picking up a bit, and it would mean an agency in the Valley."

"Well, isn't business picking up?" Aunt Meggie asked. "Isn't it better, anyway, than it was when the banks were all closed? And even if we have to ask help, it won't be for long. Taking charity isn't nearly so bad as losing someone you love. Besides"—her voice broke for an instant—"if it would be any real help, I could go to the City Home. I haven't as much dread as some people have of coming to that. I don't mean I'd choose to do it," she added, "but I could make out with it, if I felt God thought it was best for me."

"Don't be too hasty, Meggie," John Fincastle rejoined lightly. "if that is God's will, we'll do our best to circumvent it." Turning to glance out of the window, he remarked with a smile, "Have you noticed how well my grey suit looks in the street?"

"I'm glad you helped that boy, John, but I can't help begrudging your good clothes."

"I saved the black tie, my dear. Many a man has worn less when he met his Maker. Besides, Bertie will take better care of those clothes than I did."

"When Boscobel School moves into the country, his salary will be seventy-five dollars a month, with his board. That isn't much, but I hope Mrs. Rawlings will at last be able to rest her back."

"Whether she does or not, she will be happy. Bertie has learned his lesson in a hard school, and he will make a little happiness go a long way. The iron may not have entered his soul, but it has probably singed his feathers."

"I can't see what has got into you, John. You never used to be flippant."

"You're right, Meggie, as usual. Flippancy is one of the infirmities of a mature point of view. I only wish, my dear," he continued, after a pause in which his gaze followed the tall grey figure from the shadow under the mulberry tree into the sunshine beyond, "that I could be flippant about ourselves and old Midkiff. Perhaps because I am old, too, I find that Midkiff is rapidly becoming a centre of gravity."

The next morning he awoke at dawn with a feeling of extraordinary anticipation. He had felt this way before, as a boy at the manse, when he had awakened, light-hearted, in the sunrise, and had known that some great day, to which he had looked forward for months, was beginning. Rising softly, he dressed himself with shaking fingers, and descended the stairs as soundlessly as the light glided down through an upper window. In the kitchen he drank a little milk and ate a crust from the end of a stale loaf. I must keep up my strength, he thought. Yet he knew, as surely as an animal that slips away from the herd toward finality, that his strength would not fail while he needed it. This sense of elasticity, of buoyant upspringing, was not physical. Whatever the source, he felt, it was superior to matter; it used his body as a vehicle that would be soon discarded.

In the street sunbeams were rising, sinking, advancing in waves. He moved carefully, lifting his feet and putting them down again with the slowness of a man who has learned to walk after an illness. The world had worn so thin that he could see through it. People and objects, earth and sky, buildings and trees, bricks in the pavement, a milk wagon trundling past—all these appearances were so transparent that he looked into them and beyond. Only beyond there was nothing. Nothing but vapour. Nothing but a universe dissolving into a void.

For weeks he had saved, bit by bit, the price of his ticket on the omnibus to Charlottesville. There he could change for the Valley. Or perhaps the driver of a van or a car would offer him a ride for a part of the way. There was no shadow of doubt, no quiver of apprehension. All his life he had weighed, pondered, considered; he had obeyed reason. Now, at the end, he was controlled by some faculty deeper, stronger, wiser, than the power he had called reason. Even the hours of waiting on the street corner belonged not to time, but to an undivided eternity.

The omnibus, when at last it set out, was more than half empty. There were three women inside, large, medium, diminutive in figure, and a little girl, who played with a bouncing ball on the end of an elastic string. Behind him two men, one slow and elderly, and one speaking with a brisk Northern accent, pursued an argument back and forth and round again through a labyrinth. In the seat ahead an old farmer, stooped, crooked, with long twisted arms and knotted hands, chewed tobacco and spat through the lowered window down into the road. When he turned, as he did once in a while, to join in the argument, he showed a ruddy, humorous face covered with a crisscross pattern of obstinate wrinkles. In his hand he held a new fishing-rod, while he steadied, between his feet, a basket of groceries with a few purple petunia plants trailing from one end.

Sinking down into his corner, John Fincastle tried to doze away a sensation of nausea. Impressions skimmed over the surface of thought. Sounds came and went, and among these sounds —the grating of wheels, the shrieking of horns, the tinkling of words—there was no distinction in quality. All were meaningless, shrill, and as piercing as tin whistles.

Women's voices mingled: "I stayed over to have a permanent. There's a place on the other side of Broad Street where they're doing them for two dollars and a half." ... "Well, I don't favour a permanent. I had one once and it turned my hair yellow." ... "It's hard not to turn grey hair yellow in streaks. What you need is bluing. You need to put so much bluing in the water that your hair comes out purple. My man's an Eyetalian. He sets the wave all right, but he burned places in my scalp. I went straight back and showed it to him. I said, 'You've burned my scalp, and I'm going to tell everybody I know.' But he just laughed at me. 'You don't know anybody to tell,' he said." . . . "Ma, I've lost my ball. The string broke, and it fell out of the window. Oh, Ma, make the man stop, and let me run back and find it." . . . "Hush, Mamie, sit right down, and stop crying. You can't go back. Don't you hear me? Stop crying. I'll get you another the next time we go back to Queenborough." . . . "But we ain't goin' back, Ma, and I want my ball. I want to show it to the others. I want it now." . . . "I can't help it. You hadn't any business to bounce it out of the window. If you don't keep quiet, I'll give you something to cry about as soon as we get home." . . . "Yes, I was just going to say, even a poor permanent is better than none. I wonder if you happened to see that bargain sale at Spender's on Merchant Street. They had a nice lot of dresses, odd sizes, reduced to three dollars and ninety-five cents. They were imitation silk, too, all made after expensive models. My niece said she saw her identical dress in the moving pictures. Some were reduced from sixteen-fifty. I got one real pretty print, mustard-colour, piped with green. All I've got to do is to let it out a little over the hips."

Men's voices mingled: "All I want to know is what you're going to do when you've got your revolution, Mister. When you've turned the country over to the down-and-outs, what are they going to do with it? If they couldn't make anything of themselves, how as they going to make anything of a world?" . . . "The trouble with you Southerners is that your class hatred has soaked out into race hatred. You haven't enough guts to hate anybody but negroes. When the class struggle comes in the South, if it ever does, it will be all the white people against all the negroes. You can't even see the value of a planned economy." . . . "So far as I can make out, you radicals ain't never done anything but planning. It's all this damned theorizing that's the ruination of the country. When you talk about this planned economy, what I want to know is, Who's to do the planning and whose economy it's going to be? It seems to me that it's always the other fellow's economy that's being planned. The folks who've got something don't want the planning. What they aim to do is to hold on to what they've got left." . . . "But they can't hold on to it. It's going to be taken away from them for the good of the whole." . . . "What whole? Ain't they as much the whole as all the folks that are trying to eat out of your hand? . . . "It all comes back to social consciousness. There isn't enough social consciousness in the South to make a proletarian revolution." . . . "Gabble, gabble, gabble." The old farmer had looked round. "I tell you right now, I ain't no proletarian, and I ain't never seen one, unless it's the darkey that don't want to work." . . . "All I say is you Yankee radicals had better stand aside and give this new President a chance to see what he's doing." . . . "A proletarian dictatorship will mean security and leisure for the worker." . . . "And where's your dictator coming from? If we can't elect the right President, how are we going to elect the right dictator? If we can't run a veterans' hospital without stealing, as some folks say, how are we going to run a government? Anyway, I don't want a glorified ward boss telling me how I'm going to work, and when I'm going to loaf, and the way I'm going to manage my own business." . . . Rattle, rattle, grind, grind, lurch, lurch, the bus protested in varied tongues of machinery.

The sun shone; the wind blew; the dust whirled; the unsteady old bus clattered and rumbled. But there was no substance. All was insubstantial and fugitive. He had waited for his first glimpse of the hills, but when the long rhythms of the Blue Ridge flowed out of the sky, they were as limpid as the April clouds on the horizon.

A woman's voice: "I don't want to start anything. This is as secret as the grave between us. No, Mamie wouldn't understand what we're talking about. Well, they do say that the minister and Ida Watson didn't get home till near daybreak. Of course he said the car had broken down, but all the same a member of his congregation who doesn't want his name mentioned told me he had seen them together at a soda fountain in Staunton." . . .

A man's voice: "People don't want wine any more. Wine's a fancy drink. They want cawn. It takes more'n a fancy drink to tickle our prohibition palate. Yes, sir, you can get right good cawn almost anywhere, if you know the way to go about it. Up in the mountains they make a first-rate apple brandy, but that ain't as easy to get as moonshine whiskey. When you Yankees have tasted 'em all, you'll most likely agree with me that it's hard to beat the real old Virginny cawn." . . .

A second man's voice: "What I want to know is, When you get your working-class dictator, is he going to let us have all the chicken fights we want? Folks are tired of being too decent. They want strong stuff, like they have in the movies. Only they want it real blood and thunder. I believe in letting people do what they want to do, as long as it brings tourists and money into the State. Look at betting now. This State is roused, I tell you, and it's going to have betting made legal the next time the legislature gets together. Just watch out and see. We're darn sick of reforms, and of trying to make people better than God Almighty did. In the olden time we had chicken fights and dog fights and darkey gougings too. It wouldn't surprise me, the way folks need to be toned up, if we even get gouging back again. No, sir, I don't reckon I'm set on politics. I want a President that makes people happy." . . .

An echo within the shell of the mind—"*May all that have life be delivered from suffering.*"

Beyond Charlottesville he sat by the roadside until a friendly young man in a shiny new Ford car offered to take him to Staunton. Farther on, as they crossed the Blue Ridge above Rockfish Valley, where beauty ravished the eyes, he heard the friendly young man, who represented a Baltimore manufacturer of insecticides, glowingly describe the new prosperity among exterminators. He had been selling insecticides for the past two years, and in that time he had sold thirty thousand dollars' worth to one orchard man in Virginia. "You'd know his name if I told you. He's the biggest apple-grower in the Valley. I tell you, if the insects don't get the better of us before we invent a killer for every kind, we're going to get rich out of pests. It's a rare bug, I say, that won't make a fortune for somebody. Looks as if it was a race between man and bugs in this old world, don't it?" he inquired cheerfully. "Seems as if God Almighty is making pests faster than he can make human beings, though some scientists do say that we're pests like the others, only more so. But, you may take my word for it, there ain't any slump among exterminators. It's news to us that old man Depression has been hanging round. We've got more business than we can handle, and it grows bigger and better. When the bugs wanted a heaven, God gave them the Shenandoah Valley, Judge Simpkins said the last time I was travelling between Staunton and Harrisonburg. But he was fooling. Our bumper crop, I hear, is raised in the Middle West, and even in old Virginia, the Valley makes a poor showing beside the Tidewater. When you come to think of it, they don't have seed ticks in the Valley, or even in Piedmont. I've had to do with a lot of pests in my time; but I've never seen one yet that I'd trade for the seed tick."

In July, he continued after a period of meditation, he would go on his vacation for two weeks, and he expected to be married before he began travelling again. "She's a good-looker all right, but not a blonde. I don't trust blondes. They get too much newspaper publicity. What I want is a good sport, who knows a thing or two and can take care of herself with men, especially old ones. Old ones are the worst when they get going. This girl of mine has worked in an office ever since she was seventeen, and I don't believe there's a man alive that could put anything over on her."

At Staunton, John Fincastle tottered when he stepped to the pavement. Immediately, he was submerged in blackness through which red dots were sailing. From the clouds overhead he heard the voice of the exterminator asking solicitously, "Couldn't you manage a bite of lunch? I wish I could take you on to Ironside, but I'm travelling through the Shenandoah." Then, as there was no response, "Good God! It looks like starvation!"

A glass of milk was put to his lips, and a new voice said, "I've dashed it with brandy. It may bring him round, but he isn't fit to go on. Does anybody know who he is?" A pause, and then, "He didn't tell me his name. He's going to Ironside. He said he had friends in Ironside." Another pause, before a sound slashed like a pair of shears into darkness, "Then he'd better get there as quick as he can. If you think he'll last, I'll put him on the back seat of my car, and drop him as I pass Ironside. But I don't want a corpse on my hands. Wonder who he is, anyway? Looks as if he'd seen better days."

From an abyss within, it seemed to John Fincastle, his will soared up on wings, as a great bird, before it turned and seized his suffering frame in its claws. He knew he was dying. He knew also that he should not die until his will had relinquished him. Without surprise, he felt that he was stretched on the pavement, that people were gathering round him, that a hand was feeling his pulse. His will closed and tightened over sensation. Opening his eyes, he stared up at a single white cloud. Death was like that, infinite and serene.

"I must go to Ironside." The voice was so strange, so reedy, that he did not recognize it as his own. "I have important business in Ironside."

"Business? Have you no friends? You're too weak for business."

" I have friends. My friend is expecting me."

"Then I'll take him," a man said. "Ironside is on my way. I live sixteen miles beyond Teesdale. There's a pile of empty sacks in my car. He may ride easier if he is propped up on them. Hadn't he better finish that glass of milk?"

He sipped the rest of the milk, though for days he had felt unable to swallow. In one instant, by a single act of relinquishment, he knew that he could free himself with a gesture from the burden of pain. But the time had not come. Before his will released its prey, he must help where he could, he must save what he could, he must spare when it was possible. If he died in Iron-side, they would be saved the trouble and cost of the journey. Even dying, Meggie had said, was not so dear in the Valley, and his body, which would have fared as well in a pauper's grave, would require little spending before it was laid away beside Mary Evelyn in the churchyard. A hundred dollars, perhaps a hundred and fifty, might be saved, he had figured carefully, by the lower cost of burial in a mountain village. It would be like them, especially like Ralph, to wish the best for him when he was dead, but the best and the worst of death were both cut alike and of the same quality. Things had never mattered. He had none of old Midkiff's pride—or was it self-respect? Old bones were only old bones to him wherever one laid them.

Propped on empty sacks, he watched the road sliding into the hills. Now and then, the tight-lipped driver (he liked that silent sort) would call back, without turning his head, "Are you all right there?" or, "How are you coming?" And at every question he would spur himself into a dull consciousness.

Spring was running in a thin green flame over the Valley. There was a mist of green on the trees; luminous patches of green and blue sprinkled the earth. The deeper hollows were thatched with shade, and all the little hills, just touched by sunlight, were carved into stillness. Suddenly, as the road looped round a shaggy ridge, the heavens parted, and the friendly shoulder of God's Mountain marched with them on the horizon. Only, he told himself in astonishment, this was not the mountain that he remembered. For he could look through this swimming shape. God's Mountain, which had once seemed immovable, was floating on, with other fragments of the actuality, into bottomless space—with the scudding clouds, the sun-flushed river, the scattered farms, and the diminished figures of men and horses in the April fields.

He looked over the hills to where a flock of crows were crossing and recrossing the sky. His legs were dying, he thought, but his heart was still strong and urgent. A single wish drummed in his mind, now loud, now faint, now near, now distant, like a beating pulse in the centre of a vast loneliness. He must live to reach Ironside. Only in Ironside could he find release from this terrible will. Only in Ironside could he find the freedom to sink back into changeless beatitude, into nothing and everything.

The car jolted and stopped in the road below the flat rock and the big pine. While the jar still grated on his nerves a bland voice inquired out of the air, "Is there any place you'd like to go? We're coming to Ironside."

"No, no place. Put me down here. I don't go any farther." His will was bearing him up. He felt the sharp teeth and claws, and the pain brought him to life. When the driver had helped him from the car to the roadside, he stood looking vaguely over the fields to the red chimneys beyond a veil of green. "I know my way, thank you. It isn't far. I can easily find it."

"Are you fit? I don't like to leave you like this by the road."

"Oh, I'm fit. I'm perfectly able to make my way home. I thank you for bringing me," he continued as tonelessly as if he were reciting words in a foreign tongue. "I'm sorry I've nothing to offer you."

The man had expected no money and wanted none, he replied. Only he wasn't sure he was doing the right thing when he left a sick old man by the road. "I'll take you anywhere you want to go," he insisted. "You look as if you ought to be taken care of."

John Fincastle shook his head, and immediately the darkness shot with fiery sparks was spinning before his eyes. "I'm going home. It's just over the fields. You can see the house."

"Do you live there? I thought that house was deserted."

"Yes, I live there. I was born there. I've always lived there. Sometimes"—he smiled with an effort that seemed to crack his lips—"I think we always live where we're born."

Then at last, after a moment's indecision, the man drove away, turning to look back until he disappeared beyond the dip in the road, and so on past the railway station and the main street of the village.

When the car was out of sight, but not until then, John Fincastle crawled through a broken place in the fence, and sat down in the tall weeds beneath a cluster of willows. He knew these fields, he told himself, as well as he knew the palm of his hand. As a boy he had sprained his great toe on that sharp rock over there. Suddenly, surprisingly, his heart was overflowing with happiness. I've had a good life, he thought. I'd like to live it again, and live differently. In a little while he would get up and go on, but until that tremendous purpose seized him, he was incapable of an effort. When he tried to move, everything was blotted out by the old sensation of dizziness, as if he were blown in the April wind between earth and sky. And this dizziness, or this wind, stripped him of all that he had once thought of as his immortal part, as his inviolable personality. Nothing remained but a blind faith in some end that he could not see, in some motive that he could not understand. He knew his direction as the crow flying overhead knew its way in the air.

"It will come back," he said aloud. "My strength will come back." But when he rose to his feet and struggled to go on, he was struck down by a blow from within.

Lying there, in the midst of the spring meadows, he passed into a state that was not death and not sleep, while a strange dream stemmed up from below against the tide of his consciousness. In this dream, which was more vivid than life, he was a little boy again, riding behind his mother on one of her journeys of mercy into the mountains. He could feel the bulging saddlebags under his toes; he could see the nodding bunches of indigo in the bridle of old Bess. They were near Burned Timber Ridge, he knew, and they rode deeper and deeper into woods that had been burned a hundred years before, and had grown up again thick and strong. Once they passed an abandoned lumber camp, with the magnificent forest despoiled, the wild creatures trapped or slaughtered, and even the birds hurrying by overhead at a safe distance. Presently, they approached the few cabins in Panther's Gap, where women, in drooping sunbonnets, hoed rows of thin vegetables, and men lounged about with guns and lean hounds, or busied themselves with the stealthy making of mash. Then, at last, after a journey that seemed to the child to lead always deeper and deeper and yet higher and higher, they stopped at a cabin in the centre of some charred stumps, and his mother dismounted, unpacked her medicine case, and knocked at a closed door. He was left sitting alone on a stump, with only old Bess, patiently nibbling leaves from a scrub oak, as a protector. While he waited there a sudden dread, a panic terror, clutched at his heart. He knew, without knowing how he knew it, that something horrible was about to happen, was stealing toward him. I must run away, he thought, but he couldn't run; he couldn't detach his feet from the bare ground between the stumps. He couldn't loosen his tongue from the roof of his mouth when he tried to open his lips and call out to his mother. While the sweat broke out on his skin, and every pore seemed dripping with fear, the family flocked from the cabin and began to dance round him, singing and jeering. And as soon as he saw them he knew what he had dreaded—for they were all idiots. His mother had brought him to one of the mountain families that had inbred until it was imbecile. Two generations of blank, grinning faces and staring eyes and drivelling mouths danced and shouted round him as they pressed closer and closer. A world of idiots, he thought in his dream. To escape from them, to run away, he must break through not only a throng, but a whole world of idiots. . . .

Pain brought back consciousness, that strangling pain in his chest. For an instant it seemed to him that his breathing was over. Then the clutch of the agony withdrew slowly, winding back into itself. The field rolled before him like an ocean of space, rising and falling in billows. But there was only a little way to go. It would not take many minutes if he went straight and fast. One could bear anything for one minute . . . for two minutes . . . for three minutes. The grass and the trees and the distant hills were all a part of the running waves. A clod of earth was as large as a mound. God's Mountain was merely a hummock. The world and life were all one. Yet he struggled on, in this anguish of breathlessness, toward an end that was beyond the end of the living.

Behind him was the long—or was it short?—journey. He had reached the gate of the manse, where there was no gate. He walked through the gap and approached the house, which stood there in changeless quiet, near and yet far, like a house in a legend. I'm better now, he thought, for the pain had stopped suddenly. I'll have a spell now of quiet.

The manse was dilapidated, crumbling to ruins, smothered in weeds and in rubbish, but he saw it as one sees an image that rises quickly to the surface of memory, fresh, vivid, unaltered. While physical pain was suspended, a peace too deep for happiness, too still for ecstasy, poured into his mind and heart. Every dandelion, every clover-leaf, every pointed blade of grass, stood out in a spear of light that would melt at a breath, at a touch, at a whisper. Was this vision the reality? Not brick and mortar, stone and iron, but this vision?

Vertigo seized him again, and he sank down between the house and the garden. A strange, wild odour surrounded him. Gypsies had camped here. Or was it a man with a bear? Yet that was a lifetime before. He couldn't remember when or where he had heard it. But the smell of an animal, heavy, sour, curiously dark, seemed to drag him back to the earth, to all that had happened or had not happened in life, to the old ache, the old bitterness, the old despair of mortal identity. For he took a long time to die. A strong old man, somebody had called him. Or was somebody speaking of old Midkiff? A name floated into his thoughts. Mary Evelyn. Was she named Mary Evelyn? And how long ago had he known her? His mother he could remember. All his childhood was perfectly clear in his memory. He could recall every incident, every person and object that had filled in the pattern. But between his childhood and the present moment when he was old and dying there was nothing but loneliness. The sunset blazed on the broken window-panes of the house, and the dark face—dark and stern and bright—watching beyond the panes was the face of his mother. "It's time to go in," he thought. "I must get up and go in." But when he stood up, the pain leaped at him, and he dropped back on the earth.

CHAPTER 18

OD'S MOUNTAIN was lower, Ada thought, than she remembered it. Shut-in Valley was smaller. The manse was nearer the church. After her father's funeral, when the mourning village had scattered, she had left Aunt Meggie with Mrs. Black while she walked with Ralph up the steep road to the house.

"I wonder why he came back," Ralph said. "It must have killed him, that day's journey."

"I think he knew he was dying, and he held death off till he came home. He did it to spare us. The only thing that worried him, he used to say in fun, was the high cost of dying. It would be so much more reasonable, he told me, if he could arrange to die in Ironside. And he wanted his coffin made by Mr. Tinsley. I pretended I thought he was joking."

"Everything, even death comes back to that damned money in the end," Ralph answered moodily.

Ada wiped her eyes and tried to smile up at him. "I know. It was always that way. I suppose it always will be that way."

How forlorn the house looked under the spring sky! What had they done to it? How brutally it must have been treated! The shingles were rotting away beneath the golden green of the moss; the swallows were wheeling above a fallen chimney; the drain-pipes were choked with trash and last year's leaves; the air was tainted by that wild, roving smell.

"That must be the smell of a skunk," she said, looking round from the western wall.

"Why not of a menagerie?"

"I hate to leave the house like this. I wish we could clean it up. I feel that it suffers."

"Nobody would interfere with you. It isn't nearly so far gone as it looks, but the work would be wasted unless somebody came here to live. They've even cut down the pioneer oak for wild honey."

"Dr. Updike said he would let anybody come who would look after the place. He has always kept up the garden. Toby and old Marcellus Geddy are planting it now." She pointed to a hoe, stained with fresh earth, beside the gap where the gate used to be. "There are always plenty of vegetables coming on after May. I wonder . . ." She broke off and turned her eyes to the narrow pasture and the stony hill.

"I wonder too. I've been wondering the whole way up."

"You mean?" Her voice had come to life.

Without answering her question, he looked down on her with that sudden smile which would be the last thing about him she could ever forget. "Mr. Rowan wants me to take the Duncan agency for the Valley," he said.

"Then we might come back to live? Oh, Ralph . . . There's nothing to keep us in Queenborough."

"Nothing but the soup kitchen."

"Well, we shan't stay for that. I'd rather live in this village, and raise my own vegetables in my own back yard."

"Why not in this garden?"

"Why not?" She caught her breath with a sob. "We might buy it with Father's money. It would be what Grandmother used to call 'perpetual remembrance.'"

"It would take a lot of work. Look at that drain-pipe."

"But you think it isn't so ruined as it looks. And we have plenty of time."

"How could we live after we get here?"

"Oh, we'd find a way. Aunt Meggie can raise chickens, and the garden will take care of itself if we keep the seeds every year. Toby Waters or some old Geddy will be glad to work it in return for his living. That's the good thing about a village. There's always somebody to do nobody's job."

Ralph shook his head. "We'd be peasants," he replied bitterly. "Peasants without land."

"No, we shouldn't. Oh, Ralph, we shouldn't. . . . Nothing can make peasants of us but ourselves. Grandmother had less when she grew up, but she wasn't a peasant. Living with the savages didn't turn Great-great-grandmother Tod into a savage." Her gaze flew to the huddled stones on the hillside. "No matter how little we have, we shall have more than the first Fincastle owned when he cut down the trees and built the log manse here. What would he have thought if he had stumbled upon a brick house, a garden with seeds in the ground, a well, a springhouse, and the whole of Smiling Creek, with no Indians in the willows?"

"There's a difference. He had something else too. He had not only civilization, but Heaven and Hell, within himself. It takes conviction to set out to despoil the wilderness, defraud Indians of their hunting-grounds, and start to build a new Jerusalem for predestinarians. I'm not sure," he concluded grimly, "that predestination didn't conquer the land. It's a doctrine that has made history wherever it found itself."

"Don't be bitter, Ralph. It doesn't help to be bitter."

"If you're like me, it does."

She brushed away his rejoinder. "I might be able to do a little dressmaking. I learned about clothes at Shadwell's—though, of course, it's easier nowadays to buy everything ready-made."

"I'd think your hands would be full of dirt. . . . I'm not sure that any animal left that stench. It's foul enough to be human."

"What we need is lime and more lime. I'll ask Dr. Updike to start Marcellus cleaning."

"Are you sure, then, that we're coming back? I was only half serious."

"Yes, I'm sure. I felt it from the beginning." She had a sense, more a feeling than a vision, of the dead generations behind her. They had come to life there in the past; they were lending her their fortitude; they were reaching out to her in adversity. This was the heritage they had left. She could lean back on their strength; she could recover that lost certainty of a continuing tradition.

"It will be starting over from the very bottom."

"Well, we're at the bottom, so it's high time for us to start."

"Have you thought of Ranny?"

"I've thought of him every minute. The Bergens will take care of him till school is over. He would love the summer in Ironside, and if he wins that scholarship, as he is sure to do, he will be away all next winter. When he gets on in the world, he may like to have this place for his children."

"You're a dreamer, Ada. It's queer that a dreamer should be a rock to lean on." There was a sullen twist to his lips, but tenderness was welling up in his eyes. In the brilliant sunlight, surrounded by the pale green of the landscape, his face was the face of an old man—creased, hardened, hollowed, and stained by time.

"And you . . . Oh, Ralph, we have been happy together!"

He did not answer, and she wondered whether she had said too much. Always, she told herself, he would suffer from his fear of softness, from his incurable hostility to life. Because he had been in youth a disappointed romantic, he would inherit a middle age, and even an old age, if he lived, of cynical realism. But he depended upon her. The human tie was still strong. And even if his flesh had ceased to desire her, or desired her only in flashes (she looked down at her withered hands; she remembered her faded cheeks), some hunger deeper and more enduring than appetite was still constant and satisfied.

"Yes, we've had a poor life," he said at last, "but we've been happy together."

He reached out his arm, and while she leaned against him, she felt the steady beating of his heart as she had felt it—how long ago?—when they were lovers. Never, not even when we were young, she thought, with a sudden glow of surprise, was it so perfect as this.

ELLEN GLASGOW saw herself, and many critics agree, as the first southern realist. One gave her credit for initiating the whole movement. Reviewing her *Barren Ground*, Stuart Sherman wrote: "Realism crossed the Potomac twenty-five years ago, going north!"[1] Later other observers, including especially her friend James Branch Cabell and the literary scholar Louis Rubin, disputed this claim, but however literary critics of various persuasions assess her books today, not only the work but Glasgow's life marked important milestones in the history of southern fiction and of southern women.[2] From the first she aspired to the kind of realistic treatment of human behavior and human emotions that had only been attempted hitherto by an occasional southerner. She chose, too, to step boldly out of the required life of a proper southern lady, especially a single lady, by living independently and putting her career ahead of all other considerations. When she wrote in the preface to her feminist novel, *Virginia*, "nowadays, as I am made increasingly aware, the lady has become almost as extinct as the dodo,"[3] she was describing a change which she herself —however inadvertently—had helped to bring about.

Born in 1873 into the post–Civil War Richmond society of impoverished gentility, Glasgow was an anomaly in a society where women were valued for family connections, for beauty and grace, for piety, domestic skills, and a gift for motherhood.

Family connections she had. Her mother, she tells us, came from the clan sired in the seventeenth century by the all-too-

fecund William Randolph of Turkey Island, which meant she
was kin, one way and another, to most of the first families of
the tidewater. Her father, descended from Scotch-Irish Presbyterians in the Valley of Virginia, was a successful business-
man, director of Virginia's leading industry, the Tredegar Iron
Works. Hers was not a happy family, but it was certainly a distinguished one.

She was also appropriately beautiful and graceful. But there
her similarity to the prevailing definition of "southern lady"
ended. Although she would say that she had spent her life
searching for a philosophy of life which would enable her, in
Henry Adams's words which she loved to quote, to "find a
world that sensitive and timid natures could regard without a
shudder," she could in no sense have been called pious. And
though she would develop strong attachments to a succession
of men, and even from time to time consider herself engaged,
she would never be drawn either to domesticity or to motherhood. "I had not ever," she wrote late in life, "felt even the
faintest wish to have babies."[4]

In her teens, under the tutelage of an admired brother-in-
law, she embarked upon a heavy course of reading in novels,
philosophy, Henry George, and of course Darwin. Before long
she was calling herself a socialist. Quite early she conceived
an ambition to write fiction, and to write differently from the
prevailing mode of southerners whose books dwelt on romantic images of the Old South. In retrospect she would describe
herself as the first in her region to move away from the romantic style of popular authors like Thomas Nelson Page and
would suggest that her realism was thirty years ahead of its
time.[5] By 1973 Louis Rubin had come to agree. Speaking on
the occasion of her centenary, he said, "She was, simply, the
first really modern Southern novelist, the pioneer who opened
up for fictional imagination a whole spectrum of her region's
experience that hitherto had been considered inappropriate for
depiction in polite letters."[6]

In the 1920s she began to say that her books, taken together,
were meant to provide a comprehensive social history of Vir-

ginia "in the more freely interpretative form of fiction."[7] The
idea came from her friend James Branch Cabell in his review
of *Barren Ground*, but she enthusiastically adopted it and from
that point forward spoke as if it had been her settled purpose
from the beginning.[8] She did not, however, use the term *social
history* as it is most often used by present-day historians. Chal-
lenged by Cabell to define the term, she replied, "the customs,
habits, manners and general outer envelopes human nature has
assumed in a special place and period," adding that "the inner
substance of my work has been universal human nature."[9]

Ellen Glasgow also believed that her novels represented a
"straightforward facing of realities" rather than the "evasive
idealism" she thought characteristic of many American writers
(and politicians), especially those from her own part of the
country. "Great fiction," she wrote, is "great truth telling, and
the true novel is . . . history illumined by imagination."[10]

To develop the historical setting for *Vein of Iron*, her eighteenth novel, Glasgow undertook a period of "total immersion" in the records of the upper reaches of the James River,
which had been settled by Scotch-Irish Presbyterians, the
people from whom her father was descended. She admired
what she called the "Presbyterian spirit" and decided that the
most important element in that spirit was "fortitude."[11] She
invented a town and a family and set out to show the "customs,
habits and manners" of mountain people and to picture the
society built by the descendants of the pioneers who had first
settled there in the eighteenth century, bringing with them—
like the New England Puritans a century earlier—a stern Calvinism. Through their story she said she hoped to measure the
durability of the "vein of iron"—a phrase she often used—for
a new generation exemplified by Ada Fincastle who, when her
fiancé is trapped into an unhappy marriage, bears his child out
of wedlock and later leads her family out of its traditional
world into the urban maelstrom of Richmond in the turbulent
years of the First World War. Ada and her father, John Fincastle, an unfrocked minister and philosopher, sustain the family through the frenetic 1920s and the Great Depression until,

in despair with urban life, they conclude that salvation lies in a return to the mountains. The "vein of iron" had prevailed.

Glasgow saw herself as a supremely architectural novelist. She tells us that she weighed and measured her material and shaped it in "masses"; that she polished her prose, and especially the dialogue, with infinite care. She spoke of having instincts that told her the difference between excellence and "second best." Her characters, she said, came to her mind fully formed and ready to play their assigned parts. She thought all her books after *Barren Ground* were significant artistic achievements. She also wrote once that she cared more for the opinion of posterity than for that of her contemporaries.[12]

What posterity will find in *Vein of Iron* may not be exactly what she anticipated. A social historian who admitted that her work was partly fiction would be suspect; a novelist who aspires to write history may indeed be doing so, though not necessarily exactly in the way she thinks.

Glasgow's understanding of the social realities of the past was somewhat deficient. Despite her negative feelings, so often expressed, about her father, she had come to romanticize his forebears as representing indispensable values that she felt were disappearing from the modern world. However much she wanted to import irony into fiction, Glasgow did not look for it in history, beyond an occasional recognition that the pioneers had indeed appropriated land belonging to other people. Nor did she recognize the fact that many westward-moving pioneers had been more interested in speculative wealth than in establishing a godly community. For her these forebears represented the quality she most admired in herself (the only quality she admitted to having inherited from her father)—the ability to endure.

The unconscious or only partly conscious evidence for the social historian of the future lies in what the book reveals about the way Glasgow and many of her contemporaries looked at the world. Race does not figure largely in this book, but insofar as African Americans appear, the assumptions Glasgow shared with nearly all of her contemporaries are clear. Her black characters are just there, as they were just there for most southerners of her generation: figures occasionally admirable, sometimes useful as symbols, but always fulfilling their assigned roles.

Then there are attitudes toward sex. Readers under fifty may have trouble grasping the fact that Glasgow's picture of a young man forced into marriage as a result of spending five minutes in a young woman's bedroom accurately reflects the mores of the early twentieth-century South. The social historian must also ponder Grandmother Fincastle's sense of disgrace, not only about her son's intellectual apostasy but also about Ada's pregnancy. Spinsters of Aunt Meggie's type represent another important element of the social past, now virtually disappeared but once part of almost every family.

Although Glasgow saw the novel as being principally "about" the Valley and its people, the depiction of urban life in the 1920s and early 1930s is much the most powerful part of the book, the part most useful to a present-day social historian. She herself suffered hardly at all from the economic collapse of the thirties, but she had, she wrote Allen Tate in January 1933, "seen so much destitution among educated people in this depression" that she was able to create an altogether convincing portrait of a family struggling first to stay afloat and then, rather desperately, simply to survive.

In real life Virginia—like the rest of the country—had a very rough time after 1929. The economic breakdown heralded by the stock market crash was followed in the summer of 1930 by a devastating drought which in a predominantly rural state had far-reaching consequences. Crops were ruined, cattle died, and unemployment spread. Wheat at fifty cents a bushel was ruinous, and men at tobacco auctions wept when their crops brought less than it had cost to produce them. In Danville a wage cut and the imposition of what was called the "stretch-out" precipitated a violent textile strike which led the governor to call out the National Guard. By 1933 one out of five Virginia workers was unemployed. In the Southside, heavily dependent on tobacco as it was, children lacked shoes or clothes in which to go to school. When a visiting Communist organized a peaceful hunger march at the state Capitol, clubs were used and leaders were arrested.

There was no way for people to know that these desperate times would pass. Just as some people had assumed that the middle-class prosperity of the 1920s would become permanent, so now many people wondered if there would ever be jobs again. Even had they known what the future held, people do not eat in the long run but day to day.

However much Glasgow romanticized some individual characters, she effectively evoked the desperation of the times—especially the dreadful fear brought on as banks collapsed. The scenes showing John Fincastle in the breadline or giving away his carefully saved burial suit to a young man who might thereby get a job represent her best work. They must be illuminating for a generation to whom the reality of the Great Depression is often on a level with the reality of the Albigensian wars.

The Richmond section of *Vein of Iron* also reveals the reaction Ellen Glasgow shared with many other southerners (one thinks especially of the so-called Agrarians, authors of *I'll Take My Stand*) to the increasing urbanization of the South. The interior monologues of Ada and especially of John Fincastle as they contemplate the streets and shops of Richmond voice Glasgow's own extreme discomfort with the society that emerged in full force after the First World War.

These reflections reinforce similar strictures in *A Woman Within* and *A Certain Measure* and indeed in most of Glasgow's nonfiction writing after the mid-1920s. Once she had thought southern society was stifled by an outmoded code of conduct; now, in increasingly bitter terms, she deplored the enthusiastic materialism that seemed to be taking its place. However much she had enjoyed exploding the traditional images of old Confederate officers, former planters, and ladies and gentlemen of the old school, the new middle class of clerks, white-collar workers, and automobile salesmen did not please her any better. She disliked almost everything about the emerging society—from social workers to installment buying. In the poorer neighborhood in which she had placed the Fincastles and McBrides, she depicted some carryover of village mores, of mutual aid and sharing of trouble. But everywhere else—in department stores, in big houses, on the streets—she painted a quite dreadful mass society from which the "vein of iron" had departed. She contrasted members of the new middle class with artisans, especially those who worked in wood, and self-sufficient village folk who raised their gardens, spun, wove, and sewed, canned and pickled, baked and churned.[13] Using John Fincastle's experience she tried to show what she took to be the total absence of appreciation among her countrymen for the life of the mind.

With *Vein of Iron*, Glasgow was sure she had achieved her "best and truest work." "I am thrilled by its quiet power and poetic insight," she wrote one friend and, to another, "No novel has ever meant quite so much to me . . . it is long, thoughtful, tragic." She assured still another that she had "never written a novel which made so wide and so deep an appeal." While it was still in progress, she predicted that it would be a "triumph."

In careful instructions to Stark Young who, in response to her urging, had agreed to review the book, she cataloged the book's virtues. Its theme, she said, was: "What is it that has enabled human beings to endure life on the earth . . . Religion? Philosophy? Love? Simple human relationships? Or merely the character that is fortitude? What is the vein of iron that has enabled not only families, but races, nations, strains to survive and even to forge (or weave) some continuing traditions? In my book the vein of iron is of course this Scottish strain of fortitude that has come down from the earliest pioneers in the Valley."[14] She hoped Young would recognize her success in finding the appropriate rhythm for the speech of each person in her narrative. She trusted he would admire the device, early in the book, of seeing one scene through the eyes of each of five characters and added that she was particularly proud of the passage in which the grandmother ruminated while falling asleep. She also thought she had been exceptionally successful in analyzing "our age and the modern tone of that section."[15]

At the outset the book was a critical success, the triumph the author had predicted. Glowing reviews filled the first pages of the *New York Times Book Review* and the *Herald Tribune Books*. Other favorable reviews followed. It was a Book of the Month and outsold all but one of the other works of fiction published in 1935.[16]

There were a few dissenters. Randall Jarrell writing in the *Southern Review* observed that John Fincastle's judgments "are not so much those dramatically proper to the character of a great philosopher as to those that Miss Glasgow happens to have herself." Nor did he share Glasgow's evaluation of her carefully polished prose: "Miss Glasgow's style may be called commonplace; she is fond of the most obvious and familiar rhetorical devices, and these are most evident in important scenes."[17] Glasgow dismissed this review as representing an extreme view.

Yet Jarrell had a point. Measured by the standards of narrative art (and in contrast to some of her earlier books), the dialogue is often wooden and people do not always come alive. The philosopher, the indomitable grandmother, the lovers all speak in clichés. The story is built on the stereotypical plot of the admirable, upright, poor girl robbed of her lover by the spoiled, selfish rich girl.

Ada and her grandmother, like Dorinda in *Barren Ground*, are strong women who lead us to examine Glasgow's claim to be a feminist. She wrote proudly that she had been the first person in Virginia to say a word in favor of woman suffrage. This may have been a reference to her first published short story, called "A Woman of Tomorrow," in which the heroine was not only a feminist and a lawyer but also a voter.[18] This in 1895 when the mere idea of woman suffrage was in many parts of the South considered to be the most extreme radicalism. Several times in the years when suffrage was high on the political agenda she gave strong statements of support to reporters who interviewed her on the subject, but she left the demanding political work for women's right to others, excusing herself on the ground that people like Lila Meade Valentine were better suited to organize a cause.

When compared to the work of Valentine and dozens of other Virginia suffragists, Glasgow's role in the movement was slight. Perhaps the most apt comparison would be with Mary Johnston, also a Richmond novelist, who—though a shy, retiring person—put her talents at the disposal of the suffrage movement. The suffragists worked indefatigably to develop popular understanding and support for the idea on the one hand and to persuade the mostly unsympathetic Virginia legislature on the other. With extraordinary skill they cultivated powerful male politicians and community leaders. Their papers, preserved in the Library of Virginia, bear witness to the energy and dedication required when a disfranchised group seeks to make headway in a traditional political setting. They did not succeed—the Virginia legislature, like most southern legislatures, refused to ratify the Nineteenth Amendment—but their painfully accumulated experience and effective organization laid the groundwork for an extraordinary efflorescence of women's political activism in the 1920s. In the first year after suffrage, these veterans of the Virginia movement brought a long agenda to the legislature and accomplished a good deal of it. In all of this Glasgow played no part.

Ellen Glasgow would have said, and perhaps rightly, that her chosen role was different. Independent, feminist in her sentiments, aspiring realist, outspoken in certain ways—Glasgow was all these. But there was, as she herself sometimes recognized, quite another side to her life and thought. In outward appearance, in the tone and diction of her personal letters, in dealings with publishers, in the entertaining she did so lavishly for those whom she accepted into her inner circle, she was the very model of the proper southern lady. And after the First World War, the woman who had called for a southern literature of "blood and irony" was profoundly troubled by the disappearance of the very manners and behavior that she had earlier seen as emblematic of the destructive grip of tradition on Virginians. This woman who took pride in making the illegitimate son of a poor white mother the hero of one novel, and who claimed to want to understand Virginians of all social classes, was in daily life, as well as in her literary judgments, an elitist to her fingertips. Such contradictions are not uncommon in human experience, but they need to be recognized by the readers of Glasgow's work.

When Ellen Glasgow died in 1945, Virginius Dabney identified her in the *Richmond Times-Dispatch* as Virginia's greatest woman—so far had some Virginians come from the days when friends and critics alike had quailed at her radicalism. Identifying "greatness" is a risky business at best, and Dabney's accolade suggested just how blind most Virginia men were to all those other women, members of Glasgow's generation, who had helped to transform the life of many Virginia communities, women such as Lila Valentine, Mary Cooke Branch Munford, Mary Johnston, Adele Clark, Maggie Lena Walker, Janie Porter Barrett—astute and hardworking political activists. It was easier for an editor to point with pride to a best-selling novelist who introduced literary lights to Richmond society than to admire women who were openly dedicated to upsetting the social order of Virginia life.

He could justly have said, however, that almost alone of Virginia writers of her generation she had aspired to a higher standard for fiction than any that had gone before. And in so doing, she left behind works worthy of note, works still useful to historians and others who try to understand the American South. If, in the end, she was not the American Tolstoy she had once hoped to be, she fills an important niche in literary history. And *Vein of Iron*, like many another important novel, takes on new meanings as new generations of readers are further and further from the time of its composition.

Anne Firor Scott

1. Stuart P. Sherman et al., *Ellen Glasgow: Critical Essays* (Garden City, N.Y.: Doubleday, Doran and Co., 1929).

2. For Louis Rubin's incisive 1959 estimate of Glasgow, see his book, *No Place on Earth: Ellen Glasgow, James Branch Cabell, and Richmond-in-Virginia* (Austin: Univ. of Texas Press, 1959).

3. Ellen Glasgow, *A Certain Measure: An Interpretation of Prose Fiction* (New York: Harcourt, Brace and Company, 1938), p. 77.

4. Ellen Glasgow, *The Woman Within* (New York: Harcourt, Brace and Company, 1954), p. 108.

5. *A Certain Measure*, p. 9. If Glasgow had known the work of a few other southerners of her day, she would have been a bit more modest. Julia Flisch, for example, author of *Hurricane*, Sara Barnwell Elliott, *Some Data and Other Stories of Southern Life*, and Charles W. Chesnutt, who wrote *The Wife of His Youth, and Other Stories of the Color Line*, could all lay claim to the label "realist" before Glasgow began publishing. Rubin notes that she had not read books of George W. Cable, another early realist.

6. M. Thomas Inge, ed., *Ellen Glasgow: Centennial Essays* (Charlottesville: Univ. Press of Virginia, 1976), p. 4.

7. *A Certain Measure*, p. 3.

8. In a newspaper interview in 1913, she told the reporter that her purpose for the future was to write a series of novels about women. She did not, at that time, say anything about a social history of Virginia (Julius R. Raper, *Ellen Glasgow's Reasonable Doubts: A Collection of Her Writings* [Baton Rouge: Louisiana State Univ. Press, 1988], p. 120. The interview appeared in the *New York Evening Post*, Feb. 1913, p. 6). In an ironical assessment of Glasgow, parts of which were written after her death, James Branch Cabell argued that southern women had indeed been the center of her interest, whether she realized it or not. The main theme of her books, he wrote, was "The Tragedy of Every Woman, As It Was Lately Enacted in the Commonwealth of Virginia" (James Branch Cabell, "Miss Glasgow of Virginia," in his *Let Me Lie* [New York: Farrar, Straus and Company, 1947], pp. 230–67). Cabell claimed to know Glasgow better than any other single person, and his comments on her work written over a period of many years cut through her pretensions in ways

that often ring true. She was, he once said, "a mistress of parenthetic malice," who could not forgive critical reviewers.

9. E. Stanly Godbold, Jr., *Ellen Glasgow and the Woman Within* (Baton Rouge: Louisiana State Univ. Press, 1972), p. 291.

10. Interview with Joyce Kilmer in *New York Times Magazine* March 5, 1916, and Symposium on "What Is a Novel . . . ?" in *Current Opinion* 60 (March 1916), both reprinted in Raper, *Ellen Glasgow's Reasonable Doubts*, pp. 122–23, 198–99.

11. *A Certain Measure*, pp. 168–70.

12. Glasgow vastly enjoyed talking and writing about herself. She makes these points in letters, in *A Certain Measure*, in *The Woman Within*, and in many of the pieces collected in Raper, *Ellen Glasgow's Reasonable Doubts*.

13. This romanticization of the joys of self-sufficiency comes oddly from a woman who was in time unable even to sharpen her own pencils.

14. Blair Rouse, ed., *Letters of Ellen Glasgow* (New York: Harcourt, Brace and Company, 1958), p. 179 (to Stark Young), p. 171 (to Bessie Zaban Jones), p. 208 (to Edwin Mims), p. 155 (to Irita Van Doren).

15. Glasgow had flattered and cultivated Young for quite a while, and in July 1934 she had given his *So Red the Rose* a very favorable review in the *New York Herald Tribune Books* section. In several letters she told him of her efforts to promote his book. She wrote carefully constructed flattering letters to other influential literary figures of the time, including J. Donald Adams, Howard Mumford Jones, Irita Van Doren, Van Wyck Brooks.

16. Godbold, *Ellen Glasgow and the Woman Within*, p. 214.

17. Randall Jarrell, "Ten Books," *Southern Review*, Autumn 1935.

18. *Short Stories* 19 (1895): 415–27; reprinted in Raper, *Ellen Glasgow's Reasonable Doubts*, pp. 1–14. Certain Virginia women had spoken in favor of suffrage before Ellen Glasgow was born.